Contentious Politics and Democratization in Nepal

Contentious Politics and Democratization in Nepal

Edited by
MAHENDRA LAWOTI

SAGE

Los Angeles | London | New Delhi
Singapore | Washington DC | Melbourne

SAGE Publications India Pvt Ltd
B1/I-1 Mohan Cooperative Industrial Area
Mathura Road, New Delhi 110 044, India
www.sagepub.in

SAGE Publications Inc
2455 Teller Road
Thousand Oaks, California 91320, USA

SAGE Publications Ltd
1 Oliver's Yard, 55 City Road
London EC1Y 1SP, United Kingdom

SAGE Publications Asia-Pacific Pte Ltd
3 Church Street
#10-04 Samsung Hub
Singapore 049483

Published by Vivek Mehra for SAGE Publications India Pvt Ltd, typeset in 10/12pt Sabon by Star Compugraphics Private Limited, Delhi and printed at Sai Print-o-Pack, New Delhi.

Library of Congress Cataloging-in-Publication Data

Contentious politics and democratization in Nepal/edited
by Mahendra Lawoti
p. cm.
Includes bibliographical references and index.
1. Democratization—Nepal. 2. Multiculturalism—Nepal. 3. Nepal—Politics and government—1990–I. Lawoti, Mahendra, 1965–

JQ628.A91C66 320.95496—dc22 2007 2007014172

ISBN: 978-93-528-0576-1 (PB)

SAGE Team: Ashok R. Chandran, Vaijayantee Bhattacharya,
Rajib Chatterjee and Sanjeev Kumar Sharma

Dedication

For the activists who are working to extend democracy to traditionally marginalized groups, in Nepal and beyond.

Contents

PART III: Identity Politics

PART IV: Collective Public Protests

PART V: Contentious Politics and Democratization

List of Tables

List of Figures

List of Abbreviations

ABNES	Akhil Bharatiya Nepali Ekta Samaj
ANNFSU	All Nepal National Free Student Union
APF	Armed Police Force
BASE	Backward Education Society
BJP	Bharatiya Janata Party
CDO	Chief District Officer
CHHE	Caste-Hill Hindu Elite
COTW	Causes of Conflict in Third World
CPN (Democratic)	Communist Party of Nepal (Democratic)
CPN (Fourth Convention)	Communist Party of Nepal (Fourth Convention)
CPN (M)	Communist Party of Nepal (Maoist)
CPN (Mashal)	Communist Party of Nepal (Mashal)
CPN (Marxist)	Communist Party of Nepal (Marxist)
CPN (ML)	Communist Party of Nepal (Marxist-Leninist)
CPN-UML	Communist Party of Nepal-United Marxist Leninist
CPN (Unity Centre)	Communist Party of Nepal (Unity Centre)
CRC	Constitution Recommendation Commission
CZR	Compact Revolutionary Zone
FNTE	Federation of Nepali Transport Entrepreneurs
GDP	Gross Domestic Product
GoN	Government of Nepal
GPMG	General Purpose Machine Gun
HMG	His Majesty's Government
INGO	International Non-Governmental Organization
JTMM	Janatantric Tarai Mukti Morcha
KNF	Khambuwan National Front
LMG	Light Machine Gun
LWE	Left-Wing Extremists
MMM	Madhesia Mukti Morcha
MNO	Mongol National Organization

MRD	Movement-for-the-Restoration-of-Democracy
NC	Nepali Congress
NDC	National Defence Council
NDP	National Democratic Party
NEFIN	Nepal Federation of Indigenous Nationalities
NGO	Non-Governmental Organization
NNC	Nepali National Congress
NRC	Nepali Rastriya Congress
NSP	Nepal Sadbhavana Party
PLA	People's Liberation Army
RIM	Revolutionary Internationalist Movement
RJP	Rastriya Janamukti Party
RNA	Royal Nepal Army
RPP	Rashtriya Prajatantra Party
RSS	Rashtriya Swayamsevak Sangh
RW	*Revolutionary Worker*
RWB	Reporters Without Borders
SAARC	South Asian Association for Regional Cooperation
SLC	School-Leaving Certificate
SLR	Self Loading Rifle
SMG	Submachine Gun
SPA	Seven-Party-Alliance
SPM	Second People's Movement
SSB	Special Services Bureau
TADA	Terrorism and Destructive Activities (Prevention) Act
TSA	Trans-Stakeholder Approach
ULF	United Left Front
UN	United Nations
UNPM	United National People's Movement
UPF	United People's Front
US	United States
VDC	Village Development Committee
VHP	Vishwa Hindu Parishad

Preface

Nepal witnessed a plethora of contentious activities after 1990. They were made possible by the restoration of democracy. Their effects on democracy, however, have not been investigated. This volume analyses different types of contentious activities and their effects on democratization. It brings together the work of scholars and journalists institutionally based in South Asia, Japan, Europe and North America.

The chapters were written and revised by mid-2006 and analyse activities that occurred prior to 2006 in Nepal. I have, however, incorporated the effects of the second people's movement for democratization, of April 2006, in the conclusion.

Many people have helped in bringing this book together. Most of the chapters were presented at the four panels I organized during the 34th Annual South Asia Conference in Madison in October 2005. I would like to thank the participants of these well-attended panels and especially Professors Jim Fisher and Arjun Guneratne for questions and comments that were very useful in revising the chapters.

Susan Hangen supported the project and provided comments on the theme and on my chapters from the beginning of the endeavour. My graduate assistants Bonfas Odour Owinga, William Owusu and Emily A. Zerndt read the chapters and provided comments, and also helped in the editing and formatting of the chapters. I thank the commissioning team at Sage, Mimi Choudhury, Anamika Mukharji and Ashok R. Chandran, for smoothly taking forward the publication of the book. Finally, I express my deep gratitude to my wife Geeta and sons Sajjan and Sumbon for their love and support during my researching, writing and editing the book.

Mahendra Lawoti
Department of Political Science
Western Michigan University, Kalamazoo, MI 49008
November 2006

PART I

Context and Framework

1

Contentious Politics in Democratizing Nepal

MAHENDRA LAWOTI

Nepal witnessed an explosion of contentious activities, both violent and non-violent, after the restoration of democracy in 1990. Why did the democratic years witness so many collective public protests? Did those activities promote or hinder the democratization process, which had, ironically, provided space for them? Often the Nepali state and the fledgling democracy seemed to be overwhelmed by those activities. Can the fundamental democratic rights to dissent, mobilize and protest work against new democracies?

The contentious activities ranged from the identity and gender movements, numerous public protests and strikes, and the Maoist rebellion. What were the causes and consequences of these activities? The aim of this volume is to understand these collective struggles and their relationship with democratization in Nepal. Did the Maoist insurgency increase people's power or undermine it? Did the frequent strikes and close-downs of markets and roads facilitate the mobilization of people or constrain the work and lives of others? Did the identity and women's movements expand the democratic polity toward the traditionally marginalized groups or did they overwhelm the fledgling democracy?

Scholars have argued that collective mobilization can help deepen democracy by empowering more people (Markoff 1996; McAdam et al. 2001). Others have said that it can empower the state as well, in addition to the social forces. The former could be strengthened through reforms forced by the mobilizations, while the latter could benefit from concessions received from the state (Migdal 1994).

Indeed, despite the various shortcomings of the democratic period in Nepal, the mobilization of marginalized groups was a positive aspect. The poor, downtrodden and the traditionally excluded national/ethnic, caste and gender groups took advantage of the open space to articulate their aspirations, make demands and mobilize to fulfil them. However, since the public space is open to anyone, including the powerful and the privileged, the elite can also use it to maintain their domination and privilege. Did the well-off and more organized groups benefit more from the political space? Mobilization requires resources, and hence could it be that the resourceful groups in the society, as the interest group literature informs us (Lowi 1969), are more often successful in getting their interests served and protected, including their traditional privileges?

On the other hand, mobilization could have unintended consequences, especially if these occur in large numbers and too frequently, and overwhelm the emerging democratic polity. Huntington (1968) has argued that when a lot of groups mobilize in changing societies, if the existing political institutions are unable to accommodate the new demands, polities could witness violence and destabilization. Is his classic argument relevant in Nepal? Are the conflicts in Nepal due to the incongruence between societal aspirations and state institutions, and were they exacerbated by the gaps between the demands of the mobilized groups and the inadequate response and incapability of the state?

Since those who mobilize often seek resources or favourable policies from the state, it could intensify conflict among groups who control the state and its resources and those who want a voice in the state and a share of its resources. Indeed, the Maoists launched the insurgency after the state repeatedly ignored their demands and received support from the population ignored by the state. In this context of varied and sometimes opposing possibilities, what were the impacts of different collective political struggles in Nepal? Specifically, have they contributed to or hindered the democratization process?

Defining Contentious Politics and Democratization

An open polity can encounter various forms of collective mobilization and conflict, especially if its structures and norms, both traditional and modern, privilege some groups while disadvantaging others. In this book, we are concerned with a subset of struggles that are often called contentious politics. McAdam et al. (2001: 5) define contentious politics as 'episodic, public, collective interaction among makers of claims and their objects when (*a*) at least one government is a claimant, an object of claims, or a party to the claims and (*b*) the claims would, if realized, affect the interests of at least one of the claimants. Roughly translated, the definition refers to collective political struggle.'[1] This book broadly concurs with this definition and will investigate collective struggles that have targeted the state. We will specifically analyse the Maoist insurgency, identity movements and collective public protests that have occurred in Nepal after 1990. The contentious activities that occur within the formal political realm, like those that are part of the repertoire of activities that contribute to the forming and breaking up of a government, are outside the purview of this book.

In general, contentious politics can be analysed in terms of the mobilization process and structure, framing process, opportunity, repertoires of contention, and the interactions among the various collective political struggles. What processes and available structures have these groups used and exploited? How do they frame their struggles? How do the shifting opportunities, which could become available through mobilization, networking or changes in the external environment, affect the struggles? On the other hand, how does the perception of a threat, or lack of it, affect the activities? How do the mobilizing groups and organizations build networks and tap resources? How do they exploit the existing ones? What forms of contentious actions and activities have been employed and how do their impacts vary?

The contentious activities could also be analysed in terms of the claims of different groups, the response of the state and other groups to the claims, the trajectories of the struggles, and the activities' effects.

Democratization of a polity means extending the political rights and civil liberties to more citizens as well as increasing the responsiveness of rulers. In the words of McAdam et al. (ibid.: 266), democratization 'means any net shift toward citizenship, breadth of citizenship, equality of citizenship, binding consultation, and protection'. At an operational level, it could mean several things. First, all adult citizens should be included in the polity as equals. All should enjoy full political rights and civil liberties, including unhindered rights to express themselves and to form associations. Second, the contest for public offices should be open to all, in principle as well as in practice, so that all citizens have an equal opportunity to reach the decision-making bodies (Dahl 1989). Third, the public officials should be responsive to the needs and aspirations of citizens and should be accountable to them as well—not only during periodic elections, but throughout their term. Fourth, unelected individuals or groups should not have special privilege over any public policy realm. Public policies should be made by elected officials (O'Donnell 1996). Fifth, the rule of law should exist so that citizens' lives and rights are protected and elected officials are held accountable for their actions. After getting power to the people (represented by the elected officials), which is the first step in democratization, the next challenge is to ensure that elected officials are held accountable if and when they abuse power (Schedler et al. 1999). Sixth, in multicultural societies, the tyranny of the majority should be prevented. Not only does a majority not have the right to take away the political rights and civil liberties of an individual, it also does not have the right to constrain the cultural rights of minorities (Kymlicka 1995; Lawoti 2005; Young 1990).

In the Nepali context, democratization could mean, among other things, expanding and deepening democracy by reforming the polity to include the traditionally excluded groups and extending civil liberties and political rights to them. It could also mean making public officials accountable and responsive to peoples' aspirations. Contentious activities can contribute toward achieving those objectives. However, what is the empirical reality? Have they fostered inclusion and accountability and deepened democracy?

The collective activities discussed in this book were launched against the state, or rather, the 'democratic' state. Herein lies the paradox that this book intends to explore. Have the collective actions, facilitated by a democratic dispensation, weakened or strengthened democracy? Did the collective actions of people against the democratic state contribute to the democratization process or have they disrupted democracy? Specifically, have such activities empowered underprivileged groups or constrained citizens? Did they fuel the Maoist insurgency by portraying the futility of peaceful collective struggles? Did they invite the King's 2002 and 2005 interventions by increasing the craving for order among a large number of people?

This volume seeks to examine the various collective political struggles and their contribution to or hindrance of democratization. The volume brings together outstanding work on contentious politics in Nepal by leading scholars, journalists, and intellectuals based in South Asia, North America, Europe, and Japan. The chapters are based on primary empirical research as well as on secondary analysis.

Contentious Politics in Democratizing Nepal: The Literature Reviewed

Scholarship on formal politics in Nepal abounds. The works deal with the formal development of the state, the state and political leadership, mainstream political parties, and so on (Baral 2004; Hachhethu 2002; Kumar 1995; Shah 1993; Stiller 1973). There are many works that deal with political conflict and transition as well (Chauhan 1989; Gupta 1993; Joshi and Rose 1966; Kumar 2000). These, however, are also mostly limited to discussing conflict in the formal political realm—conflicts and competition among mainstream political actors and parties, often for the attainment of state power.

Among the earlier works, only occasional studies have covered the phenomenon that we have defined as contentious politics (Joshi and Rose 1966). Baral's (1977) work is one of the few that has studied in detail the oppositional politics during the Panchayat regime.

Recently, more work on non-formal political activities, labelled as contentious politics in this volume, has appeared. Writings on identity politics began to appear from the mid-1990s. They have pointed out the discrimination faced by the various ethnic and caste groups and discussed the development of the movements in the post-1990 period (Bhattachan 1995, 2000; Gellner et al. 1997; Guneratne 2002; Lecomte-Tilouine and Dollfus 2003; Neupane 2000). A few of them also look at the relationship between democracy and identity movements (Lawoti 2005; Serchan 2001). These studies, by their scope, were limited to looking at the relationships among different types of contentious politics, and their relationship with democratization.

After the turn of the century, hordes of books and articles on the Maoist insurgency have appeared. They have discussed a wide range of variables—inequality, political exclusion, ethnic dimension, state repression, the weak state, the lack of development, environmental degradation and so on—as the causes and/or factors contributing to the growth of the insurgency. Some of the works have discussed the consequences of the insurgency as well. The negative impact on the economy and development, increase in the militarization of the society and restriction of human rights have been pointed out. A few of them have discussed connections between ethnic grievances and the Maoist mobilization of the ethnic groups (Bhurtel and Ali n.d.; Hutt 2004; Karki and Seddon 2003; Kumar 2005; Lawoti 2003a, 2003b; Mishra 2004; Onesto 2005; de Sales 2003; Thapa and Sijapati 2003; Upreti 2004). Some of these literature have linked the initiation of insurgency with the failure of the parliamentary regime to deliver, but they do not provide a systematic discussion of its consequences on democratization.

Works on the social movements in Nepal, besides the identity movements and the Maoist insurgency, are rare (Aziz 1993; Neupane 2001; Uprety 1992). Surprisingly, there is not much work on the street protests and strikes that were a regular feature of the post-1990 democratic period in many urban and semi urban centres. In such a context, it is not surprising that the available literature on these movements do not explicitly examine the relationship between them and democratization, or among different types of contentious activities, or between such activities and democratization. Gellner's (2003) edited volume, *Resistance and the State*, is an exception, which analyses ethnic activism and the Maoist insurgency from the common framework of resistance; however, its focus is on the state rather than democratization.

A number of works have focused on democratization after 1990, including the analysis of various obstacles that the nascent democracy faced (Baral 1993; Brown 1996; Kumar 1995; Lawoti 2002b; Parajulee 2000). These studies too have mostly confined themselves to studying democratization in terms of the formal political realm. They do not analyse the link between the various types of contentious politics and democratization.

This volume aims to fill these gaps. It aims not only to look at the various types of contentious activities with a common framework, but also to analyse the relationship among various contentious activities and democratization in post-1990 Nepal.

Before delving further into the themes to be covered in this volume, it is necessary to lay down the contemporary sociocultural context and historical background of state building and conflict in Nepal. The next section aims to do that.

Socio-economic Structures and Exclusionary State Building

Scholars have lamented that even though Nepal was brought together territorially by the Gorkha conquest, it has not been unified psychologically and economically even after more than two centuries (Gurung 2003). This is partly because the Nepali state was captured and exploited by a small elite caste group ever since its formation. The ruling group defined the rights and duties of citizens toward the state by conflating it with its own interests and adopting political institutions that concentrated power within the group. This disjunction between the state and society is the underlying cause for the eruption of many of the contentious activities in present day Nepal. I will briefly discuss this major disjunction below.

Exclusion of National/Ethnic and Caste Groups

More than two-thirds of the population, including the indigenous nationalities (Adibasi Janajati), Dalits (traditional 'untouchables') and Madhesis (plains people), are excluded from the influential realms of governance in Nepal.[2] The caste-hill Hindu elite (CHHE) are 31 per cent of the population, but overwhelmingly dominate the state, politics, economy and society. For instance, in 1999, the CHHE occupied around 70 per cent of the positions in the legislature, judiciary, Parliament and top administration (Lawoti 2002a; Neupane 2000).[3] According to the *Nepal Human Development Report 1998*, the elite caste group occupied 98 per cent of the top positions in the civil administration in 1854 and still occupied 92 per cent of the top administration positions in the mid-1990s

(NESAC 1998: 145–46). Among other factors, historical exclusion and discrimination have contributed to the contemporary exclusion.

Historically, discrimination and exclusion were rooted in the caste-based Hindu hierarchical order. The civil code introduced in 1854 codified the top positions of hill Bahuns and Chhetris in the society. The elite have further strengthened their position in the state and society since then. Till the abolishment of the caste system in 1963, the legal system treated different ethnic and caste groups unequally, perpetuating inequality. Many opportunities, such as education and jobs, were not available to marginalized groups, and for the same crime, the 'low-caste' groups were punished more severely (Bista 1991; Hofer 1979; Levine 1987). The juridical end of the caste system during the Panchayat period by King Mahendra was a step forward, but the Panchayat system undermined different native languages, religions, and cultures through its assimilation policies. It promoted one religion, one language and one set of values in a multicultural society. In fact, the Panchayat promoted the upper-caste hill Hindu culture and values behind the façade of modernization and development.

The hill Hindu state ideology promoted by the pre-1990 Shah and Rana rulers was continued, though to a lesser extent, even in the democratic period. Even though the 1990s ushered in extensive democratic rights, the marginalized ethnic and caste groups continued to face cultural discrimination and political exclusion. The 1990 Constitution defined the kingdom as 'multiethnic, multilingual' but the other articles and state institutions it adopted discriminated against marginalized ethnic and caste groups (Bhattachan 2000; Lawoti 2005; Neupane 2000). Not only was the state declared Hindu by the Constitution, but the native languages and different cultures of indigenous nationalities and Madhesis incurred unequal treatment from the state. Ethnic parties were banned and minority rights were not recognized or protected. Dalits, indigenous nationalities, Madhesis, and women faced many other forms of legal and social discrimination (Bhattachan 1999; Biswakorma 2000; FWLD 2000; Serchan 2001). The demands for ending the historical and contemporary discrimination have fuelled the identity and women's movements, which seek equitable inclusion of these groups in the state—politics, economy and society.

Rising Inequality, the Extractive State and Neglected Peasants

Nepal is not only poor, but it has also become a more unequal society in terms of material well-being. In the 1990s, Nepal was the most unequal country in South Asia. It had the highest Gini Index at 0.426. Inequality, as measured by the Gini Index was less in the 1980s in Nepal (0.300) than in India (0.312), Sri Lanka (0.341) and Pakistan (0.326) (Wagle 2006). The rise in inequality is despite the improvement in overall Human Development Indicators (HDIs) in the 1990s. I will demonstrate that the growth in a few select areas and the stagnation in others has led to this ironic situation—rise in inequality despite a moderate rise in HDIs. Inequality in Nepal exists among different sectors, ethnic and caste groups, and geographic regions (mountains, hills and the Terai); between men and women and between rural and urban areas.

The stagnation of the rural regions during the 1970s was portrayed vividly, among others, by the book *Nepal in Crisis*—it showed the neglect of the rural regions, the increasing pressure on the limited land in the hills, and the erosion of traditional jobs and sources of income (Blaikie et al. 1980). Different economic and demographic indicators—as presented by Deraniyagala (2005) and Sharma (2006), which I will discuss, demonstrate the continuous neglect of the rural regions. This neglect contributed to the rising inequalities in the 1990s in various spheres. Poverty levels were 33 per cent in 1976–77 but rose to 42 per cent by 1995–96. The 'income share of the top 10 per cent of the people increased from 21 per cent in the mid-1980s to 35 per cent by the mid-1990s, while the share of the bottom 40 per cent shrank from 24 per cent to 15 per cent by the mid-1990s' (Sharma 2006: 1245).

Some regions face more inequality than others in Nepal. Poverty level was significantly higher in rural areas (44 per cent) than in urban areas (20 per cent). Poverty is also more widespread in the mountains, where its incidence is 56 per cent, compared to around 40 per cent in the hills and plains. The incidence of poverty in the rural central (67 per cent) and mid- and far western (72 per cent) hills and mountains also far outstrips that in the eastern (28 per cent) and western (40 per cent) regions (Deraniyagala 2005: 52). On the other hand, inequality within the rural regions may have increased due to a rise in migration. Migrants generally come from higher-income groups and could be physically more able than non-migrants. Increased remittances to migrants' families may also have worsened intra-rural inequality (Deraniyagala 2005).

Poverty and economic stagnation had a more detrimental impact on the rural residents (87 per cent in 2001) because they are dependent upon agriculture, which has stagnated. Annual growth rates of agricultural output (major crops) declined from 1961–62 to 1991–93. The growth rate was negative (–0.07) for all crops in Nepal during this period even while other South Asian countries witnessed an increase in growth rates. The stagnation in agriculture was due to the government policy of import-substitution industrialization, following which it invested in industrialization in the urban areas at the cost of the peasants and rural areas. This neglect occurred despite the importance of agriculture as a major source of employment and national income. Sharma (2006: 1241–42) writes that agriculture, in which more than 80 per cent of Nepal's people are engaged, 'has not received more than 26 per cent of development expenditure in any development plan since the mid-1950s … Nepal, which had the highest agriculture yield (per hectare) in South Asia in the early 1960s fell significantly behind other countries by early 1990s'.

Land-ownership patterns also contributed to the inequality. Despite the relatively small average land ownership, inequality in land ownership reflects the persistence of the feudal system: '44% of households in the country are marginal landowners [0–0.5 hectare], but this group only accounts for 14% of total privately owned agricultural land. In contrast, the 5% of agricultural households who own plots greater than 3 h[ectare] account for around 27% of total agricultural land' (Deraniyagala 2005: 54). Land ownership, on the other hand, may hide poverty in the hills and mountains, as 'over 40% of medium and large landowners in the hills were classified as "poor" in 1996' (ibid.: 55). Macfarlane's (2001) ethnographic study also supports the pictures painted by the broad aggregate data. In a hill village in Central Nepal, to which he has frequently returned, a labourer could buy a chicken with a day's wages in the late 1960s, whereas in the mid-1990s, it took eight days' wages to purchase a chicken.

The opening up of the market since the mid-1980s has led to an improvement in some economic indicators such as the GDP, growth in output, and exports and forex reserves. This was mainly brought about by an expansion of the urban-based modern sector and did not close the inequality gap. For instance, the nominal income of the people living in urban areas increased by 16 per cent per annum (from US$126 to US$285) during the 1988–96 period, as against only 4 per cent for the rural population (from US$95 to US$125). Sharma (2006: 1242–43) argues that 'when the average annual rate of inflation is taken into consideration, the growth in rural income is in fact negative. This not only increased poverty in the rural areas but also increased rural–urban inequality'. Large parts of the rural areas stagnated, while the urban areas, especially in the Kathmandu Valley, developed into centres of wealth. The urban growth and the stagnation in the rural areas may have further increased the perception of inequality among rural residents (Deraniyagala 2005).

The problems of poverty and inequality in Nepal were not helped by the inadequate public investment in the social sectors. The 1990s saw considerable improvement in public-service provisions, but the expenditure by the state on basic social sectors such as education and health was still low. Annual public expenditure per primary-school child was around US$20 in Nepal in the late 1990s, compared with US$40 in India. Public-sector expenditure on health in Nepal is among the lowest in the world at US$2 per person per annum in 1999, compared with US$12 for the average developing country (UNDP 2001, cited in Deraniyagala 2005: 56).

The neglect of the rural regions and the poor by a centralized state is, however, nothing new for a student of Nepali history. The Nepali state-building process involved the extraction of a heavy price from the peasantry by the state and ruling groups (Regmi 1965, 1978). The state gave land as *jagir* (compensation) and *birta* (land grants) to various central government and military functionaries as rewards and compensation for their services. The peasantry had to turn in a large proportion of their products to these often distant landholders. The elite extracted as much as they could from the peasantry, often to build 'stucco palaces'. During wars, the peasantry had to cough up extra taxes and provide free labour for carrying weapons and war supplies. The peasantry was also taxed during births, marriages, coronations and so on, of the ruling Shah and Rana family members. Often middlemen, who were employed to collect land revenues, also extracted profits from the peasants. In the process, the peasantry was pushed into deeper penury.

According to Stiller (1973), the exploitation of the peasantry had its basis in the land–military complex developed during the Gorkha conquest. Prithivi Narayan Shah promised land to his military force, composed of land-hungry middle-hill people. The promise swelled the ranks of the conquering army. As long as new territories were conquered, land was available for distribution. However, after the 1814–16 war with the East India Company and the Sugauli Treaty of 1816, the borders became more or less fixed. There was no more land to be conquered. As land was the primary source of revenue for the state, the exploitation of the peasantry increased—the regime had to maintain its security apparatus, the government and the lavish lifestyle of the courtiers with revenue from limited land.

Despite forming the backbone of the economy, the peasants had no representation in the state, nor did the state invest in their well-being. The voices of the peasants were seldom heard or heeded. Occasional rebellions brought the issues to the forefront, but they were often brutally repressed. The state's neglect of the peasants continued even after 1990. The 1990 changes, despite formally ushering in the fundamental rights of expression and organization, ended up mostly expanding the ruling group (Brown 1996). The state is still controlled by an elite caste group that has largely failed to represent the peasantry, the poor and the marginalized ethnic and caste groups. What this has meant is that the needs and aspirations of the rural poor have rarely been represented in the corridors of power and decision-making processes. This resulted in the deep economic inequalities, as the elite monopolized economic resources through political domination.

The continued marginalization of the peasantry is ironic, because one of the major political parties is the Communist Party of Nepal-United Marxist Leninist (CPN-UML), which claims to speak for the poor.[4] However, which segments of the poor the CPN-UML and other parliamentary communist parties really represent is another question. Definitely they represent the less well-off, as opposed to other large mainstream parties, but their core constituency is not the poorest of the poor. The trade unions, college students, and primary- and high-school teachers who form its core constituency are the relatively well-off members in an impoverished country like Nepal. Only the village elite can send their children to college. The claim to represent the downtrodden itself is not sufficient to become their representative. The attraction of the rural people to the Maoist insurgency, which promised radical transformation, also illustrates that the parliamentary communist parties had failed to represent the interests of the poor.[5]

The inequalities across different sectors and regions and the neglect of those on the periphery contributed to the dissatisfaction among the rural people, especially the youth. They created a fertile ground for the rise of various forms of contentious activities, especially the Maoist insurgency. The lack of representation of the peasantry's interests in the state apparatus and their continued marginalization increased the possibility of a peasant rebellion or a radical movement capturing their support.

The Centralized Polity and Political Conflicts

The small ruling elite dominated society by concentrating most of the state power at the centre. Even the democratic polity envisioned by the 1990 Constitution was highly centralized. The state was unitary. The political, administrative and fiscal decentralization was minimal. This centralization created a peculiar situation of powerlessness. Since the local governments were not given power, they were weak. They did not provide meaningful services and had no significant role in development planning or in providing law and order or security to the people. They had an insignificant role in people's lives. This meant that the Nepali state had a very tenuous presence in rural areas. In this way, the centralization created powerlessness.

Meanwhile, the political power at the centre was mostly concentrated in the executive. The Parliament was weak. It had no power to introduce bills with any budgetary provisions. Parliamentary committees were weak as well, further reducing the authority of the Parliament in terms of its relationship with the executive.

Most central agencies (such as the Election Commission) were dependent upon the executive for nomination, budget and personnel. As a result of this extreme level of centralization, almost all state power was enjoyed by the top leaders of the ruling party.

The democratic state that was established by the 1990 Constitution was exclusionary at the political as well as the ideological level. There was little political space in the polity even for the major opposition parties. They could not influence public policies. As a consequence of the limited role of the opposition parties in the formal political process, they often had no option other than informal methods (strikes and protests) to make themselves heard. In extreme cases, such as that of the Maoists, who had the third largest contingent in the 1991 Parliament, they went underground and launched a violent insurgency after repeatedly being ignored by the government.[6]

An extremely centralized polity meant that there were very few points at which people could access the government. It meant that the collectivities had to target the executive at the centre, as it was the only institution that had the authority to deal with their grievances. However, the executive could respond only to a limited number of issues or groups at a time, due to time and resource constraints, leading to the neglect of many issues and problems. As a result, frustrations piled up among those whose problems had not been addressed, often increasing alienation.

The exclusion, inequality and centralization contributed to contentious politics in a number of ways. First, when the government was not responsive to the people, the people became alienated and launched protests and social movements. When the alienation was high, they even launched violent activities and movements. Second, people not happy with the state would not support the government with enthusiasm. This meant that if the government came under attack, they would not defend or support the government. Third, an alienated people could mean that they would support the rebel forces. This is what happened with regard to the Maoists as many people joined or supported the insurgents because the government had not done much for them.

History of Rebellions and Contentious Politics in Nepal

Nepal has been described as a peaceful country in popular discourse and academia for a long time. This has happened despite the occurrence of many conflicts and rebellions in its history. In this context, a brief discussion of the history of contentious activities and violent rebellions is essential in order to demystify the myth and obtain a balanced perspective. The successful suppression of the history of these activities that did not comply with the mono-ethnic nationalism project of the state (Onta 1996) also makes their discussion more relevant.

As Table 1.1 shows, the Nepali state has faced collective contentions and rebellions ever since its formation. The table records rebellions and contentious activities from 1770 onwards (Gurung and Bhattachan 2004; Neupane 2001; Regmi 1995; Uprety 1992). The criterion for including events in Tables 1.1 and 1.2 is a large participation of people in collective, public political struggles or rebellions that resulted in suppression and executions. More than two dozen such activities occurred before 1990. In the beginning, some of these rebellions were led by the recently defeated or accommodated groups. For instance, after the repeated defeats of the advancing Gorkha troops, the Limbus of eastern Nepal were brought into the Gorkha kingdom under a treaty that provided them with political, economic and judicial autonomy. However, as the Gorkhali state consolidated, it began to undermine the Limbus's autonomy. The Limbus, in various instances, resisted the erosion of their autonomy. It is beyond the scope of this chapter to discuss other contentions and rebellions; Tables 1.1 and 1.2, though incomplete, are just an attempt to list some of the activities.

In addition to the identity, peasant (most were mobilized by communists) and student movements, revolts, and protests, Nepal also witnessed collective struggles by trade unions, teachers, government employees, and socio-religious groups (Neupane 2001; Uprety 1992). The *makaiko kheti* (maize farming) repression (1920) and Yogmaya's political-religious reform movement (1936–40) are examples of non-political party-oriented rebellions.[7]

Table 1.1
Ethnic and Caste Mobilizations and Rebellions in Nepal before 1990*

Year	*Event*	*Locality/Region*
1770	Ten Limbuwan rebellion and expulsion	Pallo Kirant (far east)
1773–81	Majh Kirant rebellion	Dudhkosi-Arun region**
1778	Limbu language repression	Pallo Kirant
1792–93	Nepal–China War: Limbus and Bhotes assist China	Arun-Tista (Limbus) and Nuwakot (Bhotes)**
1793	Tamang (Murmi) rebellion	Nuwakot
1790s	Jumla rebellion led by Sobhan Shahi	Jumla**
1808	Khambu rebellion (two executed, properties of 15 confiscated)	Bhojpur
1858	Sukhdev Gurung rebellion (killed after 17 years in jail)	Lamjung
1867	Dashain boycott (Ramlihang and Ridima killed)	Dhankuta
1870	Limbu language repression (Sirithebe exiled)	Pallo Kirant
1876	Lakhan Thapa Magar rebellion (seven hanged)	Gorkha
1877	Supati Gurung rebellion	Gorkha (execution at Tundikhel)
1908	Atal Rai, Bharatsing Rai and Kanthabir Rai executed	Manjh Kirant***
1925	Chiring Norbu Lama and four Buddhist monks expelled	Patan
1926	Nepal Bhasa Sahitya Mandal (Newar language) movement	Calcutta
1927	Buddhist monks expelled	Kathmandu
1941	Four rebels given capital punishment (three Newars)	Kathmandu
1947	Anti-untouchability movement—failed	Bhagat Sarbajit Biswakorma***
1950–51	Kiranti movement	Majh and Pallo Kirant (east)
1954	Dalit temple-entry movement (Pashupati and Shaileshowri)	Kathmandu and Doti***
1956	Movement against making Nepali the only language of instruction	Terai****
1961	Tamang rebellion	Nuwakot
1964	Kirant movement against elimination of *kipat* (indigenous land ownership)	Eastern hills*****
1965	Dalit temple entry at Sidhakali—failed	Bhojpur***
1979	Nepal Bhasa Manka Khalah (The Association of Newar Speakers) established	Kathmandu,****** large public rallies, etc. organized

Source: Gurung (2004: 136, Table 35).
Notes: *Non-public protests and individual resistances are not included in the lists.
**from Regmi (1995: 17, f.n. 30),
***from Neupane (2001),
****from Gaige (1975),
*****from Caplan (2000),
******from Shrestha (1999).

Table 1.2
Peasant and Student Mobilizations before 1990

Peasant Mobilizations		*Student Mobilizations*	
18 November 1950	Firing at a rally (several killed), Gaur, Rautahat	1947	Jayatu Sanskrit movement
3 May 1951	Anti-landlord movement—several killed in firing, Bardia	1951	Chiniya Kaji death episode
1952	Rautahat, Bara, Parsa, Sarlahi, Mahottari (began from Rautahat) repressed	1966	National College-related movement
1953	Peasant–landlord conflict, Pyuthan	1976	Four month-long movement—failed
4 August 1953	Peasant leader Bhim Dutt Pant killed, west Nepal—Indian security personnel involved	1979 April	Bhutto death protest that turned into a movement and forced the 1980 referendum
1979	Chintang killings, Dhankuta		
1980	Wage-increase movement, Dhanusha		
1981	Jute price-increase movement in Jhapa, Morang, Sunsari		
1984	Piskar killings, Sindhupalchowk*		
1986	Chitwan (30,000 signatures collected)		

Source: Neupane 2001.
Note: *Peasants were mobilized in 1969, 1972, 1979 and in 1981 as well.

This brief discussion clearly demonstrates that Nepal had a long history of collective struggles prior to 1990, even though the regimes were extremely repressive. Many dissenters and rebels were imprisoned, expelled or executed. The repressive methods became less severe after 1951, but nevertheless continued. A major difference between the earlier and more contemporary collective struggles is that the activities analysed in this volume occurred in an open polity and less-repressive environment.

Taxonomy of Contentious Politics in Nepal

The collective mobilizations that have occurred after 1990 in Nepal varied in nature and hence their effects differed as well. The contemporary contentious activities emerged from the backdrop of historical and contemporary exclusion, neglect, and changing social and political conditions. The open polity after 1990 facilitated the process by providing a space for mobilization. People began articulating their problems, needs, and aspirations in this open environment. They began to organize and make demands upon the state. If the polity had been responsive and met some of the progressive demands, it could have contributed to the deepening and consolidation of democracy. However, when the polity did not respond, some of the activists began employing more coercive methods, while a few turned violent. This volume analyses the major contentious activities that have occurred after 1990: the Maoist insurgency, national and ethnic movements, and collective public protests such as *bandhs*.

The Maoist Insurgency

The insurgency, launched in February 1996, has had varying degrees of influence in almost all the 75 districts of the country.[8] More than 13,000 people have been killed, thousands have been injured and displaced, and millions have been affected psychologically, economically and politically. The death toll increased sharply after the failure of the second peace talks at the end of 2001 (see Figure 1.1), when the Maoists attacked an army barrack, after which the army was mobilized against the insurgency. Media, civil society and human-rights monitors have accused both the Maoists and the security forces of gross human-rights violations.

The Maoists initially attracted popular support by punishing or killing well-off locals who they labelled as exploiters. However, many social activists and political opponents have also become victims of their wrath. They increased their domination in many parts of the country by terrorizing people who did not support them into submission with threats of dire consequences. This strategy worked because of the state's failure to provide security to the people: the state withdrew from rural regions when the Maoist activities increased.

Figure 1.1
People Killed during the Maoist Insurgency

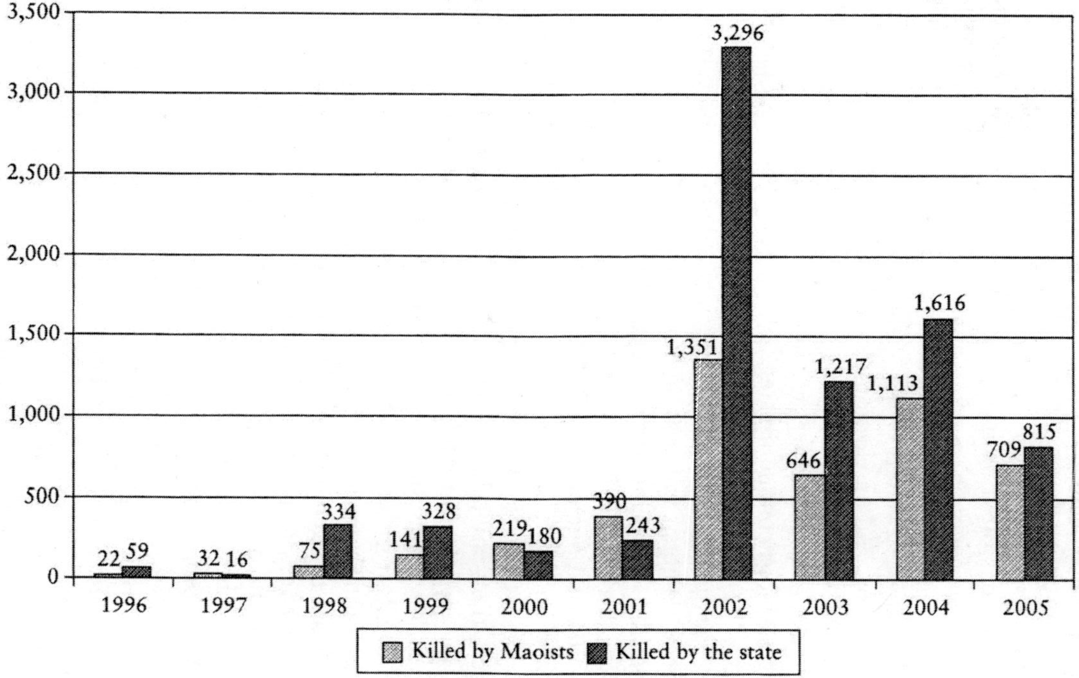

Source: INSEC (2006).

By openly championing the use of violence for social transformation, the Maoists have affected more people, both negatively and positively, than other contentious activities discussed in this book. Their impact has been such that the Nepali state's legal monopoly over coercive force in its territory has been severely undermined. The state has often been limited to urban areas and district headquarters, and its presence in many rural areas was often limited to the occasional foray by the security forces.

The major demands of the Maoists were a republic, an all-party government, and an election to the constituent assembly to design a new Constitution. The Maoists launched the insurgency when the parliamentary democracy was in place. Their overall objective is to form a Maoist communist state, or what they call a 'people's democracy.' The other prominent issues raised by the Maoists include class inequality, issues of the marginalized ethnic and caste groups, women's rights, and 'nationalism,' which implies their concerns about the sovereignty of the Nepali state.

The dialogue between the government and the Maoists failed in 2001 and again in 2003. The public nature of the first round of negotiation has been cited as a major reason for its failure. The uncertainty created by the change of government during the negotiations could have derailed the second round of negotiation.[9] During the second round, the Maoists initially seemed more serious about the negotiations, judging by their high-level team and its concerted efforts to interact with different stakeholders, such as civil society and the business community. However, some commentators suspected the genuineness of the Maoists' intentions during both the ceasefires, arguing that the Maoists could have been using the ceasefire to train and consolidate their rapidly swelling ranks of cadres, militia and the People's Liberation Army.

At the time of writing this book, the Maoists and the government are negotiating for the third time. This round of negotiation is based on more serious preparations than earlier ones. The Seven-Party-Alliance (SPA)—which has been heading the government after the king was forced to give up power by the Second People's Movement (SPM) of the SPA and the Maoists in April 2006—reached a 12-point understanding with the Maoists in November 2005. One significant achievement of the understanding was the Maoists' declaration that they would join the mainstream multiparty system. Even though this change of attitude seems genuine, based on their previous policies of changing positions depending upon strategic considerations and continued killings of and extortions from civilians, caution is warranted in taking the Maoist statements at face value. Further, the Maoists themselves have said that they have opted for a settlement due to their analysis that neither the government nor the rebel forces are in a position to win the civil war. If the perception of the stalemate changes, they could change their strategy as well. Still, there is a greater chance for the negotiations to succeed this time. There is much more trust between the rebels and the political leadership in the government. Prachanda, the top Maoist leader, has appeared in public for the first time since the insurgency began, perhaps indicating his serious intent to join open politics, as declared, if the negotiations succeed.

Identity Politics

National/ethnic conflict has occurred throughout Nepal's history (see Table 1.1). However, it is safe to say that the identity movements of the indigenous nationalities, Dalit, Madhesi, and religious minority groups gained momentum and became much more visible after 1990, utilizing the space provided by the open polity. National/ethnic, caste, and regional groups are fighting for the equal recognition of their languages, religions and cultures as well as equal opportunities in the polity, economy and society. The associations of different ethnic and caste groups have highlighted primarily cultural and political issues, while their community members are concerned about economic opportunities as well. The identity movements till now have not demanded secession, interpreting self-determination rights as a demand for autonomy. Till now, except for the Khambuwan National Front (KNF) and Janatantric Tarai Mukti Morcha (JTMM), national/ethnic movements have not launched violent rebellions.[10] However, many riots and violent conflicts have taken place among different groups, as Table 1.3 shows.

There have been several Hindu–Muslim conflicts, riots targeting the Muslim community, and riots against and involving the Madhesis. Nepalgunj witnessed five violent conflicts between Hindus and Muslims from 1992 to 1997, but they seem to have petered out since 1997. The KNF, which subsequently joined the Maoists, launched an ethnic insurgency demanding autonomy for the group. The Mongol National Organization (MNO) has threatened violent

Table 1.3
Non-Maoist Violent Conflicts (Riots and Insurgencies) in Nepal since 1990

Year	*Events/Actors*	*Location*
1992 October	Hindu–Muslim riots during Deepawali	Nepalgunj
3–4 November 1994	Hindu–Muslim riots during the parliamentary election	Nepalgunj
3–9 December 1994	Hindu–Muslim riots during well renovation at a temple	Nepalgunj
25–28 October 1995	Hindu–Muslim riots during Deepawali	Nepalgunj
1997 May	Hindu–Muslim riots during local elections	Nepalgunj
26–27 December 2000	Parbate–Madhesi (Hritik) riots	Kathmandu and Terai
Since 1999, increased in 2001–02	Khambuwan insurgency*	Khotang, Bhojpur, Solukhumbu, Okhaldhunga
1 September 2004	Riots against Muslims (reaction to Iraq killings)	Kathmandu
January 2005; April and July 2006	Madhesi insurgency**	Rautahat, Saptari, Siraha, Sunsari

Sources: Gaunle (1997); Sharma (2004); Khadga (2006) and various other newspapers.

Notes: *The KNF began violent activities in Sawan 2054 v.s. (July–August 1997) by detonating a bomb in a Sanskrit school in Dingla, Bhojpur. Since then, they have killed opponents, looted an agricultural hank, destroyed a power station, kidnapped opponents, and expelled Bahun Chettris from the area of their influence. The KNF has merged and split from the Maoists several times. In Asoj 2058 v.s. (September–October 2001), the KNF and the Limbuwan National Front (LNF) were merged with the Maoists to form the Kirant National Front. The violent activities of the KNF increased during 2001 and 2002, even though they began killing opponents in April–May 1999 (Sharma 2002; Shrestha 2004).

**The Janatantrik Tarai Mukti Morcha (Tarai People's Liberation Front) (JTMM) split from the Maoists and has killed Maoist cadres as well as others, including a parliamentarian.

rebellion and has declared that it has formed an army (Hangen, Chapter 7 of this book).

The Dalits, on the other hand, have faced numerous violent backlashes in their struggle towards equality and the end of untouchability. Table 1.4 shows that the Dalits' collective struggles have largely been directed towards ending exclusion from public spaces such as temples and accessing opportunities that should be available to any citizen, such as selling milk to publicly owned dairies. The Dalits' problems have arisen largely because the state has failed to enforce laws ending untouchability in public places.

Table 1.4
Some Contentious Activities by Dalits after 1990

Year	*Event*	*Location*
1991	Mobilization to sell milk to dairies	Udiyachaour, Syangja
1991	Temple-entry movement	Nawalparasi
1994	Mobilization to sell milk to dairies	Chitwan
1994	Gorakhkali temple-entry movement	Gorkha
1994	Right to water from a public source	Sipapokhari, Sindhupalchowk
March 2000	Anti-carcass-disposal campaign	Lahan, Siraha*
12 June 2000	Mobilization to sell milk to dairies	Gaindakot, Nawalparasi

Sources: JUP (2001); Neupane (2001); Uprety et al. (2005).
Note: *Similar campaigns were conducted in neighbouring Saptari district in 1999 (at Dultpur in July and at Madhupatti in October 1999), but these were low key compared to the Siraha district campaign.

In recent years, many activists of mainstream ethnic and Dalit movements have begun to urge taking up arms against the state if their demands go unmet. The change in discourse from non-violence to violence is significant because Apter (1997) argues that the discourse of violence legitimizes violence when it occurs. The emerging discourse on violence has special significance because of the situation in which the country finds itself: violence has entered into the society because of the Maoist insurgency, the deteriorating law and order, and the emergence of self-defence committees and vigilante groups. In such a context, the move to a violent movement from a peaceful one may not be too difficult.

Collective Public Protests: Voluntary and Coercive

The third category of socio-political collective activities is more apparent with actions and events, rather than any specific group of actors. *Bandhs* (shutdowns), strikes, *chakka-jams* (traffic blockades), *masal juluses* (torch-lit processions) and *dharnas* (sit-ins) have been used by various groups, ranging from the parliamentary political parties to the Maoists, identity movements, political interest groups, economic associations, students' groups affiliated to political parties, teachers' associations, bus-owners' associations, social-justice movements, and even spontaneous collectivities (such as when the locals bring the traffic to a halt along the highways, often after fatal vehicle accidents). These repertoires are mostly employed in urban and semi-urban areas. The political parties, including the Maoists, have more often used street protests, enforcing their protest calls with threats as well as real violence.

The public protests are a medium for the disgruntled and the political–economic interest groups to protest against government policies and make their demands heard. These activities could contribute towards democratization if the activities were progressive and such demands were met. On the other hand, neglect of progressive demands could lead to an increase in alienation and the emergence of violence or even protracted violent conflict, as demonstrated by the Maoist insurgency.

Some of these street protests have gained positive results, such as the emancipation of Kamaiyas (bonded labourers); but others, especially the activities that have been imposed with coercive methods, have often shut down businesses and schools, disrupted normal life, and destroyed public and private property. This has alienated the larger public from such movements and methods. These activities have been carried out very frequently, but scholarly work on the topic is rare.

Chapter Plan

This book is divided into five parts: context and framework; the Maoist insurgency; identity politics; collective public protests; and contentious politics and democratization. The book does not contain chapters on the Dalit, Madhesi, and women's movements, despite a concerted attempt to include them. I have provided some information on them in this introduction. This volume also does not contain issues that have been covered extensively elsewhere (such as the economic dimension of the Maoist insurgency).

Part I consists of two chapters. In Chapter 1, I lay down the framework for the book and provide background information on the activities this book investigates. In Chapter 2, I discuss the exclusionary constitutional-engineering process in 1990. I show how the under-representation of marginalized groups and women in the engineering process led to the neglect and exclusion of issues relevant to them from the Constitution. The exclusion has subsequently fuelled the gender and identity movements.

Part II brings together chapters on the Maoist insurgency. The chapters in this section bring out new and important dimensions that have not yet been analysed. In Chapter 3, Khanal points out that the commitment of the insurgents and the lines of division across the mainstream political actors contributed to the initiation and growth of the insurgency. In Chapter 4, Crawford, Kaufmann and Gurung show the different ways in which the conflict has increased the vulnerability of women and children, the group that is perhaps the most vulnerable in society and usually the last to come into consideration while analysing violent conflicts. This chapter provides much-needed empirical research on the consequences of the insurgency. In Chapter 5, a Maoist journalist who conducted extensive field coverage during the early phase of the insurgency presents the international Maoist perspective. Onesto credits the growth of the Maoists to a large extent to their following the broad strategy developed by Mao half a century ago. She also discusses the achievements of the Maoists in their base area and concludes the chapter by discussing the different challenges the insurgency faces. In Chapter 6, Somlai shows the role of multiple stakeholders in the insurgency, going beyond the usual discussion of the Maoists, the palace, and the mainstream political parties. The stakeholder analysis of the insurgency is important, but surprisingly has not been achieved yet. This chapter attempts to flesh out how different actors may be influencing the insurgency, both negatively and positively (during insurgency as well as during talks and settlements). He argues that any attempt at settling the insurgency has to take into consideration these numerous stakeholders and their varied interests.

Part III brings together chapters on identity politics. In Chapter 7, Hangen demonstrates how a small ethnic party contributed to the democratization process in Nepal. She argues that by facilitating the participation of people who would otherwise not have got the opportunity to find representation in the larger parties and the mainstream social movements and by bringing up issues important to them which the larger parties did not address, the Mongol National Organization (MNO) contributed towards democratization in the rural margins. Chapters 8 and 9 bring together two articles on Newars: one on nationalism and the other on the religious aspect of the Newar movement. Shrestha traces the development of Newar nationalism in Chapter 8. He discusses different challenges the Newar nationalists face in mobilizing a group that is divided along caste and class. In Chapter 9, Maharjan discusses the spread of Theravadin Buddhism among Newars in Kathmandu. He argues that dissatisfaction with the socio-political system, as well as insecurity in a modernizing and changing world, has contributed to the growth of Theravadin Buddhism.

Part IV contains two chapters that deal with collective public protests. In Chapter 10, Lakier argues that some contentious activities could empower people while others could protect the interests of the privileged group. She argues that many contentious activities and movements of the 1990s undermined the rights of individuals as the organizers forcefully implemented their call for strikes and protests. She calls this illiberal democracy as it constrains the civil liberty of citizens. Snellinger, in Chapter 11, argues that although student activism contributed to the restoration of democracy during the autocratic period, during the democratic period such activists were often perceived by commoners as foot soldiers of the political parties. The students, however, projected their activities as social movements.

Part V concludes by discussing the different effects of contentious politics on democratization. In Chapter 12, Rademacher discusses the attitudes of those unhappy with the environmental degradation in the Kathmandu Valley and how they attribute it to the failure of democracy. She shows that the failure of democratic governance in maintaining law and order led to support, at least initially, for the post-democratic government. Perhaps herein lies one of the challenges for democracy in Nepal. Democracy has to *work* so that people are not alienated and do not support non-democratic regimes and leaders. In the final chapter, Chapter 13, based on materials presented in this book and other sources, I argue that some types of contentious politics contributed to democratization by expanding the rights of people, whereas others undermined liberal democracy by constraining the political rights and civil liberty of citizens.

Acknowledgement

I would like to thank Susan Hangen, Mukta Singh Lama, Sanjay Serchan, Bal Gopal Shrestha, and an anonymous reviewer for helpful comments on an earlier draft.

Notes

1. The term 'episodic', again following McAdam et al. (2001: 5), 'excludes regularly scheduled events such as votes, parliamentary elections, and associational meetings—although any such events can become a springboard for contentious politics'. If these structures are used by mobilizing marginalized groups, who

are not part of the state, as part of their collective struggles, they will be considered as contentious politics in this volume.

2. The CHHE made up 30.89 per cent of the population in 2001, indigenous nationalities 36.41 per cent, the Dalits 14.99 per cent and the Madhesis 30.49 per cent (if Madhesis, indigenous nationalities, and Dalits are included in the Madhesi count—note there is some overlapping among Dalits, indigenous nationalities and the Madhesis) (Bhattachan 2003).
3. The Newars (5.48 per cent of the population) also occupy a disproportionate share of influential positions, but are discriminated against in cultural matters; and they are involved in the social justice movements of the indigenous nationalities. The presence of the Newars in politics and administration has been on the decline after 1990.
4. The CPN-UML was the major opposition party during two parliamentary tenures and the largest minority party in another. Many other smaller communist parties also exist.
5. The CPN-UML did not rule at the centre for long—hence even if it had wanted to, it was not in a position to make much difference. However, the increasing influence of the World Bank and other international regimes in pushing liberal marketization policies and its acceptance by the CPN-UML meant that its hands would have been tied when it came to initiating substantive socialist policies even if it had had an opportunity to rule longer.
6. This is not to argue that it was the major reason for initiating the insurgency. My position is that it increased alienation and helped the Maoists push towards it.
7. The palace also witnessed many intra-faction squabbles among regents, queens, princes and courtiers that resulted in numerous expulsions, factional warfare and massacres (Acharya 1998; Willesee and Whittaker 2004).
8. Only Mustang and Manang, two mountainous and isolated districts where indigenous nationalities reside, did not have any insurgency-related deaths till the writing of this chapter in mid-2006.
9. The media often project the killings of Maoist supporters by the government security forces in Doramba as a catalyst for the break-off, but Prakash Chandra Lohani, a government negotiator in the second round, says that the Maoists had already decided to break off the negotiations and showed reluctance to sit down for dialogue when the government representatives reached Harpure (the venue for the talks), before the Doramba incident (personal communication).
10. The KNF joined the Maoists (it split and joined again—this occurred a couple of times again) and the JTMM split from the Maoists.

References

Acharya, Baburam. 1998. *Aba Yasto Kahilei Nahos* (*May This Never Happen Again*). Kathmandu: Sri Krishna Acharya.

Apter, David (ed.). 1997. 'Political Violence in Analytic Perspective', in *The Legitimization of Violence*. New York: New York University Press.

Aziz, Barbara Nimri. 1993. 'Shakti Yogmaya: A Tradition of Dissent in Nepal', in M. Brauen and C. Ramble (eds), *Anthropology of Tibet and Himalaya*. Zurich: Ethnological Museum of the University of Zurich.

Baral, Lok Raj. 1977. *Oppositional Politics in Nepal.* New Delhi: Abhinav Publications.
———. 1993. *Nepal: Problems of Governance.* New Delhi: Konark.
——— (ed.). 2004. *Nepal: Political Parties and Parliament.* New Delhi: Adroit Publishers.
Bhattachan, Krishna B. 1995. 'Ethnopolitics and Ethnodevelopment', in D. Kumar (ed.), *State, Leadership and Politics in Nepal.* Kathmandu: Centre for Nepal and Asian Studies (CNAS).
———. 1999. 'Minority Rights in the Predatory Nepalese State', in S. Banerjee (ed.), *Shrinking Space: Minority Rights in South Asia.* Lalitpur: South Asian Forum for Human Rights (SAFHR).
———. 2000. 'Possible Ethnic Revolution or Insurgency in Predatory Unitary Hindu State, Nepal', in D. Kumar (ed.), *Domestic Conflict and Crises of Governability in Nepal.* Kathmandu: CNAS.
Bhattachan, Krishna B. 2003. 'Indigenous Nationalities and Minorities of Nepal'. Final report submitted to the Minority Rights Group (MRG) International, London.
Bhurtel, Jugal and Saleem H. Ali. n.d. 'The Green Roots of Red Rebellion: Environmental Degradation and the Rise of the Maoist Movement in Nepal', *Environmental Conflict Resolution.* Available at http://www.uvm.edu/~shali/Maoist.pdf.
Bista, Dor Bahadur. 1991. *Fatalism and Development: Nepal's Struggle for Modernization.* Hyderabad: Orient Longman.
Biswakorma, Hira. 2000. *Nepalko Dalit Andolanma Dalit Sangathanko Bhumika* (The Role of Dalit Organizations in the Dalit Movement of Nepal), in H. Jha (ed.), *Nepalma Dalit Utthanka Rananiti* (Strategy for the Uplift of Dalits in Nepal). Kathmandu: Centre for Economic and Technical Studies (CETS).
Blaikie, Piers, John Cameron and David Seddon. 1980. *Nepal in Crisis: Growth and Stagnation at the Periphery.* New Delhi: Oxford University Press.
Brown, T. Louise. 1996. *The Challenge to Democracy in Nepal.* London and New York: Routledge.
Caplan, Lionel. 2000. *Land and Social Change in East Nepal*, 2nd ed. Lalitpur: Himal Books.
Chauhan, R.S. 1989. *Society and State Building in Nepal.* New Delhi: Sterling Publishers.
Dahl, Robert A. 1989. *Democracy and Its Critics.* New Haven and London: Yale University Press.
de Sales, Anne. 2003. 'The Kham Magar Country: Between Ethnic Claims and Maoism', in D.N. Gellner (ed.), *Resistance and the Nepalese State.* New Delhi: Social Science Press.
Deraniyagala, Sonali. 2005. 'The Political Economy of Civil Conflict in Nepal', *Oxford Development Studies* 33 (1): 47–62.
FWLD. 2000. *Discriminatory Laws in Nepal and Their Impact on Women: A Review of the Current Situation and Prospects for Change.* Kathmandu: Forum for Women, Law and Development (FLWD).
Gaige, Frederick H. 1975. *Regionalism and National Unity in Nepal.* New Delhi: Vikas.
Gaunle, Shiva. 1997. 'Nepalgunj: Dharmik Kachingalko Bisphotak Thalo (Nepalgunj: Religious Conflicts Explosion Centre)', *Himal* (June–July): 8–16.

Gellner, David N. (ed.). 2003. *Resistance and the State: Nepalese Experience*. New Delhi: Social Science Press.

Gellner, David N., Joanna Pfaff-Czarnecka and John Whelpton (eds). 1997. *Nationalism and Ethnicity in a Hindu Kingdom: The Politics of Culture in Contemporary Nepal*. Amsterdam: Harwood Academic Publishers.

Guneratne, Arjun. 2002. *Many Tongues, One People: The Making of Tharu Identity in Nepal*. Ithaca and London: Cornell University Press.

Gupta, Anirudha. 1993. *Politics in Nepal: 1950–60*, 2nd large ed. Delhi: Kalinga Publications.

Gurung, Harka. 2003. 'Trident and Thunderbolt: Cultural Dynamics in Nepalese Politics'. Paper presented at a seminar on 'The Transformation Agenda: Inclusion in Nepali Democracy,' 24–26 April, Kathmandu.

———. 2004. *Janajati Serophero*. Kathmandu: Nepal Federation of Indigenous Nationalities (NEFIN).

Gurung, Harka, Malla K. Sunder, Krishna Bhattachan and Om Gurung (eds). 2000. *Janajati Bikasko Jukti* (Ideas for Nationalities' Development). Kathmandu: Janajati Bikash Samanoya Kendra.

Gurung, Sumitra Manandhar and Yashokanti Bhattachan. 2004. *Content Analysis of the Position of Minorities in Relation to the Constitution of Kingdom of Nepal.* Kathmandu: Institute for Democracy and Electoral Assistance (IDEA) International.

Hachhethu, Krishna. 2002. *Party Building in Nepal: Organization, Leadership and People*. Kathmandu: Mandala Book Point.

Hofer, A. 1979. *The Caste Hierarchy and the State in Nepal: A Study of the Muluki Ain of 1854*. Innsbruck: Universitatsverlag, Wagner.

Huntington, Samuel P. 1968. *Political Order in Changing Societies*. New Haven: Yale University Press.

Hutt, Michael (ed.). 2004. *Himalayan People's War: Nepal's Maoist Rebellion*. Bloomington and Indianapolis: Indiana University Press.

INSEC. 2006. *No. of Victims Killed by State and Maoists in Connection with the 'People's War' 13 Feb. 1996–29 Jun. 2006*. Informal Sector Service Centre (INSEC). Available at: http://www.inseconline.org/download/Killings.pdf. (Accessed on 8 July 2006)

Joshi, Bhuwan Lal and Leo E. Rose. 1966. *Democratic Innovations in Nepal: A Case Study of Political Acculturation*. Berkeley: University of California Press.

JUP. 2001. *Dalit in Nepal and Alternative Report for WCAR: 2001*. Kathmandu: Jana Utthan Pratisthan (JUP).

Karki, Arjun and David Seddon (eds). 2003. *The People's War in Nepal: Left Perspectives*. Delhi: Adroit Publishers.

Khadga, Jitendra. 2006. 'Maobadisanga Maramar (All out War on the Maoists)', *Nepal National Weekly* (online edition), April 23.

Kumar, Dhruba (ed.). 1995. *State Leadership and Politics in Nepal*. Kathmandu: CNAS.

——— (ed.). 2000. *Domestic Conflict and Crises of Governability in Nepal*. Kathmandu: CNAS.

———. 2005. 'Proximate Causes of Conflict in Nepal', *Contributions to Nepalese Studies* 32 (1): 51–93.

Kymlicka, Will. 1995. *Multicultural Citizenship: A Liberal Theory of Minority Rights*. Oxford: Oxford University Press.

Lawoti, Mahendra. 2002a. 'Defining Minorities in Nepal', *Nepali Journal of Contemporary Studies* 2 (2): 22–52.

———. 2002b. 'Exclusionary Democratization: Multicultural Society and Political Institutions in Nepal'. Unpublished Ph.D. thesis, Graduate School of Public and International Affairs, University of Pittsburgh, Pittsburgh.

———. 2003a. 'Maoists and Minorities: Overlap of Interests or the Case of Exploitation?', *Studies in Nepali History and Society* 8 (1): 67–97.

———. 2003b. 'Centralized Politics and the Growth of the Maoist Insurgency in Nepal', *Himalaya: The Journal of the Association for Nepal and Himalayan Studies* 23: 49–58.

———. 2005. *Towards a Democratic Nepal: Inclusive Political Institutions for a Multicultural Society*. New Delhi: Sage Publications.

Lecomte-Tilouine, Marie and Pascale Dollfus (eds). 2003. *Ethnic Revival and Religious Turmoil: Identities and Representations in the Himalayas*. New Delhi: Oxford University Press.

Levine, Nancy E. 1987. 'Caste, State, and Ethnic Boundaries in Nepal', *Journal of Asian Studies* 46 (1): 71–88.

Lowi, Theodore J. 1969. *The End of Liberalism: Ideology, Policy, and the Crisis of Public Authority*. New York and London: W.W. Norton & Company.

Macfarlane, Alan. 2001. 'Sliding Down Hill: Some Reflections on Thirty Years of Change in a Himalayan Village', *European Bulletin of Himalayan Research* 20 (1) (double): 105–24.

Markoff, John. 1996. *Waves of Democracy: Social Movements and Political Change*. Thousand Oaks, California: Pine Forge Press.

McAdam, Doug, Sidney Tarrow and Charles Tilly. 2001. *Dynamics of Contention*. Cambridge: Cambridge University Press.

Migdal, Joel S. 1994. 'The State in Society: An Approach to Struggle for Domination', in J.S. Migdal, A. Kohli and V. Shue (eds), *State Power and Social Forces: Domination and Transformation in the Third World*. Cambridge: Cambridge University Press.

Mishra, Chaitanya. 2004. 'Locating the "Causes" of the Maoist Struggle', *Studies in Nepali History and Society* 9 (1): 3–56.

NESAC. 1998. *Nepal Human Development Report 1998*. Kathmandu: NESAC.

Neupane, Govinda. 2000. *Nepalko Jatiya Prashna: Samajik Banot ra Sajhedariko Sambhawana* (Nepal's National Question: Social Composition and Possibilities of Accommodation). Kathmandu: Centre for Development Studies.

———. 2001. *Nepali Samajko Rupantaran* (Transformation in Nepali Society). Kathmandu: Centre for Development Studies.

O'Donnell, Guillermo. 1996. 'Illusions about Democratic Consolidation', *Journal of Democracy* 7 (2): 34–51.

Onesto, Li. 2005. *Dispatches from the People's War in Nepal*. London and Ann Arbor: Pluto Press.

Onta, Praytoush. 1996. 'Ambivalence Denied: The Making of Rastriya Itihas in Panchayat Era Textbooks', *Contributions to Nepalese Studies* 23 (1): 213–54.

Parajulee, Ramjee P. 2000. *The Democratic Transition in Nepal*. Lanham: Rowman & Littlefield Publishers.

Regmi, Mahesh C. 1965. *The Land Tenure and Taxation in Nepal, Volume III: The Jagir, Rakam, and Kipat Tenure Systems*. Berkeley: Institute of International Studies.

———. 1978. *Thatched Huts and Stucco Palaces: Peasants and Landlords in 19th-century Nepal*. New Delhi: Vikas.

———. 1995. *Kings and Political Leaders of the Gorkhali Empire, 1768–1814*. Hyderabad: Orient Longman.

Schedler, Andreas, Larry Diamond and Marc F. Plattner (eds). 1999. *The Self-Restraining State: Power and Accountability in New Democracies*. Boulder and London: Lynne Rienner Publishers.

Serchan, Sanjaya. 2001. *Democracy, Pluralism, and Change: An Inquiry in the Nepalese Context*. Kathmandu: Chhye Pahuppe.

Shah, Rishikesh. 1993. *Politics in Nepal: 1980–1991*. New Delhi: Manohar.

Sharma, Kishor. 2006. 'The Political Economy of Civil War in Nepal', *World Development* 34 (7): 1237–53.

Sharma, Sudheer. 2002. *The Ethnic Dimension of the Maoist Insurgency*. (Unpublished report for DFID). Kathmandu.

Sharma, Sudhindra. 2002. 'Lived Islam in Nepal', in I. Ahmad and H. Reifeld (eds), *Lived Islam in Asia: Adaptation, Accommodation and Conflict*. New Delhi: Social Science Press.

Shrestha, Bal Gopal. 1999. 'The Newars: The Indigenous Population of the Kathmandu Valley in the Modern State of Nepal', *Contributions to Nepalese Studies* 26 (1): 83–117.

Shrestha, Damber Krishna. 2004. 'Kirant Rastriya Morcha ra Maobadi Gathbandhan (Kirant National Front and Maoists Alliance)', in R. Dahal and M. Mainali (eds), *Bandukko Bojh* (Weight of Guns). Lalitpur: Himal Books.

Stiller, L.F. 1973. *The Rise of the House of Gorkha*. Ranchi: The Patna Jesuit Society.

Thapa, Deepak and Bandita Sijapati. 2003. A *Kingdom Under Siege: Nepal's Maoist Insurgency, 1996 to 2003*. Kathmandu: The Printhouse.

Upreti, Bishnu Raj. 2004. *The Price of Neglect: From Resource Conflict to Maoist Insurgency in the Himalayan Kingdom*. Kathmandu: Bhrikuti Academic Publications.

Uprety, Laya Prasad, Indra Rai and Him Prasad Sedhain. 2005. *A Case Study of the Grassroots Anti-Carcass Throwing Campaign of Saraswoti Community Development Forum*. Kathmandu: ActionAid.

Uprety, Prem R. 1992. *Political Awakening in Nepal: The Search for a New Identity*. New Delhi: Commonwealth Publishers.

Wagle, Udaya R. 2006. 'Inclusive Democracy and Economic Inequality in South Asia: Any Discernible Link?', in *School of Public Affairs and Administration, Western Michigan Univeristy*. Kalamazoo (unpublished). Available at: http:// homepages.wmich.edu/~uwagle.

Willesee, Amy and Mark Whittaker. 2004. *Love and Death in Kathmandu: A Strange Tale of Royal Murder*. Australia: Pan Macmillan.

Young, Iris Marion. 1990. *Justice and the Politics of Difference*. Princeton, New Jersey: Princeton University.

2

Democracy, Domination and Exclusionary Constitutional-Engineering Process in Nepal, 1990

MAHENDRA LAWOTI

INTRODUCTION

The indigenous nationalities (Adibasi Janajati),[1] Dalits (traditional untouchables) and Madhesis (plains people) who collectively form more than two-thirds of the population, and women were highly excluded from governance in Nepal during its second democratic experience, from 1990 to 2002. The men of the CHHE dominated most influential realms of governance. For instance, the CHHE—along with the Newars, an indigenous group doing fairly well in accessing resources but facing cultural discrimination[2]—constituted 36.37 per cent of the population in 2001 but occupied more than 80 per cent of positions in the executive, Parliament, judiciary, and the top civil administration in 1999 (Lawoti 2002; Neupane 2000).

Lately, especially after the king's dismissal of the elected government in 2002, political exclusion is being recognized as a problem in the political circles as well.[3] Attention on the issue had increased in the society earlier with the spread of the Maoist insurgency countrywide and high participation of some of the excluded groups in it. Increasingly, the majoritarian political institutions adopted by the Constitution have been identified as a major cause of political exclusion. They failed to share power among different groups in a multicultural society. The unitary state's failure to provide autonomy to various groups, the first-past-the-post (FPTP) electoral method's bias towards larger political parties dominated by the CHHE, and discriminatory constitutional provisions have contributed to the political exclusion of various socioculturally marginalized groups (Bhattachan 1999; Lawoti 2005; Neupane 2000). In this context, the question is why and how did a democratic constitution, despite introducing a number of remarkable reforms such as freedom of speech and association, ended up adopting exclusionary institutions? This is the question this chapter attempts to answer.

The constitutional questions have gained importance in Nepal as a new constitution is being planned to address the concerns of the Maoists and issues of political exclusion. An analysis of the exclusionary constitutional-engineering process may help prevent repetition of such processes in Nepal and in other emerging multicultural democracies.

Diversity, Constitutionalism and Domination

Nepal's cultural diversity emanates from various races, several religions, numerous ethnic and caste groups, around 100 languages and diverse regional cultures. In terms of mobilization and self-identification, they can be broadly divided into four major identity groups. The indigenous nationalities consist of more than 60 Tibeto-Burman linguistic groups from the mountains, hills and the Terai. The Dalits mostly consist of hill and Terai Dalits. Madhesis consist of Terai Hindu caste groups, Muslims and indigenous nationalities.[4] The CHHE, consisting of Bahun, Chettri, Thakuri, and Sanyasi, have dominated Nepal since its conquest in 1769. Though a numeric minority, the CHHE have effectively excluded other sociocultural groups from the state apparatus. Gender inequality is also rampant across the country.

Most of the excluded groups are economically deprived as well.[5] Some of the 'upper-caste' Madhesis are well-off economically, but they also face political exclusion and sociocultural discrimination.

Overall, class and identity often coincide in Nepal, potentially an explosive mix if not handled carefully. The focus of this chapter is the exclusion of identity groups from the constitutional-engineering process without denying the importance of class.

The 1990 Constitution of Nepal is the fifth in half a century. Dissatisfaction among successive generations over the constitutions has only increased, as all of them were mostly designed to protect the interests of the rulers. I will show that the 1990 Constitution also fails to extend political and sociocultural equality to marginalized groups. The realm of power and political space were broadened, but mostly accommodated more actors of the traditional elite groups in it.

This chapter distinguishes between the discriminatory provisions in the Constitution and discrimination that occurs in practice despite ideal constitutional provisions, and focuses only on the former.

Some of the constitutional articles espouse equality to all Nepali citizens, but discriminatory articles have been inserted in other places that constrain the marginalized sociocultural groups in various ways. The Constitution has contributed to four types of discrimination. First, banning ethnic parties and citizenship based on father's lineage only are some examples of explicit discrimination. Second, the lack of equal recognition of differences among cultural groups and adoption of dominant values and norms by the Constitution are examples of implicit discrimination, which privilege the dominant group. Third, the Constitution does not protect substantive minority rights. Finally, the Constitution has adopted majoritarian state structures that favour the dominant group (Lawoti 2005).

The 1990 democratic Constitution is favourable to the CHHE because their domination of the engineering process enabled them to influence its outcome. It ignored the aspirations and demands of the marginalized groups. Domination of influential political and social institutions by one group has led to unequalizing consequences for public policy in Nepal.

Identity movements have exploded since 1990 in Nepal. They have demanded group-differentiated rights to address specific problems faced by particular groups. The demands are not for dominating other groups but show a desire to participate in mainstream society as equal citizens. They are not communal in nature, as they aim at furthering integration of excluded groups into the society. Nor are they aimed at imposing their views and values on others or at isolating the groups from the rest of the society. However, the method of integration they espouse is not assimilation but equality and justice across groups.

The social-justice movements do not threaten the integration of Nepal. None of the groups has demanded secession. Additionally, the large number of groups and their individual small populations also reduce the potential threat. However, the threat could rise if they unite along broader cultural lines due to the continuation of discrimination in common arenas such as language and culture. If the groups collectively feel that their aspirations are not being met, the alliances may resort to violent activities.

Culturally Plural Societies and Inclusive Polities

Exclusion occurs in plural societies when the dominant group defines the collective identity of the state according to its values and norms (Taylor 1998: 146–47). The state, instead of being neutral or relatively autonomous, adopts and imparts the dominant values through its institutions. The alien dominant values and standards hurt minorities because they have to live with and be judged by values and standards that are not their own. Control of or influence over the state by one group becomes detrimental to other groups because the state is a resource and a distributor of resources as well as a set of repressive institutions.

Recognizing that different sociocultural groups have different values and ways of life is essential for overcoming exclusion and domination in plural societies. Equality in plural societies can be achieved not by eliminating group differences, but rather by ensuring equality among different groups by attending to the specific situations of particular sociocultural groups. Absence of group-differentiated rights for marginalized groups facilitates the continuation of domination by the traditional elite groups. Since they dominate the state and society, they define and interpret norms and standards and formulate public policies based on their values and priorities. Often, to promote equality among groups, it is necessary to recognize the disadvantages the minorities face and compensate them in arenas where they are disadvantaged (Kymlicka 1995; Mahajan 1998; Parekh 1994; Young 1990, 2000).

Scholars have shown that established plural democracies generally have power-sharing political institutions that accommodate various groups. Federalism diffuses power by providing cultural autonomy, strong bicameralism, and constitutional protection of minorities. Consociational democracy is a more comprehensive power-sharing arrangement that consists of grand coalition, mutual veto, proportionality, and segmental autonomy and federalism (Lijphart 1977, 1999).

Even though by and large constitutions are idealistic and, as a consequence, may not inform the real-world behaviour of political actors and institutions, they become obstacles when they lack these ideal provisions. 'Constitutions are "forms" that structure and discipline the state's decision-making processes. They establish how norms are created' (Sartori 1997). Constitutional provisions have provided institutional solutions for incorporating diverse social groups within polities through the introduction of innovative accommodative structures and measures, such as veto power given to minority groups on matters that affect them fundamentally, proportional electoral systems, and federalism.

Democratic Processes for Establishing Democracy

Tons of scholarly works have discussed and debated various aspects of democracy. The earlier 'classics' discussed the emergence of democracy, the conditions associated with it, and its advantages over other governance systems. Much of the later work has focused on defining and evaluating democracies. However, no scholar except Robert Dahl (1989, 1998) has proposed testable criteria for forming a democratic association. Dahl (1989) argues that for forming democratic associations, either a state or other entities, the process must meet certain democratic requirements. They should be based on and aid in ensuring political equality among members of an association. He has proposed (ibid.) five criteria for making a process democratic: effective participation, voting equality, enlightened understanding, control of agenda, and inclusion of all persons for whom the rules made will become binding. If 'any of the requirements are violated, the members will not be politically equal' (ibid.)

since those violated in a particular requirement become disadvantaged in that realm.

Dahl does not specifically discuss these criteria with regard to their applicability in culturally plural societies. The non-western and developing nature of the societies may also call for revising the criteria. Taking these issues into consideration, I will adapt Dahl's democratic criteria to evaluate the constitutional-engineering process in Nepal.

Effective Participation

'Throughout the process of making binding decisions, citizens ought to have an adequate opportunity and an equal opportunity for expressing their preferences as to the final outcome' (Dahl 1989: 109).

A democratic process requires equal opportunities for members to make their preferences known while deciding on matters that will be binding on them. If 'some members are given greater opportunities than others for expressing their views, their policies are more likely to prevail' (ibid.: 39). Effective participation during the constitutional-engineering process in multicultural societies can occur at two levels. At the level of the general public, citizens and their associations should have opportunities to express their preferences so that the engineers of the Constitution hear and heed them. At the decision-making level, dialogue and discussions among representatives of different groups and parties are measures of effective participation.

Voting Equality

'When the moment arrives at which the decision about policy is finally made, every member must have an equal and effective opportunity to vote, and all votes must be counted as equal' (Dahl 1998: 37).

Voting becomes necessary when issues cannot be settled amicably through discussion and negotiation. However, the voting need not necessarily follow only the majoritarian principle; in plural societies, such a principle may result in the tyranny of the majority (Horowitz 1994). Principles of equal consideration for all ideas and for the rights of minorities should be combined with majoritarian principles to arrive at just and fair decisions.

Enlightened Understanding

'Within reasonable limits of time, each member must have equal and effective opportunities for learning about the relevant policies and their likely consequences' (Dahl 1998: 37).

'Enlightened understanding' calls for a thorough deliberation on all important issues and alternative policies as well as sufficient time and resources for making inquiries and becoming informed, so as to enhance members' ability to participate in the decision-making process. The length and scope of the consultation process, the quality of deliberation in different forums, tolerance and openness towards differing perspectives, and access to media for all groups in terms of voice, representation, and readership are necessary for an enlightened understanding.

Control of the Agenda

'The members must have the opportunity to decide how—and, if they choose, what—matters are to be placed on the agenda' (Dahl 1998: 38).

If members do not have control over the agenda on which decisions are to be made, then even if the first three criteria are met, they may not be able to discuss and decide on matters that are important to them. Whoever controls the agenda can effectively exclude certain issues by not bringing them up for deliberation and vote. This can be judged by the inclusion of contested issues in the agenda.

Inclusion of All Adults

'All, or at any rate most, adult permanent residents should have the full rights of citizens implied by the first four criteria' (Dahl 1998: 38).

This criterion becomes very significant in culturally plural societies because even when the first four criteria are met, the process becomes democratic only to those who are included. The democratic process becomes meaningless for those who are excluded. 'If you are deprived of an equal voice in the government of a state, the chances are quite high that your interests will not be given the same attention as the interests of those who do have a voice' (Dahl 1998: 38).

The inclusion criteria in this chapter will relate to the inclusion of sociocultural groups in the constitutional-engineering process. Inclusion is essential because in particular cases only those who experience them can represent the issues effectively. Exclusion of minorities will prevent representation of minority input—preferences, needs, and perspectives—and may result in injustice towards them and inequality (Guinier 1994; Phillips 1996). The degree of formal or informal representation of different sociocultural groups in the constitutional-engineering process will determine whether this criterion has been met.

Demands for Inclusion and the 1990 Constitution

Table 2.1 lists the major demands of the marginalized groups and their treatment in the Constitution. Some of the major demands included secularity of the state; linguistic equality; ethnic and regional autonomy and federalism; proportional distribution of resources; fair access to citizenship certificates; gender equality; an end to caste-based discrimination and reservations for deprived groups.

The debate regarding a secular state evoked intense controversy during the process. Marginalized-group activists opposed the declaration of the state as Hindu, fearing that other sociocultural discrimination would spring. However, various dominant group organizations and individuals worked towards declaring Nepal a Hindu state. One of the palace nominees in the interim cabinet threatened to fast unto death if Nepal was not declared a Hindu state. Hindu organizations such as the Sanatan Dharma Seva Samiti and the Nepal branch of the Vishwa Hindu Parishad also actively lobbied for declaring Nepal a Hindu state (Hutt 1994; Raeper and Hoftun 1992). The king's wish to declare the nation a Hindu monarchical kingdom is understandable as it would help legitimize his position. However, the political parties were also responsible for it. A cabinet member who argued for a secular state says that the supreme commander of the movement, Ganeshman Singh, and the then Prime Minister Bhattarai wanted Nepal to be declared a Hindu state.[6] The Constitution Recommendation Commission (CRC) inserted 'Hindu' in the article defining the state. Some CRC members have defended it saying that it was necessary to clarify the position of the king as Hindu. However, the defense is not plausible because Article 27(1) clearly fulfils the purpose. It states that the king is a descendent of Prithivi Narayan and 'an adherent of Aryan culture and Hindu religion'.

Table 2.1

Demands for Inclusion during the Constitutional-Engineering Process and the 1990 Constitution

Contested Issues	*Marginalized Groups' Claims*	*Provisions in the Constitution*
Religion and state	The state should be secular.	Nepal declared a Hindu state.
	Religious freedom for practice and conversion.	Religious conversion banned.
Language	Equality of all native languages.	Khas-Nepali made the only official language.
Education	Mother-tongue instruction in schools.	Khas-Nepali made the medium of instruction.
	The state should preserve different native languages.	Mother-tongue instruction up to primary-school level only.
Citizenship	Citizenship laws should guarantee that all citizens will be able to acquire citizenship certificates easily.	Citizenship through mother's lineage denied. Continuation of Panchayat citizenship articles led to the denial of citizenship to more than 3 million adults.
Electoral system	Proportional electoral systems.	'First-past-the-post' method.
Political	Right to form ethnicity-based parties.	Ethnic parties banned.
	No restrictions on any sort of association.	Certain restrictions on associations for maintaining harmony among different groups.
Cameral structure	Proportional representation of minority groups in the Parliament.	No proportional representation.
	Powerful Upper House constituted as House of Nationalities.	No House of Nationalities.
Regional autonomy	Federal system of governance.	Unitary system of governance.
Rights	Group-based as well as individual rights.	Only individual rights.
Cultural equality	Equality between different cultural groups.	Hindu culture promoted.
Minority protection	Provisions necessary for protecting minorities.	No substantive provisions to protect minorities.
Untouchability	Tough measures to prohibit it and special policies and programmes necessary to eliminate it.	Untouchability banned and laws directed to be legislated to make such acts punishable.
Reservations	Reservation in education, employment and decision-making bodies necessary.	Nominal reservation for women only in the Upper House.

Source: Author's compilation.

As Table 2.1 shows, most of the claims of the marginalized groups were ignored by the Constitution while many provisions favouring the dominant group were included. The Nepal Federation of Indigenous Nationalities (NEFIN) claims that more than 25 articles of the Constitution discriminate against them. Women and Madhesis have also decried the discrimination in the Constitution.[7]

The Politics of Exclusion

Exclusion through Non-representation in the Process

Socioculturally marginalized groups were excluded in all the three stages of the constitutional-engineering process that lasted for nearly six months. First, organizations of marginalized groups had no formal representation in the process. Second, very few leaders involved in the process belonged to the marginalized groups. The three stages and the actors involved are summarized in Tables 2.2 and 2.3.

Table 2.2
Issues and Representation of Marginalized Groups in the Three Stages of the Constitutional-Engineering Process

Stages	*Process and Actors*	*Representation of Marginalized Groups*	*Time*
First stage: Consultation and drafting	CRC mandate	No mention of the cultural diversity of the country or the problems of minority groups	3 months
	CRC formation	No formal representation of marginalized groups; weak representation from political forces involved	
Second stage: Revision	Cabinet formation	No formal representation of marginalized groups; very weak representation from political forces	3 months
	Subcommittee formation	No representation	
Final stage: Negotiation and promulgation	NC and ULF leadership	Very insignificant representation	
	Palace	No representation	

Source: Author's compilation.

The exclusionary process began without any mention of the cultural diversity of the country in the mandate of the CRC. The formation of the CRC further continued the exclusion. The CRC was composed of representatives of three political forces—the Nepali Congress (NC), the United Left Front (ULF) and the palace.[8] The CHHE heavily dominated the composition of the commission at 66.67 per cent. Interestingly, all the CHHE members were Bahuns. The three nominees associated with the palace included a Bahun, a Hindu Newar and a Madhesi Janajati member.[9] The three NC nominees were all Bahuns. The ULF nominated one Janajati candidate and two Bahuns. There was neither any woman nor a Dalit despite the groups' demands.

The exclusion continued when the CRC rejected the major demands of the marginalized groups. The marginalized groups held seminars and public rallies, provided written and verbal suggestions, and lobbied with the CRC and influential political leaders. They proved more competent at presenting their views at this initial stage. In fact, the number of suggestions to the CRC from marginal groups was very substantial. The chairman of the CRC, a male Bahun, showed public dismay at the large number of suggestions dealing with language, religion and culture (Hutt 1994; Raeper and Hoftun 1992).

The second stage consisted of submitting the draft drawn up by the CRC to the cabinet. The CHHE dominated the cabinet in similar proportion as in the CRC (63.64 per cent)—interestingly, all male Bahuns again.[10] With an additional 'upper-caste' Hindu from the Terai and a Newar woman (the ULF representative), the 'upper-caste' Hindus constituted 81.82 per cent of the cabinet. There was a Buddhist Newar from the NC. The influence of marginalized groups at this stage was further diluted by the formation of a cabinet subcommittee to recommend revisions on the CRC draft. No marginalized-group members were included in the subcommittee. It proved detrimental to them. According to an interim cabinet minister, the subcommittee's recommendations were decisive, since most of the cabinet members were busy running the day-to-day affairs of the country and did not get drawn into the detailed discussions on the proposed revisions by the subcommittee. Even the minimal provisions the CRC had sought, such as the reservations for Janajatis and Dalits in the Upper House, amongst others, were eliminated.

The exclusion of marginalized groups became complete in the final stage. Even weak and indirect representation was absent in the negotiation between the palace versus the cabinet and the political parties. The king and most of the supreme leaders of the political parties belonged to the dominant group. Ganeshman Singh and Bishnu Bahadur Manandhar are Newars, but the former was luke-warm towards marginalized groups' issues. Table 2.3 shows their decreasing participation in the three stages. For the sociocultural groups, the whole process of drafting, revising and promulgating the Constitution did not meet the criterion of inclusion for a democratic process.

Table 2.3
Marginalized Groups in the Three Stages of the Constitutional-Engineering Process

	Palace	*NC*	*ULF*	*Independent*	*Total*	*%*	*% CHHE*	*Population, 1991 (%)**
				Stage I: Composition of the CRC				
CHHE	1	3	2	–	6	66.67	66.67	31.6
Janajati	1	0	1	–	2	22.22		22.2 (9)**
Madhesi	1	0	0	–	1	11.11		30.9***
Dalit	0	0	0	–	0	0		8.7 (2.8)
Women	0	0	0	–	0	0		50.06
Total	3	3	3	–	9	100		
				Stage IIa: Composition of the interim cabinet				
CHHE	2	2	2	1	7	63.64	81.82****	31.6
Janajati	0	1	0	1	2	18.18		22.2 (9)
Madhesi	0	1	0	0	1	9.09		30.9
Dalit	0	0	0	0	0	0		8.7 (2.8)
Women	0	0	1	0	1	9.09		50.06
Total	2	3	3	2	11	100		
				Stage IIb: Composition of the cabinet subcommittee				
CHHE	1	1	1	0	3	100		31.6
Janajati	0	0	0	0	0	0		22.2 (9)
Madhesi	0	0	0	0	0	0		30.9
Dalit	0	0	0	0	0	0		8.7 (2.8)
Women	0	0	0	0	0	0		50.06
Total	1	1	1	0	3	100		

(Table 2.3 contd)

(Table 2.3 contd)

Stage III: Supreme leaders involved in the negotiation of the Constitution

Affiliation	*Leaders*	*Ethnicity* 88.89*****
Palace	King Birendra	CHHE
Nepali	Ganeshman Singh	Newar
Congress	Krishna Prasad Bhattarai	CHHE
Party	Girija Prasad Koirala	CHHE
United Left	Madan Bhandari (CPN-ML)	CHHE
Front	Manmohan Adhikari (CPN-M)	CHHE
(Communist)	Bishnu B. Manandhar (CPN-U)	Newar

Source: Author's compilation.

Notes: *The ethnic/caste division is based on Neupane (2000).

**The figure in brackets indicates the Madhesi Janajati and Dalit percentages that have been added to the Janajati and Dalit category to get the national total for each category.

***The Madhesis can be divided into Dalit (2.8 per cent), Janajati (9 per cent), other Hindu castes (15.6 per cent) and Muslims (3.5 per cent). The Madhesi, Dalit and Janajati proportions are based on Whelpton (1997).

****This is an average of the cabinet (63.64 per cent) and cabinet subcommittee (100 per cent) compositions.

*****This is an average of the composition of the supreme leadership of the three forces involved in the negotiations. The palace has been assigned 100 per cent and NC and ULF 83.34 per cent each. The NC and ULF percentages were calculated by considering Ganeshman Singh and Bishnu B. Manandhar as half-marginalized groups to account for their Newar ethnicity but mixed attitude towards marginalized groups' demands. In the cabinet and the CRC, the Newars have been treated as marginalized groups since they supported marginalized groups' interests.

The Lack of Effective Participation

The participation of marginalized groups was limited to providing suggestions, and not as equal members who could 'express their preference as to the final outcome'. The CRC's requests for suggestions from the public and its travels to different parts of the country were positive steps for enhancing effective participation. However, the consultative process became a facade for gaining legitimacy for the process rather than incorporating real inputs from the society, as demonstrated by non-incorporation of a large number of suggestions from the marginalized groups.

Input from the marginalized groups in the second stage was minimal. The cabinet sought no outside input. Some marginalized-group cabinet members supported some of their groups' demands.

However, they were few and were in the cabinet not as group representatives. It was generally assumed that the cabinet would not revise the draft drastically.[11] However, it went on to make significant changes that affected the marginalized groups negatively (see Table 2.4).[12]

An important factor for lesser articulation of marginalized groups' issues by marginalized-group members in the CRC and the interim cabinet was their loyalty to political ideology and party leadership, since they were representing the political forces. Further, many of the marginalized-group members in the CRC and cabinet were not involved in the sociocultural movements and/or were not fully informed about the issues. A women's-movement leader claimed that not only were women under-represented in the whole process but that the only woman cabinet member was more concerned with general political issues. The leader in question justified her approach saying that women leaders should not just raise women's issues, as it would marginalize them within party politics. Likewise, Janajati activists claimed that some of the Janajati members showed little empathy for group issues. However, the marginalized groups' representatives claimed that they were able to insert some issues, such as schooling in native languages up to the primary level, despite being in a minority. Thus, the issue perhaps was not always that the representatives were unaware of group issues, but rather that a minority status within the decision-making bodies affected their ability to garner majority support for marginalized groups' agendas.

Among the three Janajati members in the CRC (out of nine), only the nominee associated with the palace worked for the inclusion of marginalized groups' issues in the draft, while another showed moderate interest. In the cabinet, there were three Janajati representatives and one Madhesi Hindu. Of them, only two Janajati representatives argued strongly for a secular state, an issue that was ideologically compatible with the NC and ULF, which are avowedly secular. This demonstrates that not all marginalized-group members stood for their group issues. On the other hand, some of the CHHE cabinet members actively worked to declare Nepal a Hindu state.

Among the dominant members in the cabinet, only one communist fought till the very end for declaring Nepal a secular state. At later stages of debates, all others favoured declaring Nepal a Hindu state or were ambivalent on the issue. This is quite revealing. It shows that a dominant group, which dominates political leadership

Table 2.4

Marginalized Groups' Issues in Different Drafts and the Constitution

Constitutional Issues	*CRC Draft (A)*	*Palace Draft (B)*	*Cabinet-approved Draft (C)*	*Final Draft (D)*	*Remarks*
State	Hindu constitutional monarchical kingdom	Hindu, constitutional monarchical kingdom	Same as B	Same as B and C	Hinduism as state religion made specific in later stages
Citizenship	Father as the sole source of hereditary citizenship; birthright to citizenship omitted	Same as A	Same as A and B	Same as A, B and C	More illiberal than 1962 Constitution—hereditary citizenship based on both parents earlier; birthright at commencement of earlier Constitution.
Language	Nepali the 'language of the nation' and link language; other native languages as 'national' and media of instruction up to primary level only	Same as A	Same as A and B	Same as A, B and C	Instruction in native language up to primary level only
National party	5% vote requirement	3% vote requirement	Same as B	Same as B and C	Lower percentage helpful to marginalized groups' parties
Lower House	175 members	205 members	Same as B	Same as B and C	One rationale for the increase was to increase participation of marginalized groups
National anthem	Valid until the law changes it	Cannot be changed	Same as A	Same as B	Some marginalized groups and radical communists object to the anthem
Above the preamble	–	*Swasti shree*... (an eulogy to royalty in Sanskrit)	–	Same as B	Hindu religious connotations
Reservations	Upper House: 3 seats for women, 3 for Dalits and 9 for Janajati members	3 for women	3 for women	3 for women	Removal of seats for Dalit and Janajati members

Sources: CRC (1990); Hachhethu 1994; Uprety et al. 1997.

will either promote their cultural values or support them indirectly by remaining silent when others push them or not oppose strongly, even if such views clash with their political ideology and democratic principles. Hence, despite their formal secular stand, the NC and ULF ended up declaring Nepal a Hindu state.

During the process, the rational self-interest of the actors also undermined the marginalized groups' issues. The marginalized group members in the cabinet and the CRC followed party directives that were formulated by the CHHE leadership and infused with dominant values. It was not in their personal interest to risk antagonizing the leadership. For the dominant leadership, continuance of more or less a status quo in sociocultural policies served their interests. It facilitated the continuity of their dominance. In the same process, the CHHE leadership evoked loyalty to party and political ideology over cultural issues from marginalized-group members, whereas they conveniently brushed aside political ideology when it came to promoting their groups' sociocultural values.

Organizations and Networks

Effective participation was also hampered by the infancy of the organizations and networks of the marginalized groups. Many organizations and ethnic parties were formed after the opening up of the polity in 1990, and their outreach and strength were limited. The social-justice movements were in the initial stages of building organizations, elaborating on their ideologies, mobilizing constituencies, engaging in self-development of members, and constructing collective identities. The marginalized groups' discourses were still new and they had yet to develop a common set of demands and coherent set of arguments in support of their demands. This limited the movements from being more effective during the constitutional-engineering process. On the other hand, the fragmentation of marginalized groups' organizations and tendencies among leaders associated with mainstream political parties to exploit social-justice organizations for narrow partisan interests also hampered their effectiveness.

The emerging social-justice movements faced opposition from the established and resourceful organizations of the dominant group. The CHHE were well entrenched in the state and societal institutions. Padma Ratna Tuladhar, a prominent human-rights activist, said the main reason for the dominant 'group's' victory 'was the simple fact that Brahmins were in the majority in all the relevant political institutions. Either consciously or unconsciously, they had put their own vested interests first' (Raeper and Hoftun 1992: 176).

The Lack of Enlightened Understanding

The short duration of the constitutional-engineering process also contributed to the undermining of marginalized groups' aspirations and demands. The three-month mandate for the CRC meant less research, information, consultations and deliberations. It can be safely said that the marginalized groups' voices would have been louder and more audible had the process not been so short. The populace also was not informed of various alternatives before they were adopted. It clearly deprived the people from learning about different alternatives and providing inputs on them. The CRC decided and the cabinet revised and negotiated the Constitution with the palace.

The movement-for-restoration-of-democracy (MRD) leaders tried to keep the process within their control by allocating a short time span to the process. They may have felt that a longer time frame would produce challenges to their leadership and their influence on the ongoing process. The MRD leaders' claim of a potential palace conspiracy if a longer time frame was allowed is not entirely justified, for the palace also benefited from a short time frame. Longer discussions and debates would have meant more possibility of palace privileges coming under general public scrutiny at a time when the palace's popularity was at its lowest ebb. The NC and the palace, on the other hand, were worried that the MRD movement would be taken over by more radical elements.

The political forces negotiating the change did not opt for a constituent assembly or propose to ratify the draft through a referendum. Such methods could have made the process more deliberative and enhanced the understanding of various issues. In Eritrea, for instance, the constitutional-engineering process involved ratification of the new constitution after three years of debate (Selassie 1998). The historic debates in the American Constitution Assembly were also long.

The Constituent Assembly in India lasted almost for three years, and the Indian Constitution has been widely acclaimed for its social-justice content (Mathew 1998). Despite pressure from the dominant Hindus, India did not declare the state Hindu. It provided reservations for Scheduled Castes (Dalits) and Scheduled Tribes (indigenous people) in educational institutions, civil administration and political offices. Further, it recognized the land rights of the indigenous peoples and established a form of federalism that went on to provide autonomy to different linguistic groups and nationalities. Many of these minority sensitive provisions became feasible in India because the dominant party, the Indian National Congress, facilitated the election of minorities to the Constituent Assembly. The assembly had around 30 per cent of minorities,[13] including Dr Ambedkar, who headed the Drafting Committee. A minority sub-committee was formed to make recommendations. The Assembly adopted most of the recommendations (Chiriyankandath 1999; Galanter 1998).

The deliberate aim of narrowing down the process in Nepal also became evident when the Scandinavian, Indian and other foreign experts and teams were discouraged from providing suggestions to the CRC. For a country, whose leaders always seek advice and aid, the refusal of voluntary advice from foreign experts was an unusual phenomenon. It suggests that the leadership was suspicious of external suggestions that might have worked against their wish of designing the Constitution to suit their interests. In retrospect, the events of the 1990s support this hypothesis. The NC has returned to power, despite not getting a majority of popular votes, partly with the aid of an electoral law that favours the larger parties.

The CHHE's hegemonic influence over even progressive institutions such as the media, academia, and human-rights organizations was also instrumental in undermining the marginalized groups' voice. The negligible access to mainstream media put the marginalized groups at the receiving end of negative propaganda. Their issues and events were ignored and often distorted. They were frequently faced with ill-founded charges imbued with racism, such as their being divisive and communal. The control of the popular intellectual discourse by the CHHE was influential in the continuation of their hegemony. For instance, at the early stages of CRC activities, democratic politicians and intellectuals seemed in favour of a secular state. However, the reaction of the dominant—group-dominated media to the proposal for a secular state was very negative (Raeper and Hoftun 1992: 156–62). The media bolstered the campaign of the conservative and fundamentalist Hindus and spread fear among the general Hindu populace regarding the increasing influence of non-Hindu groups, such as the Christians and the Muslims. The Nepali experience supports Snyder and Ballentine's (1997) argument that in ethnic matters, a 'free press' can become a problem when one group controls it.

Voting Inequality and Lack of Control over the Agenda

The voting equality criterion for different sociocultural groups became insignificant because the exclusion of marginalized groups from the process deprived them of 'an equal and effective opportunity to vote' (Dahl 1989). In terms of political forces, only three political forces voted, and in terms of sociocultural distinctions, the CHHE males voted overwhelmingly.

Similarly, the marginalized groups lacked control over the agenda. The limited influence the marginalized groups had over the agenda was through public lobbying. Even then, however, it was the three political forces dominated by the CHHE, the palace, the NC and the ULF that had the final say on the agenda. Many of the marginalized groups' demands, such as federalism, were not even considered.

Exclusion from the process rendered the two criteria ineffective for the marginalized groups, showing their inadequacy. Thus, to make the criteria relevant for emerging plural democracies, inclusion of all sociocultural groups should be made explicit and various criteria should also be adapted to recognize the dimension of plurality.

The Dynamics of the Transition Process

Another reason for the adoption of articles and institutions favouring the dominant group in the Constitution is that the dynamics of the constitutional-engineering process favoured the group by default. The existing sociocultural and political institutions were based on CHHE norms and hence favoured the CHHE interests, whereas the marginalized groups, as outsiders, were disadvantaged because of them. Marginalized groups' interests and perspectives have to be included by special effort, which requires considerable energy and resources to overcome the inertia of existing institutions. For emerging organizations with a shortage of material and other resources, this is a formidable task.

The values of the dominant group got incorporated in the Constitution through the adoption of a universalizing notion of 'same equality' for everyone. Universalizing notions benefit dominant groups because they define their values as the universal norms for society (Mahajan 1998, Young 1990).

Optimism among the citizens and faith in the political leadership during the constitutional-engineering process also favoured the dominant group. The general public assumed that the leadership that had made sacrifices for democracy would induce true democratic values, including sociocultural reforms. This optimism turned out to be false. In the words of a woman activist: 'We never expected them to take away the rights women already had even in the earlier Constitution' (referring to citizenship rights from both parents' line-age in the earlier Constitution).

The tension that cropped up when the palace draft became public also helped the dominant-group leaders. The MRD leadership successfully created an impression of threat to the nascent democracy from the palace. They called upon the people to rally behind them. This sense of urgency helped the leaders to get away with their proposals. In such an environment, one strategy used for pushing the dominant group's agenda was to promise future revisions in the Constitution. In the debate over secularism in the cabinet, the three members who resisted were finally persuaded by promising future reforms. However, not a single article of the Constitution was amended during the democratic years, despite the NC and CPN-UML controlling more than two-thirds of the Parliament.

The Undemocratic Culture of Democratic Forces

The insertion of undemocratic elements into the Constitution shows that the 'democratic forces' were not truly democratic. The 1990 changes broadened the elite base to include ideological opponents from the traditional social elite group, but it did not include all sociocultural groups. Dahl describes this phenomenon of public contestation among the restricted elite as an initial stage in the democratization process, but which is not yet a democracy (Dahl 1971). The experience of the 1990s supports the notion that the democratic forces were not serious about ushering in a real democracy through the inclusion of various sections of the society. They did not introduce any Constitutional amendments to the discriminatory articles, suggesting that the exclusion in the Constitution was through tacit consent of the CHHE leadership, if not by design.

During the constitutional-engineering process, the MRD leaders were keen to take powers away from the king and consolidate power within political parties, which they controlled. The MRD leaders successfully fought for political rights to strengthen their positions in the polity, but gave in to the king on traditional cultural rights because giving such rights did not undermine their power. In fact, the king's and the MRD leadership's sociocultural interests overlapped. It would help the leaders to maintain their sociocultural and political superiority in the society. When the king attempted to take control of the Constitution-framing process, the MRD leaders fought back, even threatening dire consequences. They successfully manoeuvred to put the army under a defense commission despite the king's wish to have it under him and the army's pressure to remain under the king (Hachhethu 1994; Hutt 1994).

Several explanations have been forwarded for the exclusionary behaviour of the political leaders. Some argue that the MRD leadership was influenced by the hegemonic monocultural nationalism of the pre-1990s assimilative state in the absence of alternative discourses. However, the explanation fails to hold once we take into account the continued ignorance and opposition to the demands put forth by marginalized groups, despite the emergence of diverse alternative perspectives after 1990.

Another explanation is that the mandate of the MRD did not include extending cultural rights to minority groups. However, the mandate of the movement was extended beyond its initial demand for the legalization of political parties once the MRD leadership realized they had the power to do so. They made 'four successive upward revisions' (Hachhethu 1994), but these revisions did not incorporate the sociocultural issues of marginalized groups. All the revisions were directed at the consolidation of the MRD leadership's power by limiting the king's power.[14]

A more plausible reason for the undemocratic tendencies of the MRD leaders is their self-aggrandizement, their desire to usurp power, and promote monocultural nationalism (racism). This became evident from the power-at-any-cost culture among the political parties and leaders in the 1990s, especially when coalitions were formed through frequent horse-trading during the 1994–99 hung Parliament and the packing of the party positions with relatives, caste brethren, and personal loyalists.

The marginalized groups' claims threatened CHHE leaders' interests. Incorporating more groups in the power structure would have broadened the competition for power. Introduction of cultural rights would have opened up unknown territories and increased uncertainties and unpredictability in Nepali politics. The MRD leadership may have construed this as a threat. It served the CHHE leadership better if power politics remained within a smaller group.

Conclusion

This study of the Nepali constitutional-engineering process demonstrated that the Dahlian democratic criteria were useful in analysing the exclusionary process. However, the study also demonstrated that they were not fully adequate for the analysis of democratic processes in a culturally plural society. The Nepali experience provides inputs for making the criteria more relevant. It calls for the inclusion of minorities to be made more specific.

This chapter shows that the discriminatory articles in the Constitution were inserted and inclusive elements were omitted for valid reasons, with or without conscious intentions, and the dominant group will maintain them if not challenged, because these have served them well. A comparative survey of inclusive processes reveals that favourable policies come either with representation in the decision-making process or with social movements.

In Nepal, marginalized groups were partially successful in broadening their rights through incorporation of a few issues in the constitutional-engineering process at the stages where they were represented and failed where they were excluded. In India, proportionate representation of minorities in the Constituent Assembly made it possible to incorporate exemplary inclusive provisions in the Constitution, whereas the absence of women and African Americans in the American Constitution Assembly delayed their political participation. On the other hand, the Civil Rights Movement in the US and the social-justice movements among the oppressed groups in India have extended political rights.

Given these experiences, the marginalized groups have to fight for their rights in Nepal. These will probably not be handed over to them by the dominant group. Global historical trends provide hope. Freedom, the associated organizing opportunities, and social movements have usually led to more freedom in the long run.

Notes

1. In the early 1990s, the indigenous nationalities mostly identified themselves as simply 'nationalities' (Janajati).
2. A large segment of the Newars is involved in the indigenous nationalities' social justice movement.

3. The excluded groups have been publicly protesting against discrimination since 1990.
4. Overlaps occur between the Dalits and the indigenous nationalities. Terai Dalits and indigenous nationalities can be included under both Madhesi and indigenous nationalities. Indigenous nationalities are 36.41 per cent, Dalits 14.99, Madhesis 30.49 (including Terai Dalits and indigenous nationalities) and the CHHE 30.89 per cent of the population.
5. This is not to deny the existence of poor people within the CHHE, but they do not face cultural discrimination and hence face lesser constraints in social mobility.
6. Interviews with CRC and cabinet members were taken in 1999.
7. See Dhungel et al. (1998) for a defence of the Constitution on these issues. They even call the 'Hindu and Constitutional Monarchical Kingdom' secular.
8. Extreme leftists such as the Samyukta Rastriya Janandolan (those who became Maoists were part of this coalition), Rightists and some others were not included in the CRC.
9. The chairman of the CRC, who subsequently became close to the NC, claimed that the king nominated him, but he had nominated the two other non-party members to represent the Terai and Kathmandu.
10. Perhaps the public role of Bahuns in defining political and social norms is the reason behind the identification of Bahunbad (Brahmanism) as a cause of various social ills in Nepal (Bista 1991). Here it should be pointed out that Dalits and Janajatis do not show as much anger against other CHHEs—Chhetris, Thakuris and Sanyasis.
11. The ULF called for promulgating the draft without revisions. The palace and the NC ganged up against it.
12. The changes included making the preamble non-amendable, forming the Raj Parishad Standing Committee, increasing the strength of the Lower House, lowering the minimum vote requirement from 5 to 3 per cent for recognition as a national party, and eliminating 3 and 9 reserved seats respectively for Dalits and Janajati members (Hachhethu 1994; Uprety et al. 1997).
13. If members of princely states are not counted, 37.5 per cent were from the minorities. The population of India was 37.8 per cent non-Hindus, Scheduled Castes and Scheduled Tribes in 1951.
14. Some attribute the tendency to concentrate power in the executive and the political parties to the coup by King Mahendra in 1960, when he dismissed the elected NC government. However, that power could be snatched back easily from parties and cabinets as shown by the king's 2002 and 2005 actions; but it is more difficult to take power away if it is widely distributed, something the 1990 Constitution failed to do.

References

Bhattachan, Krishna B. 1999. 'Minority Rights in the Predatory Nepalese State', in S. Banerjee (ed.), *Shrinking Space: Minority Rights in South Asia*. Lalitpur: SAFHR.

Bista, Dor Bahadur. 1991. *Fatalism and Development: Nepal's Struggle for Modernization*. Hyderabad: Orient Longman.

Chiriyankandath, James. 1999. 'Constitutional Predilections', *Seminar*. http://www.india-seminar.com/1999/484/484%20chiriyankandath.htm.

CRC. 1990. *Nepal Adhirajyako Sambidhan, 2047—Mashouda* (Constitution of Nepal, 2047—draft). Kathmandu: Constitution Recommendation Commission (CRC).

Dahl, Robert A. 1971. *Polyarchy*. New Haven: Yale University Press.

———. 1989. *Democracy and Its Critics*. New Haven and London: Yale University Press.

———. 1998. *On Democracy*. New Haven and London: Yale University Press.

Dhungel, Surya P.S., Bipin Adhikari, B.P. Bhandari and Chris Murgatroyd. 1998. *Commentary on the Nepalese Constitution*. Kathmandu: DeLF.

Galanter, Marc. 1998. 'The Indian Constitution and Provisions for Special Treatment', in G. Mahajan (ed.), *Democracy, Difference, and Social Justice*. New Delhi: Oxford University Press.

Guinier, Lani. 1994. *The Tyranny of the Majority*. New York: The Free Press.

Hachhethu, Krishna. 1994. 'Transition to Democracy in Nepal: Negotiations Behind Constitution Making, 1990', *Contributions to Nepalese Studies* 21 (1): 91–126.

Horowitz, Donald. 1994. 'Democracy in Divided Societies', in L. Diamond and M.F. Plattner (eds), *Nationalism, Ethnic Conflict, and Democracy*. Baltimore: Johns Hopkins University.

Hutt, Michael. 1994. 'Drafting the 1990 Constitution', in M. Hutt (ed.), *Nepal in the Nineties: Versions of the Past, Visions of the Future*. New Delhi: Oxford University Press.

Kymlicka, Will. 1995. *Multicultural Citizenship: A Liberal Theory of Minority Rights*. Oxford: Oxford University Press.

Lawoti, Mahendra. 2002. 'Defining Minorities in Nepal', *Nepali Journal of Contemporary Studies* 2 (2): 22–52.

———. 2005. *Towards a Democratic Nepal: Inclusive Political Institutions for a Multicultural Society*. New Delhi: Sage Publications.

Lijphart, Arend. 1977. *Democracy in Plural Societies: A Comparative Exploration*. New Haven and London: Yale University Press.

———. 1999. *Patterns of Democracy: Government Forms and Performance in Thirty-Six Countries*. New Haven and London: Yale University Press.

Mahajan, Gurpreet. 1998. *Identities and Rights: Aspects of Liberal Democracy in India*. New Delhi: Oxford University Press.

Mathew, P.D. 1998. *Constitution of India Simplified*. Rev. ed. New Delhi: Indian Social Institute.

Neupane, Govinda. 2000. *Nepalko Jatiya Prashna: Samajik Banot ra Sajhedariko Sambhawana* (Nepal's National Question: Social Composition and Possibilities of Accommodation). Kathmandu: Centre for Development Studies.

Parekh, Bhikhu. 1994. 'Cultural Diversity and Liberal Democracy', in D. Beetham (ed.), *Defining and Measuring Democracy*. Thousand Oaks: Sage Publications.

Phillips, Anne. 1996. 'Dealing with Difference: A Politics of Ideas, or a Politics of Presence?', in S. Benhabib (ed.), *Democracy and Difference*. Princeton: Princeton University Press.

Raeper, William and Martin Hoftun. 1992. *Spring Awakening*. Delhi: Viking.

Sartori, Giovanni. 1997. *Comparative Constitutional Engineering: An Inquiry into Structures, Incentives and Outcomes*. 2nd ed. New York: New York University Press.

Selassie, Bereket Habte. 1998. 'Creating a Constitution for Eritrea', *Journal of Democracy* 9 (2): 164–74.

Snyder, Jack L. and Karen Ballentine. 1997. 'Nationalism and the Marketplace of Ideas', in M.E. Brown (ed.), *Nationalism and Ethnic Conflict*. Cambridge: MIT Press.

Taylor, Charles. 1998. 'The Dynamics of Democratic Exclusion', *Journal of Democracy* 9 (4): 143–56.

Uprety, Bharat Raj, Kalyan Shrestha and Kanak Bikram Thapa (eds). 1997. *Nepalko Sambhaidhanik Kanoon* (The Constitutional Law), 2nd ed. Kathmandu: Kanon Anusandhan tatha Bikash Forum (FRIDIL).

Whelpton, John. 1997. 'Political Identity in Nepal: State, Nation and Community', in D.N.Gellner, J. Pfaff-Czarnecka, and J. Whelpton (eds), *Nationalism and Ethnicity in a Hindu Kingdom*. Amsterdam: Harwood Academic.

Young, Iris Marion. 1990. *Justice and the Politics of Difference*. Princeton, NJ: Princeton University Press.

———. 2000. *Inclusion and Democracy*. Oxford: Oxford University Press.

PART II

The Maoist Insurgency

3

Committed Insurgents, a Divided State and the Maoist Insurgency in Nepal

SHISIR KHANAL

A common argument in both popular and academic discourses is that the rise and success of the Maoist insurgency is a result of archaic social and economic conditions that have long existed in Nepal. However, this hypothesis, based on historical grievance, fails to explain why the insurgency started and rapidly expanded in the mid-1990s, at exactly the time when both political and economic opportunities were expanding? In this chapter, drawing on recent political theories on violence, I argue that persistent commitment to violent means by a determined and organized Maoist party, pre-existing support for communist parties in Nepal, ambivalent attitudes within the major political parties, and a divided state better explain the onset and success of Maoist insurgency.

CIVIL-WAR LITERATURE: GRIEVANCE AND OPPORTUNITY

A common argument in printed media and academic journals is that civil wars and insurgencies are ultimately an expression of grievances. It is argued that poverty, income inequality, ethnic cleavages, social and political exclusion as well as political repression create civil wars. Summarizing research on Causes of Conflict in Third World (COTW), Luc van de Goor (1996) writes:

> [I]n particular, the rights and access to political power and decision-making of regional, religious, ethnic, tribal or other

> groups appeared to be key factors. Denial of the rights and identities of minority groups and mismanagement of the processes involved by the state often lead to violent conflict.

Other researchers have argued that ethnic and religious fractionalization better explains the onset and prevalence of civil war (Elbadawi and Sambanis 2002) or point to the gradual increase of violence from peaceful protest to violent struggle (White 1989).

In Nepal's context, academics, journalists, international donors and politicians explain civil war in terms of Nepal's underdevelopment, income inequality, regional disparity (Pyakuryal 2001; Shrestha 2001), ethnic and caste discrimination (Bhattachan 2001; Onesto 2003; de Sales 2003), and failure of democracy (Pfaff-Czarnecka 2004, Shaha 2003).

Recent studies have tended to move away from the grievance model to a focus on opportunity as a better way of explaining the onset of violence. In an influential study, Fearon and Laitin (2003) propose that ethnic, religious or broadly held grievances are not detrimental factors in civil violence. They argue that 'conditions that favour insurgency', such as 'financially, organizationally and politically weak central governments render insurgency more feasible and attractive due to weak local policing or inept and corrupt counterinsurgency practices' (ibid.). Furthermore, they propose that rough terrain, local knowledge, a large population, foreign base camps or international support help sustain insurgency.

Collier and Hoeffler (2001) argue that nothing explains violence better than the availability of financial opportunities. They claim that financial opportunities, such as extortion of natural resources, donations from diasporas, low cost of recruitment, a cheap conflict-specific capital (military equipment), and a weak government capacity predicate a civil war better. Using data from 78 large civil conflicts from 1960 to 1999, they find that primary commodity exports increase the risk of conflict, but that male secondary-education enrolment and per-capita income growth reduce conflict risk. Similarly, large and dispersed populations and mountainous terrain increase conflict risk, but inequality, denial of political rights, ethnic polarization, and religious fractionalization have insignificant relation to the onset of violence.

Violence and Political Institutions

Besides grievance and opportunity, political institutions also have received significant attention in the literature on civil war. It has been argued that the presence of a certain type of political institution—democratic or authoritarian—is likely to promote or negate the possibility of violence. Following Kant's 'perpetual peace' argument, several authors have asserted that democracy is associated with a low risk of violence. Even in recent studies, several authors have found that 'democracy is negatively associated with civil violence' (Elbadawi and Sambanis 2002). The institutional mechanisms that exist in democratic societies are believed to provide an outlet for competing political and economical agendas or have mechanisms to address them and reduce the danger of violence.

However, others find democracy as reducing the risk of violence 'only where the conditions for stable democracy are present: relative high per capita income, high literacy rates, and (to a lesser extent) a diversified economy' (Hegre 2003). Similarly, a number of authors have maintained that an inverted-U relationship exists between democracy and violence (Ellingsen et al. 2001). This argument holds that both highly democratic and highly authoritarian states are related with low risks of violence because complete democracies have institutional mechanisms to prevent violence and highly authoritarian states prevent violence with the threat of strong repression. On the other hand, weak democracies are associated with higher risk of violence because these democracies lack both institutional mechanisms to prevent violence and state capacity to repress it. With a decade-old democracy, low level of development, high illiteracy rate, lower per-capita income, ethnic diversity and difficult geographical terrain, Nepal presents a mix of both weak democracy and 'factors that favour insurgency'.

At a cursory look, Nepal, with a per-capita income of US$240, is one of the poorest countries in the world. More than 60 per cent of the adult population is illiterate, life expectancy at birth is a mere 60, and almost 40 per cent of the population is considered poor. Similarly, with as many as 60 different ethnic and caste groups that speak around 100 different languages or dialects, Nepal is heterogeneous in terms of ethnic (or caste) diversity. Despite its diversity, Nepal was officially a Hindu kingdom ruled by the Shah dynasty for almost 250 years. Because of the Hindu character of the state, the higher-caste Bahuns, Chhetris and Newars have a monopoly over state instruments.

The grievance-based arguments have received considerable attention in Nepal. However, seeing the Maoists' insurgency as a product of economical and political grievances fails to explain why the insurgency started and rapidly expanded in the mid-1990s, at the time when both political and economic opportunities were expanding. The most common argument is that democracy failed to live up to expectations and inequitable social and economic conditions were exacerbated during the democratic era in the 1990s. However, these socio-economic conditions, such as poverty and inequality, were not the by-products of democratic politics; macro-economic data show that Nepal achieved a significant growth in infrastructure development during that period.

Both political and economic opportunities were expanding in the 1990s. After the establishment of democracy, an interim government composed of representatives of the Nepali Congress Party, a coalition of communist parties, and the Royal Palace-nominated candidates oversaw a successful promulgation of a democratic Constitution and an election was held within a year. Even though the intra-party feuds led to the collapse of the majority government of the Nepali Congress, a mid-term election was successfully held which made the Communist Party of Nepal-United Marxist-Leninist (CPN-UML) the largest party in the Parliament. Similarly, local-level elections were held peacefully and reasonably fairly. Since then, several coalition governments have ruled the country and power has been transferred peacefully from one party to another.

Democratic political opportunity provided an open environment to popular organizations. Issues relating to ethnic identity, gender- and caste-based discrimination, and human rights came to the forefront. The elderly and the widowed started receiving monthly allowances; public education up to the 10th grade was provided free; and in certain regions, scholarship programmes to promote education among girls were introduced. For the first time in Nepal's history, village-level local governments received direct funding as a grant from the central government. Notwithstanding the capacity of local institutions in Nepal, the inflow of cash to villages helped in creating local-level initiatives in infrastructure development, such as rural roads and micro-hydroelectricity projects.

During the 1990s, the macro-level economic indicators were robust. The annual GDP growth rate of 5.28 per cent from 1991 to 1996 exceeded the annual growth rate of 4.7 per cent during the second half of the 1980s and sustained that pace even after the initiation of the insurgency. Despite the rise in violence, the overall annual GDP growth for the decade of 1991–2001 was 5.09 per cent. Similarly, the per-capita GDP grew from US$187 in 1990 to US$221 in 1996 and to US$249 in 2001. By any measure, this increase of 33 per cent in a decade is a significant achievement. Further-more, both the literacy rate and the education enrolment rate grew significantly. The adult literacy rate of 30 per cent in 1990 increased to 43 per cent in 2001 and youth literacy rate (for the age group 15–24) grew from 47 per cent in 1990 to 62 per cent in 2001 (World Bank 2006).

Table 3.1
Some Economic Indicators

Economic Indicators	*1990*	*1996*	*2001*
GDP growth	4.7% (1985–90)	5.28% (1991–96)	5.09% (1991–2001)
Per-capita GDP	US$187	US$221	US$249
Literacy rate—adults	30%	37%	43%
Literacy rate—youth (15–24)	47%	56%	62%
Road networks	6,840 km	7,700 km	13,223 km*
Telephone connections (per 1,000 persons)	3.16	5.40	13.1

Source: World Bank (2006).
Note: *as of 1999.

There were improvements in infrastructure (see Table 3.1). The road network increased from 6,840 km in 1990 to 13,233 km in 2001. The 1990s also saw phenomenal growth in communication and media. The availability of telephone connections (per 1,000 people) increased from 3.16 in 1990 to 13.1 in 2001 (ibid.). The country that had only one state-owned radio channel, a television station, and only two daily broadsheet newspapers at the beginning of the decade could boast several private publication houses with daily broadsheet papers in Nepali and English languages, several local FM radio stations (both commercial and community-based) and five different Nepali-language television stations at the end of the decade. This increase was not only limited to urban centres; rural sectors grew as well. Thus, it is wrong to assert that the democratic decade failed to produce any socio-economic development.

In this light, I argue that other factors better explain the origin and growth of the Maoist insurgency. First, I argue that committed and persistent Maoist ideologues who believed only a violent movement could end the socio-economic ills of the country began a violent political campaign and achieved rapid success because of the strong support for communist ideologies in Nepal. Further, a divided state that was weak, a lack of functioning democratic institutions and a power struggle between the palace and the political parties also helped in the rise of the insurgency.

Committed Insurgents

Insurgency as a Product of Ideology

Almost all communist parties in Nepal espoused violence as a means to achieving their political objective—that is, the establishment of the new People's Democracy, socialism, and finally communism. Thus, my assertion that the Maoists were committed towards violence might sound like a non-argument or even seem naïve at first. However, what differentiates the Maoists from other communist parties in Nepal is that they actually picked up the arms. Despite rhetoric, not all political parties or groups that threaten the use of violence actually employ it. In Nepal, after the restoration of democracy, communist factions—notably CPN-UML, despite its history of political violence—moved towards embracing a multiparty democracy. The Maoists, on the other hand, remained disdainful of and hostile to the entire system. They believed that total and radical transformation of the society could be achieved only through a protracted 'People's War'. In Nepal's context, why the Maoists picked up arms and others did not can be determined by the ideological choices each party made. Beyond the rhetoric of Marxism, Leninism and Maoism and aside from the name 'communists' that these parties shared, subtle differences in political ideology separated them.

To understand these subtleties, it is important to navigate through the complex history of Nepal's communist movement.

The first communist party, the Communist Party of Nepal (CPN), was established in September 1949 under the leadership of Pushpa Lal Shrestha. The party divided into numerous factions in the decades of the 1960s and 1970s. The first such division came after the royal coup in 1960. The Communist Party divided into two factions: one, led by then General Secretary of the CPN Kesharjung Rayamajhi, supported the king; the other, led by Pushpa Lal, opposed the dissolution of the democratically elected government. However, the division and imprisonment of several influential leaders rendered the communist movement very ineffective for almost a decade.

Such divisions remained endemic in the Nepali communist movement for the next few decades. These divisions reflected several factors such as the Sino-Soviet rift, differences in application of communist ideologies in the Nepali context, and leadership rivalries. These divisions led to the formation of small and weak communist parties with their own niche areas where they were active and strong. While the divisions diminished the influence of a unified communist party, they helped to preserve a pure breed of ideologues who saw a protracted People's War as the only way out of Nepal's socio-economic and political problems.

In 1971, young communist cadres in Jhapa district in eastern Nepal organized themselves to initiate a violent political campaign, popularly known as the 'Jhapa Movement'. Under the strong influence of the ongoing Naxalbari movement in neighbouring West Bengal, India, the Jhapali youth announced their 'People's War'. Several actions against the 'class enemy' were carried out and five of them were killed (KC 2003). The Panchayat government launched a repressive campaign. The violent war was subdued and senior party leaders were arrested.

Many of the leaders who spearheaded this political violence reorganized to form the CPN (Marxist-Leninist) or CPN (ML), which slowly moved towards peaceful political activities and successfully began to organize underground political networks during the Panchayat years. The party even used the Panchayat-era election and successfully sent elected representatives to the National Panchayat. In 1990, the CPN (ML) formed a coalition with the Nepali Congress and other smaller communist parties, and launched the People's

Movement to re-establish multiparty democracy. After the establishment of democracy, the CPN (ML) and CPN (Marxist) united to form the CPN-UML. The CPN-UML established itself as the dominant communist party in the 1990s, became a major opposition party for most of the 1990s, and participated in several governments.

In the early 1970s, several communist leaders made an attempt to regroup and reorganize the communist party in Nepal. Mohan Bikram Singh and Nirmal Lama transformed a radical and pro-Beijing group into the Communist Party of Nepal (Fourth Convention) in 1965 (Nickson 1992). The Communist Party of Nepal (Maoist) can trace its roots to the CPN (Fourth Convention). Early on, the CPN (Fourth Convention) advocated 'armed revolution' and adopted proposals for 'training of guerrillas, proletarization of party cadre, creating base areas, taking action against local cheats, and initiating an agrarian uprising' in 1979 (Thapa 2004).

However, the CPN (Forth Convention) continued to split and merge in the next three decades. Soon after the formation of the party, the party split due to both international and national political conditions. The overthrow of the 'Gang of Four' in China (Nickson 1992) and announcement of a nationwide referendum on the Panchayat system in Nepal (Thapa 2004) created divisions in the party. While a group led by Nirmal Lama was in favour of taking part in the referendum and supported the new Chinese leadership, another group led by Mohan Bikram Singh maintained an ortho-dox stand and denounced the new Chinese leadership as counter-revolutionary and expressed their allegiance to the Cultural Revolution. The group led by Mohan Bikram formed a separate party called the Communist Party of Nepal (Mashal).

Soon differences appeared within the CPN (Mashal) too. The party further split into two factions called CPN (Mashal) and CPN (Masal). The CPN (Masal) led by Mohan Bikram adopted armed movement as its guiding policy. However, as the People's Movement approached in 1990, both the CPN (Mashal) and CPN (Masal) stayed out of the United Left Front (ULF), a coalition of left parties, in order to form their own coalition called the United National People's Movement (UNPM). The UNPM advocated the overthrow of monarchy. By the time of the first general election in 1991, yet another split had occurred in the CPN (Mashal). Later, the CPN

(Mashal) and the CPN (Fourth Convention) merged to form the Communist Party of Nepal (Unity Centre).

The CPN (Unity Centre) brought together individuals and parties that had originally founded the CPN (Fourth Convention). Despite this unification, the CPN (Unity Centre) was an amalgam of individuals with differing strategic visions about Nepal's communist movement. For instance, among them was Nirmal Lama, whose CPN (Fourth Convention) had aligned with ULF during the People's Movement in 1990. Further, Nirmal Lama for a long time was an advocate of using non-military means to achieve communist political objectives. He was at one time in favour of participating in the 1979 referendum and afterwards had advocated the use of the National Panchayat elections to further larger political objectives. He was also a member of the Constitution Recommendation Commission (CRC). These differences had caused splits in the past and were bound to do so in the future as well.

Despite some differences, the unity general convention in 1991 took some major and important decisions. Among them, the CPN (Unity Centre) decided to remain underground, in spite of an open democratic environment. The decision said, 'Even though multi-party democracy is a step ahead [*sic*] than autocratic Panchayat, in essence the class characteristics between [*sic*] the two systems remain the same. Thus, it would be a mistake to open revolutionary communist parties like ours [*sic*]' (KC 2003). The party also adopted programmes to establish a people's republic on the basis of a revolutionary communist party, united front, and people's army. The party further accepted protracted People's War as a fundamental party line (ibid.).

To accommodate different views, especially the views of the factions that wanted the party to participate in elections, the CPN (Unity Centre) grudgingly agreed to participate in the first general election. Among the advocates for the participation was Nirmal Lama, who from the hospital bed wrote that 'election is an opportunity for Unity Centre to establish itself nationwide. There is no doubt such an opportunity would allow us to organize Nepali people of various classes and groups towards nationwide struggle' (ibid.). In deciding to participate in the election, the CPN (Unity Centre) said, 'Owing to especial circumstances of party formation, after a long discussion and interaction, the party has decided not to fully participate in the election but to use various mechanisms and support independent candidates close to party ideologies [*sic*]' (KC 2003). The CPN (Unity Centre) floated the United People's Front (UPF) as an overt political organization under the leadership of Dr Baburam Bhattarai. The UPF participated in the first general election with an explicit goal of 'exposing the shortcomings and inadequacy of parliamentary democracy'.

However, differences emerged soon within the CPN (Unity Centre)—between General Secretary Prachanda and senior leader Nirmal Lama—regarding the timing of the People's War. While Nirmal Lama was opposed to the initiation of the insurgency, Prachanda advocated a 'People's War'. The differences led to the division of the party. Prachanda's faction held the 'Third Plenum' meeting, during which the party decided to take up arms (Thapa 2004). The plenum also decided to change the party's name to 'Communist Party of Nepal (Maoist)'.

Because the CPN (Unity Centre), later the CPN (Maoist), had made a strategic decision to initiate an insurgency, the party moved towards violent politics from the early years of democracy. As early as 1990–91, its cadres in Rolpa and Rukum districts in western Nepal, the Maoists stronghold, began 'physical action' against the 'local cheats and usurers' (Onesto 2003). Such actions often led to inter-party conflict as powerful and wealthy people in the area were often aligned with the Nepali Congress (NC) that had formed the government at the centre. The NC was able to mobilize the state machinery, especially the police force, against the Maoist cadres. As this inter-party struggle intensified, the CPN (Maoist) launched a campaign called SIJA in 1995. The objective of the campaign was to 'intensify class struggle'. During this process, Maoist cadres not only used peaceful means such as cultural programmes to reach out to the public, but physical force was also deployed against opposition party members deemed as the 'class enemy' (ibid.).

After several such violent encounters, the NC government launched a repressive police campaign called the Romeo operation. During the operation, the police resorted to unconstitutional means, such as arbitrary arrest, vandalism of private property, rape and 'encounter' killing. This campaign is often categorized as a catalyst for the Maoist declaration of their 'People's War'. While there is no doubt that brutal police repression provided a suitable impetus to launch the violent political campaign, nevertheless the CPN (Maoist) was already committed to the insurgency and the initiation of the 'People's War' was well underway. A Maoist cadre interviewed in western Nepal by journalist Li Onesto supports this claim, saying, 'During this time, party was prepared to launch the People's War. And the Romeo operation was the objective situation that came together with this subjective situation on 13 February 1996. The People's War would have been launched without the Romeo Operation. But the government campaign of repression presented good conditions and an opportunity' (Onesto 2003).

Popular Support for Communists in Nepal

Once the CPN (Maoist) declared its 'People's War', the Maoists were significantly helped by the reservoir of popular support for the communist parties in Nepal. The communist parties have a long history of political activism in Nepal. By 1990, communist parties had a network of grassroots organizations all over Nepal; were also strongly active across different sectors and classes organized as students' groups, teachers' organizations and labour associations. For the most part, these organizations were meticulously built by the CPN (ML), the latter-day CPN-UML of the 1970s. However, different factions had strongholds in different areas as well. For instance, the Nepal Workers and Peasant Party was strong in Bhaktapur and Jumla; factions of the CPN (Unity Centre) and CPN (Mashal) were strong in the mid-western hills and in parts of Gorkha and Sindhuli.

In the first election after the restoration of democracy, the communist parties secured a strong presence in Parliament with a combined total of 82 seats. They presented strong opposition to the NC, which had a simple majority of 110 seats to form a government. The overall share of votes further illustrated the strength of communist parties in Nepal (see Table 3.2). All the communist parties in the House of Representatives received a total of 38.1 per cent votes, only marginally less than the 39.5 per cent of the NC (Nickson 1992).

Of the several communist parties, the CPN-UML emerged as the dominant communist party in the country. The CPN-UML formed

Table 3.2
Share of Votes in the General Elections of 1991, 1994 and 1999

	1991		*1994*		*1999*	
Political Parties	*Seats*	*Votes (%)*	*Seats*	*Votes (%)*	*Seats*	*Votes (%)*
Nepali Congress	110	37.75	83	33.38	113	36.14
CPN-UML	69	27.75	88	30.85	68	30.74
United People's Front	9	4.83	0	1.32	1	0.84
CPN(Democratic)	2	2.43	–	–	–	–
Nepal Workers and Peasant Party	2	1.25	4	0.98	1	0.55
National People's Front	0	0	0	0	5	1.37
CPN (ML)	0	0	0	0	0	5.00

Source: Lawoti (2005).

a minority government in 1994 and gradually adopted more centrist policies including, among others, those which supported a free-market economy and accepted the monarchy in Nepal. The CPN-UML was also an active partner in the 'petty politics' that defined the decade of Nepali democracy. Coalitions were formed or broken every few months. Between 1994 and 2001, Nepal saw five different coalition governments. Members of Parliament were 'bought' and 'sold' with the lure of money and powerful positions in the governments. The governance crisis generated disillusionment in a significant portion of the population, especially among the communist cadres of the CPN-UML. They were further disillusioned at the 'bourgeois' tilt of their party leaders and were attracted by the opportunity to participate in the 'People's War'. To a large part, the supporters of the CPN-UML provided local leadership and cadres to the Maoists insurgency.

Without the pre-existing support groups and communist activists already trained in communist ideologies, it was difficult to imagine the rapid spread of the Maoists. 'Converting communist sympathizers into Maoist supporters are [*sic*] much easier than indoctrinating non-communists into Maoist cadres' (Lawoti 2005). Perhaps one key reason for the failure of the earlier Jhapa Movement was that a widespread support base and sophisticated network of the communists did not exist then in the country.

Acceptance of Violence as a Political Tool

Despite the rhetoric of a peaceful Nepal, violence has been used to achieve political objectives. In 1950–51, the NC initiated a violent struggle to rid Nepal of the Rana oligarchs. In the following decade, especially after the dismissal of the elected government by King Mahendra in 1960, the NC launched several other violent insurgencies, albeit unsuccessfully. Similarly, Nepali communists had their own violent struggles, most notably the Jhapa Movement. Another attempt was a little-known incident in 1986 caused by the CPN (Mashal).

In an oversimplification of Marx's philosophy, the communist 'revolutionary' justified 'capture of state power as direct path to revolution without realizing that social and cultural transformation must by and large precede it' (Mikesell 1999). The use of violence to capture state power has been justified by communist movements worldwide. Mao's famous dictum that 'power comes through the barrel of gun' summarized the attitude of many communists towards political violence.

Many Nepali communists have espoused violence in principle. Any loss of life during the violent struggles is glorified as a *shahaadat* or martyrdom. This glorification 'creates symbolic capital which legitimizes and even encourages violent activities' (Shneiderman 2003). Martyrdom is central to the Maoist movement. To encourage 'sacrifices', they create public markers such as gates named after a martyr. The Maoists have also attracted communist cadres who have often dreamed of initiating a revolution in Nepal. Public discussions, debates and discourses on violence legitimize violence (Lawoti 2005). The communist parties in Nepal legitimized violence for a 'just cause' through ideological discourse.

A Divided State

While the CPN (Maoist) displayed its skills at long-term strategic planning, unified leadership, and a strong commitment to insurgency, the Nepali state was characterized by extreme incompetence, incoherence, and severe rifts and contradictions. Several successive governments had neither policies nor necessary tools to combat the insurgency. Similarly, all the mainstream political parties were full of contradictions and the royal palace saw violence as an opportunity to weaken the political parties and their governments in order to destabilize democracy. By acting to strengthen their own interests, each mainstream political actor eventually strengthened the Maoists.

Incompetent Governments

When a leader of the UPF, Baburam Bhattarai, presented '40-Point Demands' to the Prime Minister Sher Bahadur Deuba in February 1996, the list came with a threat of insurgency. However, that threat was largely ignored. When the Maoists actually acted on their promise with attacks on several police posts and declared their 'People's War', the initial state reaction was denial. Then Home Minister Khum Bahadur Khadka infamously proclaimed 'the police force would crush the so-called insurgency in four days'.

The state took the insurgency as a 'minor law and order problem' and the ill-equipped police force trained to maintain civilian peace was ordered to undertake counter-insurgency operations. Traditionally, most of the lower-level police carried 'bamboo sticks' to maintain order; a police post would carry only a few of the World War II era three-nought-three rifles. Motivated insurgents were able to over-power several police posts in isolated rural areas. Soon it became apparent that these isolated police posts were unable to defend against the onslaught of insurgents. The government decided to pull out several polices posts and consolidate them in district headquarters or larger centers. By 1999, there were only six police posts out of 23 in Rukum district. Similarly, Rolpa had only six posts out of 39 (Sharma 2000). As a result, a huge section of the rural hinter-lands in the western hills was in effect handed over to the Maoists.

This provided the Maoists with a free environment in which to organize. Soon they began expelling opposition-party members and local elected officials. Under the threat to life, many elected representative became internally displaced refugees in district headquarters or in the national capital. The Maoists consolidated their base areas by holding their own elections to village governments, establishing cooperatives, collectivizing land, and collecting a 'people's tax'.

Such a circumstance arose because power was highly centralized in Nepal, with little authority vested in the local governments. Even though centralized, the Nepali state, however, was weak and had only a marginal presence in the hinterlands (Lawoti 2003). Despite the rhetoric of decentralization in the democratic period, not a single significant law had been enacted until the late 1990s to facilitate decentralization. The local self-governance act of 1999 was too late, too little. The local governments had neither authority nor institutional mechanisms to curb violence or respond to it.

Incoherent Parties

The Maoists consolidated their hold in the western hills and began to mount offensives in other parts of the country. As the insurgency gained strength, political parties used the 'Maoist problem' to ascend to power. For the most part, all the national political parties refrained from formulating any specific policy in relation to the insurgency. Party agendas reflected both inter-party and intra-party fissures. While all the political parties presented vague agendas of socio-economic development, strengthening of the state machinery and a negotiated settlement with the Maoists, the NC for the most part advocated negotiation from a position of strength. This meant 'first crushing the insurgency and then sitting down at the negotiating table' (Hachhethu 2004). However, when Krishna Prasad Bhattarai ascended to power in the aftermath of the 1999 election, he refused to even recognize the insurgency as a serious problem and contended that the problem was unnecessarily exaggerated by his political foes, especially the Girija Prasad faction within the party (Dahal et al. 1999).

On the other side, the CPN-UML, the main opposition party for the most part of the 1990s, presented shifting positions. As a communist party, the CPN-UML faced difficulties in condemning the 'People's War' as terrorism and labelled the insurgency as a misguided CPN (Maoist) strategy and called it 'Left adventurism'. The CPN-UML considered the Maoists a 'friendly' force. It was also helped by the fact that the Maoists attacked only the NC supporters in the initial stages. Violent confrontations between the Maoists and the supporters of the CPN-UML were rare, if any. At various times, the Maoists shifted their position so as to exacerbate the differences within the political parties. In 2000, the Maoists announced that they were willing to form a united front with all political forces, except the Nepali Congress. In the aftermath of the 2001 royal-palace massacre, Prachanda called for such an alliance to be formed against what he called the 'Girija–Gyanendra clique', an attempt to play on the factional politics brewing within the NC between the Koirala and Bhattarai factions. The Maoists successfully exploited the existing inter- and intra-political rivalries in the two large parties. However, as the Maoists consolidated their strength, the CPN-UML cadres also came under fire and the UML started to adopt a more stringent attitude.

The political parties' positions reflected their position vis-à-vis power. They used the insurgency to strengthen their own electoral or power positions and weaken that of their opponents. For instance, Home Minister Bamdev Gautam of the CPN-UML, during a coalition with the Rashtriya Prajatantra Party (RPP), made an unsuccessful bid to introduce an anti-terrorism bill. Under heavy criticism from human-rights groups, civil society, and other left parties, the government withdrew the proposed legislation. But when the CPN-UML was ousted from power in October 1997, it opposed the same legislation (Hachhethu 2004). Furthermore, Gautam sought a close alliance with the Maoists when he split from the CPN-UML to form the CPN (ML). In an attempt to garner more votes, Gautam lavished praise on the Maoists from an open forum in Kathmandu (Dahal et al. 1999).

To some degree, the constant power squabbles could be attributed to Nepal's power structure, which entrusted too much power with the executive (Lawoti 2003). Since Nepal had a highly centralized, unitary, majoritarian system of government, power was concentrated in the cabinet. All the political appointments and national policy decisions were made by the cabinet, whereas the legislature acted almost as a rubber stamp. Thus, there was an overwhelming temptation for politicians to form a cabinet at any cost. This resulted in frequent changes of government, rampant corruption, and portfolio hunting as legislators always made an attempt to gain the highly profitable ministries of home, water resources or finance.

Palace–Government Division

As the government weakened due to the lack of consensus among political parties vis-à-vis the Maoist insurgency, the political capital of the royal palace increased. The palace, already disgruntled as it had lost significant political power under the new Constitution, saw the rising political violence as an opportunity to weaken the political parties and eventually democracy. Despite the republican rhetoric of the Maoists, the palace was emboldened by two factors: first, the victims of insurgency were mostly political activists, mostly of the NC; and second, the palace had control over the loyal Royal Nepal Army (RNA), which was believed to be far superior in numbers, combat skill, and military hardware than the insurgents.

The rift between the government and the palace started to emerge as the elected governments sought to mobilize the RNA. The RNA, with the king as its commander-in-chief, was for all practical purposes outside the authority of the government. Even though the Constitution of Nepal created a National Defence Council, comprising the prime minister, defence minister and army chief, the army remained under the king. Attempts to gain control of it by several governments were thwarted by the palace and the army on technical and political grounds such as logistics, resources and political mandate (Hachhethu 2004). Similarly, the RNA opposed the purchase of weapons and military hardware for the use of the police force (Sharma 1999). Several cabinet ministers questioned the loyalty of the RNA to the government. In an article published in *Himal Khabar Patrika*, Jaya Prakash Gupta, minister during the 1990s, summarized the attitude among the NC ministers and police officers: 'Even a woman sold to a brothel in India, if she has enough money she can easily rent RNA helicopter when returns [*sic*] home, but police and home minister cannot use it for operations [*sic*]' (Gupta 1999).

The government sought to develop an armed police unit under civilian authority. The RNA initially opposed the creation of such a force but agreed when it received *de facto* control over the training and equipment of the newly created force. Furthermore, even when the RNA was mobilized in some Maoist-affected districts under the rubric of an Integrated Security and Development Program (ISDP), the RNA refrained from engaging with the Maoists. When the Maoists overran Dunai, the district headquarters of Dolpa in western Nepal, the army stayed in the barracks while a large number of the police were killed. When the army was criticized by then Home Minister Govinda Raj Joshi, he had to resign (Sharma 2001). Similarly, the Maoists never attacked the RNA during the first five years of insurgency. The reluctant RNA was drawn onto the battleground when the Maoists broke a four-month-long ceasefire in November 2001 and overran an army barrack in Dang.

Conclusions

The Maoist insurgency is commonly seen as an expression of frustrations caused by economic, political and social inequalities that plague the country. It is believed that the low level of development, the low per-capita income, the high ethnic fractionalization, and the failure of democracy are the major causes of the insurgency. However, in this chapter, I have argued that opportunity and not grievance is the major cause of the violence. I show that despite the common perception that democracy failed to deliver on 'development', Nepal witnessed a significant growth in terms of gross GDP and per-capita GDP during the 1990s. The development indicators show gain in infrastructure such as roads, electricity and telecommunications. Similarly, both school enrolments and the literacy rate continued to increase during the decade.

I have argued that the high level of support for the communist parties and the monolithic ideology of the Maoists' leadership and their adoption of violent struggle, and the divided state presented a good opportunity for the insurgency to grow. The Maoists' leadership also displayed strong coherence in policy and political foresight, exploiting existing frictions in the political parties and the fissure in the state machinery.

References

Bhattachan, Krishna B. 2001. 'Peace and Good Governance in Nepal: The Socio-Cultural Context', in P. Shrestha (ed.), *Quest for Peace*, pp. 73–88. Kathmandu: SAP-Nepal.

Collier, Paul and Anke Hoeffler. 2001. 'Greed and Grievance in Civil War'. <http://econ.worldbank.org/files/12205_greedgrievance_23oct.pdf>, World Bank. (Accessed on 15 November 2004.)

Dahal, Rajendra, Shiva Gaunle and Sudhir Sharma 1999. 'Partyharu ko Bhagne Taun Chhaina', *Himal Khabar Patrika* (Lalitput), 17 November-1 December.

Elbadawi, Ibrahim and Nicholas Sambanis. 2002. 'How Much War Will We See? Explaining the Prevalence of Civil War', <http://econ.worldbank.org/files/13211_ WarPrevalence.pdf>. World Bank. (Accessed on 15 November 2004.)

Ellingsen, Tanja, Scott Gates, Nils P. Gleditsch and Havard Hegre. 2001. 'Toward a Democratic Civil Peace? Democracy, Political Change, and Civil War, 1816–1992', *American Political Science Review* 95 (1): 33–48.

Fearon, James D. and David D. Laitin. 2003. 'Ethnicity, Insurgency, and Civil War', *American Political Science Review* 97 (1): 75–90.

Gautam, Pushkar. 2000. 'Prachanda ko Baktabya le Dina Khojeko Sandesh', *Himal Khabar Patrika* (Lalitpur), 13 February-27 February.

van de Goor, L. 1996. 'Major Findings of the Research Project, Causes of Conflict in the Third World: Executive Summary', <http://www.clingendael.nl/cru/research/ CODW.htm>, Conflict Research Unit, Netherlands Institute of International Relations 'Clingedael'. (Accessed on 23 November 2004.)

Gupta, Jaya Prakash. 1999. 'Maobadi Sambandhi Tin Prashna', *Himal Khabar Patrika* (Lalitpur), 17 September-2 October.

Hachhethu, Krishna 2004. 'The Nepali State and the Maoist Insurgency, 1996–2001', in M. Hutt (ed.), *Himalayan People's War: Nepal's Maoist Rebellion*, pp. 58–78. Bloomington: Indiana University Press.

Hegre, Havard. 2003. 'Disentangling Democracy and Development as Determents of Armed Conflict', <http://econ.worldbank.org/files/24637_ddcwwb.PDF>. World Bank. (Accessed on 23 November 2004.)

Informal Sector Service Center (INSEC). The Chronology of Human Rights Violation (1996–2004), Kathmandu: INSEC. http://www.insec.org.np/download/ Killings_ Data.pdf. (Accessed on 5 April 2002 and 15 November 2004.)

Kantipur Daily. (20 October 2000). http://www.kantipuronline.com. (Accessed on 20 October 2000.)

KC, Surendra. 2003. *Nepal ma Communist Aandolan ko Itihas* (History of Communist Movement in Nepal): *Part* 2. Kathmandu: Bidhyarthi Pustak Bhandar

Lawoti, Mahendra. 2003. 'Centralizing Politics and the Growth of the Maoist Insurgency in Nepal', *Himalaya, the Journal of the Association for Nepal and Himalayan Studies* XXIII (1): 49–58.

———. 2005. *Towards a Democratic Nepal: Inclusive Political Institutions for a Multicultural Society*. New Delhi: Sage Publications.

Mikesell, Stephen. 1999. *Class, State, and Struggle in Nepal*. New Delhi: Manohar.

Nickson, Andrew R. 1992. 'Democratisation and the Growth of Communism in Nepal: A Peruvian Scenario in the Making?', *Journal of Commonwealth and Comparative Politics* 30 (3): 358–86.

Onesto, Li. 2003. 'Report from the People's War', in D. Thapa (ed.), *Understanding the Maoist Movement of Nepal*, pp. 151–80. Kathmandu: Martin Chautari. Available at <http://www.rwor.org>.

Pfaff-Czarnecka, Joanna. 2004. 'High Expectations, Deep Disappointment: Politics, State and Society in Nepal after 1990', in D. Thapa (ed.), *Himalayan People's War: Nepal's Maoist Rebellion*, pp. 166–91. Bloomington: Indiana University Press.

Pyakuryal, Bishwambher. 2001. 'Response to Poverty,' in P. Shrestha (ed.), *Quest for Peace*, pp. 45–72. Kathmandu: SAP-Nepal.

de Sales, Ann. 2003. 'The Kham Magar Country, Nepal: Between Ethnic Claims and Maoism', in D. Thapa (ed.), *Understanding the Maoist Movement of Nepal*, pp. 59–88. Kathmandu: Martin Chautari.

Sambanis, Nicholas. 2001. 'Do Ethnic and Nonethnic Civil Wars Have the Same Cause? A Theoretical and Empirical Inquiry (Part I)', *Journal of Conflict Resolution* 45 (3): 259–82.

Shaha, Rishikesh. 2003. 'Idea and Reality: Nepal and Rolpa', in D. Thapa (ed.), *Understanding the Maoist Movement of Nepal*, pp. 49–52. Kathmandu: Martin Chautari.

Sharma, Sudhir. 1999. 'Yahan baat Kataa Maobadi? (What do the Maoists want Next?)', *Himal Magazine*, 3–17 October.

———. 2000. 'Char Jilla Maobadi ko Hatma', *Himal Khabar Patrika*, 16–30 July. Lalitpur: Himal Publications.

———. 2001. 'Antatah: Aamne Samne', *Himal Khabar Patrika*, 16–30 July. Lalitpur: Himal Publications

Shneiderman, Sara. 2003. 'Violent Histories and Political Consciousness: Reflections on Nepal's Maoist Movement from Piskar Village', *Himalaya, the Journal of the Association for Nepal and Himalayan Studies* XXIII (1): 39–48.

Shrestha, Bihari K. 2001. 'Maoist Movement and the Peace Building Process,' in P. Shrestha (ed.), *Quest for Peace*, pp. 12–28. Kathmandu: SAP-Nepal.

Snyder, Jack. 2000. *From Voting to Violence: Democratic and National Conflict*. New York: W.W. Norton and Company.

Thapa, Deepak. 2004. 'Radicalism and the Emergence of the Maoists', in M. Hutt (ed.), *Himalayan People's War: Nepal's Maoist Rebellion*, pp. 21–37. Bloomington: Indiana University Press.

UNDP. 1998. *Nepal Human Development Report 1998*. New York: The United Nations Development Program (UNDP).

White, Robert W. 1989. 'From Peaceful Protest to Guerrilla War: Micro-mobilization of the Provisional Irish Republic Army', *The American Journal of Sociology* 94 (6): 1277–1302.

World Bank. 2006. *World Development Indicators (WDI) Online*, http://publications. worldbank.org/ecommerce/catalog/product?item_id=631625. (Accessed on 25 November 2004.)

4

Women and Children Last: The Effects of the Maoist Insurgency on Gender-based Violence

Mary Crawford, Michelle R. Kaufman and Alka Gurung

The Maoist insurgency in Nepal has had a devastating effect on Nepali life. Many people have been forced to flee their villages as a result of violence or the fear of violence. Families are being uprooted and displaced, and those who stay behind, most often women and children, scrape by on very little income. International aid agencies have suggested that the insurgency has increased particular kinds of risks for women and children. For example, the daughters of displaced families may be at increased risk of being trafficked for sex work (Asian Development Bank 2003). Meanwhile, Nepal-based non-governmental organizations (NGOs) and their international counterparts (INGOs) are increasingly being hampered, both directly and indirectly, in their work by the insurgency.

In this chapter, we explore how the insurgency has affected girls and women in rural Nepal, as well as the work of the NGOs dedicated to helping them. First, we look at patterns of gender-based violence and increase in sex work in other countries and how they may serve as a prediction of what is occurring in Nepal as a result of the insurgency. Then, based on analysis of our visits to regional transit homes, interviews with NGO staff, village mobilizers, and victims of sex trafficking, we explore how the dearth of donor funds and the lack of access to rural areas are blocking attempts to educate and inform rural residents.

Gender-Based Violence: Definition and Scope

Sarita was born into a poor farmer's family and her parents sent her to school only for one year. When she was just 14, a young man from her village convinced Sarita to leave with him, took her across the border to India, and sold her to a brothel (SAATHI 1997).

This is just one example of the gender-based violence experienced by Nepali women and girls. Gender-based violence is a worldwide problem. In virtually every culture, some kinds of violence against women are taken for granted. They include sexual harassment, rape, incest, forced marriage, physical and emotional violence in relationships, and even persecution for witchcraft. Some forms of gender-based violence, such as stoning women (but not men) for adultery, may be officially permitted by the state; others represent a kind of unofficial terrorism. Although they are not technically legal, everyone knows these forms of violence occur and the government rarely intervenes (Sidanius and Pratto 1999).

Research has documented many examples of the prevalence of gendered violence around the world:

- One-third of women have been physically assaulted, coerced to sexual activity, and victimized by severe emotional abuse (Heise et al. 1999).
- Infanticide—the murder of unwanted infants—has been culturally accepted at various times and places in history. About 9 per cent of cultures have practiced sex-biased infanticide. In the majority of these, the unwanted sex was female (Hrdy 1988).
- In some countries, over half of all female murder victims are killed by a current or former partner (Neft and Levine 1997).

According to the World Health Organization, gender-linked forms of violence share an underlying cause: 'The lower social status of women and the belief that women are the property of men' (Murphy 2003: 208). Patriarchal social structures that accord more value and rights to men create a climate that condones violence against women (Crawford 2005). When patriarchal societies are under threat, violence against women often increases. Disruption of communal social norms and displacement of people due to political unrest increases the risk of gender-based violence.

Political Conflict and Gender-based Violence

Violence against women, including rape, abuse and assault, is a horrifying but common tactic of war. Such atrocities have occurred throughout history. Brownmiller (1975) cited rape of women as a tactic of war in World War I, World War II, and in Bangladesh and Vietnam. More recently, as many as 500,000 women were raped in Rwanda during the 1994 genocide (Organization of African Unity 2000). Hutu men who knew they were HIV positive purposely tried to infect Tutsi women by raping them repeatedly (Rehn and Sirleaf 2002). During the Bosnian War in the 1990s, an estimated 300,000 unwanted pregnancies, the result of systematic rapes, were documented (Kozaric-Kovacic et al. 1995; MacKinnon 1993). In Sierre Leone, 50 per cent of women experienced sexual violence of some degree during the conflict (Physicians for Human Rights 2002). Some researchers have argued that the incidence, savagery, and systematic organization of rape as a tactic of war have increased in the late twentieth-century conflicts (Barstow 2000; MacKinnon 1994).

Violence against women does not arise solely as a result of political conflict; often, it is directly related to the violence women suffer during peaceful times. However, conflict tends to dramatically increase the level and incidence of violence against women (Rehn and Sirleaf 2002). In cultures where violence against women is tolerated, it becomes an accepted norm during wartime. Fortunately, there is a growing recognition that human-rights abuses that occur in the context of civil unrest pose special threats to the health and lives of women (MacKinnon 1993). However, such abuses continue to occur.

Researching Gender-based Violence in Nepal

In this chapter, we analyse gender-based violence in Nepal, with special attention to the effects of the ongoing Maoist insurgency on violence against women. In particular, we focus on a form of violence that we hypothesize is highly likely to be exacerbated by the social upheaval of the insurgency: trafficking of women and girls.

The research on which this chapter is based was conducted from 2004 to 2006. The main research site was a leading non-profit NGO with a focus on the prevention and remediation of sex trafficking and other forms of violence against women and girls. The NGO, established in 1987, maintains a central office in Kathmandu and five regional facilities, and conducts a number of programmes aimed at empowering rural women and fostering health and development among the disadvantaged. These include women's leadership training, educational programmes for at-risk villagers on such topics as HIV/AIDS, sex trafficking and domestic violence; and gainful-employment programmes for women who teach marketable skills such as driving, cooking in hotels, and working in the field of community health. The NGO also has founded and sustained 200 women's micro-credit cooperatives in rural areas. Most relevant to trafficking, this NGO maintains six shelters, one in Kathmandu and five in areas where women and girls are at especially high risk for trafficking. These shelters, or transit homes, provide temporary accommodation, basic counselling and medical services, and a supportive community for women and girls who have been trafficked or subjected to other kinds of gender-based violence. The Kathmandu shelter, the largest, usually has about 35 women and girls in residence.

Our research methods included interviews with NGO staff, the head of Nepal's women's-police unit, trafficking victims, and women's rights activists; analysis of NGO publications and mass-media reports; field observations; interviews with people directly affected by the conflict; and archival research on NGO case files, assessing survivor characteristics and long-term outcomes.

The NGO case files for the years 1996 (when its first shelter opened) through December 2004 showed that during this period, 321 women and girls entered the NGO's shelters because they had been rescued from a trafficking situation. Other shelter residents were survivors of domestic violence (n = 236), rape (n = 85), other forms of sexual exploitation (n = 95) or child victims of trafficking into circus work (n = 102). Overall, this NGO had sheltered 839 women and girls since 1996.

TRAFFICKING: DEFINITION AND SCOPE

Trafficking is defined as buying and selling or coercive capture of human beings for purposes of exploitation (especially commercial sex work), forced labor or enslavement of any sort (UNFPA 2004). Between 700,000 and 2,000,000 girls and women are trafficked across borders annually worldwide (ibid.). The sextrafficking problem is most acute in East and Southeast Asia, which are currently estimated to contribute nearly a quarter of worldwide cases each year. Although accurate figures are difficult to obtain, the best estimate is that 5,000 to 7,000 Nepali women and girls are trafficked each year, primarily to India, and at least 200,000 Nepali women and girls currently work in Indian brothels (Huntington 2002).

Root Causes of Trafficking in Nepal

Nepal's status as a source country for sex trafficking is not surprising. In general, countries that are less developed, less wealthy, and less politically stable serve as source countries from which women and girls are trafficked. More developed or affluent countries serve as destination sites, where trafficked women and girls are enslaved in brothels or otherwise constrained to participate in prostitution (Farr 2005). Nepal is one of the world's poorest countries, ranking 136 on the UN Human Development Index (UNDP 2006). The overall poverty rate hovers around 40 per cent, and poverty incidence is almost double in rural areas (46 per cent), where the majority of the population lives, as compared to urban areas (23 per cent) (ibid.). His Majesty's Government estimates (HMGN 1996) that some 46 per cent of Nepali children are malnourished. The economic situation has been worsening for the past decade, as political violence has disrupted tourism and agriculture.

In addition to economic factors, the disadvantaged status of women and girls in Nepali society figures as a root cause of trafficking. The cultural devaluation of women is expressed in Nepalese proverbs such as '*Choriko janma, hareko karma*' (to be born a daughter is to have an ill fate). Other folk wisdom recognizes that a daughter's contributions move to her husband's family upon her marriage, and thus investing in a daughter is in some sense a waste of scarce resources: 'Educating a daughter is like watering your neighbour's garden.' A woman's status and material security are closely linked to marriage and bearing sons.

Inequities of legal status, schooling and citizenship combine with symbolic subordination to create a climate in which individuals internalize gender hierarchy. Subjectivity—one's personal identity—is socially and culturally formed. In other words, men in patriarchal cultures often feel entitled to dominance, whereas women feel that they deserve to be treated as second-class citizens, and both genders monitor their own behaviour in accordance with social norms. In general, Nepali women, especially those in the dominant Hindu tradition, are socialized to embody modesty, shyness, shame, and a strong sense of propriety, especially in duty to husband and family. With this background, we turn to examining women's vulnerability to sex trafficking.

Trafficking into Commercial Sex Work

Trafficking of women and children can take many forms. In this chapter, we focus on trafficking into commercial sex work. As might be expected, there is little quantitative data on this form of violence against women and girls because of its criminalized status, its secrecy, and the stigma attached to its survivors. Most of the evidence on sex trafficking comes from survivors' case studies compiled by NGOs and, to a lesser extent, government-sponsored reports. These accounts document the deceptive and violent tactics that traffickers use to ensnare women and young girls: fake marriages, promises of jobs, and abduction are common modes of trafficking. Once they have been taken across the border to India, their lives become night-marish. Case studies document multiple occurrences of rape, gang rape, burning of breasts and genitals with cigarettes, beating, chaining, imprisonment, perpetual debt bondage, and other forms of physical and psychological degradation (Institute for Integrated Development Studies 2004; Pradhan 1994).

One of the brothel survivors we interviewed described her initiation into sex work and her living conditions in the brothel. She was 13 when she was deceived into leaving her village and sold to an Indian brothel, and at first she did not realize what was expected of her:

R: For me... *dhanda* was like doing the work of the household, like cleaning, washing dishes, and everything. In Nepali, that is what *dhanda* means, right? But there, it's different. There, it's like when you take a man [provide sex to a customer], they call it *dhanda*. But I didn't know, and I was told to go and get ready for *dhanda*. And I went and looked everywhere for a broom, but I couldn't find one. Then they started scolding me in Nepali, saying, like, 'Will your father earn money and give it to us for you?' [sobbing]. I cried so much when they said that. Then I realized that I was sold [cries again].

DK: Were you allowed to go out for shopping, or just, you know, go out?

R: No, not at all. I couldn't even see the light outside. Everywhere, there were high walls and pillars. Only very small windows. If sometime we wanted to look outside, we looked through that very, very small window. And sometimes, when we got sick, we were taken outside for injections. That was the only time we could see sunlight. Our only air, inside, was from a fan. .. and that sound of the fan... .

The Insurgency's Effects on Nepali Society

The conflict between Maoist rebels and the security forces is now a decade old and shows no signs of abating. About 13,000 people have been killed in ongoing violence;. the security forces are responsible for about two-thirds of these deaths. Many more Nepali citizens are being displaced by violence or the threat of violence: estimates range from 200,000 to 400,000 people since the beginning of the conflict (Singh et al. 2005). The insurgency has also had a grave effect on Nepal's economy: tourism is down 50 per cent, business activities in Kathmandu have suffered tremendously too, and education, health, and other development programmes have been compromised as more effort has been made towards resolving the political unrest (Yogi 2002).

Displacement, even without direct exposure to insurgency-related violence, reverberates throughout the lives of victims and their families. For example, one young woman came to the NGO for help early in 2005. Widowed before she was 20 when her husband died in a road accident, she had a three-year-old son and no means of support. She could not return to her husband's village to live with his parents, because it was under Maoist control. Her own parents, displaced by the conflict, were extremely poor and living in a tiny rented room in Kathmandu. She begged for funds to pay school fees for her son, but the NGO had no funds to give.[1]

In another case, a young widowed mother of three whose husband had recently been killed by the Maoists appealed to the NGO for help.[2]

In both of these cases, the NGO provided job training for the women—in the first case, cooking training, and in the second, computer training. The NGO director reported that the second woman 'wept throughout the training, but she did it'. However, neither was able to find a job after completing their vocational training, probably a side-effect of the economic upheaval caused by the insurgency.

Some women, men and children join the Maoist cause through conviction; others are coerced. Others migrate to escape the army or the insurgents. In many parts of rural Nepal, migration has become a matter of survival. Villagers are caught between the Maoists and the army, both of whom use brutal tactics, and neither is held accountable because the government is largely non-functional outside the Kathmandu Valley and district headquarters.

Looking at data from many conflict-ridden countries around the world, such as the former Republic of Yugoslavia, Liberia, Afghanistan and Northern Ireland, it becomes apparent that native civilians often become innocent and accidental victims of internal political armed conflicts. While there are a myriad of international and domestic reasons for armed conflicts around the world, in Nepal the conflict is rooted in the lack of good governance, economic stagnation, overt dependence on the regional superpower of India, and, above all, in the disparity of wealth and resource distribution between the upper castes/classes and the peasantry. While the issue of the status of women and girls in the Nepali society is beginning to be well documented, the effect of the 'People's War' since 1996 and the role of women and girls within this prolonged armed conflict have received scant attention.

As in any significant conflict, propaganda is one of the most crucial weapons. The war that has ensued since the inception of Maoist insurgency in Nepal is no exception. Newspapers, TV stations, internet sites, radio, and public speeches have been used by both sides to give their 'side of the story'. Not surprisingly, both sides have consistently given completely opposite accounts of their treatment of young Nepali women since the conflict began. From the outset, the Maoists have claimed they were fighting for gender equality by challenging Nepal's patriarchal culture. They demonstrated this by highlighting the number of Nepali women who had voluntarily joined their military ranks in order to fight for equal rights. In press releases, written doctrines, and an interview with Comrade Prachanda, leader of the Maoist Party,[3] the Maoists claim Nepali women are being unfairly subjugated and suppressed by the male-dominated patriarchal culture that completely undermines their civil liberties and rights.

Some female rebels even claim that the Maoists have managed to curtail the entry of young Nepali women into prostitution in big Indian cities such as Mumbai (Douglas 2005). The government, on the other hand, insists that most young Nepali women in the Maoist ranks are being physically forced away from their rural villages by armed Maoists who threaten and kill them and their families if they do not go with them. While it is difficult to establish the facts, the following accounts by individuals who have lived and continue to live at the epicentre of the conflict may elucidate the complexities of this war. Each person conveyed similar stories of aggression and unnecessary force and cruelty exercised by both the Maoist and the government forces on the villagers. Many of the informants talked about living with their families under fear of abduction and extortion and of being sympathizers of one or the other party.

The destructive ramifications of the Maoist insurgency, such as economic dislocation and the unchecked outflow of displaced and terrorized refugees fleeing from the atrocities, have been felt throughout the country and the region as a result of the violence perpetrated both by the Nepalese police and army and the Maoist guerrilla fighters, as the following conversations with a displaced family from Dolakha revealed. According to Mr Karki, the headmaster of a village school until he was forced to flee from the village several months ago,[4] the insurgency has ruined his life:

> I have three children, a son and two daughters. When the Maoists came to our village, they told me that I should send my children to

a Maoist camp for three months to be trained by them. I was told that if my children followed the training regimen of the camp, they would be released and allowed to come back home.[5] Reluctantly, I let my children go. After three long anxiety-ridden months, my children returned home on leave. A few days after their arrival, I secretly sent them to Kathmandu.

About 10 days later, a group of Maoist soldiers came to my house, ready to take my children back to the camp for the second phase of their training. When I told them that my children were in Kathmandu seeking treatment for a stomach ailment that one of my daughters had developed, they did not say anything. They left as silently as they had come. A week later, three Maoist soldiers returned to my house, telling me that they had been told to bring me back with them. After much debating and cajoling from me, they finally left along with an increased donation of rice and a full month's salary of Rs 5,000 from me.[6]

However, my relief was very short-lived. Within five days, two Maoist soldiers returned to my house, informing me that their leader had ordered them not to return without me. I was very worried. I convinced the soldiers that I would leave with them the next morning. That evening, after dinner, the two insurgents fell into a deep slumber. I whispered to my wife that we would have to flee from the village, and as such she should walk down the stairs and out of the front door as quietly as possible. Should the squeaking stairs wake the soldiers up, she should tell them that she was going downstairs to heat some water. Fortunately, the soldiers did not wake up. My wife left through the front door and I jumped out of the second-floor window.

We fled in the middle of the night with only the clothes we were wearing—with no food, no money. Although we had some money in the closet, we were afraid to take it, in case the jingling keys woke the insurgents up. I keep moving from place to place every few months because I worry that the Maoists will find us. We have since found out from a village friend that they terrorized my old mother by breaking open the closet, taking the money and kicking our pots and pans across our kitchen floor. She has moved out of the house and is living with one of my brothers in a neighbouring village. In any event, the Maoists have locked up our house and have the key.

The Maoists have threatened to kill us wherever and whenever they find us. We don't feel safe even here in Kathmandu.

While it appears that, like many rebel leaders around the world, the Nepali Maoists' leaders have also resorted to violence in an effort to 'generate a hegemonic discourse which seeks to subsume subjectivity and its multiple forms of representation into a singular entity involved in a confrontational interaction with another assumed/ constructed monolithic entity' (Miall et al. 1999), the effects of such a tactic have been devastating for the villagers, especially for women and children. Their strategy of 'intimidation, extortion and brutality to exercise control' (*National Geographic* 2005) over the population, the rural territory and its subsistence economy has annihilated the very fibre of rural Nepali life. However, according to Nye (2003), such a tactic makes the proponents of violent conflict make their fight for political ideology and power 'appear more concrete, measurable and predictable', and hence a necessary means of bringing about social change.

Although articles such as 'Inside Nepal's Revolution' (*National Geographic* 2005) portray the Maoist militants as brave and angry fighters willing to take up arms against a corrupt and unjust government, it appears that for the majority of Nepali women and children, this militancy is much more traumatic and tragic, as the following account highlights.

Durga is a 19-year-old former Maoist recruit from Jiri. She and her two friends joined the Maoists after seeing them in a recruitment rally in a nearby village:

> We were bored. I was 16, Mingma was 22 and Laxmi was 15. Mingma liked a fellow in the Royal Nepalese Army. Maybe that was the reason why the Maoists were keen to recruit us.[7] They made the whole rally appear so much fun. They sang songs of freedom, danced and performed sketches highlighting the nature of our oppression. Towards the end of the performance, they asked the audience if anyone would like to go with them for a three-month training camp.
>
> On a whim, we decided to go with the Maoists. As day broke, we left the village. We were given big, heavy bags to carry, which we later discovered contained rifles and guns. After walking for nearly five hours, we arrived at a new village. The leaders of the group went inside some homes to ask for food and drink.
>
> Just as we were getting ready to rest, we saw a group of men approaching us from a nearby hillside. When our commanding

> leader saw the men, he ordered us to get our arms ready. Mingma, Laxmi and I were very scared. The men (older Maoist recruits) ran to the opposite hillside. We followed them, not knowing what was happening. Suddenly, we heard loud bangs. I saw bleeding bodies falling to the ground. Amongst them were Laxmi and Mingma. Laxmi just slumped to the ground, but Mingma struggled to get up while shouting angry, incomprehensible words at the men, who had run down the hill to capture us. The remaining members from the Maoist party ran helter-skelter and dispersed over the opposite hill. Suddenly, one of the men who had shot at us picked up his rifle and hit Mingma on the side of her face. Her skull caved in and she died instantly.
>
> The men then rounded us up, handcuffed us and ordered us to sit on the floor. We watched as they brought out combat fatigues and a can of diesel from their bags. They put these fatigues on Mingma, Laxmi and a few other dead men/boys and smeared their faces with diesel to make them unrecognizable. Soon they were taking pictures of themselves standing over the dead bodies. After they finished taking the pictures, I was ordered to carry several bags of guns and ammunition, while the captured men/boys were told to carry the dead bodies and start walking. When we finally arrived at a river, the boys were ordered to throw the bodies into the river.
>
> After dumping the bodies, we walked for several more hours until we came to a house that was being used as a police station. It was here that we found out that we had been arrested as Maoist rebels. We were shouted at, hit and threatened with death if we did not reveal the location of training camps and their war strategy. After keeping me for about 10 days, they finally let me go home. It was much later that I found out that these men were members of the government forces. Although my family was relieved to see that I was alive, they were really angry with me for joining the rebels and endangering the lives of our family members. They told me to leave for Kathmandu the same night. I am currently living in Kathmandu with some relatives. Me and my family in the village now all live in fear of both the Maoists and the government forces.

Even as we write this article, the front pages of the Nepali newspapers are plastered with images of grieving widows and family members, with headlines outlining atrocities committed by both the government forces and the Maoists against each other and innocent civilians. For a great majority of the Nepali population, this protracted armed conflict has meant little other than fear, violence, displacement and the deaths of family and friends. While ideologues on both sides of this war continue to believe that under the current circumstances, 'it is their function to resort to arms against one another' (Miall et al. 1999), the tragedy continues, with no constructive solutions emerging on either side of this bloody war. It is too soon to tell if the conflict will die down.

Political Conflict, Sex Work and Trafficking

Is the insurgency leading directly to an increase in prostitution and sex trafficking? As discussed earlier, during conflict, women and girls may be abducted and forced to serve armed groups and forces, both domestically and sexually. In areas where local economies are devastated due to conflict, many women have no other options for employment and survival other than sex work (Carballo et al. 1996). Sex work consistently accompanies militarization internationally (Enloe 2000). Armed conflict also raises the danger level for sex workers because armed men are granted absolute authority, and so the vulnerability of everyone considered outside of the law (such as sex workers) is increased (Tambiah 2004). In addition, the breakdown of law and order during conflict, including border controls and police functions, creates an environment where trafficking of women and girls can flourish. In fact, traffickers often use routes through countries or regions in conflict for this very reason. These countries also become sources for trafficked women because of the level of poverty and desperation usually caused by destroyed economies (Rehn and Sirleaf 2002).

Is the familiar pattern of gender-based violence and a rise in the sex industry occurring in Nepal as a result of the Maoist insurgency? It is clear that women and girls have been severely affected by the conflict through displacement, and those who remain in areas where the conflict is taking place are at an especially heightened risk of sexual assault and gender-based violence (Sazaki and Ryan 2005). There have been very few reports of violence against women on either side of the conflict, most likely due to selective news coverage. The reports that do exist are confirmatory, however. According to the 2003 US Department of State *Country Reports on Human Rights* (2004), violence against women in Nepal, including in refugee camps, and the trafficking of women and girls for prostitution, remains a serious problem. The ongoing conflict has escalated sexual assault exponentially, and often the law-enforcing authorities are the perpetrators. Reports from NGOs and INGOs hold that security forces are increasingly perpetrating sexual violence against women, especially young girls in military barracks in the villages. Many young militia girls have reported being sexually abused by their colleagues and seniors (Dhakal 2005). According to the Asian Human Rights Commission (1997), cases of rape, murder after rape, and trafficking increased from 1992 to 1997, which marked the early years of the Maoist insurgency.

A few specific examples of violence against women have been reported in Nepal. In April of 2002, two Royal Nepal Army (RNA) officers raped two teenage girls at an army barrack. When the case was made public, the girls recanted, probably because they were pressured to do so. The RNA acquitted one of the officers of rape charges, finding him guilty only of unlawful detainment. Similarly, in December 2002, two members of the parliamentary Armed Police Force (APF) allegedly raped a 16-year-old girl in Banke district. The APF dismissed the case and turned it over to the civil police for criminal action, but it is not clear whether any action was taken (US Department of State 2004). According to the National Network Against Girl Trafficking in Nepal (Dahal 2001), there have been numerous reports of women and young girls being abused by the Maoist insurgents in rural areas of the country.

In a recent study by Rana et al. (2005) for Save the Children Norway, female sex workers in Banke and Bardiya districts and nearby Village Development Committees (VDCs) were interviewed. Nineteen per cent of the interviewees reported that they had entered sex work because of the conflict and 85 per cent believed that the sex trade would decrease if the conflict were to end. Moreover, recent reports indicate that sex traffickers are taking advantage of the conflict- related economic and social decline in rural Nepal by focusing their efforts in the most affected areas, Rukum and Rolpa (Singh et al. 2005).

As the conflict increases hardship for rural villagers, it also increases the risk of exploitation. Village life has been disrupted and the social fabric changed. In these times of economic crisis, caring for daughters may become such an insurmountable problem that sending them away seems the best solution. As one of our NGO counselors (whose own parents had been displaced) explained:

> Right now, because of the Maoist problem, some don't even get to eat and live properly. There are so many reasons behind girl trafficking. There are lots of daughters; to get them married you need lots of wealth. You are not allowed to sell your land (because of the Maoists). In villages, they sell their land and crops and get their daughters married. It's hard if you are not allowed to sell....[8]

With the increased political tension between the Maoist insurgents and the RNA and APF, we hypothesize that there has been an increase of both gender-based violence and sex work, including trafficking of women and girls. Anecdotal reports from those living in Kathmandu show an increase in sex workers and 'cabin bars', restaurants that include with a meal a woman who will perform services (usually sexual) for the customer as needed. Women and girls who are fleeing the villages to escape being inducted into the Maoist camps and the political violence are often left with few options for income other than sex work.

Our review of the root causes of sex trafficking in Nepal shows that the women and girls most at risk are those who are already disadvantaged on many dimensions. If there is a 'typical' victim of trafficking, she is of lower caste, rural, uneducated, and very poor, and she desperately wants to migrate in search of a better life.

For example, two of the authors talked with Manu and Ranju (names changed), who left their home village in their early teens because they were so poor and because the Maoist presence was increasing. They went on foot to the Everest region, where so far the army has been in control, to work in a tourist lodge. They said they are a lot happier and a lot better off. They have a warm kitchen floor to sleep on and plenty of food. In migrating, they acted on their own behalf to improve their hard lot in life. It is true that bad things could happen to them. For example, their employer, a relatively rich and worldly man of a different ethnic group, could sexually abuse them or sell them. They definitely fit the profile of 'at-risk' girls. However, in their case the risk is mitigated by the fact that they can still keep in touch with their families, and a relative comes periodically to visit them. As the insurgency increases rural poverty, forces displacement, compels migration, and erodes communal social norms, girls like Manu and Ranju will be increasingly vulnerable to sex trafficking.

One of our NGO staff expressed this view when asked if the Maoist problem had affected trafficking risk:

> Yes, there are so many reported cases... and we have been hearing this news from different organizations working in Maoist- affected areas. .. that girls are crossing the borders every day because they are not feeling secure, because the senior member(s), the boy(s) (male family members) already are in the Maoist force. And some youth, they are also crossing the border in search of jobs, not only to India but to different countries like the Gulf countries. Many times they are the victims of violence. And girls are crossing the border in search of jobs, and when it is not possible to get a job, they work as prostitutes. Some girls leave their village or district, come to the city and work in a dance restaurant or massage parlour.[9]

According to one of the staff members we interviewed at the NGO, women and girls who are being displaced by the conflict are the ones most likely to be trafficked:

> Because of this conflict... these innocent women are trapped by the Maoist forces as well as the arm[ed] forces of Nepal. Recently my friend, who is in one of the most backward districts of Nepal, said that there are more than 1,000 women who have been raised [displaced] from the conflict, and how they are in such a position that they might get trafficked or involved in the prostitution. The conflict had made them vulnerable.... The main cause today [of trafficking] in this context is displacement, and when we control this displacement ratio, then automatically we can control girl-trafficking.

Effect of Insurgency on Trafficking Prevention and Remediation

Government agencies and NGOs alike have initiated many interventions aimed at reducing gender-based violence in the past two decades. Many of these were directed at the root causes of trafficking and other gender-based violence: income-generating programmes for rural women, support of formal and non-formal education for girls, educational programmes to raise awareness about trafficking and reduce the stigmatization of survivors, and so on. Others were directed at providing help to survivors: shelters, medical and psychological care, and reintegration into Nepalese society. Within the legal system, there have been efforts to develop and pass anti-trafficking legislation and to prosecute offenders: the traffickers and pimps who ply the brothel trade. We will examine the effects of the insurgency on prevention and remediation of trafficking in turn.

Prevention

Clearly, preventing gender-based violence is a multi-pronged effort that involves grassroots education, income-generation programmes for women, and anti-trafficking legislation and enforcement. To the extent that the insurgency disrupts any of these aspects of Nepalese society, it blocks or interferes with prevention efforts. Here, we focus on the disruption of rural education and income-generating programmes for women.

The insurgency has disrupted outreach work by NGOs in rural areas, particularly in western Nepal. For example, Save the Children's projects in Accham have been disrupted by fighting between the army and the rebels since 2002 (Rana et al. 2005) and Medecins Sans Frontieres had to curtail its projects in Jumla in 2004 (Singh et al. 2005). Problems increased after the king suspended constitutional rights, dismissed the Parliament, and declared a state of emergency in February 2005. In March 2005, the staff from our NGO's site in Dhanusa reported that they were not able to work in the villages around that area, although they remained active at their headquarters.[10] A month later, a planned visit by Kathmandu staff to Bhairawa to supervise ongoing projects was cancelled after long discussion simply because it was too dangerous to travel there.[11]

Throughout the countryside, the rural schools and clinics that provided the venues for grassroots educational programmes have been targeted for violence: many have been destroyed or abandoned. Accounts of such violence are common in the Nepali press. In February and March 2005, as students across the country were preparing for school-leaving exams, Maoists were reported to have bombed and destroyed six schools near Musikot, Rukum district, accusing the students and teachers of supporting the local administration (*Kathmandu Post Report* 2005), and another six in Nepalganj, leaving students terrorized and without the most basic educational facilities. Rural villages are even more at risk than district headquarters, and 'teachers report that hundreds of thousands of students haven't been able to prepare for their exams' (Bohara 2005).

In the NGO that participated in this research, there were mixed feelings about the magnitude of the effect on its work. On the one hand, our participating NGO had managed to sustain its five transit homes in areas outside the Kathmandu Valley. The NGO's founder reported that encounters with Maoists had ended amicably because the Maoists supported the goals of the NGO, such as empowerment of rural women and an end to sex trafficking. In an interview, she implied that the organization's pro-social focus kept NGO staff, clients, and property from being targeted by insurgents:

> I: Has the Maoist problem affected [the NGO]?
>
> R: No, actually, you know, because [the NGO] works in many different parts of the country. There are some areas which are heavily affected by Maoists, and sometimes they ask about the organization: What does the organization work for? When they come to know about [the NGO], which works for the rights of women and children, basically the victims of trafficking, and preventing violence against women....[12]

According to the president of the NGO, the Maoists never asked for a single rupee in 'donations' or 'taxes' from the staff. On the other hand, one NGO staff was directly threatened by Maoists and received ambiguous messages about what was expected of them in Maoist-controlled areas. One staff member told of her experiences in Nawalparasi, where she went to conduct a five-day leadership-training programme for local women. A threatening group of Maoist men appeared at the house where she was staying, but left when the householder told them she was not at home. Meanwhile, they apparently found out more about her activities, because their wives began to attend her leadership-development classes. Later, the male

Maoists told her that the NGO was doing good work, but that they had better not be receiving any funding from USAID.[13] For NGO staff, experiences such as these were unsettling and frightening, as the 'correct' course of action was usually unclear. At a staff meeting in Kathmandu in February 2005, regional staff were directed never to admit that they received funding from the US or from US-related agencies. Staff members recounted, in separate interviews, several frightening encounters with insurgents during the course of their work in rural areas:

> I was supposed to take the girls [trafficking survivors] back home to Makwanpur .... It was a one-day walk. It was the rainy season. I had to cross a huge river. I was all alone at that moment because I missed my way somewhere. Anyway, to cross the river, I just wrapped my shawl around my waist and turned up my trousers. I started ahead. From the opposite direction, many people came towards me who wore scarves on their heads ... oh god! They were Maoists. They thought I was one of them. They just shook hands with me and went away.
>
> And later in the same interview:
>
> At night-time, all the Maoists used to sit around the fire, burning charcoal and oil .... So on the way back also, we met them, and in fact they talked with us for a while—like they asked, 'Seems like you all are scared of us, right?' We said 'No!' But we were scared to death inside! [laughs][14]
>
> We had to take a girl [trafficking survivor] back to her home in Shantinagar, even a little further than that. So when we reached there after so many struggles, that too at night, what we saw was ... we were surrounded by Maoists.... Oh God! They started asking so many questions! But thank God, they did not do anything. Next morning, we gave the girl to her grandmother and came back.[15]

The NGO under study—founded, directed and staffed by Nepalese women and men—has had considerable experience and a great deal of local knowledge. For example, they believe that the survivor of human trafficking or gender violence should be gradually reintegrated into her family and village. Typically, a staff member working in or near the village will approach the family and ask if they would like news of their daughter, should it become available. If the response is positive, staff members would arrange for the family members to visit the shelter, without revealing that their daughter had been engaged in prostitution. If the visit is productive, the next step might be a visit to the village by the survivor and the gradual disclosure, by the survivor herself, of her history. In this way, the NGO fosters the regrowth of family bonding and eases the survivor's reintegration. Finally, if the survivor and her family were both willing, the survivor is accompanied back to the village, where she is reintegrated into communal life. Our NGO has a remarkably positive record of successful reintegration of trafficking survivors (Crawford and Kaufman, in press).

We suspect that successful reintegration is strongly linked to re-establishing family and village ties before the survivor returns home on a permanent basis. Certainly, the NGO staff believe from their own experience that this is the best, perhaps the only, way to reduce stigma for trafficking survivors. However, when travel is disrupted, optimal care practices such as family visits and follow-up contact with the NGO become difficult or impossible.

Gender-based Violence: A Neglected Problem

As recently as the 1980s, sex trafficking was a taboo topic, though it was visible to those who looked. In an interview, the founder of the NGO that participated in this research described the NGO's history in this way:

> We were going to our relatives' place, to the Terai, to Biratnagar, and on the highway, there were two minor girls. They were about 14 to 15 years of age—and there was the pimp, who was arrested. We stopped the car and my husband took a photo of the girls and we came to know that the ... pimp was (caught) selling the girls for Rs 10,000. I was deeply touched. Then I wrote an article in the newspaper about trafficking, how the girls are trafficked for prostitution to the brothels in India. No one wanted to publish that article and the photograph, and I was deeply shocked and I thought that I will do something ... even with a small seed money I'll start (an) organization and work on these issues.

The government for many years seemed reluctant to get involved in the trafficking problem. Corruption abounded. As the NGO founder said:

> It was really very difficult to speak (up) on that issue. There were reported cases that even politicians were protecting the pimps, and also [it was] very difficult to work with the police officers because there are many reported cases that they used to take bribes from the pimps. So it was discouraging and I remember 10 years ago, when I raised these issues, one night in our office at Dilli Bazaar, all the windows were broken.... If you raise this issue very strongly [your life is], not safe.

For those who did get involved, there was strong criticism and the stigma of being associated with prostitutes:

> There was a raid in the brothels of Bombay in 1996 and 238 [Nepali] girls were arrested from the brothel, and I tried my best to negotiate with our government to bring them back to Nepal. There was no response from the government for six months, and then I went myself to Bombay, rescued the girls, signed the papers, and I cried many times because when the girls were brought back to Nepal, there was big criticism about the NGOs, about ourselves. What they said is [that the] NGOs are running [a] parallel government, and some of the news media said NGOs are bringing HIV/AIDS from India. Others said Nepal would be the dumping site for HIV/AIDS. Someone said we should be publicly hanged. So many criticisms, you know? And it was really depressing, and my relatives used to ask me, why are you working on this issue? You can get [an]other good job in international agencies; why [do] you work with ... prostitutes? It was very difficult. I told them that they are Nepali citizens, they are our daughters, they have every right to come back to Nepal, and who sold them? [They weren't] trafficked [of] their own will; we Nepali people are responsible.

At present, the government can hardly provide basic security to its citizens, and attention to health and development issues is limited. In April 2005, the government called a meeting of some 300 NGO leaders to reassure them that there was no need to be frightened for their staffs' safety. The government spokesman claimed that the government had 7,000 'plain clothes' security personnel on duty. However, the director of our participating NGO wryly observed that a message of 'don't be scared' is hardly reassuring when very often a call to the police security number goes unanswered.[16]

It is clear that the political violence that continues to occur in Nepal between the Maoists and the army and police forces is creating among many Nepalis feelings of fear, instability and uncertainty about the future. These feelings are even more relevant to women and girls, who are increasingly becoming victims of gender-based violence, sexual assault, and rape, and who are at a high risk of being trafficked. We expect that human-rights abuses against women and girls will continue to increase, as it is too soon to know whether the Maoist conflict will die down. It is only through the resolution of the political unrest and sustained government intervention in addressing the root causes of gender-based violence by His Majesty's government and aid providers that women and girls, who are the most affected, can hope for lives free of fear.

Acknowledgement

This research was supported by a Fulbright Senior Scholar Grant to Mary Crawford, a grant from the Society for the Psychological Study of Social Issues to Michelle R. Kaufman, and grants from the University of Connecticut Human Rights Institute to Mary Crawford and Michelle R. Kaufman. The authors thank Deepti Khati for research assistance.

Notes

1. Field notes, 2 February 2005.
2. Field notes, 22 March 2005.
3. Interview with Comrade Prachanda conducted in the spring of 1999 by *Revolutionary Worker* (*RW*) reporter Li Onesto.
4. Conversations with several informants revealed that the Maoists often target schoolteachers and village elders for donations and information, because as 'stalwarts' of the village community, they are perceived as being privy to village politics and happenings.
5. The Maoists frequently come to villages to recruit youths and children. Often parents are coerced with tacit threats to send their children.
6. The Maoists have been 'levying' taxes on teachers and villagers who are perceived as being economically well-off. However, all villagers, irrespective of financial abilities, are expected to feed the rebels should they knock on their doors.

7. From a conversation with a male fellow villager from her village Jiri, one of the authors (Alka Gurung) found out that Mingma was considered 'loose' because of her easy and outgoing manner. Maoists regularly target such women or girls in order to curtail and 'reform' their character.
8. Staff interview 101.
9. Staff interview 115.
10. Field notes, 2 March 2005.
11. Field notes, 4 April 2005.
12. Staff interview 115.
13. Field notes, 24 January 2005.
14. Staff interview 101.
15. Staff interview 103.
16. Field notes, 6 April 2005.

References

Asian Development Bank. 2003. *Combating Trafficking of Women and Children in South Asia*. Report from regional workshop proceedings held in Manila, Philippines, 27–29 May 2002.

Asian Human Rights Commission. 1997. 'Nepal: Trend of Human Rights Violation: Past and Present'. http://www.hrsolidarity.net/mainfile.php/1998 vol08no07/1579/.

Barstow, A. 2000. 'Introduction', in A. Barstow (ed.), *War's Dirty Secret: Rape, Prostitution, and Other Crimes against Women*, pp. 1–12. Cleveland, OH: The Pilgrim Press.

Bohara, R. 2005. 'Fleeing School: Terrorized Students across Nepal Prepare for Final Exams,' *Nepali Times*, 11–17 March 2005.

Brownmiller, S. 1975. *Against our Will: Men, Women and Rape*. New York: Simon & Schuster.

Carballo, M., M. Grocutt and A. Hadzihasanovic. 1996. 'Women and Migration: A Public Health Issue', *World Health Statistics Quarterly* 49: 158–64.

Crawford, Mary. 2005. *Doing Gender in Kathmandu*. Keynote address presented at the first annual meeting of the International Society for Culture and Activity Research, 20–24 September 2005, Seville, Spain.

Crawford, M. and M.R. Kaufman (in press). 'Sex Trafficking in Nepal: Survivor Characteristics and Long-term Outcomes'. Manuscript submitted for publication to *Women and Violence*.

Dahal, B.M. 2001. 'Armed Conflict and Its Impact on Women', in *Women's Voice*, 45–47. Kathmandu, Nepal: National Network Against Girl Trafficking (NNAGT).

Dhakal, L.P. 2005. 'Rape Trauma Syndrome and Experience: 2003–2004', http://www.katmanduonline.com/featurestories/index.php?newsNo=8.

Douglas, E. 2005. 'Inside Nepal's Revolution: Who are the Maoists, and Why Have They Turned This Himalayan Kingdom into a Killing Zone?', *National Geographic, 208.5* (November) 46–65.

Enloe, C. 2000. *Maneuvers: The International Politics of Militarizing Women's Lives*. Berkeley, CA: University of California Press.

Farr, K. 2005. *Sex Trafficking: The Global Market in Women and Children*. New York: Worth.

Heise, L., M. Ellsberg and M. Gottemoeller. 1999. *Ending Violence against Women* (Population Reports, Series L. 11). Baltimore: Johns Hopkins University School of Public Health.

His Majesty's Government of Nepal (HMGN). 1996. *Secondary Education Perspective Plan*. Kathmandu: Ministry of Education.

Hrdy, S.B. 1988. 'Daughters or Sons', *Natural History* (April): 64–82.

Huntington, D. 2002. *Anti-trafficking Program in South Asia: Appropriate Activities, Indicators and Evaluation Methodologies*. Summary report of a technical consultative meeting. New Delhi: Population Council.

Institute for Integrated Development Studies. 2004. *Status and Dimensions of Trafficking within Nepalese Context*. Kathmandu: IIDS and United Nations Development Fund for Women (UNIFEM).

Kathmandu Post. 2005. 'Rebels Destroy 6 Schools, SLC Students Affected', Edit page, 20 March, p. 1.

Kathmandu Post Report. 2005. 'No Citizenship for Kids of Unwed Mothers, Unknown Fathers', Edit page, 24 March, p. 2.

Kozaric-Kovacic, D., V. Folnegovic-Smalc, J. Skrinjaric, N.M. Szajnberg and A. Marusic. 1995. 'Rape, Torture, and Traumatization of Bosnian and Croatian Women: Psychological Sequelae', *American Journal of Orthopsychiatry* 65 (3): 428–33.

MacKinnon, C. 1993. 'Crimes of War, Crimes of Peace', in S. Hurley and S. Shute (eds), *On Human Rights: The Oxford Amnesty Lectures*, pp. 83–109. New York: Basic Books.

———. 1994. 'Turning Rape into Pornography: Postmodern Genocide', in A. Stigimayer (ed.), *Mass Rape: The War against Women in Bosnia-Herzegovina*, pp. 73–81. Lincoln: University of Nebraska Press.

Miall, H., O. Ramsbotham and T. Woodhouse. 1999. *Contemporary Conflict Resolution*. Cambridge, UK: Polity Press.

Murphy, E.M. 2003. 'Being Born Female is Dangerous for Your Health', *American Psychologist* 58 (3): 205–10.

National Geographic. 2005. Inside Nepal's Revolution, November.

Neft, N. and A.D. Levine. 1997. *Where Women Stand: An International Report on the Status of Women in 140 Countries*. New York: Random House.

Nye, Joseph S. 2003. *Understanding International Conflicts: An Introduction to Theory and History*. Cambridge, MA: Harvard University Press.

Organization of African Unity (OAU) [currently African Union (AU)]. 2000. 'Rwanda, the Preventable Genocide'. Report of the International Panel of Eminent Personalities to Investigate the 1994 Genocide in Rwanda and Surrounding Events.

Physicians for Human Rights. 2002. 'War-related Sexual Violence in Sierra Leone: A Population-Based Assessment'. Report, January. Available at: http://physicians forhumanrightsorg/library/documentsreports/sexual-violence-sirra-lcone.

Pradhan, G. 1994. 'The Road to Bombay: Forgotten Women', in *Red Light Traffic: The Trade in Nepali Girls*, pp. 33–41. Kathmandu: ABC/Nepal.

Rana, P.S., B.W. Silwal, D.B. Khadka, S. Bashnet and S. Ghimire. 2005. *A Study on Impacts of Armed Conflict Pushing Girls and Women into Sexual Abuse and Sex Trade*. Norway: Save the Children.

Rehn, E. and E.J. Sirleaf. 2002. *Women, War, Peace: Progress of the World's Women 2002, Vol. 1*. New York: UNIFEM.

SAATHI. 1997. *A Situational Analysis of Violence against Women and Girls in Nepal*. Kathmandu: SAATHI.

Sazaki, J. and A.R. William. 2005. 'Nepal Conflict Aggravates Women's Reproductive Health Risks'. Available at http://www.unfpa.org/news/news.cfm?ID=721. (Accessed on: 11 June 2007.)

Sazaki, J. and W.A. Ryan. 2005. 'Nepal conflict aggravates women's reproductive health risks.' Available at http://www.unfpa.org/news/news.cfm?ID=721.

Sibbons, M. 1998. 'Approaches to Gender Awareness Raising: Experiences in a Government Education Project in Nepal', *Gender and Development* 6 (2): 35–43.

Sidanius, J. and F. Pratto. 1999. *Social Dominance: An Intergroup Theory of Social Herarchy and Oppression*. New York: Cambridge University Press.

Singh, S., E. Mills, S. Honeyman, B.K. Suvedi and N.P. Pant. 2005. 'HIV in Nepal: Is the Violent Conflict Fuelling the Epidemic?', *Public Library of Science Medicine* 2 (8): 705–9.

Tambiah, Y. 2004. 'Sexuality and Women's Rights in Armed Conflict in Sri Lanka', *Reproductive Health Matters* 12: 78–87.

UNDP (United Nations Development Programme). 2006. *Human Development Reports 2005*. Retrieved 28 June 2006 from http://hdr.undp.org/statistics/data/countries.cfm?c=NPL.

UNFPA (United Nations Population Fund). 2004. 'Trafficking in Human Misery', in *Promoting Gender Equality: Human Trafficking*. Retrieved 26 March 2004 from http://www.unfpa.org/gender/trafficking.htm.

US Department of State. 2004. *Nepal: Country Reports on Human Rights Practices, 2003*. Retrieved 28 June 2006 from http://www.state.gov/g/drl/rls/hrrpt/2003/27949.htm.

Yogi, B. 2002. 'Cost of Insurgency'. Retrieved 29 June 2006 from http://www.nepalnews.com.np/contents/englishmonthly/businessage/2002/may/cover.htm.

Zimmerman, C., K. Yun, I. Shvab, C. Watts, L. Trappolin, M. Treppete, F. Bimbi, B. Adams, S. Jiraporn, L. Beci, M. Allerecht, J. Bindel and L. Regan. 2003. *The Health Risks and Consequences of Trafficking in Women and Adolescents: Findings from a European Study*. London: London School of Hygiene & Tropical Medicine (LSHTM).

5

The Evolution of the Maoist Revolution in Nepal in an Adverse International Environment

Li Onesto

When the Maoists in Nepal initiated an armed struggle against the government in 1996, they challenged official verdicts that have declared socialist- and communist-led movements no longer relevant or viable in today's world. But within five to six years of fighting, the guerrillas had won extensive popular support and gained control of much of the countryside.

The Communist Party of Nepal (CPN-Maoist) had analysed that conditions in Nepal were ripe for launching, building and sustaining an armed struggle and that such a struggle could unite and mobilize Nepal's peasantry. The specific characteristics which they saw as a basis for launching and winning a 'People's War' included: a corrupt, semi-feudal, centralized state system with little reach outside the main cities; geographic and demographic factors favourable to revolutionary mobilization, including the fact that large parts of the population live in remote areas where the government presence is weak; deep poverty; the widespread influence of communism among the people; and large numbers of the Nepalese working in India, who could act as a kind of rear support (CPN [M]).

Protracted People's War

From the beginning, the CPN (M) conceived of their revolution as a 'protracted war'—the type propounded by Mao Tsetung as applicable in semi-feudal and semi-colonial countries. Mao's basic theory of 'protracted people's war' recognized that in semi-colonial, semi-feudal countries such as Nepal, the revolutionary forces start out weak and small compared to the government forces and that to engage in all-out military battles would only lead to getting crushed. But by avoiding decisive tests of strength and waging guerrilla warfare, the revolutionary forces can defeat and weaken the government forces in smaller battles and, through a protracted process, gain popular support, increase in strength and numbers, and extend their control. Building rural base areas and establishing military control and political authority in ever-larger parts of the countryside allow the revolutionaries to surround the cities from the countryside and to eventually seize countrywide political power (Mao 1968).

The decision to embark on such a path in Nepal was very controversial in the revolutionary movement as well as within the CPN (M) itself. Significant leaders of the communist movement in Nepal argued that such a revolution in Nepal could only be crushed, that it would be foolhardy to start such a war. In 1999, when I conducted an extensive interview with Prachanda, the chairman of the CPN (M), he told me, 'In making the plan for initiation there was great debate over how to go to the armed struggle because many people were influenced by "peaceful" struggle, work in the Parliament, rightist and petty bourgeois feelings, and a long tradition of the reformist movement. Then we said that the only process must be a big push, big leap. Not gradual change' (Onesto 2000).

With the initiation of armed struggle, the CPN (M) put forward a programme that spoke to the felt needs of many sections of Nepalese society: the rural population wants land and development, women want equality and an end to oppressive feudal and patriarchal traditions, minority nationalities want an end to discrimination and the cruel caste system, and millions throughout Nepal want democratic rights and national independence.

Within the first few years of the revolution, government officials, landlords and the police were driven out of many villages in the western districts of Rolpa and Rukum, where the Maoists had the most strength. This created a power vacuum, which allowed the guerrillas to establish military, political and economic control.

From Primitive Fighting to the Threshold of Power

The CPN (M) conceived of their protracted war as going through stages—from the strategic defensive, to strategic equilibrium to the strategic offensive. In the beginning, there was a relatively long period of the 'strategic defensive'—where the revolutionary forces were weaker than the enemy and had to accumulate strength over a prolonged period of time on the basis of guerrilla warfare. After seven years of fighting, in 2003, the CPN (M) announced that the military struggle had reached the stage of 'strategic equilibrium', where the two sides were relatively equal. Neither side was able to destroy the other side decisively. Fighting was increasingly characterized by larger-scale mobile and positional warfare. Then, after eight and a half years of fighting, at the end of August 2004, the Maoists announced they had launched the stage of a 'strategic offensive'. The decision to enter this stage meant that the party had determined that they were able to make their immediate aim the decisive destruction of the enemy's armed forces, the seizure of power and the establishment of a new government rule throughout the country.

How did the Maoists get to this point? Where had they built up enough military and political strength to put them close to the threshold of seizing nationwide power? In 1996, the fighters led by the CPN (M) were armed with only sticks, sickles, *khukuris* (knives) and a few guns. Three years later, when I travelled through the guerrilla zone, the Maoists still really didn't have modern weapons. Most of the fighters I met had old-fashioned single-shot rifles, homemade hand grenades and *khukuris*. I heard many stories about raids carried out in the first few years—attacks against local police posts and moneylenders, corrupt officials, and landlords. The guerrillas would proudly report on how many weapons they had captured—'six rifles, one pistol and 300 bullets' or 'eight rifles, one revolver and 780 bullets'. I remember wondering how they thought they were going to be able to fight and win with so few and such primitive weapons.

But by 2002, the People's Liberation Army (PLA) was using primitive as well as relatively modern weapons, including General Purpose Machine Guns (GPMGs), Light Machine Guns (LMGs), Submachine Guns (SMGs), Self Loading Rifles (SLRs) and rocket launchers captured in battle from the other side.

When the Maoists initiated armed struggle in 1996, they had no PLA, no trained fighting forces and no experience in military warfare. They started off with only small 'fighting groups'. After six months, the first squad was formed and after several more months, there were 32 squads (of 7–9 guerrillas).

In 1999, the Central Committee member in charge of the Maoist strongholds in the Rolpa, Rukum and Jajarkot districts told me,

> Sometimes the squads had to retreat when the police came into a village where the squad lived. But when the police left, the squads returned and the village would be back in the political and military control of the People's Army. There were many ambushes of police, going from smaller to larger actions and also many raids of police posts and mining of roads where police were traveling. Some were successful, some not, due to lack of experience. We were learning warfare through waging warfare. (Onesto 2005)

Again, these were notable beginnings; but still on a very small scale. The Maoists had squads and platoons (with 24–30 fighters) but had not yet formed any company-size units (of about 150 guerrillas). By 2002, the PLA had several permanent companies, and in some cases was fighting in units of brigade strength—of several hundred soldiers. By 2005, the PLA had expanded to the level of two divisions, seven brigades, 19 battalions, several companies, platoons, and sections and tens of thousands of militia. And they were able to mobilize thousands of fighters in a single battle.[1]

When I was in Nepal, the Maoists were also only in the beginning stages of establishing political authority and organization in the villages. In the countryside, there were 'guerrilla zones' where fighting was going on. But the guerrillas had only just begun a campaign to establish 'base areas' that would serve as embryos of 'red political power'.

Less than three years later, by the end of 2002, over 10 million people were living in areas under Maoist control—not just in the western strongholds of Rolpa and Rukum, but throughout the country. And 'United Revolutionary People's Committees' were exercising power, mobilizing peasants to administer production, the supply of basic necessities, education, sanitation, communications, transportation and the establishment of a judicial system.

Why and how was the People's War in Nepal able to make such military and political gains? In developing their fighting capacity, the PLA applied the principles of Mao Tsetung's military strategy—tactically pitting 'ten against one' and strategically 'one against ten' (Mao 1968).[2] The PLA recognized that on a nationwide level the revolutionary forces were (and would remain) outnumbered by government forces—and so, in an overall strategic sense, faced 'one against ten'. But tactically and in particular battles, they saw it was possible to concentrate an overwhelmingly superior force to wipe out government forces—with an orientation of 'ten against one'. So, for example, they intensified their military assaults on weak links of the government, mainly less-fortified police posts.

The guerrillas avoided all-out battles and instead took the approach of waging guerrilla warfare, luring government forces deep into 'red areas', encircling them and striking big blows at their weakest links. Support among the peasants provided the Maoists with intelligence and reconnaissance, and local militias played an important political and military role. In this way, the PLA was able to carry out successful military actions even with primitive weapons and relatively small fighting units, and the police were increasingly put on the defensive and eventually forced to stay holed up in their barracks most of the time.[3]

Such military advances allowed the Maoists to establish base areas, which is a strategic part of a 'protracted people's war' that aims to eventually surround the cities and seize nationwide power. As police, officials and landlords were driven out of the countryside, the authorities and institutions that had ruled over and oppressed the people ceased to exist—making it possible for the Maoists to set up a 'new people's power'. The more territory the guerrillas were able to liberate through military struggle, the more they were able to consolidate political authority, even if still relatively in a tenuous way.

In this way, the Maoists began to address deep economic, social and cultural inequalities that the regime could not solve. Nepal is dominated by foreign powers, principally India. This has distorted the economy, determining export and import patterns that inhibit self-reliance and reinforce severe backwardness and inhibit industry. Land ownership and control over resources in the countryside is highly unequal, leading to extreme class polarization and social inequality (Bhattarai 2003). Economic and social development, as well as the military, rely heavily on foreign assistance. The ruling class and governmental structures and institutions that promote and oversee this whole setup are highly corrupt and rest on a narrow base of political support, alien to the vast majority of people in the countryside. Nepal's ruling class has not and cannot solve the basic problems of food, water, sanitation, and health care because this would require completely tearing up these economic, social and political relationships within Nepalese society and between Nepal and other countries. This kind of transformation would destroy the very economic and social foundation upon which this class exists.

Some analysts acknowledge the dire situation of the peasants in Nepal, but say the Maoists are 'taking advantage' of and manipulating this. But real changes have taken place in areas under Maoist control: redistribution of land, equal rights for women, an end to the caste system, autonomy for oppressed ethnic groups, health care, education, and the building of roads and bridges.

Anne de Sales (2003) points out that after the 1990 Janandolan, a feeling among people that they 'could change the contours of their own social life and participate in the government of the country' penetrated even the most remote villages, including areas such as Rolpa and Rukum, where the Maoists had a history of political influence. Lawoti (2005) identifies 'push and pull' factors in the considerable support the Maoist insurgency got from socioculturally excluded groups such as the indigenous nationalities, Dalits and women. There is a 'push' in that these excluded groups have reason to support a movement that calls for radical transformation—they fare badly economically, thus their class interests overlap with the Maoist agenda. And there is a 'pull' in that the Maoists have raised sociocultural issues more forcefully than any other mainstream political party. Lawoti also points out that: 'The attraction of the rural people to the Maoist insurgency, which promised radical transformation, also shows that in the eyes of the rural people, the CPN-UML and other communist factions had failed to represent their interests'. The UML has accepted marketization policies by the World Bank and other international institutions, making it impossible for them to implement real social-welfare policies (Chapter 1 of this volume).

The real issue here is whether the Nepalese people have the right to struggle against and change the oppressive conditions they face. The revolutionary authority established through the force of arms allowed the people to transform the prevailing economic and social relations as well as the culture and thinking that go along with this oppressive setup. And the transformations that have gone on in the Maoist-controlled areas reflect the kind of society that could be built if the Maoists governed the whole country.

Base Areas as an Attractive Force and Seeds of the Future

A 'Common Minimum Policy and Programme' adopted at the founding of the United Revolutionary People's Council in September 2001 detailed the economic, social and cultural changes envisioned by the Maoists 'to guide the state after the revolution'. This programme also set the framework for changes implemented in areas governed by a new revolutionary power.

Land is a central question in the People's War and in the base areas, the agrarian revolution is seen as 'the basic foundation of the New Democratic/People's Democratic Revolution'. Here, the main policy is to 'abolish the feudal, semi-feudal and bureaucratic capitalist production relations in the land and develop national capitalist relations, in which "land to the tiller" shall be the main policy tenet'. This document also talks about the development of industry as the 'leading sector of economy' and says that 'the path for rapid industrialization in the country shall be paved by nationalizing the capital being misused in the hands of the comprador and bureaucratic bourgeoisie in the country, liberating the labor trapped in the agricultural sector and promoting internal markets, on the one hand, and by liberating national industries from the grip of imperialism and particularly Indian monopoly capital, on the other' (United Revolutionary People's Council 2001).

This corresponds to what being done in the Maoist base areas. In the mountainous areas, where peasants mainly own small plots of land, the emphasis was on forming a cooperative farming system. In the Terai region, more characterized by large landholders and landless peasants, the emphasis was to redistribute land confiscated from feudal lords to poor peasants.

Public lands previously controlled by government officers were seized and converted into 'model farm land' that produced new varieties of vegetables and grains, and small-scale irrigation, hydro-electricity, water mills, and road networks were developed, which have helped boost farm production (Parvati 2005).

In the base areas, a new revolutionary culture was developed to promote equality between men and women, puts an end to discrimination against minority nationalities, and abolishing the caste system. I remember meeting young couples in the guerrilla zones who proudly told me theirs was an inter-caste 'love marriage', going up against the norm of arranged marriages and strict taboos against people marrying outside their caste. I also interviewed young widows who were wearing bright clothes and jewellery, rebelling against feudal traditions of widows mourning for the rest of their lives. Such practices were widely popularized and institutionalized in the base areas.

With the redistribution of land, for the first time, women got equal right to own and inherit land. Arranged marriages, polygamy, and other feudal traditions oppressive to women were no longer practiced. Wife beating and rape were severely punished by people's courts. Women were given the right to divorce, go to school, and fight in local militias as well as the PLA. And women were equal participants in the new economic, political and social life of the villages.

By 2003, there were significant advances in developing the political and military leadership of women. But many things continued to work against women getting and staying involved in the revolutionary struggle, especially in the PLA, which required tremendous sacrifice. There is a struggle against entrenched feudal traditions, institutions and ideas that prevent women from equal participation in society. But these things still exert a very powerful force, including among the revolutionaries themselves. For example, there is still a lot of covert or even overt pressure on women cadres to get married. Some people still look down on women who are single, divorced or have been married more than once. There is still a lot of pressure on women to bear children, especially sons, and women are still expected to take most, if not full, responsibility for taking care of the children. And within the party, there is still the pull of the traditional division of labour, whereby men do mental work while women are left to do the physical labour (Parvati 2003). But the Maoist revolution in Nepal seriously took up this question, mobilizing, leading and waging a struggle among the people and within the party and the PLA to do away with the economic, social and ideological pillars of women's oppression.

Breaking down of caste oppression and discrimination against minority nationalities also took place in the base areas. In 2003, a man from Rolpa who had been living in India for some time took advantage of the ceasefire to visit his family, living in an area under Maoist control. He told A World to Win News Service (AWTWNS 2004b):

> One of the decisions of the party has been that the comrades don't necessarily work in the areas where they were born. This has several positive aspects. One is that the comrades gain varied experience. They come to know other regions of the country and their people, and so their view of revolution, its tasks, goals and dimensions becomes wider. The other aspect is that even though Nepal is small, it is a country of many nations and nationalities. The mixing of different people creates a situation where many fears and prejudices break down. People come to learn about each other and the feeling of unity is strengthened. This is very important, since people don't tend to migrate from one area of Nepal to another....
>
> I reached my village. With comrades who were accompanying me, I went to my father's door. I wasn't sure if I could invite them in or not. My family, even though they are not Brahmin, are from upper castes and my comrades were all from lower castes or untouchables. Previously it was impossible for my father to let them in his house. I went in. My father asked if I came alone. I said no, but [my] comrades are from lower castes. He said 'Oh! Come on! Our door is open to all. Ask them to come in and eat something. They must be tired and hungry.' I was flabbergasted. The revolution and the new political power have even broken down my old man's prejudices. This, in fact, is one of the visible changes. Most of the new party comrades are from the lower castes, those who were previously not considered whole humans. The upper castes would not eat with them or let them into their houses.

Now they are very active and respected. The red power has given them self-confidence; they know it is their own political power.

This account gives a living sense of how the Maoist revolution in Nepal brought into being a new revolutionary way of thinking and acting, including with regard to age-old prejudices and oppressive practices against minority nationalities and lower castes.

By 2003, under the leadership of the CPN (M), nine national and territorial autonomous regions had been formed, an application of the Common Minimum Policy and Programme, which says that the state shall guarantee equal treatment to all nations/nationalities and languages of the country and that all nations/nationalities traditionally oppressed by the ruling Aryan-Khas nationality shall exercise the right to self-determination (Parvati 2005).

The base areas faced the challenge of building new infrastructure and economic relations consistent with the goal of a new economy free from foreign domination, not tied into the world system of imperialism and aimed at getting rid of inequalities and exploitation. And this done, even as the PLA fought ongoing battles with the Royal Nepal Army (RNA).

The building of a new road in Rolpa is an example of how the Maoists led and mobilized thousands of people to participate in such a process. Rolpa is a remote area where the government has done little, if anything, to raise the living standards. The complete lack of roads here has meant that peasants have been unable to communicate and trade with any but their most immediate neighbours. This is a major factor keeping remote mountainous areas economically and culturally backward. The lack of roads is one of the most deeply felt needs of peasants in the countryside.

Most of the people in Rolpa are Magars, an oppressed nationality in Nepal. Under the leadership of the CPN (M), the Magarat Autonomous Region and a people's government were formed at a mass meeting of 75,000 people in January 2004 (AWTWNS 2004b). Soon after this, a decision was made to build a 92 km road through the heart of Rolpa.

Tens of thousands of volunteers participated in this project, which included the building of 100 bridges. Most came as part of a group from one or another village or mass organization. According to Santosh Buddha Magar, a leader of the Magarat Autonomous

Region, families were mobilized to send one person to work for 10–15 days (AWTWNS 2005b).

The base areas served as an attractive force—a living, material implementation of the Maoist programme that the people were able to participate in, help shape, and defend. In this way, the base areas were 'fuel' for the revolution. This was especially true in the western districts of Rolpa and Rukum, where base areas were first established in 2000. And the strength and reputation of the base areas in the west impacted on the ability of the Maoists to extend their influence to other parts of the country.

Shneiderman and Turin (2004) have written about the establishment of *jan sarkar* ('people's government') in the Dolakha district of central-eastern Nepal. They reported that, 'Against the background of widespread condemnation and even demonization of the Maoists by the national press and local political leaders, it comes as little surprise that in the village imagination they were conceived of as political demons, neither fully human nor animal' (ibid.). At the same time, villagers were hearing news of how the Maoists were attacking moneylenders and distributing the spoils, and 'from a local perspective', this seemed 'quite literally unbelievable and wonderful' (ibid.). Then, when the Maoists came to the village, the people realized that 'apart from their heightened motivation and devotion to a cause—there was little that separated them from other villagers'(ibid.). Shneiderman and Turin (ibid.) observed:

> Many villagers spoke of their sense of incredulity that such brave and powerful individuals should come to speak with them, ask them for their opinions on weighty issues, and address them with respect. This last element of the equation is crucial: villagers expected to be frightened into submission when the Maoists finally came, but instead they were addressed humanely and respectfully by people who seemed to understand the predicament of their lives. A logical extension of such experience is a sense of empowerment. As one man put it, 'If the Maoists are like us, does that also mean that we are like them?'

The New Democratic Revolution

Even after receiving increased military aid from India and the US, the RNA was unable to crush the guerrilla forces and by 2004, it was widely acknowledged that Gyanendra's regime had lost control outside of the cities and district headquarters. But to establish countrywide power, the Maoists would have to decisively defeat the RNA, take over the district headquarters, and seize power in Kathmandu and Nepal's other cities. And to do this, the guerrillas would not only face the RNA, but the possibility of intervention, and even invasion, by the Indian Army, the US or some kind of UN-sponsored force.

Nepal's ruling class was in constant crisis, fraught with deep divisions and in-fighting over how to deal with the Maoist insurgency. The monarchy became extremely isolated, especially after Gyanendra seized total power in February 2005, and then there were the events of May 2006, when weeks of massive protests led to the reinstitution of the parliamentary government.

But a replay of the 1990 Janandolan will not solve the problems that have plagued the Nepalese masses. This popular uprising united various political parties in a movement that forced the ruling class to replace the Panchayat system with a parliamentary 'multiparty democracy'. But the government remained a fundamentally oppressive one. The monarchy retained a lot of power, most importantly control of the army. The government still represented feudal and comprador classes, which depend on and serve foreign capitalist domination. And the semi-feudal and capitalist economic system remained intact.

One of the targets of the Maoist revolution is the monarchy. But the Maoist New Democratic Revolution must aim to overthrow *any regime* that represents feudalism and those big capitalist forces aligned with and serving foreign and imperialist domination.

A basic premise of the New Democratic Revolution is that in order to achieve liberation, the revolutionary forces must overthrow the bureaucratic-capitalist class and state system, which are dependent on and serve imperialism; they must uproot semi-feudalism in the countryside; and they must kick out foreign capitalism. With such goals, New Democratic tasks are carried out in the base areas. The redistribution of land is a central part of getting rid of inequalities in the countryside. Developing collective forms of owning and working the land is an essential part of breaking free of foreign domination. And criticizing and doing away with feudal traditions, culture and thinking are crucial to the building of a new revolutionary way of running society.

These essential components of the Maoist revolution are in the interest of the majority of the people in Nepal. But they run *counter* to the interests of other class forces and parties who want to get rid of the monarchy so that they can better play their role of a comprador bourgeoisie, but don't want to get rid of the essential and prevailing economic and social relations.

In the New Democratic Revolution, there is a basis for the Maoists to lead a broad united front with anti-feudal, democratic forces that address these concerns and fight for real democratic rights. This includes bourgeois forces who oppose feudalism and imperialist domination. But this is not a bourgeois revolution aimed at establishing capitalist rule.

In this light, the critique of democracy by Avakian (2005), chairman of the Revolutionary Communist Party, USA, is extremely relevant. He says:

> In a world marked by profound class divisions and social inequality, to talk about 'democracy'—without talking about the *class nature* of that democracy and which class it serves—is meaningless, and worse. So long as society is divided into classes, there can be no 'democracy for all'; one class or another will rule, and it will uphold and promote that kind of democracy which serves its interests and goals. The question is: *which class* will rule and whether its rule, and its system of democracy, will serve the *continuation*, or the eventual *abolition*, of class divisions and the corresponding relations of exploitation, oppression and inequality. (ibid.)

This question of which class will rule has posed itself very sharply in Nepal, with two futures sharply colliding. One is a continuation, in one form or another, of current society, dominated by reactionary and regressive class forces aligned with the whole international imperialist system and enforcing extremely oppressive and exploitative economic, political and social relations. The other future is a path led by the proletariat, of breaking out of this whole order, establishing a socialist society, building new economic, political and social relations, and continuing the struggle to do away with all exploitation and oppression as part of the world revolution.

With the seizure of power, the new socialist government faces transitional tasks to carry through with the aims of the new democratic phase and move to the socialist transformation of society. For example, after Mao seized power in China in 1949, there was further land reform as well as the nationalization of certain large industries and key financial levers. But such tasks are *transitional* and stay within the context of the *socialist* revolution and the building of new socialist society. After seizing power in China, Mao polemicized against those who wanted to 'consolidate the new democratic revolution'—which would have led to the building of a capitalist, not a socialist society (Revolutionary Mass Criticism Writing Group 1973).

All this illustrates that the New Democratic Revolution, from the very beginning, must be carried out with a clear strategic perspective of socialism and a communist world. This means that while the communist forces can establish a united front with other political forces, they cannot allow other class forces to lead the struggle or divert it from its communist goals.

Bob Avakian, exploring the complex relationship between the goal of communism and the revolutionary struggle at any given point, says, 'There has to be diacritical a link between where things are at, at any given point, and the final aim of communism. It is not enough for communism to be merely a "propaganda point"—something that is "thrown in" as an abstract goal and if you reduce it to that, and sever the living link between the struggle at a given point and the final aim of communism, then you have gutted the final aim of all meaning and you have cut your line and actions loose from the path leading to that final aim...' (Avakian 2002).

Revolution vs Counter-revolution

The advances by the People's War were made in spite of a brutal counter-insurgency. The RNA carried out search-and-destroy campaigns in the countryside—killing, torturing and arresting anyone suspected of being a guerrilla or 'Maoist sympathizer'. And massive disinformation and censorship campaigns by the government closed down revolutionary newspapers, jailed journalists, and spread outright lies about the Maoists (Onesto 2005). Thapa (2002), describing the November 2001 state of emergency, wrote:

> One of the first post-emergency actions of the government was to take into custody journalists from newspapers considered Maoist mouthpieces. And within days, it even came out with a controversial list of dos and don'ts for the press to follow. Further, to prove that it meant business, the government began to jail journalists seen to be deviating from its injunction. As of the end of March, more than 70 journalists had been taken into custody.

Reporters Without Borders (RWB) reported that in 2005, Nepal was responsible for *half* the number of reported acts of state censorship in the world. According to RWB, at least 425 journalists were arrested, attacked or threatened in 2005 in Nepal.[4]

The Maoist guerrillas, unlike the RNA, do not believe 'the ends justify the means' and their military policies reflected their goal of a new political consciousness that will lead to a new society aimed at getting rid of oppression and inequality. For example, the PLA released many captured POWs in good health to the Red Cross or other human-rights organizations (International Committee of the Red Cross 2005). RNA soldiers and police personnel captured by the Maoists have told reporters that while they had to listen to propaganda and were asked to join the revolution, they were not harmed. They were warned that if they were captured again, they would be severely punished, but they were given money and food so that they could go back to their villages instead of returning to the RNA. This reflected the Maoists' policy of waging a political struggle even with those who are working with the government.

The *Kathmandu Post* (2002), reporting on 18 captured police personnel, said:

> Their release has a human [*sic*] ring about it. In fact the rebels had set them free only after handing out sums ranging from Rs 800 and Rs 1,500 as expenses for their return journey.... The freed hostages have said that the rebels did not misbehave with them throughout the period they were under their control. 'Don't involve in vile deeds. You would certainly have killed had you

> taken us under your control,' rebels have been quoted as saying. They also had sent two of their cadre to guide the cops out safely.

The vast majority of the 13,000 killed since the start of the war (as of the end of 2005) were killed by the state, along with suspected revolutionaries also being tortured and murdered (INSEC 2005; Lawoti 2005). And like the US policy from Vietnam to Fallujah which could be characterized by the phrase 'destroying the village to save the village' the US-trained RNA has carried out human-rights abuses against a wide swathe of the population, killing thousands suspected of 'supporting the Maoists' which could mean simply providing food and shelter for the guerrillas. Human-rights organizations have documented how the police and RNA have burned whole villages and rounded up, tortured, murdered and jailed thousands of people. In 2003 and 2004, Nepal recorded the highest number of new cases of disappearances caused by security forces in the world (Human Rights Watch 2005).

On the other hand, the vast majority of people killed by the Maoists were police and soldiers in combat. When others, like informants, were targeted, this was because their actions have directly led to Maoists and others being jailed or killed. In many cases, the government and media reported that Maoists target people because they are teachers or members of oppositional parties. But upon closer examination, it turned out that such people were attacked not because of their profession or political affiliation, but because they collaborated with the RNA.

The CPN (M) was leading a mass armed revolution which unleashed millions of poor, angry peasants. Their families were suffering and dying in 'normal times'. And the RNA and police carried out horrendous crimes against them. When people rise up against their oppression, it isn't 'nice and neat'. There will be actions taken by guerrillas against party members and supporters who go against the policies set by the PLA and the Party—and leadership is necessary for the struggle to go beyond bitter revenge. This is exactly what the CPN (M) provided. On several occasions, the Maoists issued criticisms of actions they felt were wrong and even changed some policies after being criticized (AWTWNS 2005a; Onesto 2005; Reuters 2005).

Indian Domination

Nepal's long history of extreme dependence on India has left the country with few industries and Indian domination has been a major factor in Nepal's political history. The monarchy, as well as the Nepali Congress, have had longstanding ties with and backing from the Indian power structure. And it is largely, though not exclusively, through India that Nepal is linked to the world capitalist system. India dominates the economic life of the country—plundering Nepal's natural resources, enforcing unequal trade agreements, and exploiting the Nepalese peasants who cross the border looking for work. And India has long considered Nepal strategically important in its often hostile relationship with China.

The Maoists in Nepal have denounced the current Chinese government as 'revisionist'—socialist in name, but capitalist in fact. And the post-Mao regime in China has 'disowned' the guerrillas in Nepal and shares India's hostility to the People's War in Nepal. But India has been concerned that China could take advantage of the instability created by the insurgency to expand its power and influence in the whole region.

Millions of poor Nepalese peasants go to India in search of work and in this way become part of the working class. Some stay for years; others work for months and then return home. This created a favourable condition for the revolution in Nepal, even while it is an expression of a deep and oppressive relation that this revolution aims to abolish. There has been a strong movement of Nepalese Maoists in India who support the People's War in Nepal. And there are Indian Maoists waging armed struggle against the Indian government.

India provided truckloads of military hardware and helicopters to the government in Kathmandu and hunted down and arrested leaders of the CPN (M) in India. There has been a real threat of the Indian Army invading Nepal in order to prevent the Maoists from seizing nationwide power—which would most likely have the backing of the United States.

Geo-Strategic Concerns of the United States

After 11 September 2001 (9/11), the US government increasingly began to talk about the conflict in Nepal in the context of its 'war against terrorism'. A 2002 proposal by President Bush for US$20 million in economic and military aid to Nepal stated:

> We currently do not have direct evidence of an al-Qaeda presence in Nepal, but weak governance has already proved inviting to terrorists, criminals and intelligence services from surrounding countries... continued instability in Nepal could create the conditions in which terrorists easily could establish operations, especially in remote areas in the far west of the country.... (US Government 2002)

Behind such tortured efforts to compare the Maoists in Nepal to groups such as al-Qaeda were the real concerns of the US over the geo-strategic implications of a Maoist victory in a region of the world that is already tremendously volatile and of considerable geo-political significance.

In a speech to the Nepal Council of World Affairs on 9 August 2005, James Moriarty (2005), the US Ambassador to Nepal, said:

> I get asked all the time why the United States is so keenly interested in Nepal.... Our concern over regional stability is of course one factor. With a violent, ideological Maoist insurgency desiring to take over the state and then to export its revolution to peaceful neighbors, there is much to worry about.

The CPN (M) was put on the US's official 'terrorist list'—even though it is clear the Maoists in Nepal have nothing whatsoever in common with 'terrorist' politics, tactics and strategy. And the US made it clear that the Maoists cannot be allowed to come to power in Nepal. The US gave the RNA military training, advisers, at least US$22 million in military aid, and more than 5,000 M-16 rifles. And the US has worked on multiple tracks, reflecting different (or a combination of) preferred scenarios—all of which would have ended up with the defeat of the Maoist revolution: (*a*) the RNA, with US support, is able to militarily defeat the Maoists; (*b*) the king and parliamentary forces put aside their differences and unite to defeat the Maoists; (*c*) the king is forced to step down and the parliamentary parties unite to defeat the Maoists; (*d*) with the help of India and covert CIA-type operations, the top leadership of the CPN (M) is killed and/or arrested, leading to the defeat of the Maoists; (*e*) the

Maoists give up their goal of seizing power and establishing socialism and agree to lay down arms and participate in bourgeois democratic elections and a 'multiparty government'.

Revolution in a Globalized World

The development of and prospects for a revolution in Nepal cannot be separated from the dynamics of the international situation. The CPN (M) made a point of emphasizing that their revolution is part of the worldwide struggle for communism and has given this organizational expression through its participation in the Revolutionary Internationalist Movement (RIM), which involves Maoist parties and organizations from around the world. The CPN (M) stated that it sees the revolution in Nepal as providing both an example and a 'base area' for further Maoist revolutions.[5]

Shah (2004) argues that the conflict in Nepal is a continuation of 'a tradition that is sustained by the particular nature of South Asian intra-state relations and wider global opportunities and constraints' and that 'In linking the Maoist movement to the wider regional context, the unit of analysis must always extend beyond the national borders.' Shah makes the point that '[w]hat happens across the porous boundary often has more influence on events than what goes on inside', and then says: 'Theoretically and empirically, the challenge is to recognize the internal and external sources of the war and trace the specific pathways of their intersection' (ibid.)

Avakian (1998) also speaks of this relationship between external and internal factors and sheds light on the complicated relationship between seizing power in one country and promoting the advance of revolutions elsewhere. He says:

> Socialist countries have so far emerged and for a certain historical period are very likely to emerge one or a few at a time. So, in grand strategic terms socialist countries and, more broadly, the international proletariat and the international communist movement will be faced with a situation where it is necessary to change the world alignment of forces or face the prospect of socialist countries going under after a certain point. This doesn't mean there is some sort of mechanical mathematical or arithmetic

> equation where if you don't get more and more of the world in a given period of time, then the socialist country, or countries, that exist at the time (if there are any socialist countries right then) will inevitably go under. But there is a contradiction when a socialist country is in a situation of being encircled; and that also interacts with the internal contradictions within the socialist society. And, at a certain point, if further advances aren't made in the proletarian revolution worldwide, these things will turn to their opposites and the conditions will become more favorable for capitalist restoration within the socialist country. This doesn't mean capitalist restoration automatically kicks in after a certain point, or that it will automatically occur at all. But it means that things will begin to turn into their opposites and the conditions for capitalist restoration will become more favorable. So, in that dialectical materialist sense, it's one way or the other: make further advances and breakthroughs in the world revolution or be thrown back, temporarily.

Militarily and economically, a new Maoist government would immediately face the problem of being surrounded by unfriendly governments and the possibility of sanctions, intervention and military invasion. Politically and ideologically, it would be attempting to build a new socialist society surrounded by hostile states, in a world where communism has been declared dead and in which there are tremendous prejudices against socialist states led by communist parties. And given the military, economic, and political strength of global capitalism—and the real difficulties and challenges of building a new socialist society—there would be tremendous pulls within the revolutionary forces themselves to accommodate with imperialism. During the Chinese Revolution, Mao had to deal with what he called 'bourgeois democrats becoming capitalist roaders'—that is, those within the Communist Party itself who united with the anti-feudal and democratic aims of the revolution, but then became proponents of building a capitalist, not socialist, society. And this is certainly to be a phenomenon in Nepal, the outlines of which can already be seen in the outlook of various political parties and individuals who are proponents of bourgeois democracy, not socialism, but who have united with the Maoists to oppose the monarchy.

Notes

1. Squads are comprised of 7–9 guerrillas; platoons 24–30; companies 150; battalions 450; brigades 1,350 and divisions several thousand.
2. The numbers are not literally 10 to 1 against the Maoists, but this basic point still applies, especially in terms of things like more advanced weaponry, foreign military assistance, and so on.
3. In April 2000, the guerrillas successfully raided the Rukumkot police station, a decisive outpost of the paramilitary, a commando force. In September 2000, the Maoists captured Dunai, the Dolpa-district headquarters. Such actions put the government into an extremely defensive position and drew more attention and concern from India, the US, and other imperialist powers.
4. Human Rights Watch wrote on 1 February 2006: 'The new government has systematically attacked the media through censorship and oppressive laws, making free press in Nepal virtually obsolete. Reporters Without Borders reported at least 273 cases of arrests of journalists and 569 cases of censorship in 2005 occurred in Nepal—half of the total cases of censorship reported worldwide.'
5. See, 'International Communist Movement and Its Historical Lessons', Document of the Second National Conference of the Communist Party of Nepal (Maoist), reprinted in *A World to Win* (27), 2001 and *Himalayan Thunder*, the quarterly bulletin of the CPN (Maoist), May 2001. This document from the CPN (M) states:

> Due to the uniqueness of the economic, political, cultural and geographical conditions and the unchallenged hold of Indian monopoly capitalism, it will be very difficult for any single country of this region to successfully complete the new national-democratic revolution and; even if it succeeds following the distinct contradictions, it will be almost impossible for it to survive. The revolutionaries need to seriously concentrate on the fact that a particular country, or a particular territory of a country, shall be liberated through the force of the common and joint struggle of the people of this region following the unequal stage of development, and that it can play only a particular role of base area for the revolution in the whole region.

References

Avakian, Bob. 1998. 'Two Humps in the World Revolution: Putting the Enemy on the Run', *Revolutionary Worker*, 18 January. Available at revcom.us. (Accessed on 18 June 2007.)

———. 2002. 'Great Objectives and Grand Strategy: Seizing Power… Advancing to Communism, Keeping our Eyes on the Prize, Maintaining a Living Link', *Revolutionary Worker*, 10 February. Available at revcom.us. (Accessed on 18 June 2007.)

———. 2005. *Revolution* newspaper, 25 September. Available at revcom.us. (Accessed on 18 June 2007.)

AWTWNS (A World to Win News Service). 2004a. 'Nepal: A Walk into the Future', 12 January.

AWTWNS (A World to Win News Service). 2004b. 'Revolutionary Autonomous Region Declared in Western Nepal', 19 January.

———. 2005a. 'Nepal: Maoists offer Self Criticism after Bus Bombing', 13 June.

———. 2005b. 'Building a Road to the Future', 5 September.

Bhattarai, Baburam. 2003. *The Nature of Underdevelopment and Regional Structure of Nepal: A Marxist Analysis*. New Delhi: Adroit Publishers.

CPN (M). 1995. 'Strategy and Tactics of Armed Struggle in Nepal', *The Worker* 3 (March 1997): 26–28.

Human Rights Watch. 2005. 'Clear Culpability: Disappearances by Security Forces in Nepal'. Available at: hrw.org/reports/2005/nepal0205.

INSEC. 2005. 'Three Months of Cease Fire: An Assessment of Human Rights Situation during the Unilateral Ceasefire by CPN (Maoist) in Nepal (September 03–December 02, 2005)'.

International Committee of the Red Cross. 2005. 'Reports on Detainees Released by Maoists'. Available at: http://icrc.org/eng.

Kathmandu Post. 2002. 'Freed Cops say Weapons Let Them Down', 26 November.

Lawoti, Mahendra. 2005. *Towards a Democratic Nepal*. New Delhi: Sage Publications.

Mao Tsetung. 1968. *Selected Military Writings*. Peking: Foreign Languages Press.

Moriarty, James. 2005. Address to the Nepal Council of World Affairs, 9 August.

Onesto, Li. 2000. 'Red Flag Flying on the Roof of the World' (interview with Prachanda), *Revolutionary Worker*, 20 February. Available at: lionesto.net and revcom.us.

———.2005. *Dispatches from the People's War in Nepal*. London and Chicago: Pluto Press, Insight Press.

Parvati. 2003. 'The Question of Women's Leadership in the People's War in Nepal', *The Worker* 8 (January): 37–44.

———. 2005. 'People's Power in Nepal'. Available at: http://www.montlyreview.org/1105parvatti.htm.

Reuters. 2005. 'Nepal Rebels "Regret" Bus Deaths, Launch Probe', 7 June.

Revolutionary Mass Criticism Writing Group. 1973. *Three Major Struggles on China's Philosophical Front (1949–1964)*. Peking: Foreign Languages Press.

de Sales, Anne 2003. 'The Kham Magar Country: Between Ethnic Claims and Maoism', in D.N. Gellner (ed.), *Resistance and the Nepalese State*. New Delhi: Social Science Press.

Shah, Saubhagya. 2004. 'A Himalayan Red Herring? Maoist Revolution in the Shadow of the Legacy Raj', in Michael Hutt (ed.), *Himalayan People's War: Nepal's Maoist Rebellion*. Bloomington and Indianapolis: Indiana University Press.

Shneiderman, Sara and Mark Turin. 2004. 'The Path to Jan Sarkar in Dolakha District: Towards an Ethnography of the Maoist Movement', in Michael Hutt (ed.), *Himalayan People's War: Nepal's Maoist Rebellion*. Bloomington and Indianapolis: Indiana University Press.

Thapa, Deepak. 2002. 'Erosion of the Nepali World', *Himal South Asian Magazine*. Available at: World Wide Web: www.himalmag.com/2002/april/essay.htm.

United Revolutionary People's Council, Nepal. 2001. 'Common Minimum Policy and Programme', in S.D. Muni 2003. *Maoist Insurgency in Nepal: The Challenge and the Response*, Appendix. New Delhi: Observer Research Foundation.
US Government. 2002. FY 2002 Foreign Operations Emergency Supplemental Funding Justifications. Available at: http://www.fas.org/asmp/resources/govern/fy02_foropsemerg_justification.pdf.

6

The Web in the Shadows (*Chaayaamaa Maakuraako Jaalo*): Anatomy of Stakeholder Influences in an Insurgency

IVAN GYOZO SOMLAI[1]

PROLOGUE

> In the legendary Hindu epic, The Mahabharata, it was observed at the conclusion of the great war on the battlefield of Kurukshetra in ancient India, that Lord Krishna was the one and only who fought the battle and made the Pandavas victorious. The thousands of other men seen on the battleground were mere actors. In effect, it was Lord Krishna who did everything. (*The Telegraph* 2003)

Or was it an illusion? Having people behind the scenes, scheming, manipulating or simply influencing or advising in the background is not something new.

BACKGROUND

The Communist Party of Nepal (Maoist), or CPN (M), has been expending considerable effort in its insurrection against the government of Nepal (GoN) since 1996. By advocating the abolition of the monarchy and the establishment of a peoples' republic, the inevitable countering of such direct opposition to the government has increased fighting, making a peaceful solution through dialogue elusive.

Multifarious reasons may rationalize this struggle (Shrestha 2004); it has nonetheless been impossible to pinpoint precise cause-and-effect relationships. This is not stated in defence of serious inequities that do exist and which must be sooner or later addressed; nor is it mentioned from the perspective that the obvious socio-economic, political and cultural problems aren't the cause of the insurrection. It is stated only because in the light of empirical research (Molnar 1965), no consistent relationship has been found between insurgency and a country's state of economic development, nor with rural– urban density patterns, nor with literacy and education levels, nor with a country's percentage of military personnel. There are, however, determinants of potential conflict *per se* (Collier and Haeffler 2002), such as low per capita gross national income; high dependence on primary commodities' exports; political instability; restricted civil and political rights; militarization; ethnic dominance; and active regional conflicts. The inherent social disruptions have been abetted by reckless deference to the requisites of international financial institutions (such as privatization) and concomitant exploitation by multi-national corporations. Keeping the preceding factors in mind, 'whether the really poor have benefited from the insurgency has yet to be empirically verified' (Lawoti 2005).

Therefore, any mediation or negotiation efforts must have a very clear idea of the insurgency's meta environment so that efforts at reconciliation are able to sensibly and with dispatch take aim at root causes, and not just seek to redress the present violence. We must likewise equilibrate the distress caused by the current conflagration with its potential constructiveness in possibly catalyzing the improvement of peoples' lives.

State of Fear

Failure of the state institutions to meet citizens' needs is leading to the loss of legitimacy of the state, in the perception of the citizens; this context invites anarchy, which in turn develops fear, giving rise to pathological vulnerability, killing and sundry other behaviours normally unacceptable. This anarchical environment is spreading in the rural areas,[2] especially where district and village development committees have been rendered inactive: surveyors are unable to inspect border pillars because they are dispossessed of equipment and turned back by insurgents; teachers walk a tightrope between insurgents and the government to deliver a meagre standard of education; many health posts are empty; agricultural, irrigation and veterinary services are decreasing; normal daily security cannot be provided because security forces are compelled to congregate in select pockets, with the paths and communities in between governed by nobody or by the Maoists.

A vacuum of essential services in any society is eventually filled by individuals, non-government organizations, or—as in Nepal in many pockets—by the Maoists. The fear of death and the struggle for security affects all sides of the struggle: Maoists, government security forces and civilians. When faced with immediate death or serious trauma, any side has the potential to become a threat to those perceived to be a menace. History shows that the failure to meet human needs leads to protracted human conflict—and this is exactly what is occurring now in Nepal.

This author's experiences in Nicaragua, Cambodia, Indonesia, Russia and Vietnam clearly demonstrate that sides that are extremely at odds can, nevertheless, amicably resolve long-standing differences. Thus, it's important to note that there are precedents that Nepal can follow. Recent news from Sri Lanka indicates, however, that negotiations are delicate and can be overturned; news from Cambodia underscores that even where negotiations seem to have been successful, inadequate attention to rectifying social inequities can lead to despondency and renewed disillusionment with the system. Experience nonetheless demonstrates that there are preparatory processes for leading the adversaries to a better appreciation of (not necessarily agreement with) others' perspectives, covering aspects that need be carefully considered for negotiation.

Emphasis on Aiming for Negotiation and the Pre-conditions

The clear alternative to the earliest negotiations is a stalemate or even the perceived or real superiority of one side, resulting in a continuation of killing. Mutually acceptable resolution of a conflict can never be attained without negotiation; but constructive, effective, well-meaning negotiation can't ever occur without the assiduous preparation of three minimal pre-conditions:

Trust
This refers to arriving at a point of believing that what your adversary is saying is the truth, will be adhered to and will not be altered by some higher or hidden authority.

Security
This means that an adversary requires guarantees that during the talks, advantage won't be taken for attacks, arrests, re-arming, intimidation and other debilitating tactics. As well, there needs to be established a central authority (possibly via a foreign agency) endowed with the necessary power to judge and to employ a monitoring and controlling force greater than that of the disputants in case of disruptions.

Guaranteed Dispatch on Agreement(s)
This is defined as immediate implementation of decisions agreed on, so that delays don't result in the adversaries reverting to fighting.

Why this preparation? Because it cannot be taken for granted that the people at the table understand each other (for example, it is commonly held that a farmer has more in common with a farmer of another country than with the elite of his own country). There is insufficient understanding as to why this conflict is 'revolutionary' and not just a dispute over specific grievances, or why one side regards the confrontation as being over problems that could be debated and arbitrated whereas the other considers the issues so serious that only a violent transformation could resolve them. Therefore, when sitting at the table, although everyone would be speaking Nepali, it is more likely that delegates would be talking past rather than with each other because of differing backgrounds, perceptions, experiences, worldviews and aspirations. Anger blocks messages: this is what has happened up to now in previous negotiation attempts.

We must be aware that even if the superior side overpowers and annihilates the opposition, there is a festering, ever-present dissatisfaction in a considerable segment of the Nepali society. A peace-building process must therefore not stop at the first sign of victory; it must continue to assiduously look for, admit to and plan to remedy the inequities in the society that have caused this sad epoch in Nepal's history and ensure that an ethical system of governance is enshrined.

Success has eluded three such major negotiation attempts.[3] Possible reasons for this failure include logistical errors in choosing an appropriate location, inappropriate team compositions, unusually high expectations for progress, inadequate preparation by both major disputants—or habitual and confusing pressures from outside forces.

Thus, the purpose here isn't to reiterate causative analyses, but rather to elaborate mechanisms for improved understanding of the complexity and to proffer more effective modalities for addressing the issues, thus bringing about peace. This author's attempts have been in the realm of improved preparation prior to serious negotiation.

The approach described herein isn't new to those familiar with successful community development or participatory methodologies; however, it's obvious that many of those intimately involved in peace-making in Nepal have either a paucity of the requisite background or have, for other reasons, been incapable of synchronizing their efforts. The business community already knows that external perceptions of image, customer loyalty and satisfaction, supplier links, commercial power, negotiating capacity, and so on are barometers of a firm's sustainability. It is time that the disparate stakeholders in Nepal's future also realize that both the state and the insurrectionists depend, ultimately, on the relationships with its constituents.

Incipient Efforts

Subsequent to a request by the Maoists in April 2002 and a follow-up expression of interest by the then prime minister, Sher Bahadur Deuba,[4] this author engaged, in July of that year, in efforts to seek common grounds in preparation for negotiations. Having connections within the insurgent organization as well as the government and civil society, the initial communication was fairly productive. Each side presented certain initial demands and ultimatums regarding what they could or were unwilling to negotiate. For example, the government held the monarchy as non-negotiable, while the rebels maintained that a constituent assembly had to be on the table. Despite those demands, the deputed representatives did agree to more flexibility by the author's bringing to their attention the reality that, historically, settlements frequently have required painful compromises, and the pariah groups of yesterday are often the opposition parties of today and possibly the elected governments of tomorrow. Moreover, some tacit fundamentals about negotiation were discussed, namely that:

1. Putting something up for discussion doesn't mean necessarily losing ground on it.
2. Negotiation inherently means that while some issues will be won, others may be lost.
3. Extremely sensitive issues can be brought on for discussion after there is progress on the less sensitive issues.[5]
4. Patience is paramount.

The process was '*dohori* diplomacy',[6] but the intent wasn't mediation; rather, it was to provide support to both sides in improving preparations prior to negotiation. Meetings and travel plans were surreptitiously arranged because neither side wanted the media involved; the insurgents wanted to ensure that this author wasn't followed by security forces; and this author didn't wish to jeopardize his own connections.[7] With no desire for any personal recognition or raising of false hopes, it was agreed to avoid publicity.

Further dialogue included senior Maoists; senior and peripheral government officials; various political party leaders and cadres; senior bureaucrats and field staff in land surveys, health, tourism, security forces and education; entrepreneurs from firms of all sizes; farmers; labourers; intellectuals; the media; Service Club and other civil-society stalwarts.

As communication increased, as intents were becoming clearer and alternative approaches plausible, the need for each party to consult with others in the background increased, because the representatives didn't want sole responsibility for decisions in this complex context. One soon realized, through comments by the adversaries and private enquiries, that there was a web in the shadows that was perhaps stronger than—and could outlast—the spinner. Like a spider that secretes silk and manipulates the resulting attachment of its fine threads, major parties to negotiation extend their own threads. The spider web is built of sticky silk used to catch unwary prey and of non-sticky bits that reduce the spider's chances of getting caught in its own web. Similarly, both the insurgents and the government of Nepal exude silk to their constituents, at times getting unintentionally caught in power struggles. The considerable diversity within the shadows creates an interesting, albeit complicated background to understanding the visions, machinations, motivations and intents of all stakeholders. It is necessary to gauge the perspective of each stakeholder group with the criteria that it may use for itself in assessing the success or failure of a conflict-resolution process. This background needs to be comprehended prior to any meaningful negotiations.

The key players, who are but only at the surface, are the government of Nepal and the insurgents (see Figure 6.1). However, each of these are in turn connected to numerous subgroups or cultures—the 'mere actors' of our Kurukshetra prologue. Popular or common approaches to two-party resolutions have not been and are not portended to be effective or even possible in the Nepali culture.

Figure 6.1
The Prominent Adversaries

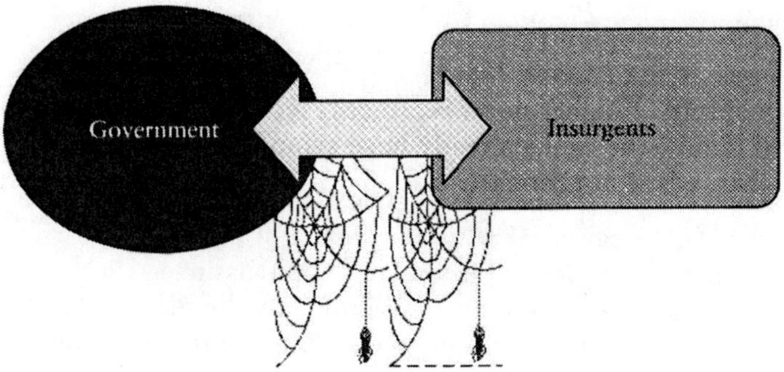

IN THE SHADOWS

What, then, does this extended web consist of? Who are its constituents? How do they relate to one another? One of the prime parties is the government, with its related constituents, including security forces, bureaucrats and the palace.

The Royal Nepal Army (RNA) (about 100,000 troops), however, is not a unitary entity except for its outer trappings and disciplinary code. Most troops have been domestically based without foreign experience, but a sizeable component in both the army and the police have seen duty overseas (Acharya 2005) and been thus exposed to other cultures and mores. Many have served as UN Peace-keepers. Therefore, this considerable untapped group within the military that has perhaps a more holistic understanding of the issues and, therefore, a correspondingly more open mind to alternative processes needs to be reached. This is an important point, because in discussions with the highest levels of the RNA, this author was informed that 'we now have new arms from abroad and we need to practice with and use them; then we'll negotiate'. The RNA feel that they have the upper hand and are relentlessly pursuing the Maoists. Casualties and setbacks to the military are usually under-reported or unreported. The Army also has a score to settle for the unprovoked attacks, embarrassments and major thefts of arms that have yet to be recovered. They have been buoyed by the substantial aid from abroad to upgrade their armaments, fortifications and living quarters in the field.

But where the loyalty of the cadre will lie in case of a magnified insurrection, an all-out civil war or heightened activities against civilians is an unknown.[8] Coming from virtually the same backgrounds as the Maoist cadre and fuelled by their knowledge that the majority of higher ranks befall only individuals connected to the royal family, the ranks already have sympathy for the cause of the Maoists, albeit not for their tactics. Although this is suppressed information, there has already been dissent in some battalions in the Far West Region.[9] The cardinal maxim guiding the Army: the conventional army loses if it does not win (Kissinger 1969); and the odds are against its winning, if we judge by the disciplinary breakdowns of most twentieth-century counter-insurgent armies (van Creveld 2005) and pronouncements by the Army's own spokesman.

Interviews with the armed police[10] (about 20,000 members) have shown dissatisfaction with usual two-year postings away from families and the constant need for vigilance. Several who are close to retirement indicated their unwillingness to go home because of fear of retribution upon themselves and their families. Many who aren't yet close to retirement are unable to visit their families during leaves because of the same fear of being targeted by the Maoists.

It is obvious that the palace wields extraordinary power within and over the government. But like any extended family in Nepal, the head of the household does not necessarily have the final word, at least not without consultation with, and at times pressure from, other motivated family members and confidants.[11]

The prime minister's office and the other ministers are a blend of people who are in 'normal times' freely elected and who are beholden to particular (and often strong) interest groups. Thus, as in the palace–family analogy, the prime minister doesn't automatically have absolute control over the composition of the cabinet, nor the composition of negotiating teams. And naturally, when the prime minister and other ministers are not permitted to discharge their responsibilities freely, they don't just become silent: they begin to oppose the strong-arm regime.

Bureaucrats, as in any government, often represent the status quo, along with some continuity of the public-service system. This may result, however, in staff dedicated to the old system undermining new initiatives. The bureaucrats' influence is, though, undergoing transformation as they abandon the periphery and gravitate towards the centre and other urban 'safe havens'. Peri-urban and rural areas are thus facing chronic deficiencies in government services, with a resulting deleterious impact on travel and work modalities. As the bureaucrats are, *ceteris paribus*, absolutely essential for the smooth operation of any government, this group definitely needs to be well oriented, advised and informed of all peace-building efforts.

Finally, there are numerous parastatal, semi-autonomous agencies, most of which used to be headed until April 1990 by a member of the royal family (and several of them still are). Examples include the National Sports Council, Social Welfare Council,[12] National Industrial Development Corporation, King Mahendra Trust for Nature Conservation, Timber Corporation and so on. Each of these has many influential constituents and has remained connected in varying degrees to the government (see Figure 6.2).

Next in the web are the political parties. We can categorize about a 100 of them (Friedrich-Ebert-Stiftung 2005) into communist, socialist, royalist, geographic/ethnic, Rightist and 'other' (for example, Hariyali), with some parties in each block having corresponding student wings and some blocks overlapping with others in terms of their platforms and principles. Political parties are considered by the Maoists as a so-called 'secondary enemy', to be utilized to gain empathy and solidarity on the road to crushing the government

Figure 6.2
Directly Related Constituents of Government

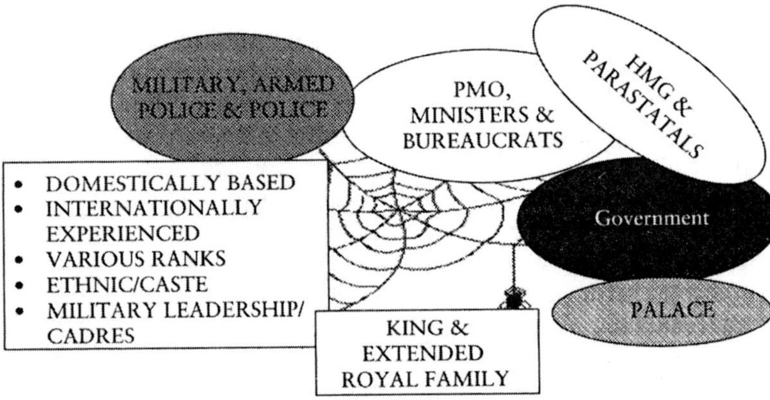

and its constituents—the 'primary enemy'. A sensitive, uncomfortable balancing act by the parties is thereby required: party members need to know that they are being used for ulterior motives by the Maoists and that, should the latter succeed in overthrowing the government, the parties themselves may be in jeopardy. However, the even temporary necessity for cooption provides an opportunity for the parties to exert reverse influence on the insurgents to seek a quicker entente.

Despite a range of philosophical underpinnings, there are many family connections among the parties and frequently amongst the respective leaderships. Thus there is an opportunity, from the perspective of seeking empathy for peace-making efforts, to exploit elite-to-élite and cadre-to-cadre connections by having them influence the key adversaries.

Trade unions, active in strikes (*hartal*), closures (*bandh*) and plugging of roads (*chakka-jam*), have to rely on the middle class to observe a strike and the inability of alternative personnel to successfully take over the running of essential services. The economic repercussions of Rs 1 billion per day (Yogi 2002) are of secondary concern.[13] Obviously, the insurgents, about 28,000 guerrillas (Samay 2005) plus seven divisions, and thousands of militia,[14] represent the other key adversary. Its constituents are varied. The tenets of Marx, Lenin and Mao aside, Nepali Maoists have distinctions within their organization. This isn't altogether unusual, in that all communist systems have had inherent inequalities, despite the common rhetoric; and local cultural contexts always influence an organization. The most obvious distinctions are that the intellectuals are primarily Bahuns, while a majority of the military wing are of other castes.[15] That aside, many armed members are native to the area where they are operating.[16] Membership is at least 30 per cent women. Occupations reflect the work patterns of the area in which they operate (that is, those in or near urban areas include bureaucrats, intelligentsia, students, the unemployed and business people; in rural areas, farmers, the unemployed, students, small business-owners, and so on). The top leaders spend much time beyond the border for personal safety reasons. An irritation for all is the claiming of tributes, vengeance and control by pseudo-Maoists cropping up sporadically in many districts.

Ethnic, caste and interest organizations oscillate in their support of the Maoists, with some overtly and consistently supportive, while others provide conditional support as and when it suits their own internal interests. Some of the support comes from not necessarily a wish to back the Maoists, but rather an opposition to the ineffective traditional organizations in what is usually called a 'protest vote' in North America (see Figure 6.3).

An oft-overlooked element is the motivation for the Maoists being much greater than for the government security forces. In the main, the reason for this is the existence of a large collective who have reached a psychological threshold, realizing that there is no hope for betterment of their own or their offspring's lives. The Maoists are tired of an expected devotion to the nation that seems to intimate 'what the individual is not allowed to want for himself, he is encouraged to seek for the… state' (Morgenthau 1946) and the state is selfish about distribution. The things up for distribution are power and authority, benefits, and burdens; the state, in their estimation, distributes only the last. They have thus nothing left to lose in laying siege to their own land. It is a parable from *Sagarmatha*: 'nothing ventured, nothing gained'! The cardinal maxim guiding the Maoists: the insurgents win if they do not lose (Kissinger 1969).

Concluding the array of stakeholders are the components of civil society: ethnic, caste and regional interest groups, businesses, the media, non-government organizations (NGOs), such as domestic and international, especially peace and human-rights agencies, and academe, together with the hoi polloi and the élite of society.

Figure 6.3
Related Constituents of Insurgents

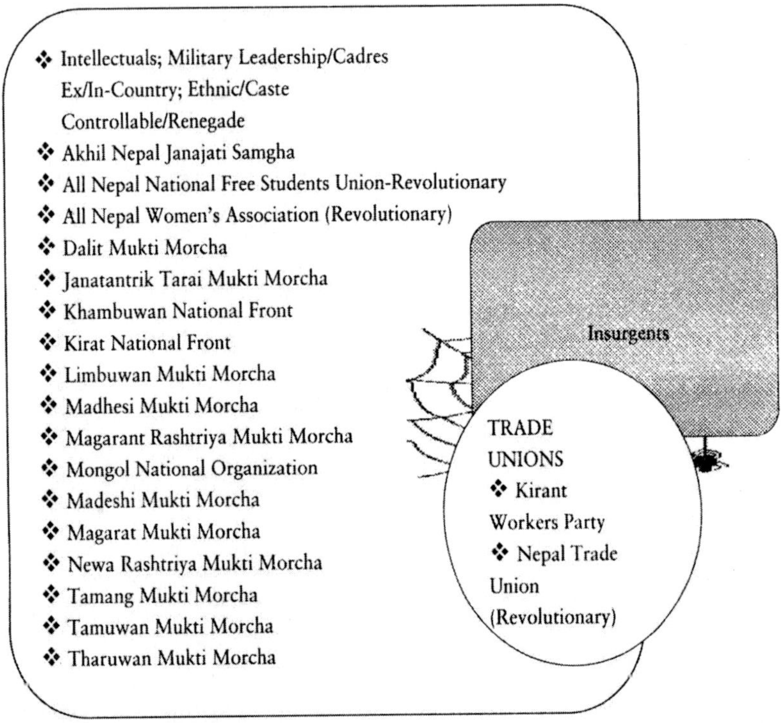

Most ethnic groups in Nepal 'feel they are overshadowed by Khas linguistic and cultural chauvinism. This situation can only lead to undesirable hostilities' (Shrestha 2003). Successive governments have failed to seek redress for ethnic, caste and regional grievances, thus propelling advocates to belligerence. Their considerable clout needs to be kept in mind during any peace-building process.[17]

Business is a crucial element of the negotiating process from two perspectives: one, there are several commercial ventures that because of their size, connections or renown can influence other stakeholders through financial support and direct access to powerful citizens; second, in any eventual peace agreement, the thousands of youth presently carrying arms and knowing no other life will be dependent on socially minded firms for retraining and employment. Gainful work for demobilized ex-combatants will be essential for effective reintegration of these people into society at large. With their guerrilla experience, demobilized soldiers are often exceptionally good candidates for conservation, wildlife, security (Hatton et al. 2001) and technical trades positions.

As to the media, some—not all—are consistently accurate, and certain publications and radio stations have risked the wrath of censors to convey the reality; but the public needs to distinguish the true reports. Blogs (web logs) and satellite communications have made it nowadays virtually impossible to hide major news or rumours for long. This new medium also provides another avenue for surveys, communication and attempts to influence disputants. In the context of stakeholder analysis, the diverse media could influence attitudes and actions and could therefore bring weight to bear on the prime adversaries.

Civil society is a catch-all for the public and the plethora of community-based and NGOs—domestic and international, religious and secular. All of these have malleable membership bases and can bring weight to bear on any number of adversarial factions. A large number of NGOs are subject to programmatic, financial and public-relations influence—if not actual direction—from abroad, creating vague allegiances. NGOs span the whole spectrum of ideologies from the government-centric to the demonstrably socially oriented. Peace and human-rights organizations have flourished in the past 11 years, but it has become apparent that their disparate views, and even territoriality, can lead them to play into the hands of outside interests; this author had recommended that they consolidate their efforts.

The middle class itself merits serious analysis. Relatively small as it is in Nepal, the middle class' support or, at a minimum, its neutrality is essential for any government. Analogously, 'a government which cannot rely upon its middle classes will, almost certainly, be unable to rely upon the unbroken loyalty of the army, or will, at any rate, be sufficiently intimidated to shirk putting the loyalty of the army to a severe test' (Chorley 1943). In this respect, we again can perceive that some mobilization of the middle class (via the media and other civil-society groups) to convince the adversaries to behave in a certain way (that is, better preparation for negotiations, negotiation on honorable terms, and so on) is possible.

It is likewise the middle class together with the lower classes that forms the majority of protesters on any given occasion. It is amazingly difficult to persuade citizens to partake in a public protest even when those citizens admit to the existence of a shocking injustice; it is well-nigh impossible to persuade others to take the risks of public sanctions entailed by the protest when they do not share the view that the injustice is shocking (Madden and Hare 1970). So those willing to protest should also be sounded out for their thoughts, because their perspectives and moral feelings are extremely insightful.

The élite, at least in the larger urban areas, are in a dichotomous state: either in a cataplexy of fear of the Pol Pot-style repercussions of any successful Maoist takeover (and once the élite convince themselves that others wish to destroy them, their perspective of choosing to destroy those others in self-defence becomes fully justified); or else it is in ostrich-like 'head-in-the-sand' mode of dismissing the current events as temporary, with the government inevitably winning or the context being so complex that it is easier to not think or do anything proactively to resolve it. The preceding needs to be balanced with the fact that a select number of the élite have also been leaders in exposing inequities and pushing for reforms.

From a more sinister governmental vantage point, civil society also harbours an average of nine underground or surreptitious supporters to each overt combatant (Molnar 1965: 74, 77). In other words, many fighters and most supporters maintain themselves through performance of their routine jobs. Such a reality most emphatically requires that pre-negotiation preparations create a deep understanding of the meta environment, meaning that the forging of links and relationships with those 'nine in the shadows' is essential for both comprehending the issues as well as for seeking backing for eventual remedies. The above statistics may bear more clout given this anecdote: several projects have had requests for donations of a percentage of their total budget from local Maoists; when the project officers claim that the request is out of consonance with the project budget, the Maoists produce the project budget, proving their calculation is viable. The import: Maoists or their supporters have infiltrated most agencies.

Religious groups, unlike in many other parts of the world, have remained tame, while some Nepali academics have tended to be amongst those on the edge of incisiveness, pushing the envelope of censorable speech. Serious interference in the peace process has been initiated by externally based groups[18] (see Figure 6.4).

Figure 6.4
External Influencers

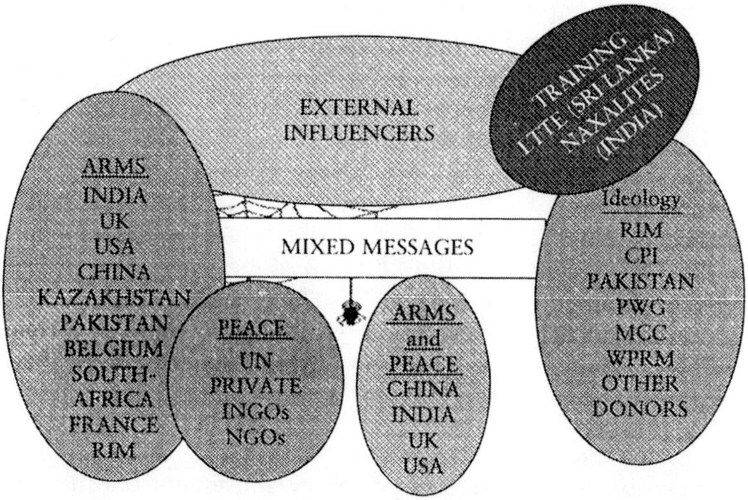

Countries and groups purveying or donating arms and training have complicated the issues by increasing the intensity and longevity of the fighting.[19] The festering insurgency has allowed the strengthening of a nexus with Indian and Sri Lankan—groups and others with allied interests (Patil 2005); this has led to varying degrees of collaborative training, economic support and other joint activities, requiring additional understanding of external actors. What has most dismayed and confused the Maoists, though, has been the attitude of the governments of the United States, United Kingdom and India, which through one department have been promoting peace-making and have via another department been shipping arms to the government side. The question is which department represents the real voice of that country.[20]

External interference also comes in purely ideological form through a full range of philosophical underpinnings, often as a political necessity for one country struggling versus another and using Nepal as a mere pawn. Overt pronouncements of support by certain Western nations are, in fact, contradicted by their covert disinterest in Nepal. Western nations proffering advice on whom to label terrorist, how to tackle firmly established inequities and how to bring about peace would do well to remember their own philosophical foundations. John Locke conceived that all men have certain natural rights anterior to all the merely conventional, legal or positive rights they may find implemented for them in their own separate societies. He had thus condoned the right to disobey all those laws that violate natural rights when a reconstitution of a just society was not provided for in the mechanics of the government in force (Locke 1924); he furthermore remarked that a civil society exists by unanimous consent (ibid.)—something sorely absent in today's Nepal.

Much like the government of Nepal itself, the insurgents require resources to allow them to carry on their struggle. Sources of finance for the Maoists include four main avenues: smuggling (timber, products obtained from endangered species such as musk deer or rhinoceros and drugs); revolutionary tithing (to tourists, through road blocks from projects); extortion (from businesses, individuals, large farms and landowners, as well as bank looting) and volunteer donors (supporters).

Official policies of 'not paying "donations"' notwithstanding, 'in many cases individual staff members contribute from their own pockets because they fear losing their jobs or even their lives' (Kievelitz et al. 2001). Such actions (fear aside) obviously play into the insurgents' hands and keep their operations solvent. Thus, aside from going after the insurgents' fighting capability, the government should rather go after their combat-making capability. But the military, on all sides, is connected to the economic system, which is connected to their cultural system, to their personal relationships. We have to understand the links among all those systems to optimize negotiations.

A True Picture of the Holistic Complexity

Thus, it became evident that the complicating factor has been not only the particular influence exerted by a discrete individual or organization; it was the diversity of opinions, of the selfish motives of stakeholders and interlocutors that, in a country noted for its paucity of coordination, has thus far strangled the efforts for regaining peace.

There is such an intimate relationship amongst many of the stakeholders that the only way to progress to meaningful negotiations is by somehow taking all of them into consideration. In Nepal, the dense web of ensnarement, family relationships and communication channels must be used to advantage. Figure 6.5 illustrates the complexity of the holistic picture—this schema could be used as a basis for determining the composition of negotiating teams and advisory committees at central as well as district levels (as suggested in Figure 6.8).

Figure 6.5
Complexity of Stakeholders

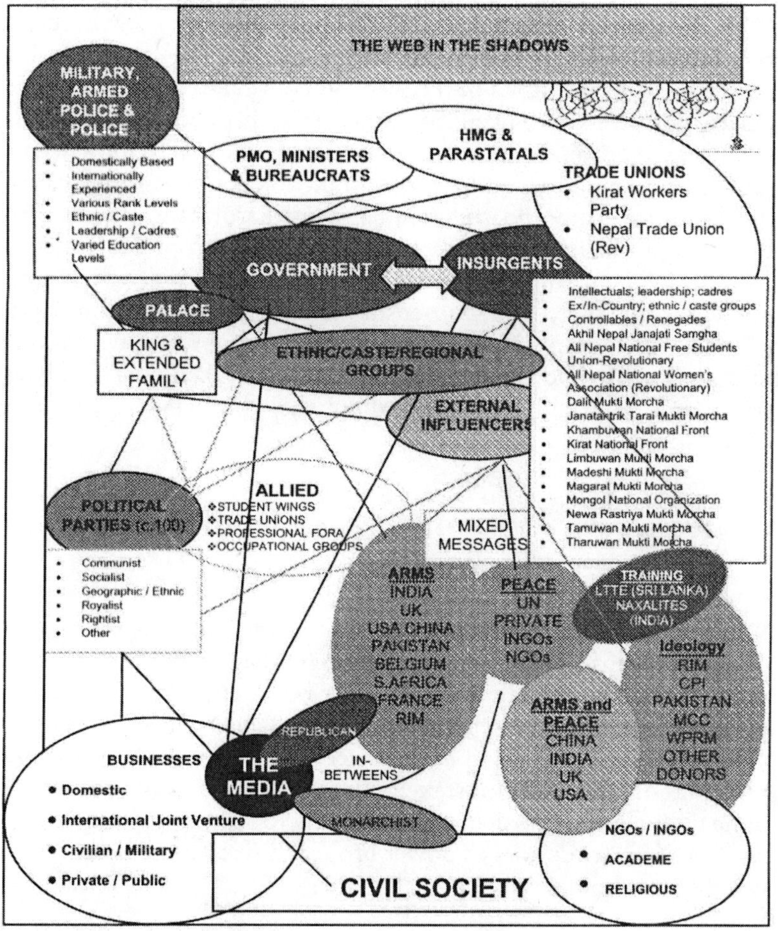

A well-articulated, iterative agenda needs to be shared via systematic connections with as many peripheral groups as possible: the élite on all sides, the often interrelated cadre and, last but not least, the inevitable family, clan and caste relationships. Probing questions need to be asked and analysed, and then there must ensue an addressing of all major socio-economic and cultural factors that have caused the insurgency.

Enquiry and Analysis

With the various stakeholders, the enquiry process itself needs to be a multidisciplinary endeavour, with a separate team serving each subgroup identified in the web, all coordinated by a respected person perceived as neutral. By gathering and collectively analysing responses to probing questions, we should be able to develop a deeper understanding and empathy for all stakeholders, in turn providing useful information and suggestions to mediators and negotiators, thereby optimizing the probability of devising appropriate strategies for a subsequent solution. 'Conflict analysis is still a fledgling field, and currently, there is no consensus on what good conflict analysis entails' (World Bank 2003). Nonetheless, a comprehensive enquiry and analysis would fairly accurately match stakeholder feedback with any claims and aspirations about the ethics and performance of the adversaries.

Alternative Modalities for Gaining Knowledge and Analysing Issues

While stakeholder involvement or engagement implies some form of egalitarianism, in fact some stakeholders wield much more power than others. The enquiry must be '...clearly committed to principles of empowerment and related measures aimed at "leveling the playing field"—giving equal voice to the perspectives and the priorities of less powerful stakeholders' (Chevalier 2001). Analyses done without their participation are likely to reflect the interests and agenda of the mediators or power brokers directing the exercise and not the stakeholders (ibid.).

That aside, we must resort to a better modality for mitigating this conflict. Holistic and trans-disciplinary perception and action (Maruyama 1974; Max-Neef 2005) can help us realize different approaches, of which this author's preference is for a trans-stakeholder approach (TSA).[21] This means essential communication with as many legitimate stakeholders as possible, with purposeful and coordinated dialogue and the nurturing of relationship building, together with feedback loops to enhance understanding and learning. Examples include the efforts of some Nepal police personnel to improve and expand the community policing scheme (Shrestha 2004) by including more stakeholders. As well, this author has attempted to develop trusting relationships with different influential groups, sought to connect disparate groups and encouraged sustained communication among groups not normally cooperating. TSA is a transformational approach: the deeper we go into the 'shadows', the more that understanding gained from the murky maze will evolve into a more lucid comprehension of the interests below the surface of the publicly espoused positions (see Figure 6.6).

Figure 6.6
Overview of Various Stakeholder Approaches

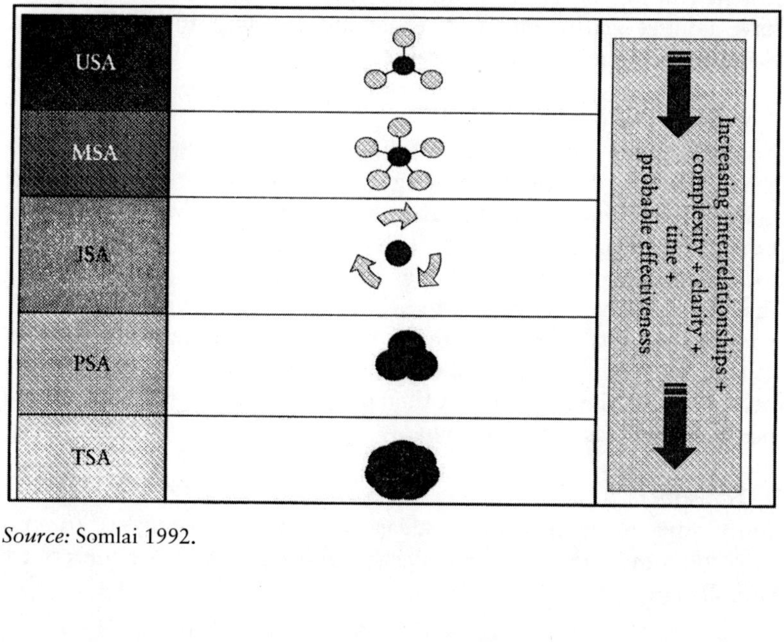

Source: Somlai 1992.

IMPACT OF TSA ANALYSIS

Overall, stakeholders have the potential to force the main disputants to negotiation, to force the inclusion of particular points, or to prolong the status quo. Thus we must try to recognize and understand the existence of comparative values and belief systems of the various subcultures. While these numerous subcultures may create control and coordination nightmares, the brighter obverse side is that the multifarious perspectives may also provide hitherto unthought-of alternatives.

TSA can thus lead to a richness of resources and solutions, a vision grander than that possible through more limited interactions. Each conjunction of stakeholders produces new insights and the resulting higher-level, more comprehensive interactions add to one's cumulative knowledge, useable at other levels. The increasing variegation of our interactions reinforces us with more confidence as we learn to cope with increasing complexity. The involvement of the subcultures in negotiation would enhance communally mediated control, increase commitment by augmented autonomy, and broaden horizons and capacities through improved communications.

An appropriate modality to understanding and respecting the salient features of the subcultures, in particular those features that have a direct bearing on effectiveness and the maturation of trust and empathy, is via a process represented by the schema in Figure 6.7.

1. Acknowledgement

You must arrive at an understanding and an acceptance of the fact that there are differences among cultures in patterns of thought, behaviours, ethics and attitudes, and admit that while you may not agree with any or all of such differences, you recognize that local context obligates or shapes these differences. As such, these differences have innate, if somewhat incomprehensible, validity. A comparison may be made with the reading of great literature (Lewis 1961): 'We want to be more than ourselves ... we want to see with other eyes, to imagine with other imaginations, to feel with other hearts, as well as with our own.'

2. Transpection

Once you are open to other ideas and ways of doing, try to step into the mind—that is, the collective culture—of your counterpart or colleague.

Figure 6.7
Infinity Empathy Loop

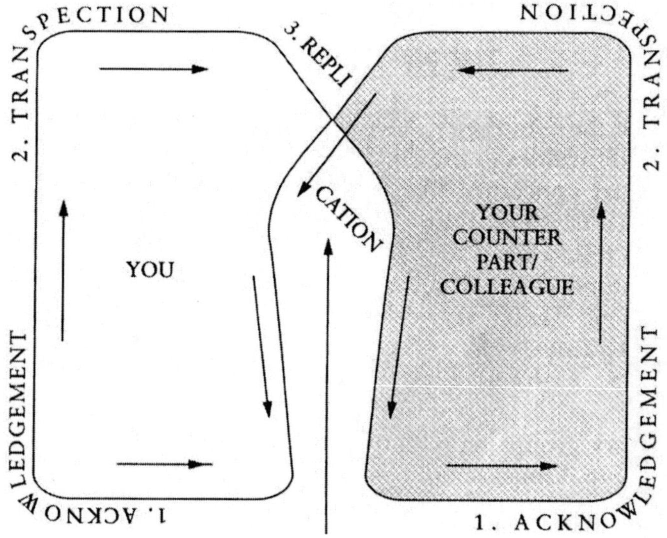

3. Replication
The junction requires the encouragement of the replication of the first two steps by the stakeholders with whom you are doing the enquiry. If such conceptual reciprocation is not done, then mutual understanding, communication and maturation of trust are halted or slowed down, because the efforts are unidirectional. Like westerners' denial or incomprehension of the Buddhist doctrine of 'no self' (*anattaa*) or the Hindu belief in reincarnation (*samsara*), the process of replication may not guarantee any resolution to a quandary—but simply a better understanding of each other's perspectives.

Initiation of this three-step process could be made by either party, and ideally should be simultaneous. Successful application of this process leads to what some might consider as antithetical results: that is, trust and friendship develop, colleagueship and dialogue flourish, blurring the distinction between different 'sides'. In turn, this implies more flexibility in roles and the potential weakening of hierarchy, a shift in our own fundamental understanding—and trust gains a foothold.

The diversity provided by the subcultures would be an asset to heighten the probability of alternative resolutions. Through the modality of TSA, we can also progressively address the three unavoidable preconditions of negotiation.

The Negotiating Team

In view of the complexity described and considering that there are inherent difficulties in the fluidity of the government of Nepal, the Maoists are concerned that negotiating with government representatives is fruitless because after some time, the actors will change, causing a restart from zero. It must be acknowledged that, looking at the history of Nepal, it is more likely than not that this fluidity will continue. Therefore, we must look at the option of a *permanent negotiating team*, representing all major stakeholder groups (using Figure 6.5 as a foundation), that would remain regardless of any further changes in government. Such a team would be supplemented by advisory groups representing regions and/or districts. Neither ought one to dismiss out of hand the participation of the king: there are numerous ways to design honourable participation.

As suggested in Figure 6.8, there may be 16 teams (more or less), each focusing on a particular subgroup but sharing and verifying its information via a negotiation coordinating body, assisted by a trusted, non-negotiating consultative team representative for all sides and issues.

Working with relatively smaller and more identifiable groups would likewise allow closer links with traditional arbitration ideas and interface with women's groups—women are yet another untapped resource for peacemaking.[22] This would not be a simple management-coordination function; the expectation of and requirement for strict ethical behaviour, confidentiality, aspirations for success and objectivity, combined with transparency, progress, urgency, validity, timing and security, demand extraordinarily perceptive and sensitive coordination and pre-enquiry orientation for all involved.

Some Other Options

High-level connections may be employed to look at hosting negotiations in another country. Cambodia, for example, has some understanding of and empathy for Nepal's situation, in that Cambodia

Figure 6.8
Simplified Schema of a Coordinated Trans-Stakeholder Approach

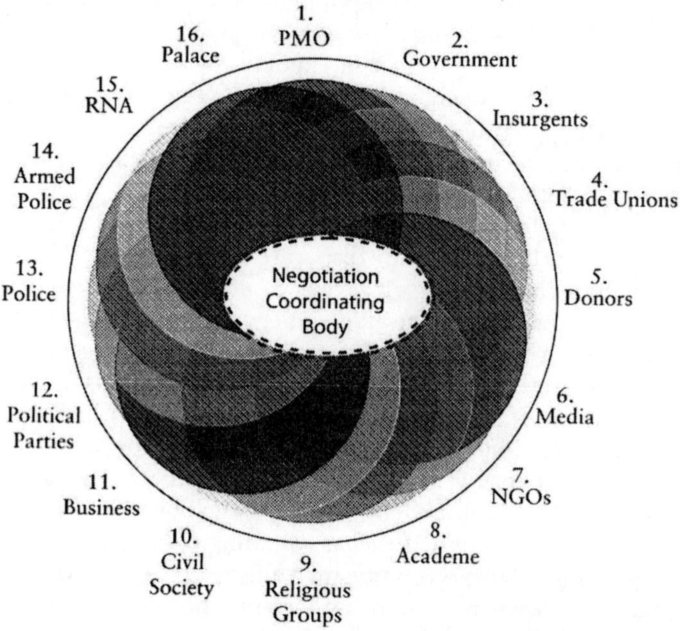

itself is a monarchy that has had fierce communist altercations. The mediator, if any be used, could still be Nepali; only the venue would be 'neutral'.

Conclusion: 'Ke Garne?'

There are scores of active conflicts around the world resulting in millions of deaths. By taking examples of successful resolutions from history, assiduously applying those to Nepal's internal issues, resolving the internal conflict bringing peace and good governance to this land, other countries will respect Nepal for its efforts—and the expertise of Nepali arbitrators would be in demand.

Presently, this author is confident that the prominent adversaries still have sufficient flexibility to be willing to compromise with the aim of resolving the insurgency and bringing relief to the citizenry; after all, as the author had publicly noted,[23] there are good and honorable people on all sides. But if the process is delayed, the Maoists would become more entrenched, stronger and less willing to compromise; and the general population would have many more people with family or friends caught in the physical or psychological crossfire, leading to an increase in vindictiveness.

All stakeholders are urged to use their connections and influence to push for negotiation. While any negotiation or mediation is an internal affair, it is also possible to improve the chances of negotiation through better preparation.

One may query the time parameters required to progressively and systematically work with disparate groups in the 'shadows': might it take three years, or seven? It could be less ... or even longer. This ought not be an impediment to trying, nor need it be thought of as a pessimistically long-time frame. Why? Because striving towards meaningful negotiations and resolutions under the current state of affairs has already taken 11 years, without bearing any fruit. Considering the activities of insurgent groups around the Indian subcontinent over the past 40 years,[24] the prognosis is not too optimistic for traditional initiatives. If each of us in our particular social position thinks of the surrounding context only vis-à-vis our own delimited responsibility and selfishly exaggerated elements that make our own role more important, then rational thinking, analysis and pro-active behaviour will remain confounded (Stagner 1967). And traditional bilateral[25] negotiations are passé—even if the two sides agree to negotiate: that modality is akin to the typical donor-government project contract, in which all arrangements for the project components, such as a village water system and supply, are agreed upon bilaterally. Only later do the locals ask why the tank was built at a particular location, why the only involvement of the locals was physical labour and why it doesn't work outside of the monsoon season!

Recriminations must also stop, if reconciliation is the aim. It has become increasingly impossible to distinguish between the guilty and the innocent. Each of the major adversaries needs moral superiority as a condition of winning; yet this is wanting. Comminatory vindictiveness often leads to selective justice and a biased morality should be rejected. We need a new paradigm for analysing, being proactive and reacting to the complexity of the conflict. 'In a changing world approaches and methods for achieving peace must also change' (Bondevik 2004). This author's recommended holistic TSA modality takes longer and requires interdisciplinary coordination, but it would elicit more buy-ins for any resolutions. Further delays in decisive and effective support shall result in more death and destruction and the unravelling of an admirable society. In order to be unequivocally justifiable from a moral standpoint, the conflagration must result in more lives being saved from starvation, disease and misery than are lost in the course of changing political power.

Lastly, South Asian neighbours beware! The current post-April 2006 interlude is but a lull: the reluctance to disarm,[26] the flow of arms and ideology[27] and the compulsive interference by donors[28] continues to destabilize the government of Nepal and fuel the protraction of secessionist and revolutionary efforts throughout the region.

Epilogue

> If I am not for myself, who is for me, but if I am just for my own self, what am I? And if not now, when? (Mishnah 14, lst-3rd century C.E.)

Notes

1. The author has been conducting personal discussions in Nepal from the perspective of one who himself has been a refugee, has worked in several international conflict environments, has since 1976 (2033 v.s.) worked many years in Nepal and has trustworthy connections with and has earned confidence of several stakeholder groups within all levels of Nepali society. Since 2002, his discussions with representatives of the UN, government and various peace-building agencies have revealed misconceptions and/or selfish motives for many trying to get involved in the Nepali context.
2. Author's personal observations and discussions in multiple districts, 2002–05.
3. Round One: 30 August 2001 at Godavari; 13–14 September 2001 at Thakurdwar, Bardiya; 9 November 2001 at Godavari. Round Two: 27 April, 1 May, 9 May, 3 July, 11 July and 17 August 2003. Round Three, agreed to on 4 May 2006 and started 26 May at Gokarna Forest Golf Resort and Spa remained inconclusive as of 10 June 2006.
4. Prime Minister from 1995–97, 2001–02, and 2 June 2004–1 February 2005. He had a sincere intent to reconstitute a peaceful nation.
5. This, indeed, happened (the topic is confidential at this time).
6. An indigenous form of bilateral social negotiation, usually with a love theme.
7. It was instructive that when this author confidentially discussed these efforts with the Canadian government representative in Kathmandu (who had expressed 'sincere interest') from the perspective of the Canadian government possibly

supporting sustained efforts, the consul affirmed this to be 'excellent progress', encouraged more talks and then asked to personally meet the Maoist delegates at the consulate. When it was pointed out that police on Lazimpat and security at the consulate may intimidate, if not actually try to apprehend, my high-level contacts and that the process didn't depend on an expansion of contacts with diplomats, the consul's interest dissipated (and this author refused to accede to such demands). This demonstrated an obvious preoccupation of the Canadians with the cachet of being able to meet high-level Maoists without serious consideration of supporting a workable process outside of the limelight. The reason the Canadians were approached to begin with was that they were considered 'understanding' by Maoists and the government alike, due to their empathy with regimes and governments shunned by the US (such as Nicaragua, Cuba and North Korea). At follow-up meetings in Ottawa, it was clarified that 'off the record, we do not have any interest in Nepal, one reason being the pressure from the Americans for increasing our role in Iraq' (Meeting with Canada, Department of Foreign Affairs at Headquarters in Ottawa, Canada, 2002). This opportunity for involvement and possible beneficial influence at a relatively early stage was, therefore, squandered.

8. There are many examples, within just the past century, of superior forces being overwhelmed: the Moscow Insurrection, 1905; the Bolshevik Uprising, 1917; the German Revolution, 1918; the Sinn Fein Revolt, 1918–19; the Franco Rebellion, 1936–39; the Vietnam War, 1956–75; the Soviets in Afghanistan, seventies and eighties, and so on.
9. Personal communication from high-level authorities.
10. By this author, in multiple districts, November–December 2004.
11. 'The king is trapped in a conspiracy,' explains retired Brigadier-General Dipta Prakash Shah. 'To hide one mistake, the royal courtiers are making a thousand mistakes' (Dixit 2005).
12. A new ordinance reported on 17 August 2005 in 'Nepal: New NGO Law Spells End of Autonomy, Say Activists', says that the semi-autonomous SWC has already come under the direct control of the Ministry of Women, Children and Social Welfare, whose minister Durga Shrestha sacked senior members of the SWC and replaced them all with her own handpicked team. Available at: http:\\www.irinnews.org/print.asp?ReportID=48618.
13. Sanjaya Dhakal 'Operation Reconstruction'. *Spotlight* 25 (40), 9 June 2006 (Jestha 26, 2063 B.S.). Available at: http:\\www.nepalnews.com.np/contents/2006/englishweekly/spotlight/jun/jun09/coverstory.php.
14. 'We amassed weapons with our ideas—Pravakar, Deputy Commander, PLA'; 9 June 2006; Interview. Available at: http:\\focus.blogsome.com/2006/06/09/we-amassed-weapons-with-our-ideas-pravakar-deputy-commander-pla/.
15. Personal observation and communication. However, this is supported even by communists: 'I was very struck by the composition of the PLA squads and platoons. They were overwhelmingly made up of those on the very bottom of society—lower castes, ethnic minorities, peasant youth and many, many young women (Onesto 2005).

16. This is in contrast to Anne de Sales 'The "people's army" is organized in such a way that the fighters in any one district come from outside it.' *European Bulletin of Himalayan Research* (Autumn), 2000. But this aspect varies over time, location and circumstance. She says 'always'; this author does not.
17. Insightful details available in Lawoti (2005).
18. One recent note is from the president of the Rastriya Prajatantra Party, Pashupati SJB Rana, warning against foreign intervention. Available at: http:\\www.nepalnews.com/archive/2005/dec/dec26/news02.php.
19. See, Sangeeta Thapliyal, 'Maoists in Nepal', *The Hindu*, 18 December 2001. Available at: http:\\www.hinduonnet.com/thehindu/2001/12/18/stories/2001121801321000.htm.
20. Question to me during interview; his answer: '*Kunni*' (How should I know?).
21. The others options are: (*a*) the unitary stakeholder approach (USA); (*b*) the multi-stakeholder approach (MSA); (*c*) the pluri-stakeholder approach (PSA); and (*d*) the inter-stakeholder approach (ISA).
22. See, Antonia Potter, 'We the Women: Why Conflict Mediation is Not Just a Job for Men'. Geneva. Centre for Humanitarian Dialogue. Available at: http:\\www.hdcentre.org/?aid=166.
23. Interviewed in Nepali on Metro FM 106.7, Kathmandu on a special programme 'Conflict in Nepal', 12 December 2004; rebroadcast on 18 December 2004.
24. In Kashmir, Andhra Pradesh, Bihar and Jharkhand (the Naxalites), Bodoland, Nagaland, Meghalaya, Mizoram, Assam, north-west Bengal (the GNLF), Maharashtra, Madhya Pradesh, eastern Uttar Pradesh, Chhattisgarh, western Orissa and Sri Lanka, for example.
25. A recent article even refers to a 'triangular struggle' among the government, insurgents and political parties. See, 'Heat on the King', *The Economist*, 376 8443: 10–16 September 2005.
26. See, Somini Sengupta, 'Nepal Rebel Vows Not to Disarm Before Vote on Charter', *The New York Times*, 21 May 2006.
27. See, *People's News*, 'Indian Maoists Encouraged from Nepalese Maoists' Success', Kathmandu, 8 May.
28. See, Devendra Raj Pandey, 'Democracy, Donors and Diplomats'. Available at: http:\\www.kantipuronline.com/kolnews.php?&nid=72415.

References

Acharya, Madhu Raman. 2005. 'Nepal has Contributed 50,000 Peacekeepers to UN: Acharya', nepalnews.com, 23 October 2005, at: www.nepalnews.com/archive/2005/oct/oct23/news01.php.

Bondevik, Kjell Magne. 2004. 'Peace Mediators' Retreat'. Speech made at Oslo, Norway, 10 June.

Chevalier, Jacques. 2001. *Stakeholder Analysis and Natural Resource Management*. Ottawa: Carleton University. Available at: http:\\www.aiatsis.gov.au/rsrch/ntru/ifamp/practice/pdfs/Chevalier_2001.pdf.

Chorley, K.C. 1943. *Armies and the Art of Revolution*, p. 78. London: Faber and Faber.

Collier, Paul and Anke Hoeffler. 2002. 'Violent Conflict in the Past 10 Years,' in *Greed and Grievance in Civil War*, pp. 1, 2, 5, 9, 10, 11, 13, 17, 26–28, 30. World Bank: Development Research Group.

van Creveld, Martin. 2005. 'Everything they did Seemed to be Wrong. If they let the (insurgents) kill them, they were idiots. If they attacked the (insurgents), they were seen as killers. The effect, in nearly every case, is demoralization and breakdown of discipline.' In, Dexter Filkins, 'The Fall of the Warrior King', *The New York Times*, 23 October, 2005. Available at: http://www.nytimes.com/ 2005/10/23/ magazine/23sassaman.html?pagewanted=all.

Dhakal, Sanjaya. 2006. 'Operation Reconstruction', *Spotlight* 25 (40: 9 June 2006 or Jestha 26, 2063 B.S.). Available at: http:\\www.nepalnews.com.np/contents/ 2006/englishweekly/spotlight/jun/jun09/coverstory.php.

Dixit, Kunda. 2005. 'The Royal Trek: King Gyanendra does the Patan Walkabout', *Nepali Times*, e-Special, 23–29 September. Available at: http:\\www.nepalitimes. com/issue266/headline.htm.

Friedrich-Ebert-Stiftung (FES). 2005. Available at: http:\\www.nepaldemocracy.org/ institutions/political_parties.htm.

Hatton, J., M. Couto and J. Oglethorpe. 2001. *Biodiversity and War: A Case Study from Mozambique*. Washington, DC: Biodiversity Support Program.

Kievelitz, Uwe, Tara Polzer and Debendra Manandhar. 2001. *Nepal Country Study on Conflict Transformation and Peace Building*. Kathmandu: German Development Cooperation.

Kissinger, Henry. 1969. *Foreign Affairs* January: 211–12.

Lawoti, Mahendra. 2005. *Towards a Democratic Nepal*, p. 58. New Delhi: Sage Publications.

Lewis, C.S. 1961. *An Experiment in Criticism*, pp. 137, 139. London: Cambridge University Press.

Locke, John. 1924 (1960). *Of Civil Government*, pp. 165, 231. New York: E.P. Dutton.

Madden, Edward H. and Peter H. Hare. 1970. 'Reflections on Civil Disobedience', *The Journal of Value Enquiry* 4 (2): 87.

Maruyama, Magoroh. 1974. 'Paradigmatology and its Application to Cross-Disciplinary, Cross-Professional and Cross-Cultural Communication', *Dialectica* 28 (3–4).

Max-Neef, Manfred A. 2005. *Foundations of Transdisciplinarity*. Available at: http:\\www.sciencedirect.com/science/article/B6VDY-4FNW4S2–3/2/ 651916c13 354d7f43067072ebf277781.

Molnar, Andrew R. 1965. *Human Factors Considerations of Undergrounds in Insurgencies*, pp. 71–73. Washington, DC: Special Operations Research Office, The American University.

Morgenthau, Hans J. 1946. *Scientific Man vs. Power Politics*. Chicago: University of Chicago Press.

Onesto, Li. 2005. 'Telling Lies in Kathmandu', *Revolution* 7 (26 June): 12.

Patil, Shivraj. 2005. 'Maoists from Nepal and India Providing Training to Each Other', *nepalnews.com*, 21 December. Available at: http:\\www.nepalnews.com/ archive/2005/dec/dec21/news15.php.

Potter, Antonia. n.d. 'We the Women: Why Conflict Mediation is Not Just a Job for Men', Geneva: Centre for Humanitarian Dialogue. Available at: http:\\www.hdcentre.org/?aid=166.

Samay. 2005. 'Maoist Expansion', *Nepali Times eSpecial*, 1 December. Available at: http:\\www.nepalitimes.com/issue275/fromthenepalipress.htm#6.

Sengupta, Somini. 2006. 'Nepal Rebel Vows Not to Disarm Before Vote on Charter', *The New York Times*, 21 May.

Shrestha, Bal Gopal. 2003. *Ethnic Nationalism in Nepal*. IIASN Newsletter #30 March. Available at: http:\\www.iias.nl/iiasn/30/IIASNL30_22.pdf.

Shrestha, Chuda Bahadur. 2004. *Nepal: Coping with Maoist Insurgency*. Kathmandu: Chetana Lokshum.

Somlai, Ivan Gyozo. 1992 (second edition, revised and expanded). *Fancy Footwork: Entrapment in and Coping with the Nepali Management Model*. Kathmandu: Ratna Pustak Bhandar.

Stagner, Ross. 1967. *Psychological Aspects of International Conflict*, p. 126. Belmont: Brooks/Cole.

The Telegraph. 2003. Kathmandu, Wednesday, 27 August.

World Bank. 2003. Conflict Analysis Framework Draft, 26 August, 2003 (p. 7, note 8; and p. 5) Social Development Department, World Bank.

Yogi, Bhagirath. 2002. 'Cost of Insurgency', *New Business Age* (May).

Additional Reading

Bhattarai, Baburam. 2003. *The Nature of Underdevelopment and Regional Structure of Nepal: A Marxist Analysis*. New Delhi: Adroit Publishers.

Hutt, Michael (ed.). 2004. *Himalayan People's War: Nepal's Maoist Rebellion*. Bloomington and Indianapolis: Indiana University Press.

Karki, Arjun and David Seddon (eds). 2003. *The People's War in Nepal (Left Perspectives)*. New Delhi: Adroit Publishers.

Muni, S.D. 2003. *Maoist Insurgency in Nepal: the Challenge and the Response*. New Delhi: Rupa & Co. with Observer Research Foundation.

Ogura, Kiyoko. 2001. *Kathmandu Spring: The Peoples' Movement of 1990*. Lalitpur: Himal Books.

Onesto, Li. 2005. *Dispatches from the People's War in Nepal*. London: Pluto Press.

Raj, Prakash A. 2004. *Maoists in the Land of Buddha: An Analytical Study of the Maoist Insurgency in Nepal*. Kathmandu: Nirala Publications.

Sapkota, Bishnu (ed.). 2004. *The Costs of War in Nepal: A Research Study*. Kathmandu: National Peace Campaign.

Thapa, Deepak (ed.). 2003. *Understanding the Maoist Movement of Nepal*. Kathmandu: Martin Chautari.

Thapa, Deepak and Bandira Sijapati. 2003. *A Kingdom Under Siege: Nepal's Maoist Insurgency*, 1996 to 2003. Kathmandu: The Printhouse.

Upreti, Bishnu Raj. 2004. *The Price of Neglect: From Resource Conflict to Maoist Insurgency in the Himalayan Kingdom*. Kathmandu: Bhrikuti Academic Publications.

PART III

Identity Politics

7

Between Political Party and Social Movement: The Mongol National Organization and Democratization in Rural East Nepal

Susan Hangen

Since the restoration of a multiparty system in 1990, identity politics has become a major force in Nepali politics. Low-caste Hindus, known as Dalits; caste and ethnic groups, who are called Madhesis, hailing from Nepal's southern region, the Terai, and ethnic groups who now call themselves indigenous nationalities, or Adibasi Janajati, have mobilized to demand greater inclusion within the political system as well as social and cultural rights. They argue that high-caste Hindus from the hills have monopolized the state since its inception in the late eighteenth century, and that this created political, economic and social disadvantages for other groups of people. To address these problems, all of these marginalized groups have formed social-movement organizations, and both the Madhesis and the indigenous nationalities have formed political parties as well. These parties include the Madhesi party called the Nepal Sadbhavana Party (NSP) and several parties representing the indigenous nationalities: the Rastriya Janamukti Party (RJP), the Mongol National Organization (MNO), and a few regional liberation fronts such as the Limbuwan Mukti Morcha and the Khambuwan Mukti Morcha.

This chapter investigates how one of these ethnic parties, the MNO, contributed towards the process of democratization in rural east Nepal in the 1990s.[1] 'Democratization' here refers to the process of establishing a political system that employs the procedures and institutions associated with electoral politics and upholds a set of political ideals and values (Dahl 1971; Held 1996). The increasing capacity of citizens to influence public policy through a wide variety of civic and political organizations is also a key part of the process of democratization (Schmitter and Karl 1996).

This chapter examines how the MNO contributed to these components of democratization by analysing the types of political activities that the MNO undertook and the political meanings and effects of these activities. I ask why this party engaged in certain activities while refraining from others and compare the MNO's activities to those of the mainstream political parties and ethnic social-movement organizations. This chapter aims to illuminate some of the limitations on and possibilities for creating social and political changes in rural Nepal during this era.

Ethnic parties in Nepal, such as the MNO, have received little scholarly attention, with a few exceptions (Lawoti 2005; Lecomte-Tilouine 2004), primarily because they are minor players in the political system. Minor political parties are often ignored in political analyses that are primarily concerned with understanding the most powerful actors. However, as Hanna Herzog (1987) argues, minor parties are relevant for understanding the boundaries of political cultures and how they change. Examining these parties can reveal what kinds of ideologies are excluded or included in the legitimate political culture and can increase 'our knowledge about potential change, about challenging groups and ideas, and about rejected alternatives' (ibid.: 318). Had scholars of Nepal paid more attention to minor parties, perhaps the Maoist insurgency, which began through a minor political party, would not have been so unexpected. An examination of minor ethnic political parties can thus help us understand the boundaries of Nepal's political culture after 1990.

Ethnic parties in Nepal have also been overlooked because political parties are usually assessed in terms of how they perform in campaigns, elections and governments. Ethnic parties have not fared well at the polls when compared with other political parties, as

I shall discuss later. However, the significance of ethnic parties is not limited to their election results.

Ethnic parties often engage in activities that are typically associated with social-movement organizations. Unlike political parties, social-movement organizations do not seek to gain direct political power; rather, they define, raise awareness about and mobilize support for a particular cluster of social issues. While the goals and political strategies of ethnic parties are different from those of social movements due to their participation in elections, they share a commitment to ending ethnic inequality. Like social movements, ethnic parties also engage a wide range of people in the political process of debating, discussing and working for social change. Ethnic parties have introduced and spread new ideologies, constructed identities and presented discursive challenges to the dominant political system, as this chapter demonstrates. Highlighting the overlap between ethnic political parties and social movements that to some extent may exist for all parties, it argues that scholars could gain new understandings of political parties by examining a broader range of political-party activities.

In the context of Nepal, it is not particularly surprising to suggest that political parties should act like social-movement organizations. After all, most political parties 'evolved as movement organizations' (Hachhethu 2002: 183) as they were not allowed to operate openly as parties. Political parties spearheaded many of the major political changes in Nepal, from the overthrow of the Rana family's autocratic rule in 1950 to the institution of a multiparty system in 1990. They continued to play this role through the 1990s and have led the current efforts to restore democracy after February 2005, as Snellinger's study (see Chapter 11 of this volume) of student movements within major political parties also illustrates. Indeed, people in Nepal expect political parties to act as agents of social change (Hachhethu 2005: 162).

Rethinking the boundary between political parties and social movements can bring insights into the role of ethnic political parties in the process of democratization. Although ethnic parties frequently emerge in new democracies, political scientists and governments alike have often regarded ethnic parties as impeding democratization, as they encourage people to vote on the basis of narrow, ascribed identities (Horowitz 1985). However, other scholars suggest that ethnic parties may play a positive role in the democratization process, by making the party system more representative of the full population and expanding political participation (Madrid 2005). By examining how ethnic parties operate like social movements, we can recognize additional ways in which these parties contribute to democratization.

Acting like social-movement organizations, these parties play many of the same roles in the democratization process that scholars and international donors attribute to civil society. Scholars and analysts have celebrated the potential of and necessity for a robust civil society to consolidate democracy in Nepal and in other new democracies. They view a strong civil society as the key to creating and sustaining a democratic system on the grounds that civil society can keep the authoritarian tendencies of the state in check, provide a space for people to engage in debates and discussions on issues of public concern, and instil democratic values such as tolerance and justice in citizens. Identifying and developing civil-society organizations became a key aim of donor countries involved in efforts to democratize Nepal and other new democracies (Carothers 1999; Tamang 2002).

In order to track the process of democratization in Nepal, it is imperative to not focus exclusively on civil-society organizations, but rather to examine all existing forms of associations, including small political parties. As Seira Tamang argues, 'A focus upon civil society may be obscuring the breadth and significance of other forms of participatory and political activity in Nepal—other forms of politics which may lead to alternative and more effective forms of democracy' (2002: 343). I suggest that small ethnic political parties such as the MNO exemplify one such form of political activity.

When analysing democratization in rural Nepal, it may be particularly counterproductive to emphasize the role of civil-society organizations while ignoring the roles of other types of organizations. NGOs, often revered by the international community as the ideal type of civil-society organizations, deliver services in much of the rural Nepal; but only occasionally do rural residents plan and execute these activities. In villages in Ilam district, I observed more popular participation in political parties such as the MNO than in any NGO.

The MNO is based in rural Nepal, unlike larger mainstream parties and civil-society organizations that are centred in Kathmandu, the capital city, and extend into the rural areas. Many scholars have lamented the lack of studies on politics in rural Nepal, which could offer insights into the growth of the Maoist insurgency and the ways the multiparty system functions outside of the capital (Gellner 2002: 25; Hachhethu 2002; Pfaff-Czarnecka 2004). Ethnic parties represent one distinct forum through which people in rural Nepal have attempted to create social change by working through the established political framework.

In the following sections, I examine the goals and political activities of the MNO as a way of understanding the changing political culture and the ways in which democratization was taking place in rural east Nepal. I show how this minor ethnic party, which advocated radical change and promoted the interests of Mongols, nonetheless participated in the process of democratization.

The MNO's Goals

The MNO was founded in 1989 by Gopal Gurung, one of the first and most influential writers to discuss ethnic discrimination.[2] After the reintroduction of multiparty politics in 1990, people in eastern Nepal who were familiar with Gurung's writings and had heard about the MNO began to mobilize support for the party. After 1990, the MNO began to mobilize support in two districts, Ilam and Jhapa, in eastern Nepal. Rural areas in these districts formed the MNO's stronghold.

The party seeks to unite and represent more than 60 linguistically and culturally diverse ethnic groups, defining them as members of a Mongol race.[3] Mongols, the MNO argues, comprise 80 per cent of Nepal's population, while the dominant group, the Hindus, form only 20 per cent. The party thus claims that it represents the majority group. The party aims to increase political power for Mongols and end ethnic inequities by instituting radical changes in Nepal's political structure, such as establishing a system of federal states, instituting a system of reservations for Mongols in the government and education system, abolishing the Hindu monarchy and redefining Nepal as a secular, rather than Hindu, state.

While the MNO seeks to transform the structure of the state, it clearly supports the continuation of a multiparty democracy. MNO activists argue that they are working to strengthen democracy, which has not yet been realized in its true form because of the Hindu monarchy and the Hindu bias of the state (Hangen 2001). The MNO does not aim to prevent high-caste Hindus from holding positions in the government; rather, they want to create a political system in which there would be greater opportunities for Mongols to participate in the government. To this end, they call for the proportional representation of Mongols in all government offices. They also propose ending the constitutional monarchy, which they see as supporting high-caste Hindu political dominance and limiting democracy, and establishing a republic. Furthermore, they advocate creating state structures that would support multiculturalism, such as a federal system of states in which ethnic languages would be used and supported by the state.

Participation in Elections

While advocating radical transformations in the political system, the MNO has upheld and strengthened the procedures of democracy by taking part in the election system. MNO candidates ran in every national and local election held during the 1990s. However, the MNO did not have official status as a political party because ethnic parties were banned, although other political parties became legal after 1990. According to the 1990 Constitution, any parties that were 'formed ... on the basis of religion, community, caste, tribe or region' could not receive recognition or registration from the Election Commission (HMG 1990).[4] The MNO is presently the only political party that continued to participate in elections despite being denied registration on this basis. The regional liberation fronts boycotted elections, while the Rastriya Janamukti Party and the Nepal Sadbhavana Party managed to secure registration by not referring to the community they sought to represent in their party names and by defining this community in broad, inclusive terms in their party manifestos. The MNO, however, refused to consider changing its party name or disguising its platform, and was denied registration by the Election Commission. Thus, MNO candidates could only appear on the ballot as 'independent' candidates.

Furthermore, while the large national parties receive election symbols that they maintain permanently, minor parties such as the MNO have no permanent election symbols. These issues limited the capacity of voters to recognize and cast votes for MNO candidates.

Despite these limitations, the MNO participated in elections and achieved a modest degree of success. In each of the three parliamentary elections held in 1991, 1994 and 1999, the MNO candidates ran for election in Ilam and Jhapa districts. The party was most successful in Ilam, where at least one candidate came in third place in every election, just behind two of the large national parties, the Nepali Communist Party (UML) and the Nepali Congress Party (NCP), beating out another large party, the Rastriya Prajatantra Party (RPP). However, it did not win any parliamentary seats. Further, as illustrated in Table 7.1, between 1991 and 1999, the MNO received progressively fewer votes.

Table 7.1
Votes for MNO Candidates in Parliamentary Elections

		Ilam District Results		*Jhapa District Results*	
Year	*Constituency*	*Votes*	*%*	*Votes*	*%*
1991	1	2,519	5.14		
	2	6,019	12.77		
1994	1	1,611	4.77		
	2	2,396	7.49	383	0.91
	3	3,403	10.19	525	1.37
1999	1	496	1.20		
	2	693	1.71	361	0.66
	3	2,321	5.72	1,098	2.08

Sources: Election Commission (1992, 1994 and 1999) and interviews with MNO members.[5]

This progressive decline suggests that voters were becoming increasingly discouraged with the fact that votes for candidates who did not win were a waste. Nepal's electoral system works to the disadvantage of small parties like the ethnic parties. Nepal employs a 'first part the post' electoral system, in which seats are allotted to the individuals who win the most votes, rather than a proportional electoral system, which would allot seats to parties according to the proportion of votes that they receive overall (Lawoti 2005: 264–65).

As people became more familiar with how the electoral system worked, they saw that MNO candidates did not have a realistic chance of winning parliamentary seats when compared with national-level parties that had formed governments, held seats or were at least registered. Thus, people may have become more sceptical about the possibility of elections achieving the goals of their party, rather than less supportive of its ethnic political platform.

In local elections, the MNO was far more successful than it was in the national elections, particularly in Ilam district (see Table 7.2). Here, in 1992, MNO candidates were elected in 24 out of 47 village governments, called village development committees (VDCs), and won the majority of the posts, including the chair and vice chair seats, in two of these VDCs. In 1997, however, MNO candidates were elected in only 19 VDCs, though they retained the majority in the two villages where they had established it. Thus votes for MNO candidates decreased in local elections as well.

Table 7.2
Votes for MNO Candidates in Local Elections in Ilam District

Year	*Number of VDCs Where Seats Won*	*Total Number of Seats Won/Total VDC Seats*	*Total Seats Won (%)*
1992	24	57/423	13.47
1997	19	123/2,209	5.5

Sources: Election Commission (1992 and 1997) and interviews with MNO members.[6]

This decline reflects a nationwide trend in the local elections: across Nepal, the ruling Nepali Communist Party (United Marxist Leninist), or the NCP-UML, won over 50 per cent of the seats in VDCs (Hachhethu 2005: 166). This decline can also be explained by people's increasing understanding of the new political system, with regard to the limited role of village governments in the new system. Despite the government's support for the concept of decentralization, VDCs have little power or autonomy. The capacity of the elected officials in VDCs to bring resources to the village depends on their networks with elected officials and bureaucrats at the district centre, who are all members of the mainstream political parties. MNO candidates were thus thwarted in their capacity to secure resources from the centre.

Among the ethnic parties, the MNO was not alone in its poor performance at the polls: the RJP also failed to secure any seats in the Parliament, despite having registration and 82 candidates in 36 districts in 1994 (Gurung 2003: 153). Only the NSP won a few seats in the Parliament: six seats in 1991, three seats in 1994 and five seats in 1999 (Lawoti 2005: 69). This party grew out of a long social movement and sought to mobilize voters on a regional identity rather than an ethnic identity (ibid.: 70–71).

Many analysts interpret this to mean that ethnic political parties are not viable in Nepal because voters do not support their platforms (Baral 2005: 46; Hoftun et al. 1999; de Sales 2002: 337–38). However, as Lawoti (2005) argues, the explosion of ethnic organizations after 1990 shows that ethnic issues were of concern to people, and there are many other reasons why ethnic parties did not fare well at the polls. These parties faced historical, internal and systemic challenges when competing for votes (ibid.: 69–73). First, the lack of registration and recognition from the Election Commission clearly limited the ability of ethnic parties to mobilize votes, as they were denied a consistent and common election symbol, access to media, and government campaign funds. Another factor that created obstacles for these parties is that they were established much later than the major parties, which had been working underground from 1962–90 despite being banned. As new parties, they lacked the funds and the experience of older parties. Furthermore, they had to compete with the established networks of other political parties, which had already gained loyal supporters. Elites from the ethnic groups the parties sought to mobilize were reluctant to leave parties with district- and national-level networks to join these small new parties.

Given this history and these structural constraints in the political system, it appears that ethnic parties could become more viable in Nepal if some of these factors were to change. The most important changes would be to remove the structural constraints by establishing a proportionate electoral system and removing the constitutional constraints on the registration of ethnic parties. Creating a federal system would also help ethnic parties get more power to local-level political bodies where they have more support. Comparative data from Latin America also suggests that institutional changes that serve to increase the representation of minor parties in the political system are necessary, though not sufficient, in order for the ethnic parties to become electorally viable (Van Cott 2003).

It is important to understand why ethnic parties have not fared well in elections in order to understand the potential for these parties to contribute to the process of democratization through the formal political channels. However, the significance of the MNO's participation in elections was not limited to the election results. Rather, these election activities were also a form of contentious politics. By operating as a political party and participating in elections despite its lack of registration, the MNO disobeyed state authority. In campaign speeches, MNO candidates cited the Election Commission's refusal to register their party as proof of the Hindu bias of the state and as an illustration of high-caste Hindus' dominance of the political sphere.

Part of the rationale for the MNO's participation in the elections was that it provided the party with an arena in which they could publicize their political agenda. This symbolic dimension of participation in elections is also found in the political behaviour of minor parties elsewhere in the world: minor parties participate in elections 'not so much for the purpose of winning, but rather as a means of being heard' and '...to draw attention to their grievances' (Herzog 1987: 321). Thus, within the framework of electoral politics, the MNO was acting as a social-movement organization by raising awareness about ethnic inequality.

Elections were the main forum in which the MNO could express their political position in a public sphere. Larger political parties also voice their positions through media coverage and through public political protest. Public protests, such as transportation strikes (*chakka-jam*) and closure of businesses (*bandh*), became central to political culture in Nepal during the 1990s, as Lakier discusses (see Chapter 10 of this volume). The MNO has only participated in one such protest. On 8 February 2006, the MNO called a *bandh* in Kakharbhitta, a bazaar town in Jhapa district on the eastern border of India, to protest the municipal elections called by the king and to call for establishing a republic. This was also an unusual form of action for the MNO because they coordinated with other larger political parties, all of which were also boycotting these elections, which were perceived as the king's attempt to legitimize his direct rule.

There are several reasons why the MNO has so rarely engaged in public protests. First, the MNO's support base is almost entirely in villages, away from bazaar towns and cities. Kakharbhitta, the site of the recent *bandh*, is one of the only bazaar towns in which it has any support. These public-protest tactics all rely on the existence of public, commercial space. A *bandh* would have no tangible effects in most villages in Ilam, which have no motorable roads and a commercial space, limited to a couple of tea and dry-goods' shops and itinerant vendors, that is open for business once a week. These forms of political action are ways of trying to control public space as a way of claiming and demonstrating political strength.

Second, it takes extensive support in these areas to enforce one of these protests. People comply with the orders of the party or organization that has called for the protest due to threats of violence. The MNO did not have the necessary degree of support in these bazaar towns to carry out these forms of protest.

Third, without media to publicize the events, the effects of the protest would be limited. Media coverage of these public protests is essential for the political party to gain public recognition as a powerful organization with the capacity to demand support. There is negligible coverage of rural events in print media or on radio stations, and a very limited circulation of print media in rural Nepal. The types of political activities the MNO could carry out were thus constrained by its rural basis and its lack of access to public space. Within the context of rural Nepal, participating in elections as an unregistered party was thus a reasonably effective mode of expressing dissent in a public forum.

Although the MNO challenged the state by acting as a party despite being denied registration, in other ways the party demonstrated its support for the democratic system. By partaking in elections, the MNO showed that it was willing to work within the established, legal political framework in its efforts to gain political power. Furthermore, aside from participating in elections without registration, the MNO abided by all of the government's rules for campaigning and elections, just as the mainstream, registered parties did.

The MNO also illustrated their support for the democratic system when its elected representatives served in village governments, VDCs. Significantly, these representatives did not try to obstruct the operations of a state that their party strongly criticized. They could not implement their party's grand plans, as this would require structural changes in the state. Despite lacking a party network that extended to the higher levels of the government, these elected officials tried to run the village-level offices much as individuals elected from other parties did. They resolved local conflicts and brought development to the village in the form of new health posts, schools and water taps. By having MNO candidates serving in these roles, the MNO sought to demonstrate that Mongols were capable leaders and should be widely included in the formal political process and institutions. Furthermore, they believed that winning these seats showed that there was popular support for their long-term goals and potential for the party's growth.

However, the MNO also clearly proclaims the limitations of its support for working within the legal political system. The party threatened to stage a revolution if they did not manage to gain control of the government through elections. In party documents and speeches, activists and leaders repeatedly declared that the revolution would begin 'within five years' if they did not achieve power—yet these deadlines have been perpetually postponed. The symbolism of the MNO party flag represents this dual approach to gaining power. The upper diagonal half of the rectangular flag shows a five pointed star on a blue background, standing for peaceful methods of political action, while the lower diagonal half of the flag depicts a *khukuri* (a long curved knife used by Gorkha soldiers and by villagers) on a red background, symbolizing the threat of violence and bloodshed. MNO party songs and other cultural productions also used images of violence to mobilize people. These images could refer to fighting through elections, but also could be read literally as a call to arms.

While the MNO may not have the strength or resources to use violence to take over the state, it could possibly stage a violent rebellion. First, the MNO has become less successful in elections over time, which could lead to increasing frustration with the legal political system. Second, as Lawoti argues (Chapter 1 of this volume), violence has become an increasingly central part of the political culture and discourse in Nepal. There have been many small-scale incidents of political violence in the country's history. The Khambuwan National Front launched an ethnic insurgency in 1997. The success of the Maoist insurgency in gaining political power and in curtailing the operations of the state will make violent political tactics more appealing to the MNO and other groups.

After the Maoist insurgency began in 1996, the MNO established a Mongol Liberation Army (Mongol Mukti Sena). This army appears to exist in so much as it publishes and signs occasional communiqués; however, it has not taken any violent action. Despite their representations and threats of violence, the MNO continues to support democratic methods.

In sum, given the party's relatively short history and lack of financial resources and registration, the MNO has had considerable success in elections, managing to gain control of several village governments in its stronghold of Ilam district and often receiving the third most votes in national elections in that district. Clearly, participating in electoral politics as an unregistered party has limited effectiveness as a strategy to gain political power. Nonetheless, elections provided a public forum on which the MNO could announce its political position and challenge the state. Elections, however, are not the only way that the party participates in the democratization process.

Expanding Political Participation

Membership in the MNO is limited to those individuals who can identify themselves racially and culturally as Mongols, thus excluding high-caste and low-caste Hindus.[7] The MNO's mobilization and promotion of an exclusive identity as the basis for a political community would, for many scholars, disqualify the organization from making any positive contributions towards democracy. However, ethnic-based associations, depending on their aims and functions, have the potential to perform the functions of civil-society associations, and have effectively done so in societies with long histories of ethnic discrimination (Varshney 2002: 42–43). Caste associations in India have played a similar role, expanding democratic structures and procedures in rural India through the locally meaningful rubric of caste (Rudolph and Rudolph 1960). Even though its membership policies were exclusive, as was the constituency that the party sought to benefit, the MNO works in other ways to strengthen the democratic system.

While its membership criteria are exclusive, the MNO is in some ways more inclusive than the large mainstream political parties. In particular, it expands opportunities for political leadership among ethnic groups and in rural areas. According to Larry Diamond (1996), this is one of the crucial roles that civil-society organizations can play in democratization 'where the recruitment of new political leaders within the established political parties has become narrow or stagnant' (ibid.: 233). Yet minor political parties such as the MNO can play this role as well as civil-society organizations.

The leadership recruitment and training patterns of the large political parties do appear narrow and stagnant. The mainstream political parties give high-caste Hindus the majority of opportunities to contest elections and to serve in party leadership positions (Lawoti 2005). The MNO facilitates greater participation in the political system for people from a wider range of ethnic groups, giving them the opportunity to participate in every level of the party.

The MNO is also inclusive in that it recruits leaders and activists, as well as supporters, from rural rather than urban areas. Large mainstream political parties like the NCP operate in a centralized fashion: they are based in urban Nepal and their networks extend outwards to the rural districts and villages. Candidates for national elections and party leaders are recruited in the urban centres. By contrast, the MNO's stronghold is in the rural villages of Ilam and Jhapa, and it gained only scattered support in bazaar towns in these districts. Aside from Gopal Gurung, the party founder and president, and a few other individuals, the MNO has no supporters in the capital city, Kathmandu.

With its rural base and its support for the politically marginalized ethnic groups, the party often gives leadership opportunities to people who lacked previous experience in politics. This is partly by default rather than by design: as a new, small, rural political party, the MNO is not able to secure resources and rewards for those involved. Joining the MNO simply does not connect people with a powerful extended network the way joining the NCP or NCP-UML does. Thus few people who have political experience and already belong to the network of a large political party are willing to give up those benefits and tie their fortunes to this unregistered party with a radical ethnic platform.[8] As a result, the

MNO recruits individuals who might not otherwise have been party activists and leaders.

Certainly, many of the typical participants in any form of village politics in Nepal were actively involved in the party: activists included ex-Gorkha soldiers, sons of former Panchayat leaders, and young people who had passed their school-leaving certificate (SLC) exams and yet could not gain employment or go on to further studies. Yet unlike the mainstream parties, the MNO was not established on college campuses and thus could not rely on college students as a source of activists who would eventually become leaders (Snellinger, Chapter 11 of this volume). In general, it is likely that MNO activists and leaders were not as educated as those in larger parties.

Several prominent district-level leaders were not educated beyond elementary or middle school and were not raised in elite political families. For example, MNO activists taught an unmarried, 30-year-old Rai woman with only a few years of education to give speeches. When she was not helping her family sell liquor and snacks from their one-room thatched house during the weekly market, she was frequently involved in party activities: she spoke at mass meetings throughout Ilam and Jhapa, attended meetings with other MNO activists and taught younger women of her village to give speeches. The general secretary of the party during the mid-1990s was from a similar background—a Limbu farmer who had studied only to the fifth grade. Both of these individuals travelled throughout Ilam and Jhapa and were known by MNO supporters for their passionate speeches, which brought new people into the party.

Individuals with this level of education and from these ethnic groups often participate at the village level of large political parties. However, it is unlikely that they would have become prominent district-level leaders in those parties. Thus, the MNO has contributed to democratization by expanding political participation by recruiting a wider range of individuals for leadership positions.

Discursive Challenges

In addition to contributing to the democratization process through its participation in the formal political arena, the MNO has also issued important challenges to the dominant political discourse. Prior to 1990, ethnic political issues were outside the boundaries of legitimate political discourse. For example, the MNO's founder and president Gopal Gurung was jailed for publishing a book that articulated ethnic grievances (Gurung 1985). Even in the early 1990s, people were often hesitant to mention the existence of ethnic inequality in front of high-caste Hindus. The MNO, along with other ethnic organizations, has played an important role in bringing demands for ethnic equality to the forefront of the political discourse. The MNO encouraged people in rural Nepal to discuss and debate these ideas and to work together to make demands on the state. Scholars have interpreted these types of activities as fundamental ways in which civil society can strengthen democracy (Diamond 1996; Edwards 2004). This further illustrates how the MNO's activities overlap with those of social movements and other civil-society organizations.

In addition to challenging the limits of legitimate political discourse, the MNO also opposed the way that the state defined the political community of the nation. The MNO does not question the existence of a Nepali nation; rather it asserts that the cultural markers of national identity should not be limited to those of the high-caste Hindus. The party aims to reverse the state's Panchayatera efforts to create a homogenous nation of Nepali-speaking Hindus, and argues that the state should support multiple cultures and languages. By altering the definition of the nation, they seek to extend the boundaries of the political community to include marginalized ethnic groups.

One way in which the MNO revises Nepali nationalism is through recounting a Mongol history in speeches, songs, plays and calendars. According to this history, Mongols had once ruled Nepal before high-caste Hindus, who originally came from India, conquered them. Since losing their sovereignty, Mongols have endured centuries of oppression under high-caste Hindu rulers. This history challenges the dominant nationalist narrative of Nepali history that depicts high-caste Hindu kings as nationalist heroes who united the country. It is also central to the MNO's justification of their political project, framed as an effort to restore this former political power to Mongols.

The MNO's use of the racial term 'Mongols' also presents a discursive challenge to the state (Hangen 2005b). By identifying their community as a racially united block of Mongols, the MNO and its supporters explicitly contest the state's categorization of their people as divided into castes or ethnic groups.[9] The MNO's presentation of Nepal's population in racial terms was initially unfamiliar to people in rural east Nepal: as many people remarked, 'Before the MNO came here, we did not know we were Mongol.'

The party also encouraged people to view themselves as political actors with the potential to change not just their own cultural practices but those of the state as well. By identifying as Mongols, people were asserting a new political identity. The MNO creates a direct link between personal and party identity that motivated some people to participate in politics. This was evident in the most common response to my question about why people support the MNO: 'We are Mongol, the party is also Mongol.' The MNO's ethnic political discourse gives people the feeling that they have something personally at stake in the political system and the capacity to create social change, as they are united with others in a political community.

The MNO initiated many changes in its supporters' everyday cultural practices. For the MNO, Mongol identity is a cultural as well as a racial identity, and the party encourages people to reject high-caste Hindu culture, abandon Hinduism and to revive their own languages, religions and other cultural practices. The party does not advocate any one religion or cultural practice, respecting the cultural diversity within the Mongol community. Rather, the party focuses on promoting cultural practices that all Mongols could share. For example, they persuaded people in rural Ilam to boycott the national Hindu festival Dasain, a way of expressing a united Mongol identity through the rejection of a Hindu identity (Hangen 2005a). In one village, MNO activists also reinterpreted and celebrated another Hindu holiday, Tihar, as a Mongol festival that had been appropriated and corrupted by Hindus.[10] These cultural changes further challenged the dominant construction of the national identity.

The MNO as Compared with Other Ethnic Organizations

Many organizations besides the MNO also promote the rights and cultural revitalization of Nepal's ethnic groups. In addition to a few ethnic parties, there are many social organizations (*samajik sansthan*) that represent single ethnic groups. They can be categorized as social-movement organizations and as civil-society organizations.[11] An umbrella organization composed of one organization from each ethnic group, called the Nepal Federation of Indigenous Nationalities (NEFIN), has become the dominant voice of the ethnic political movement. NEFIN acts as a pressure group that seeks to influence government policy and political discourse at the centre. During the 1990s, these organizations were primarily centred in Kathmandu and other urban areas, and mostly engaged elite members of society. Since 2004, however, these organizations have increasingly held street demonstrations. They have also expanded to rural areas and thus are broadening their membership.

How is the MNO different from these organizations in its role in the process of democratization? In some respects, the MNO operates like the social organizations by raising awareness about ethnic inequality and inspiring people to change their identities and cultural practices. However, the MNO employs a different political strategy and targets a different constituency. The social organizations primarily seek to create political change by convincing the government to change its policies: their leaders direct their political efforts towards the government. This lobbying strategy does not require the mobilization of rural society. As a political party, the MNO seeks votes for candidates who will run the government and implement structural changes: the primary target of its political activities is the broad base of voters. The MNO focuses on raising awareness among rural individuals and building consensus and support for ethnic politics at the grassroots level. During most of the time since 1990, the MNO has created a more mass-based form of political action.[12]

At the village level in east Nepal, the MNO mobilized a wider range of people than the social organizations because it was operating as a political party. Political parties can mobilize a wide sector of the population because there are many ways in which people can participate in and align themselves with them. In addition to voting for the MNO, people could campaign, convince others to support the MNO, attend and speak at mass meetings and meetings in their village wards, hang flags outside their homes, and sing MNO songs that spread the party's ideas. Many of these forms of participation did not require people to have a high degree of education or even literacy, although these skills were valued.

By contrast, the social organizations offer more limited ways for people to get involved. At the central level, members of these organizations write articles and books, deliver formal speeches at conferences, and network with other elite members of ethnic groups and government officials. At the village level, these organizations hold periodic cultural programme that showcase the traditional dances, songs and clothing of their ethnic groups. Some organizations such as Kirat Yakthung Chumlung are more active at the village level and sponsor youth clubs and language classes. However, there is a general perception that these are organizations for elites.[13] Thus, some villagers in Ilam who felt alienated from these social organizations supported the MNO. One uneducated Gurung woman said she wasn't involved in the Gurung social organization in her village because 'they probably only let people who can read or write take part in those organizations'. However, she voted for the MNO and called herself 'Mongol'.

Furthermore, the MNO operate across a wider swath of rural Ilam than the social organizations. The social organizations each focus on a single ethnic group and largely confine their activities to the sections of villages where that ethnic group is concentrated. By contrast, the MNO has members from and works with, all of the 'Mongol' ethnic groups in the village. There are party committees in every village in Ilam and many villages in Jhapa, often in each of the nine wards of the village. The MNO disseminates its ideas to a broad cross-section of the village, by holding regular mass meetings and campaigning door to door before the national and local elections. In two villages in Ilam, Limbu and Rai, social organizations are active but are not nearly as powerful and widespread as the MNO, which has controlled the village governments from 1992 onwards. Thus, in rural east Nepal, the MNO involved a wider range of people in the debates and discussions about the state and ethnic equality than the social organizations.

Conclusion

When seeking to understand the process of democratization in rural Nepal, scholars and international donors should not confine their attention to organizations that fit the model of civil-society organizations. Political parties can also be effective forums in which people come together to define and discuss issues of public concern. In particular, ethnic parties have generated public debate and involved people in critically engaging with the state in rural Nepal. Since 1990, the MNO as a small ethnic party has played this democratizing role in some rural areas.

The MNO contributed to the democratization process in the formal political sphere. It called attention to and critiqued the legal restraints that the 1990 Constitution placed on ethnic parties. These restraints meant that participating in elections was not a productive way for the MNO to gain power at the national level, even if it was able to gain seats in village governments. In Nepal's centralized political system, power at the village government level could not be used to enact the broad political changes that the MNO proposed. The MNO has attempted to create radical changes to the political structure by working within the system. The obstacles the party has faced illustrate the near impossibility of accomplishing this and can help us to understand the rise of the Maoist insurgency as emerging from the limitations of the formal political system.

The MNO's rural base is both its greatest strength and limitation in terms of its contributions to democratization. A minor party lacking registration could not have challenged the large, mainstream political parties at the centre, yet the MNO was able to do so in some rural areas. The MNO was able to expand the political choices available to people in these areas and to change the boundaries of the political culture. Many people in rural Nepal were receptive to the party's ethnic political discourse and actively participated in the party. The MNO also expanded political participation by recruiting leaders and activists from politically marginalized ethnic groups. However, the MNO's rural base also limited its effectiveness in gaining power and national attention: it could not engage in the politics of protest available to parties based in more urban areas.

The MNO was more effective in creating social changes than in changing the political system and it accomplished this by acting like a social-movement organization. The MNO contested the state's construction of nationalism and encouraged people to change their identities and cultural practices. Furthermore, through the MNO, issues of ethnic inequality became part of the public political discourse in rural eastern Nepal, as people discussed and debated the relationship between ethnic groups, national identity, and the state.

Many of the MNO's political ideas were extremely radical when they were first voiced: it was considered unseemly to discuss ethnic inequality in public and most people could not imagine that Nepal could become a republic or a federal system. Yet after February 2005, influential factions of many of the mainstream political parties began espousing these very ideas in the movement for the restoration of democracy that emerged. Calls for an end to the monarchy were one of the central demands of the popular movement that swept the country in April 2006. In May 2006, the reinstated Parliament curtailed the king's political power, declared Nepal a secular state and called for elections to a Constituent Assembly that would draft a new Constitution. With these dramatic changes, some of the MNO's core demands have been fulfilled; whether or not ethnic inequality in the country will recede as a result of these changes remains to be seen. If a more inclusive political system is not established, the party could possibly seek to reach its goals through violence. By paying more attention to minor political parties in Nepal and elsewhere, we may learn more about the political future, in addition to learning about often overlooked dimensions of democratization.

Acknowledgements

My greatest thanks go to Gopal Gurung and other members of the MNO for their assistance with my research. Support for field research, conducted between 1994 and 1997, was provided by a Fulbright (IIE) Fellowship, Sigma Xi, the Social Science Research Council/American Council of Learned Societies, and the Wenner-Gren Foundation for Anthropological Research. I thank Mahendra Lawoti, Deepak Thapa and members of the audience at the 34th Annual Conference on South Asia for valuable comments on this chapter. I also thank the Faculty Writing Circle at Ramapo College for their suggestions. I remain responsible for any errors and omissions.

Notes

1. I use the term 'ethnic parties' to refer to all of these identity-based parties, as this is the most common term in the literature. The Madhesi identity is regional rather than ethnic.
2. Gopal Gurung began writing about ethnic inequality in Nepal in 1972, in a Nepali newspaper called *New Light*, and published an influential book titled *Nepali Rajnitima Adekha Sachar (Hidden Facts in Nepali Politics)* (Gurung 1985).

In 1988, he was sentenced to three years in jail for his writings, under the State Offence Act, which made it illegal for anyone to damage the image of or attack the royal family, or to disturb the peace of the country in any way. He founded the MNO in 1989 while in jail.

3. I see racial identities, such as the Mongol identity that the MNO promotes, as forms of ethnic identities as well. I discuss the history of racial concepts in Nepal and the implications of the MNO's selection of a racial identity in detail elsewhere (Hangen 2005b).
4. In the 1990 Constitution, Article 112(3) states: 'The Election Commission shall withhold recognition from any political organization or any party which has been formed ... on the basis of religion, community, caste, tribe or region.' Article 113(3) states, 'The Election Commission shall not register any political organization or party if any Nepali citizen is discriminated against in becoming a member on the basis of religion, caste, tribe, language or sex or if the name, objectives, insignia or flag is of such a nature that it is religious or communal or tends to fragment the country' (HMG 1990).
5. MNO candidates are listed as independent candidates in the official election data. Thus, this election data was compiled based on the official election results from the Election Commission in combination with information about candidate's names from MNO leaders. In Ilam district, the total number of constituencies was increased from two to three in 1994 (Election Commission 1992, 1994 and 1999).
6. Election results for MNO candidates were ascertained by combining official data from the Election Commission (1992, 1997) with information about candidate's names from MNO leaders. The number of seats on each VDC was 11 in 1992; this was increased to 47 in 1997 (ibid.).
7. While the MNO leaders and activists recognize that low-caste Hindus and Mongols face similar problems with discrimination and exclusion, the party does not address this issue in its manifesto and other declarations.
8. The only people with extensive political experience who joined the MNO were those who had been active in the Panchayat era. Former Panchayat-era leaders came under heavy criticism after 1990 and the MNO offered some of them a way to refashion their political identities.
9. In the late nineteenth century, the Nepali state had categorized these people in terms of caste: they were classified as alcohol drinkers (*matwalis*) and ranked far below the purer high-caste Hindus (Hofer 1979). In the twentieth century, they were classified in the census on the basis of language and religion, until 1991, when they were enumerated along ethnic group lines.
10. The MNO was not alone in its efforts to reinterpret Tihar as a non-Hindu holiday. A Limbu organization called Kirat Yakthung Chumlung promoted and celebrated it as a Limbu festival, as I observed in Jhapa and Ilam districts. Magars have also sought to claim Tihar as their own holiday, according to Deepak Thapa.
11. Unlike many other NGOs that the international development community supported and deemed to be excellent examples of civil-society organizations, these ethnic organizations only began receiving international development support after 2000.

12. This was especially evident in the 1990s, when NEFIN and its organizations remained based in the capital. During the 2000s, NEFIN has made efforts to gain mass support for its political activities by expanding its activities outside the valley.
13. Similarly, Arjun Guneratne (2002) argues that one of these social organizations, the Tharu Kalyankarini Sabha (Tharu Welfare Society), was founded by and for elites from the Tharu ethnic group. Although this organization had district committees throughout the Tarai, they were very inactive and the actual power in the organization rested with the central committee in Kathmandu (ibid.: 146).

References

Baral, Lok Raj. 2005. 'Democracy and Elections: Trajectories of Political Development', in L.R. Baral (ed.), *Election and Governance in Nepal*. New Delhi: Manohar.

Carothers, Thomas. 1999. *Aiding Democracy Abroad: The Learning Curve*. Washington, DC: Carnegie Endowment for International Peace.

Dahl, Robert. 1971. *Polyarchy: Participation and Opposition*. New Haven: Yale University Press.

Diamond, Larry. 1996. 'Toward Democratic Consolidation', in L. Diamond and M.F. Plattner (eds), *The Global Resurgence of Democracy*. Baltimore: The Johns Hopkins University Press.

Edwards, Michael. 2004. *Civil Society*. Oxford: Polity.

Election Commission (Nirbachan Aayog). 1992 (2049 v.s.). *Pratinidhi Sabha Tatha Sthaniya Nikaya Nirbachan Parinam: Ilam*. Kathmandu: Nirbachan Aayog.

———. 1994 (2051 v.s.). *Pratinidhisabha Sadasya Nirbachan—2051: Nirbachan Parinam Bibaran*. Kathmandu: Nirbachan Aayog.

———. 1997 (2054 v.s.). *Sthaniya Nikaya Nirbachan 2054 ko Parinam: Ilam Jilla*. Kathmandu: Nirbachan Aayog.

———. 1999 (2056 v.s.). *Pratinidhisabha Sadasya Nirbachan—2056 v.s. Nirbachan Parinam*. Kathmandu: Nirbachan Aayog.

Gellner, David. 2002. 'Introduction: Transformations of the Nepalese State', in D. Gellner (ed.), *Resistance and the State: Nepalese Experiences*. New Delhi: Social Science Press.

Guneratne, Arjun. 2002. *Many Tongues, One People: The Making of Tharu Identity in Nepal*. Ithaca: Cornell University Press.

Gurung, Gopal. 1985. *Nepali Rajnitima Adekha Sachai (Hidden Facts in Nepali Politics)*. Kathmandu: Gopal Gurung.

Gurung, Harka. 2003. *Social Demography of Nepal: Census 2001*. Lalitpur: Himal Books.

Hachhethu, Krishna 2002. 'Political Parties and the State', in D. Gellner (ed.), *Resistance and the State: Nepalese Experiences*. New Delhi: Social Science Press.

———. 2005. 'Political Parties and Elections', in L.R. Baral (ed.), *Election and Governance in Nepal*. New Delhi: Manohar.

Hangen, Susan. 2001. 'Debating Democracy at the Margins: The Mongol National Organization in Nepal', *Himalayan Research Bulletin* XXI: 25–28.

Hangen, Susan. 2005a. 'Boycotting Dasain: History, Memory and Ethnic Politics in Nepal', *Studies in Nepali History and Society* 10 (1): 105–33.
———. 2005b. 'Race and the Politics of Identity in Nepal', *Ethnology* 44 (1): 49–64.
Held, David 1996. *Models of Democracy*. 2nd ed. Stanford: Stanford University Press.
Herzog, Hanna 1987. 'Minor Parties: The Relevancy Perspective', *Comparative Politics* 19 (3): 317–29.
HMG (His Majesty's Government of Nepal). 1990. *The Constitution of the Kingdom of Nepal 2047 (1990)*. Kathmandu: Law Books Management Board.
Hofer, Andras. 1979. 'The Caste Hierarchy and the State in Nepal: A Study of the Muluki Ain of 1854', in *Khumbu Himal*. Innsbruck: Universitatsverlag Wagner.
Hoftun, Martin, William Raeper and John Whelpton. 1999. *People, Politics and Ideology: Democracy and Social Change in Nepal*. Kathmandu: Mandala Book Point.
Horowitz, Donald. 1985. *Ethnic Groups in Conflict*. Berkeley: University of California Press.
Lawoti, Mahendra. 2005. *Towards a Democratic Nepal: Inclusive Political Institutions for a Multicultural Society*. New Delhi: Sage Publications.
Lecomte-Tilouine, Marie. 2004. 'Ethnic Demands within Maoism: Questions of Magar Territorial Autonomy, Nationality and Class', in M. Hutt (ed.), *Himalayan People's War: Nepal's Maoist Rebellion*. Bloomington and Indianapolis: Indiana University Press.
Madrid, Raul. 2005. 'Indigenous Parties and Democracy in Latin America', *Latin American Politics and Society* 47 (4): 161–79.
Pfaff-Czarnecka, Joanna. 2004. 'High Expectations, Deep Disappointment: Politics, State and Society in Nepal after 1990', in M. Hutt (ed.), *Himalayan People's War: Nepal's Maoist Rebellion*. Bloomington and Indianapolis: Indiana University Press.
Rudolph, Lloyd and Susanne Rudolph. 1960. 'The Political Role of India's Caste Associations', *Pacific Affairs* 33 (1): 5–22.
de Sales, Anne. 2002. 'The Kham Magar Country: Between Ethnic Claims and Maoism', in D. Gellner (ed.), *Resistance and the State: Nepalese Experiences*. New Delhi: Social Science Press.
Schmitter, Philippe C. and Terry Lynn Karl. 1996. 'What Democracy Is ... And Is Not', in L. Diamond and M.F. Plattner (eds), *The Global Resurgence of Democracy*. Baltimore: The Johns Hopkins University Press.
Tamang, Seira. 2002. 'Civilizing Civil Society: Donors and Democratic Space', *Studies in Nepali History and Society* 7 (2): 309–53.
Van Cott, Donna Lee. 2003. 'Institutional Change and Ethnic Parties in South America', *Latin American Politics and Society* 45 (2): 1–39.
Varshney, Ashutosh. 2002. *Ethnic Conflict and Civic Life: Hindus and Muslims in India*. New Haven and London: Yale University Press.

8

Ethnic Nationalism in Nepal and the Newars

Bal Gopal Shrestha

Introduction

Nepal has seen a rise of ethnic nationalism because of discriminatory policies of the state against various ethnic nationalities. Nepal is home to more than 100 'indigenous nationalities' (Adibasi Janajati). None of these nationalities, including the predominant Khas population—consisting of Hill Brahmin (Bahun) and Chhetri (Khas) castes who speak Nepali (Khas) and practice Hinduism—can be considered a single majority group. The Khas, however, remain determined to propagate their language, culture and religion through their control of state institutions. While ethnic mobilization in Nepal has largely, to date, avoided bloodshed, the frustration of minority nationalities, ethnicities, castes, and tribes is an important factor behind the growing popularity of the 'People's War' of the Communist Party of Nepal (Maoist)—the CPN (M).

At present, though the ethnic-nationalities movements have subsided because of the violent war, they might erupt any time as long as grievances of these ethnic groups in Nepal are not tackled properly. A recent study (Pathak 2005: 323) predicts that if the 'People's War' deviates from its main political ideology and fails to ensure social justice, ethnic insurgency is inevitable in Nepal.

In this chapter, an attempt is made to examine the growing trend of ethnic nationalism in Nepal and the role of the Newars, who began the earliest campaigns in the late 1970s. The Newars are important as the largest population in the capital, with a long history of association with ethnic movements. The Newars make an interesting case because of their hierarchical order of castes and internal divisions, language diffusion, and Hindu–Buddhist mixed religious culture, as well as their active involvement in the present ethnic movements (Gellner 2003; Shrestha 1999a).

Ethnicity and Nationalism

The historiography of nations and nationalities is now more than two centuries old. A vast literature on the issues of nationalism, national movements and ethnic uprisings is available. Nationalism in Nepal, on the other hand, is a more recent phenomenon, which did not prevail before the 1980s but it is on the rise in present-day Nepal.

Benedict Anderson sees a nation as an imagined community: '...[I]t is imagined as community, because regardless of the actual inequality and exploitation that may prevail in each, the nation is always conceived as deep, horizontal comradeship' (1991: 7). He goes on to say, 'A nation is constituted by the social group's (the peoples') consciousness of being a nation, or of wanting to be one, and by their demand for political self-determination' (ibid.: 11). In Nepal too, despite inequalities within the communities, they present a horizontal comradeship among themselves and are united in the fight against the suppression by the dominant group. Such a 'horizontal comradeship' is imagined not only within a group but also among oppressed nationalities in Nepal, united under the umbrella of the 'Nepal Federation of Indigenous Nationalities' to achieve equal rights for all 'nations'.

The nation is limited: certain 'borders' set the limits of the nation, and limit who belongs to the nation and who does not. These borders can be determined on the basis of ethnic divisions (for example, characteristics of religion, culture and language) or on the basis of civic characteristics. Greenfeld (1992: 11) states that the ethnic group forms the basis of the nation in 'ethnic nationalism' and that as a consequence, the group is more important than the individual human being. Not everybody can belong to an ethnic nation, because the membership is determined by certain ethnic characteristics. According to Seton-Watson (1977: 5), it is impossible to develop a scientific definition of nation: 'All that I can find to say is that a nation exists when a significant number of people in a community consider themselves to form a nation, or behave as if they formed one.'

In 'civic' forms of nationalism, in contrast, everybody in principle can belong to the nation, which is a universalistic political community and is based on civil and political liberties for every member of the nation. The civic form of nationalism stresses the attachments and connections between the members from their belonging to the same political community (for example, by having the same civil liberties), while the ethnic form of nationalism emphasizes the attachments and connections between the members by belonging to the same ethnic community (for example, sharing the same ethnic and cultural characteristics).

In Nepal, clearly there exists a tension between the civic form of nationalism and 'ethnic nationalism'. The reality is that the ruling minority has been imposing its language, religion and culture upon all other Nepalese groups on the pretext of 'national unity' or 'Nepali nationalism', while other nationalities have attempted to rescue their languages, religions and cultures from such a 'civic' form of nationalism. In his recent book, Lawoti (2005) has elaborately discussed this one-sided 'nationalism' as a 'caste-hill Hindu elite (CHHE)' nationalism.

All the nationalities have been actively participating in the recent ethnic movements, but they have different historical and socio-cultural backgrounds. On the one hand, we see the mutual understanding and interests shared by these nationalities, while on the other, internal hierarchies and competitions between these groups are a reality. In the rising phenomenon of ethnic nationalism in Nepal, the interrelations and mutual understanding shared by these contesting nationalities can be perceived within the broader framework of ethnicity and state formation, and they relate the Nepalese to the growing discourse on ethnicity and nationalism in a global context.

The History of Nationalism in Nepal

Ethnic nationalism is a rising phenomenon in present-day Nepal. The issue of minorities and their rights was ignored or suppressed during the 30 years of Panchayat rule (1960–90). Soon after the 1990 political change that re-introduced the multiparty system in Nepal, the voice of the minorities became clearer. Not only the Newars, but also many other ethnic groups of Nepal began to organize themselves to demand their rights.

The indigenous nationalities are frustrated in Nepal by the control of the state and by the Khas. The other nationalities have cultures distinct from the national mainstream—that of the Khas population. As already shown by some scholars, ethnic nationalism in Nepal is a modern phenomenon that was not prevalent before the 1980s but has been rapidly growing since the 1990s (Gellner et al. 1997; Gurung 1999; Hangen 1999; Kraemer 1996, 2003; Subba 1999; Tamang 1994; Tamang 1987, 1999).

It was only in 1990, as a result of political changes, that the non-Khas nationalities began to search for their national identity. Following the 1990 political changes, a new Constitution was introduced that presented Nepal as a multinational (*bahujati*) and multilingual (*bahubhasika*) country. However, it retained the Nepali (Khas) language as the only 'national language' for official use and Hinduism as the only 'state religion'. Although the Constitution provided enough liberty to ethnic non-Khas, non-Hindu religious communities to express themselves against the domination of the 'one nation, one language and one religion' policy of the government, they did not achieve rights for their languages and religions as the Khas in Nepal were and are determined to propagate their language, culture and religion using state mechanisms. The ruling Hindu population of Nepal articulate their nationalism by imitating Indian Hindu nationalists, whose vivid forms of activity have been discussed by some scholars (such as Jaffrelot 1996 and van der Veer 1994).

Alter (1994: 11) says, 'A nation is constituted by the social group's (the people's) consciousness of being a nation, or of wanting to be one, and by their demand for political self-determination'. Van Schendel (1994) has shown for the Jummas of Bangladesh that after having been dominated for two centuries, they are now actively striving for an identity that separates them from the Bengalis.

The search for a 'national identity' in Nepal may be a recent phenomenon, but has deep roots. Until 1769, present-day Nepal was composed of small independent states and principalities of different 'nationalities'. The Gorkhali king Prithivi Narayan Shah, forefather of the present ruling dynasty of Nepal, embarked on an expansionist campaign, bringing several small states and principalities under the control of the Gorkha. His successors continued the expansionary policy, which came to an end only after their defeat in a war with the British East India Company (1814–16). It was only in the 1930s that the Nepalese government began to adopt the name 'Nepal' in an attempt to make it a modern nation state (Burghart 1996: 255). There have been rebellions against the state for centuries in Nepal. Scholars have attributed the phenomenon of ethnic nationalism to the fact that '[t]he social relationships, which emerged from the Gorkha conquests were based on ethnic, caste and other discrimination, hence they were exclusive, discriminatory and exploitative' (Pradhan 1991: 204).

Soon after the Gorkha conquest in 1769, the Gorkhali king Prithivi Narayan Shah, announced his country to be the 'true land of Hindus' (*asali Hindustan*). In 1854, Jangabahadur, the first Rana prime minister, introduced a written law based on Hinduism, which divided Nepal into several hierarchical levels and subordinated all other ethnic communities to the Bahun and Chhetri (Khas) ruling castes of Nepal. In 1960, King Mahendra, the father of the present king, introduced the party-less political system called 'Panchayat', which proclaimed Nepal the only 'Hindu Kingdom' and 'Khas the only Nepali and the only official language', thus ignoring its multi-religious, multinational, multicultural and multilingual character. It provided legitimate grounds to the Bahun-Chhetris to impose Hindu religious supremacy and their language, Nepali, over all other populations of Nepal.

In 1964, with the implementation of the New Law (*Naya Muluki Ein*), Hindu religion-based caste discrimination lost its legal ground, but in practice this has not diminished Hindu religious domination. The ruling class came up with new slogans such as 'One nation, one language, one religion, and one culture' in favour of the Bahun-Chhetri community, their language (Nepali), their religion (Hindu) and their culture. The 30 years of Panchayat politics gave immense support to Hindu religious organizations such as the World Hindu Council (Vishva Hindu Parishad) that strengthened Hindu fundamentalists in Nepal while ignoring the issues of the minorities and their rights. Encouraged by Hindu fundamentalists in India, Nepalese Hindu extremists have become active. They have taken inspiration from Indian organizations such as the 'Shiva Sena (it draws its name from the Maratha-king warrior, Shivaji) to form groups such as the Cows Welfare Association, Nepal. It is notable that a person found guilty of killing a cow is condemned to life imprisonment by Nepali law even today.[1] It didn't surprise people when Hindu fundamentalists in Nepal announced heavy cash rewards to anyone who would cut off the head of Padma Ratna Tuladhar, a popular Newar human-rights champion and then minister of health, when he voiced the rights of the cow-eating communities of Nepal.

As the ruling class manipulating state institutions, Bahun-Chhetris are the target of other nationalities' criticism. The other nationalities of Nepal find it insulting to be categorized alongside low-caste Hindus. Mainstream scholars also define these groups as 'tribes'. Most such groups in Nepal, including the Newars, Tamangs, Magars, Gurungs, Sherpas, Limbus, Rais and Tharus, do not accept the labels 'ethnic groups' or 'minorities'. They prefer to be called 'nations' and believe they fulfil all the criteria of nationhood: language, religion, culture, territory and a history of independent statehood, which could be achieved again if rights to secession were granted. All these groups now accept the Nepali word *janajati*, translated as 'nationality' in English. In 1990, when 18 of these groups gathered to create a forum called the Nepal Janajati Mahasamgha, they translated it as the 'Nepal Federation of Nationalities', which has been transformed into the Nepal Adivasi Janajati Mahasamgha or 'Nepal Federation of Indigenous Nationalities'. Because of their close relationship, I have adopted both the words 'ethnicity' and 'nationalities' to address the present phenomenon of nationalism in Nepal.

The major demands of the non-Khas nationalities in Nepal are: the right to autonomy; political representation in the central government; equal rights for their languages in the courts, in education and in local and central administration; and an end to the domination of the Hindu religion and culture. The 'All Nepal Nationalities' Organisation' (Akhil Nepal Janajati Samgha), a Maoist sister organization to the CPN (M), has presented the most radical demands, including the right of self-determination for all nationalities in Nepal. The Maoists also initiated liberation fronts (Mukti Morchas) for various ethnic nationalities of Nepal, such as the Newar Liberation

Front, the Khambuwan Liberation Front, the Tamang Liberation Front, the Tharuwan Liberation Front, the Magarat Liberation Front,[2] and the Gurung Liberation Front. The Maoists advocate federal structure of the state, dividing the country into nine different provinces on the basis of major nationalities and languages of Nepal.

THE NEWARS

The Newars are the natives of the Kathmandu Valley, consisting of various races and castes but a single linguistic community ('nation'). The 2001 population census showed that the total population of Nepal was 23.2 million, of which the Newars were 1,245,232.[3] Although Newars live in every region of Nepal and beyond its boundaries, such as in India, the US and the UK, the majority are concentrated in the valley of Kathmandu.

The word 'Newar' is nowadays commonly used to indicate the people living in the Kathmandu Valley and those speaking Nevar or Newari or Nepalbhasa as their mother tongue elsewhere in Nepal and in India. Regarding the origin of the Newars, there are several myths. Most scholars believe that the Newars are the original inhabitants of the Kathmandu Valley. They accept that the Newar speakers lived in the valley of Nepal from prehistoric times. It is commonly believed that the word 'Newar' is derived from the name of the country 'Nepal' itself. The word 'Newar' is etymologically identical with the place name 'Nepal'. Linguists such as Ralph L. Turner assert that the words 'Nevar', 'Neval' and 'Nepal' all have developed from the word 'Nepal' or 'Nevar'.[4]

However, there are conflicting views about the origin of the word 'Nepal'. K.P. Malla confirms that an inscription from 512 AD by Vasantadev of Tistung is the first evidence that the word Nepal was used for the people of Nepal.[5] According to the oldest chronicle of Nepal, the *Gopalarajavamsavali*, the Kiratas ruled Nepal for 32 generations (Vajracarya and Malla 1985: 121–22). Many scholars believe the Newars are the descendants of the Kirata, who ruled Nepal before the Licchavis began their rule in the valley. Especially certain sections of the Newars, such as the Jyapus (farmers) and the Dyola (sweepers and guardians of temples of the mother goddess) are sometimes referred to as the true descendents of the Kiratas. Some of the inhabitants of eastern Nepal, such as the Limbu and Rai, also claim descent from the Kiratas. Newar shares a certain vocabulary with Limbu and Rai. Linguistically, the Newar, Limbu and Rai languages are classified as Tibeto-Burman languages. Because of this too, the linking of the Newars with the Kiratas has been justified (van Driem 1992). So far no recorded history of the Kiratas has been found. Only their successors, the Licchavis, who ruled Nepal from the second to the ninth century AD, have left a corpus of inscriptions, all written in pure Sanskrit. By analysing the place and river names written in these inscriptions, Malla concluded that although the Licchavi rulers were inclined to use Sanskrit, the language spoken by the people belonged to the Tibeto-Burman stock. He believes it is likely that the names of places found in the inscriptions are in an archaic form of Nepalbhasa.[6] According to Gellner (1995: 5), 'The Newari seems to have been spoken by the inhabitants of the Kathmandu Valley as far back as the records go.' Another anthropologist, Bista (1976 [1967]: 16) writes, 'The Newar people had been settled in the Nepal Valley since prehistoric time.'

After the fall of the Licchavis, the Thakuris ruled Nepal for more than two centuries (the ninth to the eleventh century AD). The Thakuris did not leave too many inscriptions either. Therefore, this period is also known as the dark period of Nepalese history. Nevertheless, it was from the Thakuri period that some of the earliest written evidences of the Newar language have remained, including the palm-leaf document from Ukubahal, Patan (dated 1114 AD, Malla 1990) and the stone inscription from Vajrayogini, Sankhu (dated 1172 AD). Later, during the Malla rule (thirteenth to eighteenth century AD), Newar language and culture flourished extensively in what is now known as the Kathmandu Valley. Numerous inscriptions and a vast literature in mixed Newar–Sanskrit and in the pure Newar language are dated from this time. Scholars agree that numerous feasts, fasts and festivals in honour of gods and goddesses celebrated in present-day Nepal date back to the Malla period and some of them even date from the Thakuri and Licchavi periods. Most Newar socio-religious and ritual activities are taken care of by the *guthi,* the socio-religious associations.

For centuries, the valley of Nepal remained a melting pot for migrants from the south and the north, and they all began to be called 'Newar'. During the Malla reign—from the thirteenth century until the dynasty's downfall in the eighteenth century—the kings did a great deal to promote literature in Nepalbhasa, as well as in other languages such as Maithili, Avadhi, Bhojpuri and Bengali. For 15 centuries, a Sanskrit literary tradition was cultivated in the Kathmandu Valley. The Malla courts supported all languages, classical and vernacular, without discrimination. The extent of the literary tradition in other languages indicates the cosmopolitan nature of the Malla courts.

Even after the 1769 Gorkha conquest of Nepal, the victorious Gorkha rulers accepted most of the Newar culture as their court culture (Hoek 1990). The court's patronage of Newar culture helped a great deal in continuing Newar culture and rituals in modern Nepal.

As traders, the Newars received more opportunities to develop their profession under the Gorkha rule. They spread all over the kingdom and opened shops wherever they went. Many new Newar settlements appeared outside the valley of Nepal.[7] The latest population census of Nepal reports that Newars are spread through all the 75 districts of the country. However, in many districts their number is very less. In the hands of the new rulers, Newar language and culture had to suffer a great deal.

From the religious point of view, the majority of Newars follow Hinduism and Buddhism, making no distinction between the two. There are also Muslim and Christian Newars in Nepal. Muslim Newars have long been living in Kathmandu and speak the Nepalbhasa. The Christian Newars were forced into exile to India as soon as the Gorkha king Prithivi Narayan Shah conquered Nepal in 1769. The composition of Newar society is highly complicated, with divisions in caste and caste hierarchies. As the nineteenth-century chronicles and oral traditions testify (Vaidya Shrestha 1991: 180–90), the early Malla king Jayasthiti (1382–95 AD) introduced the division of castes among the Newars, but the Newar caste hierarchy began to acquire after 1769 conquest of the Gorkha a rigidity it had not had before as they were made subordinated to Parbatiyas (Gellner 1995: 12; Rosser 1979 [1966]).

Later, under the Gorkha rule, the first Rana prime minister, Jangabahadur, introduced a legal code in 1854. In spite of having their own caste system, the Newars were collectively labelled one *jat* (caste) in the 1854 legal code and their castes were lumped together with other Parbate castes. The Parbates follow the Hindu *varnasram* caste hierarchies, which divide their society into four distinct levels: Brahmins at the top and Gaine, Damai, Sarki and Kami at the bottom. Other ethnic groups were also ranked under the same caste system.[8]

The 1854 legal code gave the Newars their separate ethnic identity as a culturally and linguistically distinct group. However, the language of the Newars was gradually replaced with the Gorkhali language. The latter began to be called Nepali since the 1930s and thenceforth Nepali became the only official language of Nepal. During the Rana rule (1846–1951), even writing in the Newar language was forbidden, which provoked a section of the Newar elites into defying the government policy. The suppression of the Nepalbhasa and of Newar intellectuals intensified during the reign of Chandra Shamsher (1901–28). In 1905, he banned the Newar language from the courts of justice and administration. The language of the Newars, or Nepalbhasa, began to be called 'Newari' while the name 'Nepali' was used to designate the Khasakura or Gorkhali language.

The name 'Nepali' was first made popular outside Nepal. Only in the 1930s did the rulers of the country recognize it (Burghart 1996: 253; Pradhan 1991: 203). In a similar manner, the word 'Newari' was designated for Nepalbhasa by western scholars long before it was adopted by anybody in Nepal (Shakya 1997). The suppression of the Newar language, however, gave birth to modern literature in Newar and a number of devoted activists.

In 1951, the Rana regime ended in Nepal, but the Newar language did not gain much in status. It did not achieve the right to be used in the courts or in the administration. It did not receive any recognition from the government, while Nepali alone was made the medium of government, administration and schooling. In 1957, the government of K.I. Singh declared Nepali to be the only language of instruction in schools at the cost of all other languages of Nepal (Joshi and Rose 2004 [1966]). The 1959 Constitution of Nepal declared Nepali to be the national language of Nepal, ignoring the languages of all other nationalities.

During the 30 years of the Panchayat regime (1960–90), the Newar language suffered great suppression as the government systematically imposed Nepali. Publication became more difficult with the imposition of censorship, which intended to prevent publication against the Panchayat system. For many years, no new

Nepalbhasa journals or newspapers received permission to be published. In 1971, the New Education Plan was introduced, which pushed the Nepalbhasa further back by forcing children to make a choice between Nepalbhasa or other languages, science, vocational subjects, mathematics, and so forth. Although peaceful protests from literary circles were made, the Newar people as a whole did not protest collectively. Seemingly, the notion of ethnic nationalism in Newar society emerged only toward the end of the 1970s (Shrestha 1999a), with the establishment of the Association of Newar Speakers (Nepalbhasa Mamkah Khalah) in 1979. It was only in 1995 that the National Forum of the Newars (Nevah De Dabu) was established, aiming to assert ethnic national rights for the Newars.

Newar Nationalism

The Association of Newar Speakers

The necessity of Newar unity for the sake of their language and their nation (*jati*) has been repeatedly emphasized by literary elites, but the common Newar people have yet to be convinced. At the same time, the social structure of Newar society does not allow them to unite easily. On the one hand, the unequal division of classes do not permit them to unite and on the other hand, the traditional Newar caste divisions divide them. One of the reasons is the traditional caste structure. The elaborate caste system of the Newars adds to the complexity of the society. On the one hand there is the separation between different castes, on the other hand there is their interdependency, a paradox existing in the greater part of South Asia. Social division is prevalent because of the caste structure. Especially for those low-caste groups whose traditional duties are stigmatized, it is still hard to believe that each of them is an integral part of the Newar national movement.

In 1979, following the students' movement, King Birendra announced the political referendum on whether to retain the partyless Panchayat system with certain reforms or to re-introduce the multi-party system. In April 1979, all kinds of restrictions against public gatherings and meetings were lifted. This new situation allowed the Newars to organize themselves in a new way for the cause of their language and national identity. In this regard, the formation of the Association of Newar Speakers in August 1979 was a historic step. It was the first time that the Newars expressed themselves in a collective manner and articulated the necessity of obtaining rights for their language, culture and nationality from the state. They categorically rejected the 'one language, one nation' policy of the government and urged equal rights to all languages and nationalities of Nepal. Their demands included education in the mother tongue for children, rights for all languages to be used in the courts of justice and in administration, access for all languages in the government media and equal recognition of the cultures of all nationalities (NMK 1993).[9]

In the same year, on 22 October 1979, the Association organized a big New Year's rally in Kathmandu. New Year Day was also celebrated in Patan, Bhaktapur and other Newar towns. A motorcycle rally, which was organized to observe New Year Day, went out of the Valley through different Newar settlements. In the following years, New Year Day continued to be celebrated in this manner. The Newars of other settlements began to copy this tradition. Consequently, in many Newar settlements, the Newar people have formed their own ethnic organizations.

In the 1980 referendum, the partyless Panchayat system won over the multiparty system and the old language policy continued. No changes took place in favour of the various nationalities and languages. Parties were once again banned and the press controlled. However, it had become impossible for the government to go back to the situation preceding the referendum. Parties were allowed to function using the epithet 'banned' before their names. Likewise, the Nepalese press tried to continue the freedom that it had acquired during the referendum period. In 1982, the Nepalbhasa weekly *Inaap* was launched in Kathmandu.[10] It played a vital role in developing ethnic awareness among the Newars. Its circulation spread beyond the Kathmandu Valley to many other Newar settlements.

The Association of Newar Speakers assumed greater importance, but it did not succeed in bringing under its umbrella the organizations outside Kathmandu district.

In 1986, the chairman of the Association of Newar Speakers, Padma Ratna Tuladhar, stood for election to the National Assembly (Rastriya Panchayat) as a supporter of multiparty democracy in Nepal. Those who were against his views on language and ethnic rights labelled him more as a communal (*sampradayik*) Newar candidate. He was successful, however, because of his statements in favour of the multiparty system and ethnic rights, which gained him enormous popularity. His voice in favour of minority nationalities inspired other ethnic groups of Nepal to establish their own ethnic organizations. In a way, the Association of Newar Speakers played a leading role in promoting ethnic awareness in Nepal.

In 1986, the Forum for the Rights of All Nationalities (Sarvajatiya Adhikara Mamca) emerged to take a collective stand for the equal rights of all nationalities, languages, cultures and religions. This forum was able to spread ethnic awareness, but disappeared after the 1990 change.

The National Forum of the Newars and other Organizations

Academic organizations such as the Council of Nepalbhasa (Nepalbhasa Parisad) and Cvasapasa were already there; and the Nepalbhasa Academy was also established in 1992, but the urgent need of the time was not only city-centred scholarly associations, but also a mass-based national organization to inspire the new generation of Newar society. This could be achieved only through originating a national Newar organization. The Newars continued their efforts to bring about a consensus for a national organization of their own. In February 1991, in a bid to create a Newar national organization, the Council of Nepalbhasa held a two-day conference on Newar nationality and language.

The Association of Newar Speakers, on the other hand, had long been trying to build consensus among the Newars for the establishment of a national organization. In 1992, when its second convention was held in Kathmandu, one of its main targets was to hold a gathering of the Newars to form a national organization. In December 1994, it held a two-day seminar to discuss the basic requirements for a national convention of the Newars. As a result, they succeeded in forming an ad hoc committee to hold such a national convention. On 1 and 2 September 1995, it organized a convention in Kathmandu, which was joined by participants from 38 districts. On its second day, it proclaimed the formation of the Nevah De Dabu, the National Forum of the Newars. Those who participated have formed local-level organizations in their areas. The participants from various districts also suggested keeping the organisation politically neutral.

The National Forum still has to gain unanimous support from all Newars. When the preparation for the formation of the National Forum was in progress, one group of Newars, politically close to the NCP, formed the Association of Democratic Newars (Prajatantrik Nepalbhasa Khalah) led by Hitkarvir Sing Kansakar, another well-known figure in the Nepalbhasa movement.[11] In a similar manner, the Newar Trust (Nevah Guthi, 1993), the Nepal Newar Society (Nepal Nevar Samaj) and the Great Trust of the Newars (Nevah Maha Guthi, 1997) attempted to organize the Newars of the country under their own umbrellas.

The Newar National Movement (Newah Rastriya Andolan) is another organization whose focus is on autonomy for the Newars wherever their population is dense. In 2003, yet another Newar National Organisation (Newah De Gu) was launched to achieve autonomy for the Newars. In 2005, during the second convention, it adopted a new name: Newah De Guthi Nepal Mandal or the Newar National Organisation Nepal Mandal. It also demands autonomy for the Newars where their population is dense. Furthermore, the Maoists have formed the Newar Organisation (Newah Khalah) and the Newar Liberation Front (Newah Mukti Morcha), who advocate a separate province for the Newars.

At the same time, there are several caste-based organizations within the Newar society. In Kathmandu, the Vajracaryas (the Buddhist priestly caste), Urays (the merchant castes such as Tuladhars and Kansakars), Manandhars (oil-pressers), Kapalis (tailors and musicians), Khadgis (butchers), Podes (sweepers), Citrakars (painters) and Tandukars (rice makers) have had their caste foundations for many years. In 1993, the biggest caste group in Newar society, the Jyapus, established the Great Foundation of the Jyapus (Jyapu Maha Guthi). In 2004, the Shresthas also initiated their caste organization in Kathmandu. At present, the caste associations are playing a sup-portive role in forming Newar unity.

Traditionally, there are more than two dozen distinct Newar castes. In 2005, when the National Forum of the Newars held its fourth convention, 18 Newar caste organizations appeared to have affiliated themselves with it. The National Forum of the Newars is also busy inspiring all these caste groups to produce their caste profiles and lets all of them play a helping role in its bid to achieve equal rights for the Newars as a single ethnic national group.

However, what will be the role of these caste-based organizations in the future is unpredictable, since the depressed caste groups no longer acquiesce to the traditional hierarchical order of castes. Whether these caste-bound associations will seek their separate identities or will become part of the Newar ethnic movement is a vital question.[12]

So far, despite the criticism it received, the National Forum of the Newars is the only organization that has succeeded in gaining recognition as a national organization of the Newars. The 2005 convention of the National Forum of the Newars also passed a resolution on autonomy for the Newar populations in areas where they are settled densely. In this respect, all the major Newar organizations have now spoken in one voice regarding autonomy for the Newars. However, whether all the Newar organizations can cooperate with each other or are dividing the Newar national movement into several fragments is a crucial question for the Newar nationalist today.

Challenges to Newar Nationalism

With the creation of the National Forum of the Newars, the Newars have shown their eagerness to present themselves as a separate 'ethnic group' or a 'nation' within the modern state of Nepal. Unlike the other nationalities of Nepal, it is not easy to unite the Newars as an ethnic group.

It is a hard task to unite the Newars for the cause of Newar nationalism because their culture is not based on equality among the various castes. However, from the so-called highest caste (Brahmins) to the so-called lowest caste (Pode), all are identified as Newars because of their culture and language. At present, all Newar nationalist organizations are trying to accommodate members in their organizations without caste bias. However, the abolition of caste hierarchy in Newar society is not an easy task. For instance, during most festivals, many castes participate and in such festivals, each caste has to fulfil its own duties (Shrestha 2002; Toffin 1978).

Women are subordinate to men in Newar society. Especially, married women are highly discriminated against in their homes. A few city-dwelling, educated women are being assimilated into different Newar organizations, but their representation is not insignificant. In 1989, a Newar Women's Association (Nepalbhasa Misa Khalah) was founded in Kathmandu, but this association is mainly concentrated in literary circles. Whether the Newar nationalists will succeed in receiving active support from Newar women or not is another important question.

A trend of speaking Nepali in Newar houses had already started during the Rana period. Upper- and middle-class Newar parents are more inclined to speak Nepali with their children, to the detriment of their own mother tongue. At present, the English language has captured the attention of the Nepalese, including the Newars.[13] At the same time, the new generation is more interested in western pop culture and Indian cinema than in their own music and culture. The migration of people into the valley from other parts of Nepal and from north India (mainly from Bihar and Uttar Pradesh), the growth of countless concrete buildings on the fertile land of the Valley and the sharp increase in highly polluting motor traffic continue unchecked, which has displaced the Newars from their ancient homeland (Malla 1992: 24). However, the consequence of globalization in cultural realms will not only be faced by the Newars but also by all other groups. The Newar leaders have not yet made any far-sighted plans and policies to overcome challenges surfacing from the growing intrusions of foreign cultures and languages into Newar society. In any case, there is no doubt that no culture can resist the wind of change. It is not possible that the Newars will preserve everything of their culture and tradition either, nor is it desirable; but a continuation of unique cultural traits might be a solution. At the same time, some traditions, for instance domination of women by men and caste discriminations, must be brought to an end.

During the past two centuries, the Newars of the Valley have also migrated extensively to other parts of the country and beyond. In many areas, they have mixed with other ethnic groups and lost contact with the centre of their culture, and may well have forgotten their language and culture. The Newars outside the valley of Kathmandu, especially the new generations, have lost their ancestors' language because the trend of speaking Nepali in their homes became more common. In most cases, these Newars can be recognized only by their family or caste names. Only for the past one or two decades or so have the Newars outside the Valley been attracted to their past glory and the Nepalbhasa. Newars living in many places outside the Valley are now seeking to learn the Nepalbhasa. In the past few years, the Association of the Newar Speakers has sent teachers to various places. Even from Sikkim, Newar people have made contact with the Association to acquire Nepalbhasa teachers and school textbooks. The Newars of India organized a gathering in Kalimpong for the first time on 2–3 December 1995.[14] Now there are branches of the All India Newar Organization in several Indian states. Even Newars living in the US have formed their own organizations, such as the Nepal Friends Association (Nepah Pasa Pucha, 1991), the International Nepalbhasa Seva Samiti, the Newah Organization America, and so on. They have launched publications such as *Dabu, Swonigaa a Newah Vijnana* and *Lasakusa*. They have also initiated Websites for a global network of the Newars. Most recently, in a bid to revive the Newar language, the Newah Organization America also began teaching the Newari language to their children. Similarly, the Newars in the UK have initiated the Pasa Pucha in London. Despite such activities, the Newars who have migrated away from their homeland are at risk of losing their identity.[15]

The Newar people have also been debating the creation of a new party of their own. Many Newar leaders, such as Keshavman Shakya, have been pleading for a Newar ethnic party; but a prominent Newar leader such as Padma Ratna Tuladhar is not in favour of such a party. Shakya is also of the view that the Newars need to have their own militia and army in order to achieve rights such as autonomy. From the viewpoint of present politics, not only the Newars but also all other ethnic groups are divided into as many factions as there are political parties. Shortly before the local elections in 1997, the Newar National Movement Coordination Committee (Nevah Rastriya Andolan Samanvaya Samiti) emerged. It aimed at organizing the Newars politically and ethnically to fight for equal rights for their language and nation. However, its attempt to field ethnically motivated candidates in the Kathmandu Valley during the 1997 local elections did not succeed. It was found that the Newar politicians preferred to contest the election on political party tickets rather than on ethnic lines.

With the exception of the ruling Hindu Bahun-Chhetris, Dalits and Muslims and the Madhesi Hindus, all other nationalities of Nepal accept being called Janajatis; but the debate on whether or not the Newars should be called a Janajati is going on among the Newars. Most Newar activists, such as Malla K. Sundar, who is at present the chairman of the National Forum of the Newars, strongly advocate calling the Newars a Janajati and plead for joining hands with all other Janajatis in the fight to achieve equal rights for all the nationalities, while several leaders, such as Hitkarvir Singh Kansakar, who initiated the Democratic Newar Association, believe that the Newars are not a backward community, and so it is inappropriate to call the Newars a Janajati. They also consider the Newars a 'nation' or '*rastra*' because the Newars, though consisting of various castes and races, speak a single language and follow a single culture.

Many also lump the Newars together with the Bahuns and Chhetris, and present them as economic and political elites. However, the Newar nationalists do not agree with this. They argue that while it was true to a certain extent in the past, this view does not fit the present-day reality. As the inhabitants of the Valley, the Newars had easy access to education and other modern facilities, which gave them the chances of occupying some administrative posts soon after the 1951 change, but the situation has changed drastically in the past two to three decades. They argue that those Newar individuals who occupied ministerial or administrative posts were never able to play any role to benefit the Newar society as a whole. For instance, during the Panchayat regime, Marich Man Shrestha was made prime minister and Jog Meher Shrestha was made a minister time and again, but they were not in a position to do anything in favour of the Newar community, because it was not possible for individuals to influence the decision-making processes. Similarly, those Newars who occupied high-ranking administrative posts also were unable to act in favour of the Newars. They believe the situation did not change after the 1990 political change. Even the supreme leader of the then ruling NCP, Ganeshman Singh, had to protest against the Bahun domination (*bahunbad*) (Daryn 2003; Malla 1992); and in the subsequent years, not only was his voice ignored, but also Nepal saw a growing trend of Bahun domination in every sphere of Nepalese life. Being himself a Bahun, Kanak Mani Dixit (2001) presents interesting data that shows how the Bahuns in Nepal have rapidly succeeded in sweeping up all the important administrative posts for themselves, depriving the Newars and all other ethnic groups of opportunities soon after the 1990 political change. The truth is also that there are no instances of the Newars' involvement in any decision-making bodies since the time the Gorkha conquered Nepal in 1769. Therefore, the Newar leaders perceive that the Newars are equally deprived of ethnic rights as all other ethnic groups of Nepal. Thus, they justify their claim of being an indigenous nationality or janajati.

Conclusion

With the downfall of the former communist regimes in Eastern Europe, many small nations have emerged, while others remain incipient. Tamil insurgents in Sri Lanka (Kapferer 1998) can be seen as one of the most destructive examples of national uprisings in South Asia. In Southeast Asia, Indonesia is experiencing equally violent uprisings. For decades, India has been witnessing violent national movements: in many instances, it managed to overcome them; but there are several cases that remain unresolved, for instance the case of Kashmir. In many respects, present-day ethnic nationalist movements in Nepal are heavily influenced by events elsewhere, though they are unusual in their by-and-large non-violent record. The Nepalese government has taken few steps to fulfil ethnic demands. The news is now broadcast in several languages, but the Supreme Court of Nepal infuriated non-Nepali speakers with its 1999 decision prohibiting the use of local languages in municipalities and district development committees.

At present, all ethnic groups in Nepal feel they are overshadowed by Khas linguistic and cultural chauvinism. This situation can only lead to undesirable hostilities. A number of bloody incidents have recently taken place in eastern Nepal in which local people killed Bahuns, burnt down their houses and chased them away from their villages. Up until now, however, ethnic uprisings in Nepal have been peaceful in nature and, except in a few cases, violence has been avoided. However, the beginning of 2007 in Nepal saw an extremely violent Madhesi uprising in South Eastern Tarai, costing lives of more than three dozens people. The most interesting aspect of the present ethnic mobilization is that the nationalities are united through the Nepal Federation of Indigenous Nationalities in their fight against the ruling Khas.

Restructuring of the state with federal map, the right of secession and the right of autonomy are currently under debate among the intellectuals and the political parties of Nepal. Many fear that the country might face disintegration if such demands were to be fulfilled, while others think they may be necessary to avert ethnic violence. Some scholars such as Bhattachan (2000) view Nepal as a place 'waiting for ethnic insurgency'; Bista (2005) sees that the 'country seems to be gradually turning into a major killing field' since ethnic conflicts have not been addressed in time; while others (Whelpton 1997) see that there are possibilities for 'peaceful co-existence' if wise decisions are taken.

Leaderships of all the political parties, including the republican Maoists, are in the hands of the Bahun-Chhetris. The NCP and the Nepali Congress Party Democratic as well as the CPN-UML talk about the rights of the nationalities and languages of Nepal, but have failed in implementing their programmes on nationalities and languages when they were in power. Small parties, such as the Terai-based Nepal Sadbhavana Party and the National Democratic Party, a Rightist party, participated in the government but were not in a position to affect policy changes because they were minority partners in the government. Other communist factions such as the Communist Party of Nepal (Unity Centre), the Communist Party of Nepal (Marxist-Leninist-Maoist) and the Communist Party of Nepal (Marxist Leninist) demand equal rights and autonomy for all nationalities. The CPN (M) is the only political party that presents radical demands for the oppressed nationalities, such as the right to self-determination for all nationalities.[16] Thus far, the existing political parties of Nepal have not been able to convince the oppressed indigenous nationalities in Nepal that their slogans presented in favour of nationalities are honest.

The failure of parliamentary parties in Nepal to address the grievances of these nationalities has caused the latter to turn to the Maoists for support. It has been noted that the Maoists receive active support from non-Hindu ethnic groups and oppressed lower castes (Dalits) (Bhattachan 2000). The majority of people killed by the police on suspicion of Maoist activity come from ethnic nationalities and oppressed castes. Bhattachan speculates that the Maoists' People's War played a crucial role in preventing ethnic insurgency in Nepal.

To develop mutual understanding among the different groups in a multi-ethnic country such as Nepal is a difficult task. Claims were being made that the king has served as the 'unifying symbol' of all nationalities in Nepal, but the palace massacre of 1 June 2001, in which practically the entire family of King Birendra was murdered, has jeopardized that claim. The only surviving brother of the slain king, Gyanendra, has now become king. Unfortunately, in contrast to the respect shown to his slain brother and his family, people do not trust the present king. The image of the deified kings of the past has been destroyed. On top of that, the present king Gyanendra's extra-constitutional autocratic rule has made him the most unpopular king in the history of Nepal. The 19-day People's Movement of April 2006, in which Nepalis expressed their solidarity, forced King Gyanendra to bow down and reinstate the House of Representatives on 23 April 2006. On 18 May 2006, the reinstated Parliament unanimously endorsed the historic House Proclamation 2006, which radically stripped the powers of the king. The House also announced plans to hold elections to the Constituent Assembly for drafting a new Constitution. The oppressed nationalities are speculating about possibilities for favourable changes, but no steps have yet been taken to satisfy them so far.

The majority of ethnic nationalities, including a large section of the Newars in Kathmandu Valley, are sympathetic toward the Maoists because of their populist slogans in favour of exploited nationalities. In this country with many nationalities, the government is unable to effectively address ethnic conflict. If ethnic uprisings are not handled with care, Nepal may face unpleasant violence, as has been experienced by the Balkan states and Southeast Asian countries, including neighbouring India, Sri Lanka and Pakistan. As a state with many ethnic nationalities, Nepal must find a way to address the rising phenomenon of ethnicity before it becomes too late.

Notes

1. Michaels (1997) discusses significance of the cow in the Hinduization of Nepal.
2. Lecomte-Tilouine (2004) presents intriguing discussions of the role of the Maoists in the Magars' struggle for their ethnic rights. Many scholars have discussed the Nepalese Maoist rebellions (see Hutt 2004; Karki and Seddon 2003; Onesto 2005; Pathak 2005; Shrestha 2004; Thapa 2003).

3. As a result of increasing awareness among the ethnic nationalities, more ethnic groups were registered in 2001 (HMG CBS) than in the 1991 census. However, scholars criticize the CBS census for not presenting accurate data for ethnic groups, specifically for calculating the number of Nepali speakers by deducting the numbers of the other ethnic groups from (Shrestha 1999b).
4. See Turner (1931: 353). See also Acharya (1953) and Mali (1978: 14–18).
5. For a detailed discussion on the word 'Nepal', see Malla (1983a: 63–69).
6. See (Malla 1981: 5–23, 1983b: 57–68, 1996: 1–9). Witzel (1980: 326) also saw the possibility of this being an early form of Newar; however, he preferred to call it 'Kirati'.
7. Newar settlements, such as Dolkha, already existed outside the valley in the early Malla period, but extensive migration of the Newars began after the 1769 Gorkha conquest—to escape Gorkhali persecution also, among other reasons (Gellner 1986: 102; Lewis and Shakya 1988: 25–65).
8. For a detailed analysis of the 1854 legal code of Nepal, see Hofer (1979).
9. See Nepalbhasa Mamkah Khalah (NMK) (1993).
10. See Shrestha (1995: 448–56) on Newar journalism.
11. They accused the supposedly national organisation of being controlled by the Left and alleged that the draft constitution for the proposed national organization was undemocratic because it was written to fulfil the interests of Left-inclined Newars. For an elaborate discussion of the political affiliations of the Newars, see Gellner et al. (1997).
12. A point to note here is the case of the Rais. The Rais have more than 30 languages—thus creating difficulties in presenting them as a nation. Some Rai linguistic activists have organized separate linguistic associations and demand separate recognition.
13. On the first Newar school, see Shrestha and van den Hoek (1995).
14. See *Sandhya Times*, 29 December 1995.
15. See Gubhaju (1999) and Maharjan (1999) for more on the American Newars' striving for their identity. See Shrestha (2005) on how the Newars in Sikkim are devoted to reviving ritual and identity in the diaspora.
16. See *Janajati* (1997: 8). See also Lawoti (2001, 2003).

References

Acharya, Baburam. 1953. 'Nepal, Nevar ra Nevar Bhasa (Nepal, Nevar and Nevar Language)', *Nepal Samskritic Parisad* 1 (1): 1–16.

All Nepal Nationalities Organization. 1997. *Janajati* (in Nepali) 1 (1): 5–10.

Alter, Peter. 1994 (1989). *Nationalism*. London: Arnold.

Anderson, Benedict. 1991. *Imagined Communities*. London: Verso.

Bista, Dorbahadur. 1976 (1967). *People of Nepal*. Kathmandu: Ratna Pustak Bhandar.

Bista, Purna B. 2005. 'Conflict and Ethnicity', *The Kathmandu Post*, 10 January. Kathmandu, Nepal.

Bhattachan, Krishna B. 2000. 'Possible Ethnic Revolution or Insurgency in a Predatory Unitary Hindu State, Nepal', in Dhruba Kumar (ed.), *Domestic Conflict and Crisis of Governability in Nepal*, pp. 135–62. Kathmandu: CNAS.

Brass, Paul R. 1991. *Ethnicity and Nationalism: Theory and Comparison*. New Delhi: Sage Publications.

Burghart, Richard. 1996. 'The Conditions of Listening: The Everyday Experiences of Politics in Nepal', in C.J. Fuller and J. Spencer (eds), *The Conditions of Listening: Essays on Religion, History and Politics in South Asia*, pp. 300–318. New Delhi: Oxford University Press.

Daryn, Gil. 2003. 'Bahuns: Ethnicity without an "Ethnic Group"', in Marie Lecomte-Tiloune and Pascale Dollfus (eds), *Ethnic Revival and Religious Turmoil: Identities and Representations in Himalayas*, pp. 162–73. New Delhi: Oxford University Press.

Dixit, Kanak Mani. 2001. 'Bahuns and the Nepali State', *Nepali Times* 65: 19–25 September.

Gellner, David N. 1986. 'Language, Caste Religion and Territory: Newar Identity Ancient and Modern', *Archives European Sociology* 27: 102–48.

———. 1995. 'Introduction', in David N. Gellner and Declan Quigley (eds), *Contested Hierarchies: A Collaborative Ethnography of Caste among the Newars of the Kathmandu Valley, Nepal*, pp. 1–37. Oxford: Clarendon Press.

———. 2003. 'From Cultural Hierarchies to a Hierarchy of Multiculturalisms: The Case of the Newars of Nepal', in Marie Lecomte-Tiloune and Pascale Dollfus (eds), *Ethnic Revival and Religious Turmoil: Identities and Representations in Himalayas*, pp. 73–131. New Delhi: Oxford University Press.

Gellner, David N., Joanna Pfaff-Czarnecka and John Whelpton (eds). 1997. *Nationalism and Ethnicity in a Hindu Kingdom: The Politics of Culture in Contemporary Nepal*. Amsterdam and New York: Harwood Academic Publishers.

Gellner, Ernest. 1983. *Nations and Nationalism*. Ithaca: Cornell University Press.

Greenfeld, Liah. 1992. *Nationalism: Five Roads to Modernity*. Cambridge, MA: Harvard University Press.

Gubhaju, Bina. 1999. 'The Fluidity of Ethnicity: The Case of Nepali and Newar Identity in the United States', *Contributions to Nepalese Studies* 26 (1): 135–49.

Gurung, Ganesh M. 1999. 'Ethnic Identity and Politics of Ethno-Museum in Nepal', in Ram B. Chhetri and Om P. Gurung (eds), *Anthropology and Sociology of Nepal: Cultures, Societies, Ecology and Development*, pp. 81–90. Kathmandu: SASON.

Hangen, Susan I. 1999. 'Making Mongols: Identity Construction and Ethnic Politics in Ilam District, Nepal', in Ram B. Chhetri and Om P. Gurung (eds), *Anthropology and Sociology of Nepal: Cultures, Societies, Ecology and Development*, pp. 69–80. Kathmandu: SASON.

HMG CBS. 2001. *Population Census*. Kathmandu: Central Bureau of Statistics.

Hoek, A.W. (Bert) van den 1990. 'Does Divinity Protect the King? Ritual and Politics in Nepal', *Contributions to Nepalese Studies* 17 (2): 147–55.

Hofer, A. 1979. *The Caste Hierarchy and the State in Nepal: A Study of the Muluki Ain of 1854*. Innsbruck: Universitatsverlag Wagner.

Hutt, Michael (ed.). 2004. *Himalayan People's War: Nepal's Maoist Rebellion*. London: Hurst & Company.

Jaffrelot, C. 1996. *The Hindu Nationalist Movement in India*. New Delhi: Viking Penguin India.

Joshi, Bhuwan Lal and Leo E. Rose. 2004. *Democratic Innovations in Nepal: A Case Study of Political Acculturation*. Kathmandu: Mandala Book Publications. (First edition in 1966 by University of California Press, Berkeley.)

Kapferer, Bruce. 1998. *Legends of People, Myths of State: Violence, Intolerance, and Political Culture in Sri Lanka and Australia*. Washington and London: Smithsonian Institution Press.

Karki, Arjun and David Seddon (eds). 2003. *People's War in Nepal: Left Perspectives*. New Delhi: Adroit Publishers.

Kraemer, Karl-Heinz. 1996. *Ethnizität und Nationale Integration in Nepal: Eine Untersuchung zur Politisierung der Ethnischen Gruppen im Modernen Nepal*. Stuttgart: Frans Steinier Verlag.

Kraemer, Karl-Heinz. 2003. 'The Janajati and the Nepali State: Aspects of Identity and Integration', in Marie Lecomte-Tiloune and Pascale Dollfus (eds), *Ethnic Revival and Religious Turmoil: Identities and Representations in Himalayas*, pp. 227–37. New Delhi: Oxford University Press.

Lawoti, Mahendra. 2001. 'The Maoist Insurgency and the State of Emergency Declaration in Nepal', *Economic and Political Weekly (India)*, 15 December. (Reproduced at: http://sherwa.de/publications/mahendra_2001.htm).

———. 2003. 'The Maoists and Minorities: Overlap of Interest or the Case of Exploitation', *Studies in Nepali History and Society* 8 (1): 67–97.

———. 2005. *Towards A Democratic Nepal: Inclusive Political Institutions for a Multicultural Society*. New Delhi: Sage Publications.

Lecomte-Tilouine, Marie. 2004. 'Ethnic Demands within Maoism: Question of Magar Territorial Autonomy, Nationality and Class', in Michael Hutt (ed.), *Himalayan People's War: Nepal's Maoist Rebellion*, pp. 112–35. London: Hurst & Company.

Lewis, Todd and Daya Ratna Shakya. 1988. 'Contribution to the History of Nepal: Eastern Newar Diaspora Settlements', *Contributions to Nepalese Studies* 15 (1): 25–65.

Maharjan, Tulsi R. 1999. 'Editorial: Revisiting our Culture', *Dabu* 1 (5). Available at: http://www.nppa-us.org/dabu/dabu98/index.html.

Mali, Indra. 1978. *Jhigu Bhay: Jhigu Khamgva* (Our Language Our Words) (in Nepalbhasa). Pokhara: Mam Bhay Mulukha.

Malla, Kamal P. 1981. 'Linguistic Archaeology of the Nepal Valley: A Preliminary Report', *Kailash* 8 (1–2): 5–23.

———. 1983a. 'Nepal Archaeology of the Word', *Nepal Heritage Society Souvenir*, pp. 63–69. Kathmandu: PATA Conference.

———. 1983b. 'River Names of the Nepal Valley: A Study in Cultural Annexation', *Contributions to Nepalese Studies* 10 (1–2): 57–68.

———. 1990. 'The Earliest Dated Document in Nepalbhasa: The Palm Leaf from Uku Baha N.S. 235/AD. 1114', *Kailash* 16 (1–2): 15–26.

———. 1992. 'Bahunbad: Myth or Reality', *Himal* 5 (3): 22–4.

———. 1996. 'The Profane Names of the Sacred Hillocks', *Contributions to Nepalese* Studies 23 (1): 1–9.

Michaels, Axel. 1997. 'The King and the Cow: On a Crucial Symbol of Hinduization in Nepal', in David N. Gellner, Joanna Pfaff-Czarnecka and John Whelpton (eds), *Nationalism and Ethnicity in a Hindu Kingdom: The Politics of Culture in Contemporary Nepal*, pp. 79–99. Amsterdam: Harwood Academic Publishers.

NMK (Nepalbhasa Mamkah Khalah). 1993. *Bhintuna Pau* (A Souvenir). Kathmandu: The Association of Newar Speakers.

Onesto, Li. 2005. *Dispatches from the People's War in Nepal*. London: Pluto Press.

Pathak, Bishnu. 2005. *Politics of People's War and Human Rights in Nepal*. Kathmandu: BIMIPA Publications.

Pradhan, Kumar. 1991. *The Gorkha Conquests: The Process and Consequences of the Unification of Nepal, With Reference to Eastern Nepal*. Kolkata: Oxford University Press.

Rosser, C. 1979 (1966). 'Social Mobility in the Newar Caste system', in C. von Fürer-Haimendorf (ed.), *Caste and Kin in Nepal, India and Ceylon Anthropological Studies in Hindu-Buddhist Contact Zones*, pp. 68–139. New Delhi: East-West Publications.

Seton-Watson, Hugh. 1977. *Nations and States*. Boulder: Westview Press.

Shakya, Daya Ratna. 1997. 'In Naming a Language'. Paper presented at the 3rd Himalayan Language Symposium, UC Santa Barbara, the USA, 18–20 July.

Shrestha, Bal Gopal. 1995. 'Nepalbhasaya Patrakarita: Mhigah, Thaum va Kanhay (Newar Journalism: Past, Present and Future)', in Phanindra Ratna Vajracarya (ed.), *In Memory of Maniharsha Jyoti*, pp. 448–56. Kathmandu: Nepalbhasa Parisad.

———. 1999a. 'The Newars: The Indigenous Population of the Kathmandu Valley in the Modern State of Nepal', *Contributions to Nepalese Studies* 26 (1): 83–117.

———. 1999b. 'Rastriya Janagananay Khay Bhay Lhaipinigu Mithyamka: Chagu Namuna Sakvaya Suntol GaViSa (The Deceptive Numbers of Nepali Speakers in the CBS Census: an Example—the Suntol VDC in Sankhu), *Newah Vijnana* 3: 71–3.

———. 2002. *The Ritual Composition of Sankhu: The Socio-Religious Anthropology of a Newar Town in Nepal*. Leiden: University of Leiden.

———. 2005. 'Ritual and Identity in the Diaspora: the Newars in Sikkim', *Bulletin of Tibetology* 41 (1): 25–54.

Shrestha, Bal Gopal and Bert van den Hoek. 1995. 'Education in the Mother Tongue. The Case of Nepal Bhasa (Newari)', *Contributions to Nepalese Studies* 22 (1): 73–86.

Shrestha, Chuda Bahadur. 2004. *Nepal Coping with Maoist Insurgency: Conflict Analysis and Resolution*. Kathmandu: Chetana Lokshum.

Smith, Anthony D. 1986. *The Ethnic Origin of Nations*. Oxford: Blackwell.

Subba, Tanka. 1999. *Politics of Culture: A Study of Three Kirata Communities in the Eastern Himalayas*. Chennai: Orient Longman.

Tamang, Parshuram. 1994. *Janajati ra Rastrabad* (Nationalities and Nationalism). Kathmandu: Jana Sahitya Prakasan Kendra.

Tamang, Sitaram. 1987. *Nationalities Question in Nepal* (in Nepali). Kathmandu: Palmu Tamang.

———. 1999. *Marxbad ra Nepalma Janajati Andolan* (Marxism and Nationalities' Movement in Nepal). Kathmandu: Pragati Pustak Sadan.

Thapa, Deepak (ed.). 2003. *Understanding the Maoist Movement of Nepal*. Kathmandu: Martin Chautari, Centre for Social Research and Development.

Toffin, Gérard. 1978. 'Intercaste Relation in a Newar Community', in J.F. Fisher (ed.), *Himalayan Anthropology*, pp. 461–81. The Hague and Paris: Mouton.

Turner, Ralph Lilley. 1931 (1980). *A Comparative and Etymological Dictionary of the Nepali Language*. New Delhi: Allied Publishers.
Vaidya Shrestha, Revatiramanananda. 1991. *Pracina Nepalya Juyavamgu Kham* (The Ancient History of Nepal) (in Nepalbhasa). Kathmandu: Thaumkanhay.
Vajracarya, Dhanavajra and Kamal P. Malla. 1985. *The Gopalarajavamsavali*. Wiesbaden: Franz Steiner.
van der Veer, Peter. 1994. *Religious Nationalism: Hindu and Muslims in India*. Berkeley: University of California Press.
van Driem, George. 1992. 'In Quest of Mahakiranti', *Contributions to Nepalese Studies* 19 (2): 241–47.
van Schendel, Willem. 1994. 'The Invention of the "Jummas": State Formation and Ethnicity in Southern Bangladesh', in Sekhar Bandyopadhya, Abhijit Dasgupta and Willem van Schendel (eds), *Bengal Communities, Development and States*, pp. 135–73. New Delhi: Manohar.
Whelpton, John. 1997. 'Political Identity in Nepal: State, Nation, and Community', in David N. Gellner, Joanna Pfaff-Czarnecka and John Whelpton (eds). 1997. *Nationalism and Ethnicity in a Hindu Kingdom: The Politics of Culture in Contemporary Nepal*, pp. 38–78. Amsterdam and New York: Harwood Academic Publishers.
Witzel, Michael. 1980. 'On the Location of the Licchavi Capital of Nepal', *Studien zur Indologie und Iranistik* 5/6: 311–38.

9

The Spread of Theravadin Vihar Buddhism among Newars in the Kathmandu Valley

KESHAV LALL MAHARJAN

INTRODUCTION

Some elite Vajrayana Buddhist Newars learned about Theravadin Buddhism during the early 1900s in India and tried to revive this sect in the Kathmandu Valley during the 1930s in a subtle way to protest against the then autocratic Rana regime. Initially, this sect of Buddhism was supported by the liberal Vajrayana Buddhists from the upper castes of the Newar society, who were rather well-to-do economically. It started to take root in the Kathmandu Valley during the 1950s, amicably accepted by the locals as 'Vihar Buddhism'.

It spread widely in the valley among the rural Newars and beyond in the 1980s. It became a firm trend after the democratic change in 1990. The introduction and the spread of Vihar Buddhism in Nepal and the Kathmandu Valley especially can be understood both as the cause and the effect of the political and socio-economic transformations of contemporary Nepal. Generally, the followers of Vihar Buddhism, especially the monks, the sponsors and the intellectuals, are regarded as people who have some kind of grudge against the society or dissatisfaction with the prevailing systems, institutions and networks.

Many also undertake Vihar Buddhism in order to protect themselves from the angst of this fast-changing world of globalization and economic differentiation in which they are unable to keep pace and feel consciously or unconsciously insecure. Declaring oneself as a Vihar Buddhist in the former case—that is, as monks, sponsors and intellectuals do—may be regarded as a sort of active protest against existing systems, institutions and networks, and an attempt to create an alternative for self-realization. By contrast, for the latter, that is, for a vast number of people in the laity, the adoption of Vihar Buddhism can be regarded as the passive action of the masses in search of a place or means for self-realization. This has been more pronounced since the 1980s, when Vihar Buddhism penetrated Newar society deeper and wider in terms of areas, communities, castes, economic status, gender, cultures and networks, at times incorporating diaspora Newars and non-Newars (especially after 1990). In general, these Vihar Buddhists are more liberal and progressive, as well as more concerned, hardworking and sober-living people.

Keeping this in mind, this chapter will examine the spread of Vihar Buddhism among Newars in the Kathmandu Valley. In doing so, the socio-economic dynamism of the local setting will be discussed, with a case study to understand the socio-economic nature of the place and the people involved where the Vihar Buddhism is being introduced and is spreading. Also, the actual mechanism or process of the spread of the Vihar Buddhism will be discussed, taking into consideration the perceptions of local people. Further, recent developments involving local youths in Vihar Buddhism and the Vihar Buddhists getting involved in the post-democratic activism and contentious politics (the Newar nationalistic movement, secular movements and language movements) will be discussed to put the spread of Vihar Buddhism in the contemporary societal dynamics perspective. Before that, a quick review of macro-economic trends and Newar society and religion will be made.

Macro-economic Trends

Ever since the feudalistic Rana regime was deposed in 1951, Nepal has adopted a mixed economy to manage and develop the country. However, during all these times, the national income was always less than the national expenditures and the internal incomes of tax and revenues were never available for development expenditures (Maharjan 2005). The most part of this deficit was met with foreign grants and/or aid. In the mean time, the overwhelmingly agriculture-dependent nature of the economy has not changed. The economic disparities between urban and rural regions, non-agricultural and agricultural sectors have widened, thus marginalizing the people in the rural region and making them highly vulnerable to food insecurity and welfare hazards. The people who find it hard to make ends meet also migrate to India, which ultimately makes the people and the country very much dependent on India. Tradable goods to be exported to third countries beyond India and tourism destinations in the various parts of the country have been explored to create economic opportunities to enhance people's food security and welfare. However, there has been no miracle yet. The whole economy of the country is lagging behind and the speed of development is very slow. The people, especially the middle and the lower strata, including rural residents and agriculture-dependent communities, have not yet received their share of the dividend of democracy in terms of enhancement of food security and welfare. Those who did, under niche conditions, also feel insecure under the current system that has become individualistic and competitive without safety nets. Hence, many people are living in anxiety.

Newar Society and Religion

In the Newar society of the Kathmandu Valley, Hinduism and Buddhism co-exist and they are hard to differentiate as practiced by the laity. This is especially true for Vajrayana Buddhism and Hindu Tantrism, which became intricately intertwined with each other during the late Malla period. They follow the same annual rituals and the same rites of passage (though minute details may differ). Although *ahimsa* (non-violence: avoiding involvement in fowl and animal sacrifice) is supposedly essential to the Buddha's teachings, it is relatively less important in Vajrayana Buddhism.

Vajrayana Buddhism is particularly associated with the Bare and Gubhaju castes. They are regarded by other Newars as Buddhists by birth, whereas the Dyahbramu (Newar Brahmins), Joshis and some Sheshyahs (including those who claim to be the descendants of the Malla rulers of mediaeval Nepal and their various courtiers) are regarded as Hindus by birth. Where the vast majority of the population is concerned, whether they are regarded as or claimed as Buddhist or Hindu, a stark differentiation between the two religions is neither sought nor possible (see also Gellner 1992; Gellner and Quigley 1995).

However, during the Shah-Rana regime before 1951, Hinduism received preferential treatment, as it was (and is) the religion of the rulers.[1] Buddhism was regarded as an offshoot of Hinduism and secondary to it, if not inferior. Buddhist priests were regarded as secondary to Hindu priests, regardless of their scholarly and practical ritual achievements. In the caste system supported by the state during the Rana period, they were assigned lower status than Hindu priests (Hofer 2004). Thus, claiming to be non-Hindu is often a sign of protest against the feudalistic and authoritarian regime.

In order to claim to be Buddhist and be regarded as such by others, it would be necessary for them to act publicly, with some visible performance. This means that in order to be generally recognized as a Buddhist in the locality, it is not enough simply to undertake traditional Vajrayana rituals, but to practice either (Tibetan) Lamaism or Theravada Buddhism. The first thing the laity will have to do in this case is to visit a Lama monastery or Theravadin Vihar regularly to listen to sermons and participate in regular group worship. The final step would be to become a *lama* or *bhikshu*.

In the case of the Theravada, commitment means first of all a regular visit to a *vihar*, listening to the preaching of the *bhante* (monk), taking part in Buddha puja and trying to practice the teachings of the Buddha in everyday life. They do so by not offering fowl and animal sacrifices in rituals, by becoming vegetarian, by giving up alcohol, and so on. They offer rice, money and other consumer goods to the *bhante* on the day of Buddha *puja*. Later, they start fasting during the Buddha *puja* and also take on various practices of *Panchashil* and *Astashil* ('Five Precepts' and 'Eight Precepts') and so on, in order to lead a life according to the Buddha's teachings (Bajracharya 1986; Pragya 1982; Sushobhan 1985; Vajracharya and Vajracharya 1983). They also participate in the *bhojan* (communal meal) after the Buddha *puja* sponsored by the laity. Many people do all this individually, while still participating in the rituals of traditional Buddhism and Hinduism as a member of their family or *guthi*.[2]

Annual rituals may be simplified and rites of passage may be modified according to Theravada if the practicing person is the head of the family. Visiting the *vihar* and *ahimsa* are the basic symbols of Theravada for the laity and essentially go together with the *vihar*. The laity understands it as the *Vihar dharma*. For them to go to the *vihar* is equivalent to abiding by dharma, and they use the expressions *viharay wanegu* (to go to the *vihar*) and *dharmay wanegu* (to go [to do] *dharma*) as synonyms. Hence, in order to remain close to informants' own way of describing their religious practice, the form of Theravada practiced in the valley will be referred to as Vihar Buddhism hereafter.

The Introduction of Theravadin or Vihar Buddhism in Nepal

Vihar Buddhism was revived in Nepal during 1930s by people who, dissatisfied with the Rana regime and the religious practices of the time, came in contact with it in Kolkata, India, and later in Sri Lanka and Myanmar. The Newar merchant community with trading *kothis* (houses) in Kolkata were influenced by the Maha Bodhi Society and its founder Dharmapala, a Sri Lankan *anagarika* (nun) no doubt played a crucial role in reviving Vihar Buddhism in Nepal. Since people could not protest against the Rana regime openly, they expressed their protests indirectly in the form of undertaking and or encouraging Buddha *dharma*, which was different from the Hindu *dharma* as well as being different from Vajrayana Buddhism. Another form of protest that was lurking then was the language movement. The Newars were pushing for recognition for Nepal Bhasha, the Newar language,[3] with a strong sentiment of Newar nationalism. They came together and moved forward jointly by publishing Sanskrit and Pali Buddhist texts as a journal in Nepal Bhasha called *Buddha Dharma*, published in 1925 by Dharmacharya. This was the first magazine or newspaper in Nepal Bhasha. Later, a monthly journal called *Dharmodaya* became the platform for such movements. Dharmacharya also organized the Buddha Jayanti on the day of Swanha (ya) Punhi (the full-moon day in the month of Baishakh according to the Vikram calendar) in 1926 to celebrate the day of the Buddha's birth, enlightenment and passing away.

The first monks to lead a monastic life with full Theravadin ordination were Mahapragya and Pragyananda, ordained by Chandramani, a Myanmarian monk living in Kushinagar, India, in 1932. Chandramani also ordained the Nepali nuns Dharmapali, Sanghapali, Ratnapali and Dharmachari, all from the rather affluent families of Uday, the trading community of the Newars (LeVine and Gellner 2005). But all these monks and nuns were treated in a hostile manner by the Rana regime and were exiled. In exile, they formed the Dharmodaya Sabha, the Buddhist Society of Nepal, in 1944, which still exists in Kathmandu today as an umbrella organization for Nepali Buddhists. It was only in the late 1940s that they could return to Kathmandu again and found the Ananda Kuti Vihar in Swayambhu in 1948. It was the official headquarters of the Theravada Buddhists, headed by Bhikshu Amritananda and boasted a Buddha relic brought from Sri Lanka. The All-Nepal Bhikkhu Mahasangha was formed in 1950 and Theravadin monks, with a monastic community of about 50, including *gurumas*, as the nuns were called, started activities openly in an organized way. *Vihars* were constructed at many abandoned and often ruined *bahal/bahis* (traditional rectangular housing complexes with a number of Buddhist temples and statues in the large central public space), some of which had been used as a public toilet or garbage collection centres by the local people. About 30 such *vihars* were found in the valley by the 1980s.

After the end of the Rana regime in 1951, King Tribhuvan made Buddha Jayanti a public holiday in 1952 and sponsored the recitation of *Mahaparitran* and Buddha pujas in 1953.[4] In 1956, marking the 2,500th year since the Buddha's *parinirvan* (death, salvation and supreme enlightenment), Nepal, under the leadership of Bhikshu Amritananda, hosted the fourth World Fellowship of Buddhists conference. This conference was inaugurated by King Mahendra, and delegates from more than 40 countries participated. It being the first ever international conference held in Nepal, the king and the country got much-needed publicity. This millennial celebration was remembered for a long time among the Newars of Kathmandu.

However, Vihar Buddhism was not able to develop smoothly thereafter. The introduction of the Panchayat political system after 1960 dealt it a severe blow, as it did to the Newar nationalist movement. This is also true for all other ethnic and language movements.

To convert a person from one religion to another was forbidden. Hence the Theravadin monks could only reach out to Buddhists by birth: basically to the Bare, Gubhaju and Uday among the Newar community. With few exceptions, *bhante* and *gummas* came from these communities. But the mass of the laity came from the Jyapu community. It was not a big problem for them to undertake Vihar Buddhism along with their traditional rituals, Hindu or Vajrayana, and thus their worship was still in line with the Panchayat injunction. Slowly the monastic communities started to perform rites of passage and to recite sutras to aid in the fulfilment of wishes, to heal ailing family members or to ensure safety when travelling for their laity, just like the Tibetan Lamas and Vajrayana Gubhajus, or for that matter Hindu Brahmin priests. This must have provided the space necessary for the lay community to undertake Vihar Buddhism (see also Gombrich and Obeyesekere 1988).

The Spread of Theravadin or Vihar Buddhism among Newars in Kathmandu Valley

With the fast reduction of farmland in the Kathmandu and Patan city areas, the suburban area of the valley has begun to supply fresh food—vegetables, milk, poultry, and so on—making rational use of surplus family labour. Residential and industrial areas have sprawled out into these suburbs. Governance, though slow, is becoming more systematized and more firm. The felt need for development is everywhere. Leaders with more local interests are starting to be recognized in electoral politics. More schools are being established and systematized. All these phenomena have their effects on daily life and people's ways of thinking and their perceptions of the things happening around them, tinging some with hope and some with anxiety. People have become more aware of their rights and duties, of choices and alternatives in their mode of livelihood, and of a need to create and uphold their identities.

Adopting a new religion and/or reviving an old one can be considered a way to establish social and personal identity in a time of rapid change. The move towards Vihar Buddhism can be understood in the same way.

In fact, Vihar Buddhism has spread quite widely in Nepal, especially among the Newars in the Kathmandu Valley. By the 1980s, Vihar Buddhism had spread throughout the Kathmandu Valley and its vicinity, especially among the Newars, though much more strongly in some villages and some urban contexts than in others. It had also spread beyond the valley among diaspora Newars, at times involving Tamangs, Gurungs, Magars and Tharus. In the 1980s, it began to spread faster, especially with the active participation of the second-generation monks and nuns. In the 1990s, after the democratic movement, the lay community turned to it more and more as an alternative, if not with high expectations. After 1990, the spread became faster and much wider, involving more of the diaspora Newars and other ethnic groups, and even some Parbate Hindus. Currently, there are 90 Theravadin *vihars* in Nepal, of which 57 are in the Kathmandu Valley and its vicinity (Kondanya 2003). One can find a *vihar* in almost all the Newar settlements that existed from the Malla period in and around the valley. The nearest ones from central Kathmandu would be Nakadesh (Nw. Nara), Thimi, Sunakothi (Nw. Sunagu), and others, and the farther ones would be Thankot, Dhulikhel (Nw. Dhaukhyah) and Trisuli. Besides, there are more than 30 Buddhist institutions called *sangha* or *samuha*, or centres, which are purely Theravadin and organize or sponsor Theravadin activities. As for the active monastic community, there are about 200 *bhikshus* and *sramaneras* (*bhante*) and about 120 *anagarikas* (*gurumas*), some preaching and some still studying (ibid.). Those who are studying not only learn about Buddhism but also acquire a general education, some even in foreign countries, such as Sri Lanka, Myanmar, Thailand, Taiwan, Australia, France, the United Kingdom and the United States of America.

The Case of Nakadesh

The Local Setting

The local setting discussed here is Nakadesh (also known as Nagadesh and Nara in Newar), which is regarded as a part of a bigger settlement, Thimi (see also Lachhi 1989; Malla et al. 2000). This settlement is dominated by the Jyapu, the Newar farmers, but also has a sizeable population of Sheshyah and Nay, with a few houses each of Gubhaju, Kau, Nau and Jugi (Maharjan 1994). Sheshyahs are regarded as latecomers to the village and claim to be the descendants of the concubine of the last Malla king of Bhaktapur. They all identify themselves as Narmis. The physical order of the settlement is typically Newar. The social order of the society is based on caste and the division of caste roles in performing religious and social functions is all typically Newar and basically Hindu, understood to have been formed by the end of the Malla period (see also Gutschow and Kölver 1975; Levy 1990; Muller 1981; Quigley 1985 and Vergati 1995). But at the same time, the *chibhadyah*, the basic element of Buddhism, is to be found in almost all big *nanis* (courtyard-like spaces surrounded by houses, often with a well and/or images of some Hindu deities) and *lachhis* (wide, open public spaces). Gubhajus, including those from Thimi and Bhaktapur, perform rituals for the Jyapus and act as their domestic priests. Dyahbramus from Thimi are the priests of the Sheshyahs. Some of the Jyapus also use them as domestic priests.

Contemporary Socio-economic Dynamism

Although farming is the main occupation of the majority of the people, most of them own very little land. About half of them have less than two *ropanis* (1 *ropani* = 0.05 ha) of farmland and those holding more than four *ropanis* are only about 20 per cent of all the villagers (Maharjan 1998). Life is very hard for those who depend on farming as the only source of livelihood, especially if they are producing only traditional crops, such as traditional varieties of paddy, wheat, maize and millet. It is only with the introduction of vegetable farming that the economy of ordinary farmers became better. By the 1990s, it became a typical vegetable-growing area, with almost all the farmers producing some sort of vegetables on their land. Vegetable production, in which all members of the family can be engaged, has become one of the main activities of the farmers of this village and they are able to earn a living even from the little land they cultivate. Farming as a whole in the valley has widely gone through a major transformation during this period.

However, the people of the village are no longer dependent on farming alone. The transportation of goods and people, the sale of farm products, and the running of corner shops, tea stalls and restaurants are jobs that are fast increasing in the village. Butchery, tailoring, iron-smithery and cobbling are the jobs traditionally undertaken by people of occupational castes (Dalits). Some locals are managing private schools. Government servants, bank clerks and teachers are also increasingly represented in the village. Some commute from the village to Kathmandu on a daily basis. Some locals manage broiler farms, pig farms and brick kilns. In addition to the traditional cottage industries of producing earthen pottery, masks, beaten rice and yeast, now factories making cold drinks, alcohol, medicines, electrical parts, carpets and garments have been established nearby, especially from the 1980s. Consequently, a steady polarization into the haves and the have-nots is observed to be in progress.

The Spread of Theravadin or Vihar Buddhism

Although there were Thimi-Narmi people who used to visit *vihars* in Patan and Kathmandu even in the 1950s and 1960s, Vihar Buddhism got its momentum in the region during the 1970s, when the remains of an old *chaitya* were found during the cleaning of a public toilet. The laity decided to make a *vihar* in this place and started to collect donations from various people. They finally built the Thimi Pati Vihar in the early 1980s and a *bhikshu* (monk) from Dharan took up residence here and started to preach Vihar Buddhism.

Meanwhile, more and more of the Narmis got interested in Vihar Buddhism. Most of them were those worried about the dark side of the current socio-economic dynamism. They were especially worried about the problem of ageing, the increase of nuclear families with only old couples or a lone old member living far away from the ideal Newar joint family, the lavish lifestyles and individualistic ways of thinking of the younger generation, and the polarization of society. They wanted to improve the situation and wanted to transform society into a more accommodating, more productive and more stable one. They were trying to find an answer and perhaps salvation in Vihar Buddhism and formed the Nagadesh Bauddha Samuha (Nagadesh Buddhist Group Caucus, a socio-philanthropic voluntary organization) in 1987 with a small but active membership (Nagadesh Bauddha Samuha 1988). Through this organization, they began *vihar* activities independent of the Thimi Pati Vihar. The Samuha became the donor group for a new *vihar* in the village, named Nagadesh Buddha Vihar, and they sponsor and undertake activities in the Vihar pertaining to a deeper understanding of Vihar Buddhism. The activities are all voluntary.

The Samuha had 200 members, including 75 women, in 1996. They participated actively in Vihar Buddhism and in other social activities of the Samuha. They were all active *upasakas* and *upasikas* (devotees). The activities of the Samuha include yearly celebrations of Buddha Jayanti, Dharmachakra Prabartan Divas and Ayu Sanskar Divas, mini gatherings once a week, Buddha *puja* on every *astami, amai* and *punhi* (the eighth day, new-moon day and full-moon day of the lunar calendar), daily voluntary prayer and meditation at the community meditation centre, and participation in bigger Buddha *puja* events at various *vihars* in the valley. They also organize Buddha *puja* processions in the village and worship all the *chibhadyah* in the village on the important full-moon days of the year—*Swanha (ya) Punhi, Guru Punhi, Si Punhi* and *Gunla Punhi*. Mini gatherings are accompanied by meditation, reciting of Pali *sutras*, and the exchange of ideas on the Buddha's teachings and their adaptation to daily life. The number of participants in such gatherings varies from 20 to 30; invariably about half are female. During the Buddha *pujas* in the *vihar*, a *bhante* and sometimes a *guruma* leads the meditation, recites *paritran slokas* and gives the preachings. He or she explains the Buddha's teachings—the *Panchashil, Astashil*, and so on—illustrating with various episodes from daily life. At the end of the *puja, upasakas* and *upasikas* give offerings of money, fruits, rice, sweets and incense to the priest. A *bhojan* (ceremonial meal) is arranged soon after. Members who remain in the *vihar* thereafter discuss various matters as long as time allows.

People going into or out of the *vihar* fold their hands and bow, saying '*bhagawan sharana* ([I take] refuge in the Lord [Buddha])'. The Samuha members also use this Buddhist greeting instead of the more common *namaste* or more recent (Newar revivalist) *jwajalapa*.

Some of the core members of the Samuha are rather learned. One of them was a teacher for 18 years in the Buddhist high school Ananda Kuti Vidyapeeth, in Swayambhu. Many of them are teachers in the local high school. The head teacher and social worker, who is also a core member of the Samuha, is a very diligent and hardworking person with a deep understanding of the Buddha's teachings.

He was the key person in the whole movement. He claimed to have been influenced by Ambedkar and introduced Ambedkar and Rahul Sankrityayan and their deeds to the local residents. He has written about 10 books on various aspects of Buddhism in the local context and their understanding along Theravada lines.

The Nagadesh Bauddha Samuha was registered at the district office of Bhaktapur as a non-profit organization and actively organizes eye camps in cooperation with the Lion's Club of Kathmandu and Tilganga Eye Hospital, treating eye patients from near and far. It also organizes literacy classes for adults, women and children and *pariyatti* classes on Buddhism. Often the *vihar* is used by village youths for various purposes. Some members even talked about organizing skills training to help local youths earn their living. Samuha members also voluntarily contribute to various community works (such as maintenance of roads and drainage systems). They help villagers with complicated official papers regarding bank accounts, sanction of loans, asset registration or transactions, acquiring citizenship cards, dealing with the police and civil administration, and service-delivery programmes run by the government and NGOs.

As an institution, the Samuha also acts as a pressure group along with other similar groups for achieving common goals. In this regard, in 1990 it sent an official letter with 17 recommendations—including that Nepal be declared a secular country and that citizens be granted the right to use Nepal Bhasha for official purposes—to the committee drawing up the new Constitution. Later it also wrote to protest against the Supreme Court's decision to ban the use of Nepal Bhasha in Kathmandu and Maithili by the Rajbiraj municipality for official work of the respective municipalities.

The Laity's Perceptions of Theravadin or Vihar Buddhism

This section will analyse Vihar Buddhism as perceived by the local people on the basis of a survey of 53 members (85 per cent male) of the Nagadesh Bauddha Samuha and 35 non-members (91 per cent male) during 1996–97. The members who were surveyed were active members of the Samuha and the non-members were chosen at random. The questionnaire dealt with the socio-economic condition of those surveyed, the current problems they were facing, their opinions about Vihar Buddhism, its (probable) role in the socio-economic development of the village and in making a difference to their livelihoods, on making the *vihar* more participatory and effective and on the spread of Vihar Buddhism. In addition to this, the members were also asked about the time and reason of their joining the Samuha, the ways in which they participated in or contributed to the *vihar's* activities and the changes in their daily lives after becoming Vihar Buddhists.

Almost all the Samuha members were over 30 years of age and more than one-third of them were over 60, which revealed that the Samuha members were indeed aged (Table 9.1). Most of them were living in joint families. However, 42 per cent of the families were nuclear, of which 11 per cent were made up of only aged people over 65, living either alone or with their spouse only. Two old men who earlier lived alone have started to live in the *vihar* itself. Of the families, 11 per cent had a female family head above 60. As for the non-members, almost all of them were under 60 and more than half (57 per cent) lived in nuclear families. Some 60 per cent of the families were headed by people in their forties.

About two-fifths of the Samuha members were literate, having had primary education or attended adult literacy programmes. About one-third were illiterate and the rest had education beyond high school (10 years of schooling); some were even graduates with bachelor's or master's degrees. About two-fifths of the non-members were illiterate, about one-fourth just literate and the rest had education beyond high school. Some 78 per cent of the Samuha members were farmers, 13 per cent were teachers and the rest held salaried jobs or were self-employed entrepreneurs. Six of the female members undertook virtually all the housekeeping work in the *vihar*. Almost all of them owned some piece of farmland, but half of them had less than 5 *ropanis*. About a third owned land up to 10 *ropanis* and few (9 per cent) owned more than 10 *ropanis*. With regard to the family income in cash, 15 per cent said they earned more than Rs 50,000 per year, while 26 per cent said they earned between Rs 25,000 and Rs 50,000 and 23 per cent earned less than Rs 25,000 per annum. The rest said they either had no cash income or had so little cash, which passed through their hands so quickly that they could not work out its accumulated value over a year. The main profession of

Table 9.1
Socio-economic Characteristics of Nagadesh Bauddha Samuha Members and Non-members

Description	*Members (%)*	*Non-members (%)*
1. Gender		
Male	85	91
Female	15	9
2. Family type		
Nuclear	42	57
Joint	58	43
3. Age		
Over 60	36	6
30–60	58	83
Under 30	6	11
4. Literacy and education		
Illiterate	34	43
Literate	42	23
SLC (school-leaving certificate)*	13	20
College and higher education	11	14
5. Occupation		
Farming	78	83
Teaching	13	11
Others (business, service, etc.)	9	6
6. Landholdings		
Landless	6	6
Under 5 *ropani***	49	77
5–10 *ropani*	36	14
Above 10 *ropani*	9	3
7. Cash income		
None or negligible	36	49
Less than Rs 25,000***	23	9
Rs 25,000–50,000	26	29
More than Rs 50,000	15	13

Notes: * = SLC is 10 years of schooling
** 1 *ropani* = 0.05 ha
*** US$1 = Rs 70

83 per cent of non-members was farming. The remaining included teachers, those in salaried jobs and businessmen. Although almost all had a piece of land to farm, nearly four-fifths had farmland of less than 5 *ropanis* in extent. Only one person had land more than 10 *ropanis*. Almost all had some amount of cash income, but half could not specify it, as the amount was too small. About 13 per cent

had an annual family income of more than Rs 50,000, one even having more than Rs 300,000 per year. But one-third had cash incomes of Rs 25,000 to Rs 50,000. Thus it can be said that economically there was not much difference between the two groups.

All 53 were active members of the Samuha and 80 per cent of them were founding members who joined the Samuha on their own initiative (Table 9.2). The remainder joined the Samuha after they

Table 9.2
Process of Members Getting Involved in Nagadesh Bauddha Samuha

Description	*Percentage*
1. Involvement	
Founding member	81
Influenced by friends/other members	19
2. Earlier involvement in Vihar Buddhism	
Involved in Thimi Pati Vihar	19
Involved in other *vihars*	13
None	68
3. Practice of other religious activities	
None	42
Other Hindu or Buddhist rituals	58
4. Reason for becoming a member	
Belief in Buddhism and desire to gain knowledge of it	45
Wish to listen to Buddhist precepts and gain peace of mind	36
Wish to bring about changes in life and spend a righteous life	19
5. Changes in daily life after becoming a member	
Eating and clothing habits	17
Behaviours and ways of thinking	22
Family relations	24
Relations with others and society	18
House and farm work	11
Others	8
6. Leisure	
Meditation, singing hymns and counting the rosary	17
Learning about Buddhism	32
Discussing religion with friends	26
Listening to Buddhist precepts	17
Others (visiting friends, helping with family work, resting at home)	8
7. Contributions to the Vihar	
Every possible way	23
Economic contributions	32
Physical contributions	24
Moral support (participation, administration, negotiation, planning)	21

were asked to do so by their friends and neighbours who were members. All of them had consent from their family members to their becoming Vihar Buddhists. Some 32 per cent were active in Vihar Buddhism even before the formation of the Samuha. They participated in various Buddha *pujas* and gatherings in *vihars* in Thimi, Patan and Kathmandu. More than half of them also practiced traditional Hindu and Vajrayana Buddhist rituals, including *astami brata* (fasting) and *haribhajan* (singing of hymns).

Many (80 per cent) said their reason for joining the Samuha was that they wanted to increase their knowledge of Vihar Buddhism, *thahtah thahmhaysinah mhasikegu* (to get to know and understand their own inner self) and to achieve tranquility. But some 20 per cent also said that they were looking for improvements in their lives. Most of them feel some changes have occurred, including in eating and clothing habits (17 per cent)—many became vegetarians, stopped consuming alcohol and admired simple dress, behaviour and ways of thinking (22 per cent); relationships with family (24 per cent), neighbours and society (18 per cent); and ways of performing house and farm work (11 per cent). Almost all of them spend their leisure time by being involved in Vihar Buddhism by meditating or singing hymns (17 per cent), listening to precepts and learning about Buddhism (49 per cent) and discussing religion with friends (26 per cent), mostly in the *vihar*. They were always ready to contribute to the *vihar* for its betterment, some (23 per cent) in every possible way, some (32 per cent) emphasizing donation of money, land or other material goods, some (24 per cent) volunteering to do various jobs and yet others (21 per cent) by offering moral support or aiding in planning, and management and negotiation of various activities.

There was not much difference in perception of problems, personal or societal by Samuha members and non-members (Table 9.3). However, more (64 per cent) of the members seem to have no problems in their lives than the non-members (35 per cent). Nearly half of the members opined that the *vihar* plays a significant role in village solidarity and development through promotion of goodwill and harmony among the people, whereas fewer (17 per cent) non-members shared this opinion (Table 9.4). On the other hand, more (57 per cent) of non-members opined that the *vihar* could nurture feelings of togetherness and lead to an egalitarian society. There was

Table 9.3
Problems Perceived by Nagadesh Bauddha Samuha Members and Non-member Respondents

Description	*Members (%)*	*Non-members (%)*
1. Personal problems		
None	64	35
Health	6	10
Economic	13	33
Family	15	10
Others (housing, education, social)	2	12
2. Societal or village problems		
Sanitation	46	46
Drinking water	26	30
Public service (education, health, security)	9	4
Public infrastructure (toilet, road, temple maintenance)	8	11
Commodity and farm-inputs price	5	2
Others (drug addiction, unemployment, social feelings)	6	7

Note: Multiple answers allowed.

Table 9.4
Opinions of Nagadesh Bauddha Samuha Members and Non-member Respondents on the *Vihar*

Description	*Members (%)*	*Non-members (%)*
1. Role of *vihar* in village solidarity and development		
Promotes goodwill and harmony among the people	47	17
Nurtures feelings of togetherness and an egalitarian society	19	57
Has a good effect on education and social awareness	34	26
2. Ideas on making the *vihar* more participatory and effective		
Publicize Buddhism and share knowledge with others	47	51
Strengthen activities (organize more programmes, bring residing monk)	28	17
Work together with mutual understanding and serve people	25	32

Note: Multiple answers allowed.

not much difference in the opinions of the two groups on the role the *vihar* could play in improving education and creating social awareness. The opinions of both groups were also not much different on the ways of making the *vihar* more participatory (people-oriented) and effective. They were basically positive and they wanted to publicize Buddhism and share knowledge, work together to serve the people and increase the activities, which included organizing more religious programmes, bringing residing monks to the *vihar* to raise its ascetic status in the monastic circle, and so on.

Except for the ageing and the problems that come along with it, there seemed to be basically not much difference between the socio-economic conditions of the two groups and their perception of Vihar Buddhism. Rather, non-members had higher expectations as outsiders and evaluated it more positively than the members. Hence, all of the non-members could be regarded as a pool of potential Vihar Buddhists, ready to become active Vihar Buddhists when the time came even with a very small motivation. Thus, it can be said that Vihar Buddhism will further spread in this region and beyond.

Recent Developments

This section summarizes developments between 1998 and 2004. The Nagadesh Bauddha Samuha became the Madhyapur Thimi branch of the Dharmodaya Sabha, an umbrella organization of all sects of Buddhism in 1999. The Nagadesh Bauddha Lyayemha Puchah (Nagadesh Buddhist Young People's Group), the brother association of the Nagadesh Bauddha Samuha, was formed in the same year. The Samuha uses the youth power of the Lyayemha Puchah to make the presence of Vihar Buddhism visible whenever possible.

Nine members of the Samuha (including one who was a Jugi by caste, i.e., who would have been considered 'untouchable' in the past) (see also Hartman 1993) and some members of the Lyayemha Puchah participated in a temporary *pravrajya* ('going forth') and *upasampada* (ordination) ritual organized by the Dharmakirti Adhyayan Gosthi in Lumbini in December 2000. They all became *bhantes* for a week. The *Upajjayacharya* (the presiding learned monk) at this function was Bhadant U. Nanissar Sayadaw of Sitagu International Buddhist Academy, Myanmar.

The Samuha also organizes short and long Buddha *pujas* several times a year. Not only has the frequency of such *pujas* increased, but also the timing of holding the *pujas* is thought-provoking for the villagers. For example, it commemorated Rahul Sankrityayan on the very day of Biska Jatra in April 2001, the most important traditional Hindu festival, which goes together with the local identity in the region for many people. It also commemorated the Buddhist king Ashok on the day of Mohani Nakhah, the biggest national Hindu festival, in October 2001 and Disarmament Day in October 2002. According to the secretary of the Samuha, they were just the right days to commemorate such events to make the people more aware of the Buddha and the Buddha's teachings, including *ahimsa,* piousness, detachment and the righteous way of living.

In a bid to secure a resident monk for the *vihar*, an offering of alms to *sramaneras* was held at Nagadesh Buddha Vihar and Bhikshu Varasambodhi stayed for a *varsavas* (rainy-season retreat) in the *vihar* from the month of August in 1999. The following year, Bhikshuni Keshavati started a *varsavas* in the *vihar* in July 2000. During her *varsavas*, Keshavati Guruma encouraged the children to study Buddhism and gave *pariyatti* lessons to them. More and more children of Samuha members are taking *pariyatti* exams and are becoming the pool of future *sramaneras* and *anagarikas* and perhaps *bhantes* and *gurumas* thereafter. Some have already taken ordination to become *sramaneras* or *anagarikas*. Four of them were sent to Sri Lanka for further studies where they not only learn Buddhism but also receive a general college education. The Samuha is hopeful that some of these children, if not all, will continue monastic life after returning from their studies and will become the resident monastics—*bhantes* reared by the Samuha from their own community—of the *vihar* consequently raising the dignity of the Samuha members and at the same time raising the ascetic status of the Vihar among the monastic circle.

The Samuha felicitated the government for declaring Shankhadhar Sakhwa, the eponymous founder of the Nepal Sambat in 879, a national hero. It also commemorated the understanding made between Satya Narayan Goenka and Jayendra Saraswati of Kanchikamkoti Pith (in the Maha Bodhi Society, Sarnath), in November 1999 to not regard Buddhism as a branch of Hinduism and to practice their respective forms of worship with dignity and due respect to each other as independent faiths. It campaigned for local people to write 'Bauddha' and 'Newar' in *dharma* and *jati* columns of the 2001 Census and sent a letter requesting the government to include Pali as an elective language in the courses for students of classes 9 and 10.

In addition, eye camps were organized regularly by the Samuha to treat eye patients. Furthermore, an eye donation campaign for the Nepal Eye Bank was also initiated in the village and the eyes of a Samuha member who died in July 1999 were donated to two persons from Trisuli and Dhading. Earlier, people would think that one would be reborn without eyes if they mistreated their eyes. But with the influence of Vihar Buddhism, they have started to realize that *mikhadan* (eye donation) is good as it helps others to see the beautiful world even after one's own death (see also Leve 2002). 'Anyway the inner sight is what is most needed for living a pious life and to gain Buddhist wisdom (*gyan/prajna*),' says a donor. There were already 172 men and women, old and young, both from monastic and lay communities, regardless of caste, willing to donate their eyes. In March 2001, a 'Mikhadan Mahadan' meeting was organized jointly by the Samuha and the Lyayemha Puchah in the *vihar* to make people aware of eye donation.

Besides, the most visible changes in daily life among the laity can be said to be the stopping of *ban syayegu*, a simpler observation of traditional rituals and the widespread abstinence from drinking alcohol and eating meat. Many were performing Buddha *puja* on their birthdays. Some were changing the way they observed rites of passage. About 10 cases of *samsmaran*, or Theravada-style memorial services, were performed during the period 2000–2003, instead of the *shraddha* that is carried out under the instruction of a Gubhaju as an annual homage to the ancestors. During the funeral processions of the Samuha members, all the members, including women, participated in reciting Pali *sutras*. The core members were planning to replace the traditional funeral ceremony itself and put an end to their traditional death *guthi* in the near future. Due to the thought-provoking activities undertaken by the *vihar*, people were also changing their earlier cosmological concepts, as in the case of eye donation, the worship of deities and human relations. Slowly, more and more members of the same family were joining the Samuha.

Conclusion

Vihar Buddhism was revived in Nepal during the 1930s by people who, dissatisfied with the oligarchic Rana regime, came in contact with it in Kolkata, India, and later in Sri Lanka and Myanmar. Since people could not protest against the Rana regime openly, they expressed their protests indirectly in the form of undertaking and or encouraging Buddha *dharma*, which was different from the state-sponsored Hindu *dharma*. However, Vihar Buddhism was not able to develop smoothly thereafter. The introduction of the Panchayat political system after 1960 dealt it a severe blow, as it did to other ethnic and language movements. Socio-economic transformations of Kathmandu Valley affected its 'native' inhabitants, the Newars, the most. It brought changes in all spheres of their political, economic, social and cultural life. The introduction and spread of Vihar Buddhism in Nepal can be understood both as the cause and the effect of such changes. Generally, the followers of Vihar Buddhism are regarded as people who have some kind of grudge against or dis-satisfaction with the prevailing systems, institutions and networks.

However, this may not be the only reason for involvement on the part of the laity. Most lay people also undertake Vihar Buddhism in order to protect themselves from the angst of the 'fast-changing world' with which they are unable to keep pace and feel consciously or unconsciously insecure in their livelihood. Declaring oneself as a Vihar Buddhist in the former case may be regarded as a sort of active protest against existing systems, institutions and networks, and an attempt to create an alternative for self-realization. By contrast, in the latter, the adoption of Vihar Buddhism can be regarded as the passive action of the mass in search of a place or means for self-realization. This has been more pronounced since the 1980s, when Vihar Buddhism penetrated Newar society deeper and wider in terms of area, community and caste, economic class, gender, culture and network, at times incorporating diaspora Newars and non-Newars, especially after 1990. In general, these Vihar Buddhists were more liberal and progressive, as well as more concerned, hardworking and sober-living people in comparison to their contemporaries.

This was also true for Nakadesh, where Vihar Buddhism started to take its root among the laity in the 1980s. The accidental excavation of an ancient *chaitya* provided a much-needed alternative for people who were feeling insecure in the rapidly polarizing society. Most of them were aged and have-not and are female; all are, to some extent, the victims of the ongoing paradigm change in society. They came in masses to the *vihar* to listen to talks by the *bhantes*, to take the precepts of Buddhism, to overcome familial troubles and loneliness, to heal wounds, to gain the will to guard themselves from extreme consumerism and lavish lifestyles, to control their emotions, to pass their leisure time, and to get peace of mind by following a righteous life by praying, singing hymns and discussing Buddhism—to make a difference in their lives. They were willing to contribute in whatever way was demanded by the circumstances. They formed a Samuha to perform all these activities and create solidarity and be accommodative. The Samuha, in turn, arranges the rites of passage through life needed for the laity in a simpler and *ahimsa*-led way—a Theravadin way. All of these do help the laity to gain what they seek in the *vihar*: knowledge of Buddhism, peace of mind and a righteous life. They also believe that Vihar Buddhism aids them to overcome problems in life and society, and many claim that changes have occurred in their behaviours, attitudes, ways of thinking and relationships and these have made them able to better realize the self.

With the active participation of these younger members, the Samuha could not only organize Buddha *puja* more regularly, but also urge people to become pacifists by arranging such programmes on the various Hindu festival days, which, according to the Samuha leaders, are continued by the people out of sheer habit only. Although most of the then-vibrant members of the Samuha are now aged, there are also some younger educated members who are active in the various social activities in the village, including teaching in the schools and organizing adult and female education programmes, *pariyatti* lessons, health camps, *shramadan* (for communal work), political campaigns, and so on. They also play the role of facilitators in channelling the services of governmental and non-governmental organizations and remain concerned about the causes of the local people. They often act as a pressure group along with other similar groups for achieving common goals, regarding issues of language (recognization of all languages of the nation, including Nepal Bhasa and Pali), religion (freedom of belief and equal treatment for all the religions) and social justice. All of these factors together can be understood to influence people to undertake Vihar Buddhism, and hence aid in its spread among the Newars in Nepal.

Notes

1. Nepal was the only country in the world officially declared a Hindu state. State functionaries, including the monarch, had to function according to this proclamation. The recently reinstated Parliament declared Nepal as secular, though the relevant law is still not promulgated.
2. *Guthis* are characteristic Newar institutions that bring together a group of Newar household heads for a common, usually social and ritual purpose. Many *guthis*, though not all, are based on shared kinship (see also Nepali 1965; Quigley 1985; Regmi 1978).
3. The language of Newars is called *Newah bhae* in their mother tongue, which in Nepali becomes *Newar bhasha* and 'Newar language' in English. The Newar scholars and activists, in line with the ethnic movements in the country prefer this denomination to the earlier one, 'Newari', commonly used in Nepali. Nepal Bhasha is the Sanskritized name of the Newar language used by the language activists and the literary world. The Newar language gets that name as the language of the inhabitants of the then Nepal (Mandala), the mediaeval Newar kingdom of Nepal. Here, 'Nepal Bhasha' and 'Newar language' are interchangeably used according to the context. 'Nw.' before the word will indicate any word in the text specific to the Newar language.
4. The recitation of *paritran* or 'protection' verses is, other than the worship of the Buddha, one of the main rituals of Theravada Buddhism. A *mahaparitran* refers to a collective all-night recitation by a large number of monks.

References

Bajracharya, Badri Ratna. 1986. *Buddhism of Nepal*. Kathmandu: Ananda Kuti Vihar Trust.

Gellner, D.N. 1992. *Monk, Householder, and Tantric Priest*. Cambridge: Cambridge University Press.

Gellner, D.N. and D. Quigley (eds). 1995. *Contested Hierarchies: A Collaborative Ethnography of Caste among the Newars of the Kathmandu Valley, Nepal*. Oxford: Clarendon Press.

Gombrich, R. and G. Obeyesekere. 1988. *Buddhism Transformed: Religious Changes in Sri Lanka*. New Delhi: Motilal Banarsidas.

Gutschow, N. and B. Kolver. 1975. *Ordered Space Concepts and Functions in a Town of Nepal*. Wiesbaden: Franz Steiner.

Hartman, Jens-Uwe. 1993. 'Some Remarks on Caste in the Theravada Sangha of Nepal', in Gerald Toffin (ed.), *Nepal: Past and Present*. New Delhi: Sterling Publishers.

Hofer, Andras. 2004. *The Caste Hierarchy and the State in Nepal*. Lalitpur: Himal Books.

Kondanya, Ven. 2003. 'Theravada Bhiksu, Sramanera, Anagarika Tatha Viharharu (2060)', *Ananda Bhoomi* 31(1): 32–37. Kathmandu: Buddha Vihar, Bhrikutimandap.

Lachhi, Ganeshram. 2046 VS (1989). 'Thimiya Laekuchhen wo Nagadesh (Thimi Palace and Nagadesh)', in Nagadesh Village Panchayat (ed.), *Nagadesh Gaun Panchayat—Ek Parichaya* (Nagadesh Village Panchayat—An Introduction), pp. 50–52. Bhaktapur: Nagadesh Village Panchayat (Nepal Bhasha).

Lacoul, Baikuntha Prasad. 1985. *Sthaviravada*, Kathmandu (Nepal Bhasa).

Leve, L.G. 2002. 'Subjects, Selves, and the Politics of Personhood in Theravada Buddhism in Nepal', *Journal of Asian Studies* 61 (3): 833–60.

LeVine, S. and D.N. Gellner. 2005. *Rebuilding Buddhism: Theravada Revivalism in Nepal*. Cambridge, MA: Harvard University Press.

Levy, R.I. 1990. *Mesocosm: Hinduism and the Organization of Traditional Newar City in Nepal*. California: University of California Press.

Maharjan, K.L. 1994. 'Effects of Modernization on Periurban Families in Kathmandu Valley', in Allen Michael (ed.), *Anthropology of Nepal: Peoples, Problems and Processes*, pp.193–208. Kathmandu: Mandal Book Point.

———. 1998. 'A Study on Farming of Kathmandu Valley in Nepal', *Journal of International and Cooperation* 4 (1): 127–51.

———. 2005. 'Katomanzu Toshi Kinko Sonrakuno no Henka to "Bihara Bukkyo" no Tenkai (Dynamism in Periurban Village of Kathmandu and Spread of Vihar Buddhism)', in H. Ishii (ed.), *Ryudo suru Neparu* (Social Dynamism in Contemporary Nepal), pp. 203–28. Tokyo: University of Tokyo Press.

Malla, K.P., Tej R. Kansakar, Jyoti Tuladhar, Gurushekhar Rajopadhyaya, Saraswati Tuladhar and Tulsi L. Singh (eds). 2000. *A Dictionary of Classical Newari*. Kathmandu: Nepal Bhasha Dictionary Committee, Chwasa Pasa.

Muller, U. 1981. *Thimi: Social and Economic Studies in a Newar Settlement in the Kathmandu Valley*. Giessen: Selbstverlag des Geographischen Instituts der justus Liebzig-Universitat Giessen.

Nagadesh Bauddha Samuha. 1988. *Nagadesh Bauddha Samuhako Bidhan 2051*. Bhaktapur: Nagadesh.

Nepali, G.S. 1988 (1965). *The Newars*. Kathmandu: Himalayan Book Sellers.

Pragya, Rashmi Bhikshu (ed.). 1982. *Buddha Dharmaya Ruprekha* (An Outline of Buddhism). Kathmandu: Gana Mahabihara.

Prajapati, Krishna Kumar, Birendra Bhakta, Pradhanang, Deepakraj Shahpal, Ramkrishna Duwal and Bikram Vaidya (eds). 1997. *Nagadesh—Ek Parichay* (Nagadesh—An Introduction). Bhaktapur: Nagadesh Gaun Bikas Samiti.

Quigley, D. 1985. 'The Guthi Organizations of Dhulikhel Shresthas', *Kailash* 12 (1–2): 5–62.

Regmi, M.C. 1978. *Land Tenure and Taxation in Nepal*. Kathmandu: Ratna Pustak Bhandar.

Sushobhan, Bhikshu. 1985. *Buddhism at a Glance*. Kathmandu: Ananda Kuti Vihar.

Vajracharya, Ratna Kaji and Bijaya Ratna Vajracharya. 1983. *Nepah Dehya Biharya Tahcha* (Key to Viharas in Nepal). Kathmandu: Mantrasiddhi Maha Vihar.

Vergati, A. 1995. *Gods, Men and Territory: Society and Culture in Kathmandu Valley*. New Delhi: Manohar Publishers.

PART IV

Collective Public Protests

10

Illiberal Democracy and the Problem of Law: Street Protest and Democratization in Multiparty Nepal

GENEVIEVE LAKIER

Democracy in Nepal was born in street protest and has lived with it ever since. Almost as soon as the rubble of the People's Movement of 1990 cleared, new protest programmes were announced by groups who threatened 'to take to the streets' (*sadakma orlanu*) if they could not achieve their objectives any other way. Street protests, ranging in forms from the simple rally to the national strike, played a major role in almost all important political struggles in the democratic period, up until the royal proclamation of 1 February 2005 severely curtailed the democratic freedoms of speech and assembly on which protest relied. Nonetheless, it was the resurgence of mass mobilization on the streets that eventually brought down the king's government in April 2006 and inaugurated another period of formal multiparty democracy in Nepal.

This chapter investigates the complicated power of protest in Nepal during the democratic period—and, in particular, its ambivalent role towards democratization, conceived as an ongoing social and political process. Like other analysts of social movements, I do not assume that public protest is necessarily democratic or democratizing (Guigni 1998: xxii), and indeed street protests such as the *bandh*, or general strike, proved at times to be not only highly unpopular but coercive and sometimes violent events, which functioned not to reflect 'popular will' but to demonstrate the strength of a particular social group or party.[1] The turbulence of democratic street politics contributed greatly to the undermining of faith in the democratic system, which allowed the king to establish his absolute authority in 2005 with little immediate reaction from a population weary of the political parties.

Nonetheless, protest did play a vital role in emancipatory projects throughout the democratic period. The freedom to protest publicly provided traditionally disadvantaged groups—such as the Kamaiyas (bonded labourers), women, Adibasi Janajatis (indigenous nationalities) and Dalits (untouchables)—with a means to acquire political and social rights even when still primarily excluded from the country's formal structures of political representation.[2] Street action produced results where legal and political appeals alone could not. Despite complaints by the middle classes about the instability caused by political protest, access to democratic rights and privileges in the 1990s for these groups would likely have been even more restricted than it already was had it not been for their ability to take to the streets when necessary (see Lawoti 2005).

Protest cannot therefore be said to have played an entirely positive or an entirely negative role in democratization in Nepal, even as it became increasingly unpopular. As this paper demonstrates, protests were mobilized both by groups seeking to expand the provision of rights and those seeking to defend against them. In both cases, what the centrality of protest to the negotiation of political power in Nepal reveals is that despite the formally liberal structures of the multiparty state, it was not law alone but the performance of collective power that guaranteed or foreclosed the democratization of rights.

The fact that it was only by demonstrating their *collective* power that groups like Kamaiyas could achieve the legal recognition of their *individual* rights is an irony that makes visible both the new freedom available in the multiparty period and its limits and suggests the extent to which democracy in Nepal can be described as 'illiberal'—that is, democratic rights and privileges determined not on the basis of law, or the disinterested operations of bureaucratic procedure but instead negotiated via ongoing, highly public struggles for political visibility and power.

Illiberal Democracy in Nepal

The protection of the individual's freedom of speech, including political speech, is one of the central human rights guaranteed under liberal political orders. Freedom of speech is important to liberal theory both as an end in itself—a moral good and an inalienable right—and as a means to an end. It is after all via debate and discussion in public that liberals believe, as Immanuel Kant most famously argued, men (we may assume now women as well) will learn to govern themselves (Kant 1970). Freedom of speech is one of the central preconditions, therefore, for democracy itself, insofar as it is supposed to make public reason itself the principle of political order (Habermas 1989). Protest, in this model, functions as a particularly symbolic and affective kind of political speech, one which can play an invaluable role in the ongoing process of democratization insofar as it functions to expand the participation of citizens in the political process and to ensure greater accountability on the part of the government.

But protests such as the *gherao* (sit-in), *chakka-jam* (traffic blockade) and *bandh*, however much they may assist democratization, are highly problematic practices for the liberal theory of democracy. Instead of the rallies and public meetings that characterize normatively liberal public protest, these forms of political opposition function not by simply expressing dissenting opinion, but by enforcing it. All three kinds of protest listed above operate by shutting down or interrupting public space; the *bandh*, in addition, not only impedes public space but coerces, with violence if necessary, public participation in the protest. By erecting blockades and shutting down traffic (in the case of a *chakka-jam*) or by impeding passage into or out of a public building (as in the case of a *gherao*) or by forcing the suspension of all transportation, production and commerce in a city, a district or even the entire country for a day or more (as in the case of a *bandh*), political groups exploit the extreme sensitivity of industrialized mass society to any kind of blockage in mobility and productivity.[3] In so doing, they impede the individual autonomy of other citizens and transform the neutral space of the public into a politicized domain.

Protests that take over public space and obstruct public passage can thus be called illiberal forms of political practice. Forms of action as much as examples of speech, they interfere with fundamental liberal rights (such as the right to privacy and personal autonomy) and because they so often use coercive force, they challenge the state's monopoly on legitimate violence. Most fundamentally, they demonstrate the power of collectives when liberal political philosophy and law recognizes only individuals.[4]

In Europe and North America, strikes and blockades emerged as prominent weapons of a socialist struggle that repudiated liberalism as a political and economic philosophy, and in particular rejected its differentiation of a civil public sphere from relations of production, power and hierarchy (Forman 1998). In Nepal, however, the mobilization of these techniques has not been tied to the labour movement and trade unions have not been their primary agents, in part because of the dominance of the state as an economic agent and the absence of a large industrial sector. It is, as a result, not in the name of the proletariat but on behalf of a far more varied assortment of groups that strikes and such acts are justified. As opposed to the early twentieth-century worker's struggle, these techniques in Nepal have generally been used not to overturn the democratic system, but to work within it.[5]

It is not, of course, the case that all protest in Nepal during the democratic period was coercive. The marches and signature campaigns adopted by the women's property-rights movement (Kunreuther 2002) and the peace rallies organized by human-rights NGOs in the wake of the Maoist conflict are both examples of classically liberal forms of political speech and representation. But the tendency of protest forms to escalate—particularly in the more contentious of the democratic struggles—suggests a certain failure in the effectiveness of these modes of civil protest for all kinds of groups.[6] As we shall see below in the case of the Kamaiya and the syndicate movements, *gheraos* and *chakka-jams* emerged as political options when the legal process of the law and the liberal practices of civil society proved either unavailable or insufficient for the needs of those protesting. The fact that these groups not only could, but arguably had to adopt these means in order to achieve their political ends, suggests the extent to which Nepali democracy functioned outside, or beyond, the law—and as such, can be characterized, for want of a better term, as 'illiberal'.

I cautiously borrow the concept of illiberal democracy from the conservative political analyst Fareed Zakaria, who, in a well-known 1997 article (Zakaria 1997) usefully pointed out that all democracies are not necessarily liberal, nor liberalism necessarily democratic. Although liberalism and democracy tend to be conflated in general political discussion (because democratic theory assumes that if government is 'by the people', it will also be 'for the people'), the two are analytically distinct kinds of things. Democracy is a political doctrine concerned with the legitimacy of governments, while what Zakaria calls 'constitutional liberalism' is a moral and philosophical tradition of norms and values. If the first examines *who* should get to govern, the second asks *how* they should do so. Democracy is thus defined by the formal structures of representation. Liberalism, on the other hand, depends instead on the affirmation of the substantive value of individual rights, human freedom and the preservation of both through the enforcement of the rule of law (ibid.: 25–26).

What is meant by liberal democracy cannot therefore be achieved simply by the mechanism of the vote. In the aftermath of the Cold War and the fall of the Berlin Wall, more of the world's countries (including Nepal) were democratic than had ever been the case previously. However, as Zakaria argued, many of these new democracies were governed by regimes that ignored the basic tenets of liberalism—the rule of law, for example—and sometimes radically restricted the exercise of liberal freedoms while remaining sufficiently popular domestically to win elections and to claim 'the will of the people'. Despite western self-congratulation about the spread of democracies as a force for global peace, Zakaria warned that it was precisely these illiberal democracies that were the source of political instability, because it was these kinds of societies that were particularly prone to both 'hyper-nationalism and war-mongering' (ibid.: 38). As Samuel Huntington, whom he quotes, put it: 'Democracy is one public virtue, not the only one, and the relation of democracy to other public virtues and vices can only be understood if democracy is clearly distinguished from the other characteristics of political systems' (Huntington 1991: 108, in Zakaria 1997: 25).

In Nepal, this lesson can indeed be taken to heart, given the failure of formal democracy to ensure political stability or public peace. The persistence of coercive and unpopular protest after 1990 indeed suggests that the revolution in itself did not guarantee either popular sovereignty or equality. But as opposed to the governments Zakaria describes, what may be understood as the illiberalism of Nepal's democracy did not stem from the excesses of bad governments or from an extremist and anti-western ideology, but instead from a more general and, one might say, structural inability of the government to enforce its authority and to live up to its commitments.

It was not, as Zakaria imagines, that the democratic government in Nepal was too excessive in its exercise of power (this was left to the royal regime to follow it), nor that those who governed adopted ideologies contrary to liberalism as a political philosophy. All of the democratic governments—including, to a surprising degree, the nine-month government of the Communist Party of Nepal (United Marxist Leninist) (hereafter CPN-UML)—expressed a commitment not only to liberalism but even to neo-liberalism as an economic philosophy. In its 1994 election manifesto, the CPN-UML supported the privatization of major sectors of Nepal's economy (including trade, commerce, finance, industry, tourism and urban development) and asserted that there would be 'no ideology in formulation of foreign policy' (Hachhethu 2002: 228), or in other words, that there would be no Leftist ideology.

Instead, it was because of the inability of the central government to enforce the rule of law that protest proved necessary to enforce the rights already guaranteed by the system. Protest, in other words, negotiated the role and the application of the state's law, and suggested that even if 50 years of state-sponsored 'nation building' had not achieved the kind of totalizing bureaucratic authority that both proponents and critics of development believed would come with it, it had given to groups within Nepali society new powers with which to mobilize and negotiate the conditions of their governance on the street. To see how this worked in practice, let us turn to two examples.

A Taxonomy of Protest

The kinds of movements that appropriated the techniques of strikes, lockouts, *gheraos* and blockades that this chapter examines did so for a wide variety of ends. On the one hand were movements that used protest to demand *emancipation*—the recognition by the state of their political and social rights. On the other end of the spectrum were mobilizations, such as that of the transport syndicates described below, which were organized in order to defend or demand institutional privileges and economic monopolies when these conflicted with liberalizing economic law. The protests organized by the political parties—in which category I include the protest mobilizations of groups as diverse as the National Democratic Party (NDP), the Nepali Congress (NC), the CPN-UML and the Communist Party of Nepal (Maoist) or CPN (M)—accomplished at times one or both of these aims, insofar as the demand for political power was also a demand for control of the distribution of patronage and hence a demand for institutional privilege and power.

Examining in the first case the freedom struggle of Kamaiyas—bonded labourers, most of whom are Tharu, officially 'liberated' by His Majesty's government in 2000—makes clear why sometimes illiberal and coercive methods of protest proved necessary to achieve classically liberal ends. Indeed, the emancipation from debt bondage that Kamaiyas were fighting for had been legally guaranteed to them under the democratic Constitution of 1990—which states, in Article 20(1), that 'traffic in human beings, slavery, serfdom or forced labour in any form is prohibited' and that 'any contravention of this provision shall be punishable by law'—as well as in the numerous international conventions against slavery ratified by His Majesty's Government (HMG).[7] But in practice, these rights had not been enacted. When some organizations, most famously the Backward Society Education (BASE), approached government officials for assistance in their struggles against exploitative landlords, they received little sympathy. In response, they turned to protest and to the public techniques of shame and publicity.

The movement began when Kamaiyas working for a local landlord (and one-time minister in the government), Shiva Raj Pant, began demanding that they receive a pay raise to keep their compensation above the minimum wage recently set by the new labour law passed by the Parliament in 2000. When Shiva Raj Pant refused, they filed a case in the local village development committee (VDC), demanding not only the enforcement of the minimum wage law, but also the cancellation of their debts, rehabilitation from the government (that is, land and renumeration) and the guarantee of their personal safety. The case, in other words, turned immediately away from the landlord and towards the government. In an effort to resolve the conflict, the VDC invited the 19 Kamaiyas and Shiva Raj Pant to a mediation meeting. When he did not appear, the Kamaiyas, with the help of organizers from BASE, went for assistance to a higher level of bureaucratic authority, to the district administration office in Dang and to the chief district officer (CDO) of Dang, one Tana Gautam.[8] But the CDO refused to file their case (Lowe and Kasajoo 2001: 87).

As Tatsuro Fujikura recounts, the CDO, Tana Gautam, 'insulted the kamaiyas and supporting organizations'. In response, the Kamaiyas 'immediately began a sit-in in front of the CDO office, on May 12'. Two days later, the sit-in had grown to encompass thousands—according to BASE sources, it numbered as many as 7,000 or 8,000 (INSEC 2000 in Fujikura [forthcoming]: 31). The sit-in was supplemented by demonstrations throughout the bazaar. Demonstrators marched with a black cloth tied around their mouths, to signify the government's inability to listen to their voices; they marched through the bazaar in daylight, bearing lanterns to signify their search for justice; '[o]n other days the demonstrators beat drums, pots and pans, proclaiming that they were trying to wake up the conscience of the government officials' (BASE 2000 [2057 v.s.] in Fujikura 2006: 31).

After 12 days of sit-in, the landlord, Shiva Raj Pant, gave in. Yagya Raj Chaudhary recalls what Shiva Raj Pant said at a meeting at the district office:

> 'I might have borrowed money from these people in a previous life. I grant remission of their loans. They are free from me.' After Shiva Raj Pant said this, I thought to myself: 'He is the most influential person in Kailali district. I won the conflict with such a person.' I was very encouraged. I thought all other kamaiyas should also file a case in the same way. (Lowe and Kasajoo 2001: 76)

The sit-in achieved, within a span of days, what other mechanisms (including continuous efforts to attract the support of high-level politicians)[9] could not. The use of shaming and pressure tactics served not to convince but to *enforce* the demands of the Kamaiyas, which were nevertheless understood, in the end, by all the parties as their right. The landlord Shiva Raj Pant's comment makes this clear, inasmuch as it reinterprets his defeat in the face of the determined action of the Kamaiyas in terms of the cosmological order of karma. The coercive nature of the protest did not make it illegitimate, even if its legitimacy emerged out of a very different notion of political right than that of legal process. What it produced was the belief—not only in Yagya Raj Chaudhary, but very soon in many other Kamaiya activists—that protest could reshape the existing social and economic balance of power in unforeseen ways.

Immediately, after this victory, at least 48 Kamaiyas filed cases in six VDCs in Kanchanpur district; one of them received a freedom certificate in return. Several weeks later, 676 more Kamaiyas from five districts filed petitions. The movement was growing exponentially. On 8 July, in response to its expanding support, Kanchanpur district officials come to an agreement on the emancipation of the Kamaiyas in the district (Lowe and Kasajoo 2001: 87). But in order to achieve a national rather than piecemeal success, the movement decided to continue on to Kathmandu and to the centre of political authority in Nepal.

Its tactics, however, remained the same. On 13 July 2001, protestors organized a sit-in, or *dharna*, this time around Parliament. After three days of sitting without result, however, they decided to take further and more spectacular action.Tatsuro Fujikura (2006: 36) narrates the story from a personal perspective:

> Wanting to keep up the momentum, Dilli Chaudhari and others decided that the protesters should march towards the parliament building, stop traffic, and let a few among them including Dilli [Chaudhari, head of BASE] himself be arrested. On the fourth day of the sit-in, we began to march. When the police stopped the march from reaching the parliament, Dilli and others sat down in the middle of the road. The police decided to arrest Dilli, all the kamaiyas and kamalaharis, and many of the supporters marching with them, including me [Fujikura]. In the Mahendra Police Club where we were all detained, we heard on the 5 o'clock radio news that the government, based on a cabinet meeting held earlier that day, declared that, effective immediately, all the kamaiyas were free, and any debts they owed to the landlord was void. The government also promised to implement rehabilitation measures for the freed kamaiyas. Kamaiyas and their supporters celebrated joyfully inside the Mahendra Police Club, rubbing abhir (red powder) on each other's face.

The CPN-UML and the Congress parties had agreed to liberate the Kamaiyas in the face of the ongoing uprising even prior to the dramatic march upon the Parliament (Fujikura 2006: 36–37). But the tactics of rally, *dharna* and even arrest that characterized the uprising (as it similarly characterized the People's Movement of 1990) played a central role in the success of a movement that (again similar to the 1990 uprising) even a year previously had seemed to enjoy little chance of success.[10] While negotiations with political parties had continued throughout the movement, the decisive transformation in the character and outcome of the uprising was due to the size and the drama of the demonstrators, first in the western districts and ultimately in Kathmandu itself. The attention this received from the media was a vital element in its power; but it was not the media alone that ensured the victory. Since the restoration of multiparty democracy, the emancipation of Kamaiyas had been a subject of considerable political interest (INSEC 1996); but it was only in the face of a confrontation that could not be evaded that the government took active steps to respond. Both symbolically and pragmatically, this was what the tactics of *gherao*, demonstration and arrest were intended to achieve.

The movement from its beginning was thus marked by the law and demanded the enforcement of law, but necessarily *exceeded* the law. In order to achieve their legal rights, the Kamaiyas had to find a way to transcend their invisibility before a law that was only formulated through the mediations of higher officials—such as the CDO above—who could restrict its application. Fujikura stresses the extent to which demonstrations of strength of numbers were vital to the success of the movement. Indeed, both before and after the uprising, BASE organized massive rallies throughout the western Terai, intended to function as *shakti pradarshan* or 'shows of power'. These functioned not only to celebrate the Kamaiya victory, but to 'exhibit their power to the people in the bazaar including the merchants, office workers, politicians and government officials' Dilli Chaudhari, leader of BASE, also visited the local police and administration in bazaars where the rallies took place to explain to these officials that 'the purposes of the kamaiya movement and that it was a peaceful one, and [to] ask them not to randomly arrest or otherwise persecute kamaiyas or their supporters' (Fujikura 2006: 38).

This example suggests the complex relationship between (liberal) law and (illiberal) tactics, or in other words, between insurgency and accommodation, which characterized the Kamaiya Andolan and also many other similar movements.[11] It was not that the Kamaiya organizations wanted to defy the government; they wanted, it seemed, nothing more than to be embedded within its legal order. But in order to do so, they were compelled to take to the streets to demonstrate their power—and hence the justice of their claim—and to establish, for safety as much as identity, their collective strength and the fact that they were not isolated individuals who could be randomly arrested or persecuted.

Even in this case, there were limits to the impact of legal recognition on social emancipation. Several years after the 'victory' of the Kamaiya Andolan, the 'rehabilitation' promised by the government had failed to materialize in full, although thousands of Kamaiya families had been granted some land or money or both.[12] But as for those who could not receive the landlord's signature attesting to their history as Kamaiya, they received no land.

In response, the Kamaiyas blocked the national highway in Kailali and four other districts in the west of Nepal for a day in demand of land (Lowe and Kasajoo 2001: 87). Freed Kamaiyas also began appropriating and farming unclaimed government land. This too was a form of protest and communication. When asked 'Why they decided to occupy government airfields and cotton fields, rather than for instance unclaimed patches of land in the villages or near the forests', Fujikura (2006: 47) writes, 'A number of freed kamaiyas told me that they were trying to "awaken the government".' As he also notes, this comment suggests once more the essentially democratic, rather than revolutionary, orientation of the struggle: not revolt against the existing system, but a quest for recognition within its terms. The persistent failure of the law meant, however, that the Kamaiyas had to continually transgress in order to achieve this.[13]

A Second Example

On the opposite side of the political spectrum from the struggle of the Kamaiyas for legal rights is the *chakka-jam* organized in early June of 2003 by the transportation syndicate, the Federation of Nepal

Transport Entrepreneurs (Nepal Yatayat Byabasayi Mahasangh). If the Kamaiya Andolan was waged for the expansion of liberal rights, the syndicate's chakka-jam—which eventually shut down all Nepal's highways outside of the Kathmandu Valley—was waged, and won, in defence of corporate privileges against the application of (liberal) law. The issue at stake here was one of power as well as one of money: it concerned who enjoyed the privilege of operating public transportation in Nepal in the context of the expansion and liberalization of the public-transport industry.

Public transport in Nepal emerged out of local initiatives. State regulations followed, rather than created, the industry. The first bus services started operating around 1953, almost as soon as there was anywhere to bus to, but public transport on a mass scale did not become a reality in Nepal until the 1960s. Its organization emerged at the local level first, and was initiated on behalf of local entrepreneurs.[14] In 1960, the Morang Transportation Improvement Committee was inaugurated—under the 'assurances' of the Bada Hakim of the province, but nonetheless as an entity separate from the government. A year later, the Morang Motor Syndicate was similarly founded.

Eventually, the centre got involved. In 1965, the national Panchayat passed the first major piece of transportation legislation—the National Transport Management Act—in Nepal's history. The Act sought to regulate the newly emergent entrepreneurs by placing them under the formal authority of the zonal authorities and by establishing a new office of transport authority in the zone called the Zonal Syndicate Office. Whoever wanted to operate a public-transport service had to register with the office, and in turn received a route and a position in the route. The system was organized co-operatively, via *allo pallo* (turn-taking) rather than *pratisparda* (competition).

This emphasis on taking turns, of complementarity rather than competition, was central to the Panchayat state's corporatist ideology. It was this logic that legitimated the banning of political parties and the establishing, in their place, of five separate class organizations to represent and harmonize the special interests of various sectors of the population (Kaphley 1967). The zonal syndicate offices, in a similar fashion, were supposed to encourage the growth of transport but prevent conflict and competition between transporters. But in practice, all power devolved on the syndicates, who in collaboration with the zonal offices took upon themselves the responsibility of establishing and organizing the routes and ordering the queue (Bhattarai 2002 [2059 v.s.]).

What emerged was indeed an impressive, coordinated system of syndicates that organized all human transport throughout the country. In 1978, these organizations banded together to found what is presently known as the Federation of Nepali Transport Entrepreneurs (FNTE). The FNTE operated as an umbrella organization for a host of smaller local bodies composed of small-scale bus and truck owners. Buses, even if registered, could not be used to ferry paying passengers, however, unless their owners joined the local association that assigned routes, set fares and in general organized the terms of their business.[15]

In 1992, however, in line with the rest of the market liberalization, the new democratic government was initiating under the auspices of the International Monetary Fund (Shakya 2002: 178), the rules of public transport in Nepal changed. The post-Panchayat 1992 Transport Management Law established absolute freedom in the running of buses; but by simply threatening a *chakka-jam*, the syndicates managed to convince the drafters of the bill to include an amendment guaranteeing their continued existence.[16] It was only after 1998, when the Consumer Protection Act passed a year earlier came into force, that private companies began to enter the market in any significant number. These companies, such as Agni, Makalu and Yatayat, grew dramatically in the Kathmandu Valley and in Nepal's east, but suffered pressure and intimidation from syndicate owners—particularly in the west of the country, where their control was greatest—that restricted their expansion. It was thus that in December 2001, the Consumer Protection Council established under the 1997 Act explicitly banned all transportation syndicates in Nepal (*The Rising Nepal* 2001).

At first, the syndicates used their close connections with members of the government to defy the ruling. This worked successfully in the immediate aftermath of the decision. An article in the *Kathmandu Post* (2002) explains:

> Even weeks after the government decision to ban decades old syndicate system in transportation, the uncooperative attitude of

> the government offices to materialize [sic] the decision has created a huge hurdle in ensuring healthy market competition. Despite the complete ban of transport syndicate system, department, and offices of Transport Management has been denying to grant [*sic*] permission to new bus companies to start the services in some of the existing routes [*sic*] ... Makalu and Himal bus companies are waiting for route permission. 'We asked for Bhairahawa and Nepalgunj routes, but the office refused,' says Nirmal Rayamajhi, General Manager of the Agni Transportation Company. However, officers of the transportation department turn down such [*sic*] allegation. 'We have not stopped issuing road permission and any company can get such license on the ground of necessity,' they stressed.

The private companies would not, however, give up. A year later, a jeep company in the western transport depot of Butwal tried to operate a long-distance service. Surya Bahadur Bhattarai, general secretary of the FNTE, recounted the small and seemingly unimportant confrontation in Butwal that sparked the *chakka-jam*:

> In the beginning, [the *chakka-jam]* was just a small thing ... what is the cause? (*Karen ke ho bhane*?) Well, the CDO gave the right to run minibuses to a jeep organization, gave them the license. There was no rule that they couldn't get that license. But one sector was running buses, and the other sector was running jeeps. They [had] worked with this understanding for many years .... (interview with Surya Bahadur Bhattarai, 18 August 2003)

More than a question of law, then, the *chakka-jam* was a protest against a disruption in an 'understanding' that was effective, although informally, throughout much of Nepal. The speed with which the conflict expanded revealed its extensive implications for the survival of the existing system; it also revealed the level of organization and support provided to the cartel by their fraternal associations. The *chakka-jam* moved first west and then east, but by 22 June, only five days after the small incident in Butwal, it was nationwide, with the sole exception of the Kathmandu Valley itself. The government pleaded with individual truckers and transporters to keep working and promised security for all who chose to use the highways, but to little avail. The parties met several times for emergency talks, but it took 11 days before the *chakka-jam* was finally called off, to the relief not only of the government but of rural districts facing severe food shortages, as well as the thousands of travellers reportedly stranded on the Indian border. The government and the bus operators had agreed to disagree: or rather, to form an investigation committee, charged with the responsibility of researching the cause of the strike and coming up with solutions. What this meant was that, in essence, the syndicate had won; in fact, one of the three members appointed to the investigation committee was Surya Bahadur Bhattarai, president of the FNTE. There was to be no change in the organization of transportation in Nepal, and three years later, the private companies that had emerged by the end of the 1990s were still battling to gain new route permits.

The syndicate did not win by changing the law, however. That remained as it had been, agreeably un-enforced. What lay behind the conflict was not a question of the legal rules but of what we can call the syndicate's institutional privileges, privileges that indexed a balance of power in which the state did not enjoy ultimate control but instead shared sovereignty over the passage of vehicles on 'its' roads. The director of the government office of transportation in Kathmandu put it most directly when speaking about the reasons for the *chakka-jam*: 'The syndicate thinks it owns the roads, that those roads are its own property. It has been running vehicles on them a long time. They give no one else permission to conduct service.'[17]

As is patent in the disapproval implied in the director's comment, the privileges of the syndicate were not grounded in an authorized model of a social order, one backed up by law and ideology. Nonetheless, the power of the syndicates was historical and conventional; above all, it was recognizable. And it was the *de facto* right of this recognizable authority that the government had to accede to in the face of a *chakka-jam* it could not disarm.

Law, Illiberal Rights and Democracy in Nepal

What both these examples of public protest suggest is the new power made available to collective groups under the democratic dispensation and, in particular, its guarantee of the right to assembly and to speech. The weakness of the democratic state's monopoly on violence and the publicity available in the new independent Nepali press gave political actors a remarkable new source of power: the power, as organizers frequently told me, 'to make the government listen' when it otherwise would not. In the first example, the power of demonstration achieved for the Kamaiyas their freedom—even if a freedom undermined by the domination inherent in 'free wage labor' (Rankin 1999: 24). In the second case, the same power preserved the corporate privilege of the syndicates against their new competitors, in the face of the liberalization efforts of a succession of democratic governments.

Whether operating in demand of or in opposition to the law, both examples reveal the limits of the democratic state's ability to enforce a liberal legal and bureaucratic order. This is true at least partly, as many have argued, from the fact that the state, in Nepal as elsewhere, does not stand outside of society, but is instead embedded within and composed by the hierarchies that constitute the social order. Scholars have long pointed to the exclusionary make-up of the state bureaucracy (Regmi 1978), as well as the larger indebtedness of the government administration to economic and social elites, as explanations for the enduring failure of the state's modernizing and universalistic rhetoric to translate into political and social practice (Lawoti 2005; Seddon 1987). But the patriarchal and hierarchical norms of those who compose state law and occupy government offices are not the only reasons why law fails. Instead, examples like the *chakka-jam* above suggest that the democratic period gave new powers to groups who wished to contest the rule of law by (ironically) co-opting the development infrastructure of highways and mass transportation built by the Panchayat state as a means of fostering 'national integration' (Schloss 1983).

Political theorists and historians, both in Nepal and elsewhere, have argued that the expansion of the modern state changes not only who is in power but how power operates. James C. Scott (1998) has argued that the modern state is distinguished from older forms of political authority by the efforts it expends on making society, as he puts it, 'legible' and hence subject to new and more invasive forms of order and control. Michel Foucault (1977) calls similar effects the panopticism of the modern era. In both cases, what distinguishes states as modern is their new kind of knowledge of, and hence power over, the everyday social world.[18] It is also what characterizes liberalism as a political ideology organized around the primacy of the rule of law. In its faith in law, liberalism presupposes the ability of modern governments to make their abstractions meaningful, to substitute, as Karl Marx put it, the 'unreal universality' of the citizen for the real, material existence of the man (Marx 1972 [1843]: 46).

Ironically, however, the development infrastructure built or sponsored by the Panchayat state as part of a political project that aimed to enhance its political control (Schloss 1983) has enabled various social and political groups—such as those described earlier—to not only oppose the particular policies of the various Nepali governments, but also to undermine the principles of legibility and of law that they were supposed to assist. This opposition and subversion of state authority was not always insurgent or even intentional on the parts of those who enacted it; it was not in any simple sense 'resistance'. The Kamaiyas indeed organized the uprising in order to make themselves visible before the abstracting regimes of state law. The mechanisms by which they did so and the limits of their victory suggest, however, that even those who *desire* the panoptic authority of the modern state and its law to liberate them from an inequitable social order nonetheless achieve their aim by the evasion of the legal process.

The relationship between the modern state and society in Nepal cannot therefore be characterized as simply a one-way optic of simplification, legibility and control. The power of the media, expanded under the Panchayat to be a tool of propaganda and development, has been turned into a conduit of publicity that grants to groups willing to exploit it new powers of resistance and dissent. Protest thus reveals how the 'political hybridity' of the Nepali state, its 'pragmatic tolerance of local autonomy' (Campbell 2003: 104), is negotiated and reshaped under democracy. Indeed, the act of protest itself produced sometimes unexpected new modes of identity and forms of identification, frequently in opposition to the government.

This process indeed can be understood to be a kind of democratization, but one which did not result in a horizontal liberal order composed of autonomous and equivalent citizens—instead produced a highly varied terrain of corporate interests, in dialogue with but never fully described by, the rationalizing impetus of the state's law. What conclusions can be drawn from this for the future are murky at best. It is unlikely that protests will disappear from the political horizon even *after* the new victory of multiparty democracy, and it is unlikely that all or even most of these will have purely emancipatory intent. Nonetheless, the power of corporate groups to take to the streets to make their demands known must be understood to be a power which emerges with, and not in opposition to, the process of democratization and development that has brought Nepal to the contemporary moment. Protest is therefore one of the many ways in which democratization is, has been and will continue to occur in Nepal; but one which reveals the essentially political and contingent nature of even democratic equality.

Acknowledgement

I would like to thank Omar Kutty, Amy Cohen, Biella Coleman and Tatsuro Fujikura for their helpful comments on earlier versions of this chapter. In particular, I am indebted to Tatsuro Fujikura's work on the Kamaiya andolan for my own discussion of the movement. The fieldwork on which some of this chapter is based was funded by a dissertation research grant from the Fulbright-Hays.

Notes

1. By the end of the 1990s, calls for the banning of the *bandh* had become increasingly widespread and popular antagonism towards the *bandh* emerged in a variety of ways. In August 1998, the comedian Raja Ram Poudyel assembled a mound of shoes in Tundikhel, in the centre of Kathmandu, in order to demonstrate the uselessness of the technique by making visible the pairs of shoes Nepalis had worn out walking during strikes due to the suspension of transportation. The positive reception to his performance made clear how many shared his perspective. See *Kathmandu Post*, 'Comedian against the bandh', 5 August 1998.
2. The research on ethnic and caste representation in the Nepali government tends to indicate that disadvantaged groups were less adequately represented under the multiparty system, because of the decline in the Panchayat's integrative patronage policies (see Kramer 2003; Lawoti 2005; Subba et al. 2002).
3. This is why only those areas of rural Nepal beyond the industrial infrastructure built by development—beyond the reach of roads and large shops—generally suffer the least from the call of a *bandh* or *chakka-jam*. The absence of a large industrial economy in Nepal is one of the reasons why protests take on the state-sponsored infrastructure of development rather than the private institutions of industry, such as factories.

4. There are clear exceptions to this rule, however. The Indian Constitution recognizes the rights of minorities and the separate juridical structure of Muslim personal law. See Larson (2001) for a discussion of this history. But India is an exception. Even in international treaties such as the Convention on Genocide that were drafted in the wake of the Holocaust to protect against attacks on communities, rights remain defined at the level of the individual members of the community under threat (Das 1995: 86fn).
5. It was during the anti-colonial struggle in India that already existing practices of caste and political negotiation such as the *dharna* were mobilized for the ends of mass political mobilization (Guha 1997; Hardiman 2004). In post-colonial India, just as in Nepal, they function however as almost routinized elements of democratic political practice.
6. The general failure of NGOs to adopt both liberal and illiberal protest forms is a very interesting tendency in this context and warrants further research. It suggests that public protest in Nepal remains largely organized around the relationship between the state and its citizens.
7. These include the Slavery Convention (1926) and the Supplementary Convention on the Abolition of Slavery, the Slave Trade, and Institution and Practices Similar to Slavery (1956) in 1963 (Fujikura Forthcoming: 28).
8. Yagya Raj Chaudhary, one of the primary organizers, told Lowe that it was the VDC officials who were afraid of Shiva Raj Pant, who referred the case to the district administration office (Lowe and Kasajoo 2001: 76). BASE documents cited by Tatsuro Fujikura argue that it was the Kamaiyas themselves who made this decision (Fujikura Forthcoming: 30).
9. Fujikura reports that during the sit-in, the chairman of the Informal Sector Service, Sushil Pyakurel, sent letters on behalf of the demonstrating Kamaiyas not only to the prime minister, NC leader Sher Bahadur Deuba, but also to the general secretary of the CPN-UML as well as other major political leaders (Fujikura Forthcoming: 34).
10. Fujikura provides a detailed narrative of the multiple objections to the directaction campaign provided by even supporters of Kamaiya rights and freedom. Indeed, the confrontation between BASE, engaged in an ongoing protest movement, and the human-rights NGO INSEC—which, in Fujikura's (Forthcoming: 33) words, 'argued that a comprehensive legislation for Kamaiya liberation and rehabilitation, the kind that they had already drafted, needed to be passed by the Parliament before the liberation process to begin'—can be read as a confrontation between an illiberal and a liberal programme of liberation.
11. One could think here as well of the struggle for women's property rights, which similarly involved dramatic public shows of strength, particularly in Kathmandu. The mass protest rally of reportedly 20,000 women in Kathmandu in December 2000 was similar in many respects to the *shakti pradarshan* of the Kamaiyas. This suggests that even primarily liberal and law-abiding tactics of protest tend to take on the collectivist form of the show of strength.
12. Fujikura reports on a study conducted in 2004 by several NGOs, including BASE, which reports the number of Kamaiyas who had received land from the government to be roughly 12,000. Given that by this point the government recognized officially the existence of almost 33,000 Kamaiya families, the number

who received significant material assistance from the government, while sizeable, was not even close to 50 per cent of those legally entitled (Fujikura Forthcoming: 41–42).

13. This was not, after all, the first movement on behalf of the Kamaiyas. What is known as the Kanara Andolan took place in 1992–93. It similarly involved public demonstration, but to a much greater extent relied upon the reclamation of land rather than upon political transformation. It enjoyed mixed success. In the wake of the movement, the Kamaiyas managed to get one of 'their own' elected to Parliament. But this was not sufficient to ensure their equality; further activism continued to prove necessary. See Dhakal (2000) for a discussion of the earlier movement.
14. Interview with Bimal Aryal, 14 October 2003.
15. By taking on the burdens of capital investment and maintenance, the syndicates relieved the government of a job it could not seem to fulfil. In 1961, the government began the operation of its own transport collective, the Sajha Yatayat; but while initially successful, Sajha never grew large enough to satisfy the market, and in 1991, it closed shop due to mismanagement and disrepair.
16. Interview with Surya Bahadur Bhattarai, 18 August 2003.
17. Interview with Sunir Prasad Singh, Director of the government transport office in Kathmandu district, 29 September 2003.
18. Arguments similar to those put forward by Scott and Foucault have also been made specifically in relation to the Nepali state. Seira Tamang (2000), for example, has critiqued the expansion of women's legal rights enacted under the Panchayat regime in the name of women's development and liberation. Tamang argues that precisely because changes in the law carried out over the course of the Panchayat regime rendered women *visible* as individuals (rather than simply as the property of their husbands and fathers), this in fact 'resulted in the increased power of the Nepali state to intervene directly into family relations' (ibid.: 127) and in the replacement of family patriarchy with the patriarchy of the state. Tamang argues that in fact this served not to equalize women's status but to reinforce patriarchy by explicitly tying women, in law, to the private sphere of home and family, and thus undermining the autonomy of the family itself (and the various communities within Nepal which structure their family organization differently from the Hindu norm). Reformations in abortion, marriage and property law 'led to the active re-structuring of gendered roles to fit dichotomously defined notions of masculinity and femininity in Nepal' (ibid.: 152). State law homogenizes: first, by homogenizing the various kinds of gendered relations in Nepal under the one rubric of the 'Nepali woman', but second, also by expanding the division between public and private spheres to produce the distinctive division of public and private labour found in the West. My analysis suggests something quite different.

References

BASE (Backward Society Education). 2000 (2057 v.s.). 'Kamaiya Andolan Kailalima kun Din ke Bhayo? 2057 Baisakh Jestha 17 Sammako Ghatna Vivaran' (in Nepali), *Sanghari* 3 (12): 10–12.

Bhattarai, K.P. 2002 (2059 v.s.). *Nepal Yatayat Swatantra Majdur Sangathanko Samskyipta Itihas* (A Short History of the Nepal Free Transport Workers Union). Kathmandu: Nepal Free Transport Workers Union.

Campbell, B. 2003. 'Resisting the Environmentalist State', in D.N. Gellner (ed.), *Resistance and the State: Nepalese Experiences*, pp. 83–112. New Delhi: Social Science Press.

Das, V. 1995. *Critical Events: An Anthropological Perspective on Contemporary India*. New Delhi: Oxford University Press.

Dhakal, S. 2000. *Issues and Experiences: Kamaiya System, Kanara Andolan and Tharus in Bardiya*. Kathmandu: Society for Participatory Cultural Education.

Forman, Michael. 1998. *Nationalism and the International Labor Movement, the Idea of the Nation in Socialist and Anarchist Theory*. University Park: Pennysylvania State University Press.

Foucault, M. 1977. *Discipline and Punish: The Birth of the Prison*. New York: Pantheon Books.

Fujikura, T. (Forthcoming). 'The Bonded Agricultural Laborers' Freedom Movement in Western Nepal', in D.N. Gellner, Ishii and Nawa (eds), *Nepalis Inside and Outside Nepal*. Delhi: Manohar.

Guha, R. 1997. *Dominance Without Hegemony*. Cambridge, Massachusetts: Harvard University Press.

Guigni, M.G. 1998. 'Social Movements and Change: Incorporation, Transformation and Democratization', in M.G. Guigni, D. McAdam and C. Tilly (eds), *From Contention to Democracy*, pp. xi-xxvi. Maryland: Rowman & Littlefield Publishers.

Habermas, J. 1989. *The Structural Transformation of the Public Sphere: An Inquiry into a Category of Bourgeois Society*. Cambridge, Massachusetts: Massachusetts Institute of Technology Press.

Hachhethu, K. 2002. *Party Building in Nepal: Organization, Leadership and People: A Comparative Study of the Nepali Congress and the Communist Party of Nepal (United Marxist-Leninist)*. Kathmandu: Mandala Book Point.

Hardiman, David. 2004. *Gandhi in His Time and Ours: The Global Legacy of His Ideas*. New York: Columbia University Press.

Huntington, S. 1991. *The Third Wave: Democratization in the late 20th century*. Norman: University of Oklahoma Press.

INSEC. 1996. *Plight of the Kamaiyas: A Report of the Kamaiya Conference*. Kathmandu: INSEC.

———. 2000. 'Bonded Labourers on their Road to Freedom', *Informal*, 10: 46–49.

Kant, I. 1970. 'An Answer to the Question: "What is Enlightenment?"', in H. Reiss (ed.), *Kant's: Political Writings*, pp. 54–60. Cambridge: Cambridge University Press.

Kaphley, I.P. 1967. *Fundamental Bases of Panchayat Democratic System*. Kathmandu: Ministry of Information.

Kathmandu Post. 1998. 'Comedian against the bandh', 5 August 1998.

Kramer, K. 2003. 'How Representative is the Nepali State?', in D.N. Gellner (ed.), *Resistance and the State: Nepalese Experiences*, pp. 179–98. New Delhi: Social Science Press.

Kunreuther, L.E. 2002. 'Domestic Archives: Memory and Home in Kathmandu'. Dissertation, Department of Anthropology, University of Michigan, Ann Arbor.

Larson, G.J. 2001. *Religion and Personal Law in Secular India: A Call to Judgment.* Bloomington: Indiana University Press.

Lawoti, M. 2005. *Towards a Democratic Nepal: Inclusive Political Institutions for a Multicultural Society*. New Delhi: Sage Publications.

Lowe, P. and V. Kasajoo. 2001. *Kamaiya Slavery and Freedom in Nepal (Kamaiya dasata ra mukti)*. Kathmandu, Nepal: Mandala Book Point in association with Danish Association for International Cooperation.

Marx, K. 1972 (1843). 'On the Jewish Question', in R. Tucker (ed.), *The Marx—Engels Reader*. New York: W.W. Norton and Company.

Rankin, K. 1999. 'The Predicament of Labor: Kamaiya Practices and the Ideology of Freedom', in H. Skar (ed.), *Nepal: Tharu and Tarai Neighbors*, Vol. 16, pp. 27–45. Biblioteca Himalayica Series III. Kathmandu: EMR Publications.

Regmi, M.C. 1978. *Thatched Huts and Stucco Palaces: Peasants and Landlords in 19th Century Nepal*. New Delhi: Vikas.

Schloss, A. 1983. *The Politics of Development: Transportation Policy in Nepal.* Berkeley: Center for South and Southeast Studies, University of California.

Scott, J.C. 1998. *Seeing Like a State: How Certain Schemes to Improve the Human Condition have Failed*. New Haven: Yale University Press.

Seddon, D. 1987. *Nepal: A State of Poverty*. New Delhi: Vikas.

Shakya, S. 2002. 'The Squandering of a Promising Economy', in S. Ramachandran and K.M. Dixit (eds), *State of Nepal*, pp. 176–90. Kathmandu: Himal Books.

Subba, C., A. Yonjan, N. Acharya, L. Limbu, S.K. Shrestha, S Ranamagar and D.N. Dhungel. 2002. *Adivasis/Janajatis in National Development: Major Issues, Constraints and Opportunities (Plan of Action Proposed for the 10th Plan 2003–2007)*. Kathmandu: Institute for Integrated Development Studies (IIDS).

Tamang, S. 2000. 'Legalizing State Patriarchy in Nepal', *Studies in Nepali History and Society* 5 (1): 127–56.

The Rising Nepal. 2001. 'Protect Consumer Rights, says Khadka', Wednesday, 12 December (27 Mang 2058).

Zakaria, F. 1997. 'The Rise of Illiberal Democracy', *Foreign Affairs* 76: 22–43.

11

Student Movements in Nepal: Their Parameters and Their Idealized Forms

AMANDA SNELLINGER

INTRODUCTION

Social movements matter. Historically, they have had a profound impact on states in abrupt ways. They are often considered the anti-system way to impact the system, directly accessible to the masses in ways that legislative, political and policy processes of the state are not. But their impact is broader than that: they can also affect social discourse and values. As a process, they disseminate ideas to the larger public, which in time will also impact the political process through voting trends and priorities concerning political and social issues.

In his essay 'Parties in Contemporary Democracies: Problems and Paradoxes', Juan J. Linz (2002) posits that social movements are more flexible than political parties because they are not fixed systems beholden to public opinion or votes. They can criticize the parties and foil their pragmatism with idealism. This view reflects the more functionalist argument that Herbert Kitchelt (1993) has made: social movements actually have a place in the larger political system because they are able to highlight issues both in political and social spheres that political parties cannot. In other words, transgression, the changing of the normal state of affairs (Jordan 2002), is not only the most unique, consistent character of social movements, but it is part of the political and social order of things.

In considering this categorical distinction between parties and social movements, I recall a description I have often heard from Nepali student activists and politicians that student movements are social movements within the Nepali context. During my field research of the joint students' movement in Nepal in 2003 and 2004,[1] which was connected to the five-party Pratigaman Andolan ('movement against regression'), many of those I interviewed highlighted the students' current role as being with the people and representing the public's wishes. There is a history of student movements in Nepal, both before the 1990 establishment of democracy and after. But the student organizations are sister organizations to mainstream parties. Does this affiliation exclude their movements from being social movements? This question addresses the particular treatment of social movements as a democratic alternative that can confront issues of justice and representation despite the structural limits of the system (Hachhethu 2002b; Kramer 2002; Lawoti 2005; Pradhan 2002; Thapa 2004)—which furthermore illuminates why people assign meaning to or claim the description of 'social movement' for such political action. In the context of Nepal, this question reveals the gap between the hyper-idealized category of students' movements as social movements and the view that student movements are an entrenched political tactic of the students who serve as party appendages. This brings up the question of whether this discrepancy has an impact on the effectiveness of student movements or on the students as political actors.

Most Nepali student activists and politicians are from the educated elite who have a grounding in political and sociological theory. What they believe a social movement to be is informed by historical studies, political science and sociological studies of social movements. They make these academic definitions meaningful through their own culturally prescribed notions of what is political. For me to understand social movements as an ideal, my analysis must be grounded in Nepali politicians' and students' specific definitions of the political. I cannot take for granted that society has a particular form (Escobar 1992). In other words, to analyse how Nepali politicians and students are employing the social movement as an ideal type, I need to understand the different aspects that give social movements their weight within the context of Nepali political culture and history. This involves asking what can be defined as a social movement. Moreover, can other political action have the same impact as a social movement if it is not set within the social-movement parameters?

In order to answer these questions, I will unpack the political science and sociological literature on social movements not to set up a straw man against which to contrast Nepali student movements, but as a means to understand how Nepali students imagine themselves to fit within this paradigm. I will be employing the three analytic categories of political opportunity of movement emergence; mobilizing structures; and framing processes. It has been argued that many scholars consider only one of these factors, which renders their studies incomplete because they treat these factors as independent rather than considering them in a dynamic relationship that allows conclusions to be both specific and general within a comparative study of social movements (McAdam et al. 1996; Tarrow 1998). I aim to engage these categories as parts of a synthesized social-movement theory by using analysis based on my ethnographic research and in-depth interviews. I will assess the larger implications of unorthodox social and political action through student movements in Nepal and how they are idealized as social movements.

The Political Opportunity of Movement Emergence

One of the first considerations of the political-science literature on social movements, as a phenomenon, is the emergence of a movement. It considers under what conditions we can expect a given type of movement to emerge. On a fundamental level, it needs to be understood who the movement comprises, who their enemy is, what they are fighting for and who can benefit from it. Within the political-science literature, the modern social movement is often considered a phenomenon that occurs in states that have institutionalized political systems. Kitchelt's (1993: 17) observation that the rigidity of institutions provides the bridge between more traditional political action and social movements insinuates this assumption.

Citizens expect the state to be responsive to their demands and be accountable to the voter constituency.[2] But when the state as an institution becomes so rigid that citizens do not feel the traditional democratic channels of representation are being effective, they turn to the direct democratic action of social movements. The basis for this observation is that the state must be institutionalized enough for the citizens to have expectations of it; otherwise the relationship between the states and citizens would have a different code of conduct. Albert O. Hirschman (1981) was the first political scientist to conceptually craft this pattern of wavering between traditional political participation and unorthodox forms of direct political action: he called it 'shifting involvements'. The basis for Kitchelt's argument is that the role of institutions in the state explains the cycle of 'shifting involvements'.

The contemporary state of Nepal has not established an institutional foothold (Hachhethu 2002b, 2004; Hutt 2004; Lawoti 2005; Mahat 2005; Upadhya 2002). Democracy has been so short-lived that its practices, administrations and bureaucracy have not gained the entrenched character of an institutionalized system.[3] Perhaps the Panchayat government could have been considered 'institutionalized', but there has not been enough time to re-establish it as an institution in this era of post-democratic uncertainty (Mahat 2005). Kitchelt's and Hirschman's analyses are based on the assumption of established democracy where people can assume certain democratic rights and a social movement is a reaction to those rights being rendered ineffective. The democratic rights on which they base the parameters of their analysis are not consistent in Nepal (Hutt 2004; Joshi and Rose 2004 [1966]; Roka 2004; Shah 2004). Therefore, even though it may not be particularly appropriate to consider the degree of institutionalization of the state for the Nepali context, conceptually it still provides some useful analytic points. People want access to a state that allows them another way to participate rather than having to resort to the uncertain tactic of direct democratic dissent through protest.

The concept of shifting involvements can be altered for the Nepali context. There are shifting involvements in student movements from norm-oriented agendas to value-oriented agendas.[4] When there was an active democratic process, the students concentrated on norm-oriented, limited, pragmatic agendas for their students' movements. They were using the tactic of movement mobilization—or what students call 'direct democracy'—in order to address issues that the parliament may not have been able to, such as petrol price hikes, transportation-cost increases, water shortages and educational issues. They swayed over to value-oriented ideological agendas when the state did not allow them to engage in tactics of direct democracy.

The state has taken on different forms at different times in student movements' history. During the democratic period, the state is run by the parties with which the students are affiliated, so typically the institutions against which students mobilize movements are the universities, industries or particular branches of the government. But when there is no democracy, the state as a monolithic whole[5] is the enemy, and the students and parties fight against it together (Snellinger 2005).

For example, in May 2003, after the king dismissed the Parliament and replaced it with self-appointed officials, the students had engaged in a peripheral movement to decrease the rising petrol prices. During this protest, they spoke about the need to reinstate Parliament and declared their support for the five-party joint movement against regression, but most students admitted this movement was norm-based and they limited their demands to their material agenda. It was not until Devi Lal Poudel, a student in the district of Palpa, was shot dead that this movement took a new turn. The students immediately demanded the resignation of the king's appointed prime minister and the reinstatement of the Parliament. Lokendra Bahadur Chand, the then Prime Minister, did resign, but he was replaced by another appointee of the king. A student leader said to me, 'It was at this time that we realized what was at risk. The issue was no longer about the price of petrol but the principle of protesting [*sic*] the price of petrol. Our democratic rights were at stake and that changed the nature of the movement. It had to change. There was so much more at risk, including the honour of a martyr.'[6] After this, the students stepped up their support for the five-party joint movement as sister organizations (ibid.).

Political opportunity needs to be considered in two ways within the category of movement emergence. The first consideration is of political opportunities that allow movements to emerge. Mainly this genre of the literature considers the incentives in the political environment (or cracks in the institutional system) that allow for contentious collective action. In other words, it asks, '[W]hy does contentious politics seem to develop only in particular periods. . . And why do movements take different forms in different political environments?' (Tarrow 1998: 19). The earlier analytical perspective is based on a rational-choice paradigm: it assumes that activists will engage in a movement only when the state is weak enough to allow them to be effective. But as Sidney Tarrow (1998) has established in his research, like rational-choice theory itself, this assumption needs to be balanced with a number of other considerations in order to understand political opportunity as one aspect of a larger synthesis of the social-movement theory.

Often, political action is a reaction—only through afterthought is it charged with a larger political agenda. It is the last option that people feel they have to make an impact. For example, actors are not always strategic enough to wait for the best time to react. Sometimes movements can come from bursts of frustration over unexpected events rather than strategic mobilizations, for instance, the Nepali student movement of 1979. On 6 April 1979, approximately a thousand students were marching to the Pakistani Embassy to protest the unjust execution of Zulfiqar Ali Bhutto. But the police would not let the students through one of the main thoroughfares because it would block traffic at a time when the king was scheduled to be travelling in the area. The students demanded to be allowed to proceed but were refused, and clashes broke out between the students and police. By this time, the students' gathering was no longer about the execution of Bhutto, it was about the suppression by the police. In the days that followed, there were protests throughout the country that resulted in police brutality and several deaths. After nationwide escalation of violence, King Birendra[7] ordered a royal commission to investigate the students' demands. The student action committee, which consisted of three students—Bal Bahadur K.C. (a Nepali Congress affiliate), Shai Lak Karki (a pro-Moscow affiliate) and Tanka Karki (United Marxist Leninist affiliate)—settled on a bargain with the commission that ended the new education policy, abolished entrance exams to university (which made university education accessible to all those who had passed the school-leaving certificate exam), allowed for independent unions at the national level and abolished the Rastravaadi Vidhyaarthi Mandal (National Student Forum), the pro-Panchayat student organization accused of orchestrating attacks against student protesters. For the students' movement, this was a victory—they had achieved significant reform at the university level; but they were unable to affect change at the state level.

The next day, as these three representatives were reporting the outcome of the talks, an outcry arose among the students that they had not addressed the ultimate spirit of the movement, which had since amassed martyrs. They forcibly painted the faces of two of the student negotiators black[8] and paraded them through the streets. The demonstration attracted about 25,000 protestors and culminated in the burning of a government newspaper office and the destruction of public vehicles in front of the Royal Nepal Airlines Corporation office (Hoftun et al. 1999: 90; Rana 1995: 422–25).

The next day, 24 May 1979, King Birendra announced that he would allow a nationwide referendum where the populace would choose between the multiparty system and the reformed Panchayat-style government. He allowed the underground parties to campaign in preparation for the referendum. Ganesh Man Singh, the general secretary of the Nepali Congress (NC) at that time, claimed, 'Only foolish men can believe that a free and fair referendum will be possible under Panchayat Rule'[9] (Hoftun et al. 1999: 91). Many other leaders were suspicious of such a move, although eventually the parties worked together to campaign for the national referendum (Rana 1995). Ultimately, the government won the referendum,[10] yet the process was sparked by a student reaction that is considered as a step forward in their larger movement for democracy.

As I have just demonstrated, the rational-choice analytic consideration of timing versus reaction is useful in understanding why certain movements succeed. This is true for the *jana aandolan* (people's movement) of 1990. Prior to the 1990 people's movement, India had closed the border over disagreements regarding an expired trade treaty with Nepal. At first, the Panchayat was able to use the situation to build up nationalism because they could blame the dwindling economy on a foreign aggressor. But when the situation had dragged on for over six months, the banned political parties realized that opposing the Panchayat would not be seen as being pro-Indian. This opportunity to openly criticize the Panchayat government's policies allowed the political parties to slowly build political awareness and led to the creation of links between the NC and the communist parties that culminated in the victory of the people's movement.

The joint students' movement of 2004 was another example of seizing an opportunity to push forward their political agenda. After the government was unable to charge arrested students with sedition, the students had the political advantage to transgress the normative political demands and call for a republic. Their mission was to radicalize the discourse of the political parties' movement against regression. The main point to consider here is that not only were the state's policies and actions the source of opportunities for particular movements, but that these movements served as a contentious aspect of the state-building process. In all these cases, the movements' impact on the state was that they forced the state to react and reform in order to rebuild itself (Tarrow 1996).

The second aspect of political opportunity within the category of movement emergence is the political opportunity gained by movement emergence. Social movements are about reshaping the political landscape, an investment that piques the interest of many different factions. For this reason, autonomy is an issue that is often addressed in this analytic category, although it also surfaces in other analytical aspects of social-movements literature. There is an overarching sensibility that social movements are or should be autonomous in order to maintain their legitimacy as having an agenda that transcends politics. In order to transgress the normative, it is assumed that movements need to be detached from the present political order and look toward the future beyond that known order. Yet in order for a movement to be successful, it must appeal to many sectors of society, just as politicians must do. A social movement needs to engage in politics, but should not get bogged down in partisan politics. For this reason, it should remain free of the grips of those who have other investments that may stymie the movement's ultimate visions. Some argue that this is a western sensibility that has no grounding in reality; that movements' agendas are often about efficiency, not the principle of autonomy (Ho 2003).

Yet, it cannot be dismissed that many social movements have varying degrees of connections to political parties nor that they become political parties at different points in their lifetimes. Furthermore, it must be considered that autonomy is an issue of legitimacy in Nepali political history, particularly in the post-democratic era. The public regularly dismisses the student movements as being party machinations that exploit the metaphor of social movements.[11] The students use their self-proclaimed autonomy to gain political capital in the eyes of the people, which causes them to be more of a political asset to the parties themselves. There is an insinuation in this dynamics that in recent years parties have not had the ability to carry out social movements in the name of the people; therefore, unless the students have autonomy, they cannot claim the status of a social movement.

The students claim that they gain autonomy from their mother organizations, the political parties, through the political capital they gain in running students' movements (Snellinger 2005, 2006). This was articulated to me during the 2004 students' movement. The students claimed to not only be radicalizing the political discourse while opposing the king's autocratic actions, but they were also carving a space of political autonomy for themselves. The following quote from one of the arrested student leaders sums up the change in the students' role after 2002:

> Yesterday, the student organization's role was only to powerfully assist the parties. They were treated as nurseries, which used to supply plants for the parties. In the nursery the seeds used to be watered and fertilized. The role of the student organizations was limited to this. Our work was to make [the] Nepali Congress win the election and to make the college students and school students familiar with [the] Congress's theories, by making them educated in Congress theories... and to produce cadres for Nepali Congress. We did not have the situation [*sic*] to conduct struggle within [the] Congress. But now because of the students' movement and the faith that we have obtained (from public), our role is not that.... We are the force with the most potential; the student organizations have realized this during our movement. Therefore mainstream politics should not be driven only by the political parties, but we must also interfere [*sic*] in it. Yesterday we did not interfere in it; we did not take part in how the state was run ... In 12 years of parliamentary democracy a lot of defects came and we never spoke. Our opinion is that we were limited: 'Your work is to do [*sic*] politics in the campus, your work is to take part in Free Student Union elections, your role is to assist the parties in the elections'—this is what was said to us. And we said yes; we understood in a wrong way [*sic*]. But today we are interfering [*sic*]. To be able to point a finger at the parties, saying that you cannot compromise with the king in an inappropriate way, means we are also in the mainstream of politics.[12]

Another student leader from the All National Nepal Free Student Union (ANNFSU)[13] articulated this sentiment by claiming that the public supports their movements more than they do the parties' movements. His reasoning was the political parties were at fault in their governing practices during the multiparty democracy; their incompetence brought about this political crisis. The students, on the other hand, had committed no injustice upon the public and they were aware of the mistakes of their leaders, which they would therefore avoid committing. Ultimately, he believed that the students were in an unique position between the public and the parties. Their political position allowed them to fight for the true priorities of the public (Snellinger 2005).

The students are eager to highlight any progress they make because in reality their ability to influence politics is very limited. They must rely on relations of patronage in order to rise in the ranks of the parties (Hachhethu 2002a; Pfaff-Czarnecka 2004; Upadhya 2002), while simultaneously convincing the public that they can be effective politicians who can provide alternatives to their mother organizations' policies. These idealistic articulations of autonomy are meant to both contest and conceal the underbelly of political constraint. Such perceived autonomy gives purpose to the students' struggles, which allows them to have the conviction they need to sustain the dedication and passion for their protracted movement against regression. Regardless ideals hover over reality and sometimes they fail to coalesce within the structural limitations of the political system that the students are entrenched in.

Mobilizing Structures

The analytic genre of mobilizing structures considers the structural approaches of formation, organization and sustainability. Social movements are in a unique position of power because they operate outside institutions. There are no protocols about how one engages in social movements; there are effective tactics, but there are no structural limitations on how to operate. Movements can be spontaneous, which allows them to catch the opposition off guard, and while the opposition is preparing a reaction, the activists are engaging a different tactic. When Kitchelt (1993: 25) posited that liberal representative systems can cope with substantive complexity but not temporal complexity, he was referring to social movements' orientation to the past or the future, from which activists are trying to affect change in the present. A policy may claim to be future-oriented, but it is always grounded in the present and must be executed within contemporary constraints, whereas social-movement processes are based directly in a relationship between time and transgression (Jordan 2002: 40). Social movements seek to affect degrees of structural change on the basis of which the future can be constructed. This approach could be past-oriented, future-oriented or both simultaneously, but either temporal location can be used to criticize and change the present. Most of the value-oriented movements in Nepali democratic history have demanded the end to regression and the restoration of the democracy of 1950 or 1990. They have two fixed points that allow them to frame the possibilities for the future in ways that people recognize, while allowing room for the imagined changes they want to bring (Roka 2004; Upadhya 2002).[14] The social movements' grammar of politics is not structurally confined to the tropes of the present, which can make it difficult for institutions to react to it without adopting the social movement's language, which some argue can causes subtle changes in the political order itself (Jordan 2002; McCarthy 1996).

Social movements also rely on informal networks in order to gain momentum and sustain themselves. Movements are about collective action. For this reason, anthropology has found studying social movements a useful way to understand the building of collective identity (Assies and Salman 2000; Edelman 2001; Escobar 1992; Giri 1992). Whether exclusive or inclusive, social movements rely on solidarity in order to articulate and contest meaning (Laclau 1985). This allows them to call on casual networks—family, churches, communities and professional networks—to participate. They can be mobilized by the very fact that the interaction, working together to achieve an end for the collective, is familiar within these networks. Mobilizing familiar social organizations provides an air of mass-based support because people of different affiliations are joined together in the movement.

In the context of Nepal, mobilization of external groups is contentious. Networking and relying on one's filial, professional and political contacts is a part of everyday life to such a degree that it is often difficult to distinguish between those types of networks. Politics in Nepal relies on culturally entrenched systems of patronage (Hachhethu 2002a; Panday 2000). While campaigning in villages, it is considered strategic to approach the heads of households and village chiefs to secure blocks of votes rather than campaign on an individual level.

The student organizations are not the only sister organizations of political parties: the Tarun Daal ('youth wing'), the professional unions and the women's organizations have become institutionalized in the last 40 years and are mobilized when the parties need them (Hachhethu 2002a). The students differ from the rest of these organizations because of their position in society. Often it is at university that citizens forge their political alliances. Indoctrination and recruitment are legitimately sanctioned duties of all the student organizations, and there are set processes of clientelism and coercion within the universities in order to recruit students not only on to party rosters but also on to the streets during protests. The point is, the student groups are political and so anyone they bring to the street has some degree of political affiliation. The people's movement of 1990 was the only time that the common masses came to the streets. So, although the students have a number of networks on which they rely, their informal networks have political underpinnings too—in other words this may not be an indicator of public sentiment or support as it may be in the context of other social movements.

Another strength that is often attributed to social movements is their decentralized organization with fluid boundaries and flexible leadership (Buechler 1990: 42). Social movements are about democracy, and often the organizational patterns they aspire to mirror their convictions of what society should be. Although it is difficult, movements are often characterized as using direct and communicative democracy as they move forward with their objectives. This process is usually coupled with decentralized parallel leadership rather than a hierarchical structure of authority. The advantage to this is that it keeps the organizational structure flexible so that it can react simultaneously to different situations in different places. Yet there is always a tipping point in the degree to which movements should be organized: they need to be organized enough to be coherent and effective, but once they become organized to an institutional degree, they lose their unique ability to foil their opponent with spontaneous, innovative techniques.

Although Nepali student organizations try to portray themselves as democratic institutions, the organizations reflect no parallel-leadership structure. They are highly structured organizations where internal democracy is minimal, with even fewer internal democratic procedures. The student-organizational system is elaborately hierarchical, with the central committee in direct communication with the party (Hachhethu 2002a; Rana 1995).[15] Orders are dictated downward to the district committees, who then communicate with the university committees. This organizational system is entrenched but effective: when student leaders want to mobilize campuses, they make a few phone calls in order to see results nationwide. But within this organizational structure, there is a degree of autonomy from campus to campus, which allows the student movements to be effective in engaging in tactics appropriate to the situation at hand. The overarching sensibility is that any effective tactic should be used, and if it works in one place, it is often replicated in others.

Over the years, students have fine-tuned the art of protest and dissent. With every generation, increasingly creative tactics are employed. To become known as a protest tactician is one of the best ways to gain political capital as a student politician with future political aspirations. The students and parties both recognize the students' unique position of not being accountable for the repercussions of their tactics, so students are generally encouraged to engage in whatever they feel is necessary. The public would say that this is one of the downfalls of student movements. The students claim they are protesting for the good of the public, but they are closing schools, vandalizing property, causing traffic jams, burning tyres and getting into rock fights with the police. The exasperated public views this as a disturbance of the peace that the political parties choose not to control. The parties, on the other hand, claim that the students are the new generation and their acts of semantic and physical destruction are more than just a testament to their longing to affect change. In other words, their mobilization tactics are opening up the space for the parties to speak out.

The last issue that is often considered in mobilizing structures is sustainability, which regularly comes in the shape of formalization. In the literature, it is a common topic to analyse social movements either being co-opted by parties or becoming parties themselves. This literature usually analyses whether the movement is able to sustain its momentum and address all its stated agendas after it is co-opted by or decides to become a part of the system. Why does this move seem to be an attractive step for a movement? One reason is found in the resource-mobilization theory, which claims that social movements rationally collect resources for their common goal. Typically, their resources are based on their networks, their appeals and in the unorthodoxy of their tactics. Yet if that is not enough to affect the system, then they may consider collaborating with a party in order to achieve their agenda. I would argue that this may be the progression for norm-oriented movements that have a specific policy or legislative agenda.

Tarrow (1990, 1996) argues that it is naïve to think that parties are not involved in social movements. The political parties can capitalize on social movements; they see political opportunity in them as much as the activists themselves do. Tarrow has shown that parties either co-opt or pre-empt social movements. They watch movements from the sidelines, perhaps influencing them all along or usurping them when they see an opportunity to gain from supporting the movement. Typically, the outcome of co-optation is reform, 'partial disappointment but incremental reform' (Tarrow 1990: 267). In looking at the anti-nuclear protests of Taiwan, Ho observed that co-optation could perhaps work, but expectations between the movement and the party often collapse under the pressures of *realpolitik* (2003: 708).

For value-oriented movements, there may be a natural progression toward becoming a political party rather than being co-opted. The changes that are sought to be effected in the system are not quantitative but qualitative: they perhaps cannot be measured in reform, new policy or legislation. To affect change, they either have to destroy the system in a revolutionary manner or become part of the system. This was the trend in many European countries during the 1980s with the sprouting of popular green parties. The upsurge of green parties in Europe was a direct result of social movements realizing that in order to affect the changes they wanted, they needed to address the institutional structure of the political process, and that they had gained the capital to fulfil their agendas but would need to become a part of the political process in order to restructure it from the inside (Rohrschneider 1993).

This has also been a common step for ethnic movements in various South American countries. In these cases, it is usually representation that they seek. The social movement is meant to bring attention to perhaps one piece of legislation or oppose a legislative trend. Yet in struggling for their cause, they realize that they need to provide a consistent voice throughout the political process in order to uproot the base of the problem. Becoming a party makes sense because it provides more access to resources (Van Cott 2003).

In both of these cases, being outside the system but willing to come into the system allows them the possibility of implementing the changes that they seek.

Student movements in Nepal are between these two poles of sustainability. They are co-opted by parties and they have every intention of joining the political system, but the distinction is they do not join the system as an organization but as a collective of individuals, through party politics. It is obvious that their connection to the parties is both an advantage and a disadvantage. Their interests are aligned and the parties have more resources and access to careers that the students want, so it makes sense that they would be united. Yet they are limited in the extent to which they can make political demands and see them through. It is at the transition point that historically there has been incremental reform but more than partial disappointment. The parties have always relied on the students to be more radical in order to create pressure. The students have ful-filled this role for the parties, being at the fore of making radical political demands, standing on the political ground gained by the generations before them. Yet they must wait until they are the politicians before they can implement their radical demands within the system, at which point they will face the structural constraints of the political system.

Framing Processes

The crux of my study lies within this conceptual category of framing processes. Mayer N. Zald's (1996: 262) definition of frames is worth noting:

> Frames are the specific metaphors, symbolic representations, and cognitive cues used to render or cast behavior and events in an evaluative mode and to suggest alternative modes of action.

Focusing on framing processes highlights how movements strategically articulate themselves in order to appeal to the masses. A movement must define the implications of success and failure from within the cultural system that can identify the agenda that they support. In other words, the demand for change and the means of change must exist within one common social framework that must be familiar to people yet also suggest the possibility for change. Therefore a social movement must mobilize culture, ideology and discourse in similar ways as politicians do in order to gain the attraction of the public.

The tendency of students and politicians to refer to student movements as social movements is itself an act of strategic framing. This language pitches the student movement to the masses as something done in their interest and for their progress. When I asked student activists to cite other social movements with which they were familiar, I heard the following examples: the Dalit movement, Gandhi's Satyagraha movement, Nelson Mandela's anti-apartheid movement and the Cuban revolution. There is no doubt that they understand the category they are employing both within a historic and political science frame: it is one in which people fight against a state or foreign power for their rights to dignity and self-determination. Social movements are understood as a means by which the public consciously thinks of itself and affects its own historicity. The students and parties use the student movement as a historic event that represents the higher intentions for which some student movements have fought, in order to embolden all the norm- and value-oriented movements that the students have carried out.

One may wonder why social movements? Why is it that the students do not employ other frames in order to gain the respect of the masses? It is common for social movements to frame their political goals within larger societal definitions of rights and responsibilities in order to highlight the wrongs of the current social order and the possibility for the change that they want to bring about.

Discourse plays an important role in the process of framing. It can be treated in two ways: through political speeches and through the media. Politicians and student politicians must employ rhetoric for change to convince people of the possibilities that would open up if they were to mobilize. Urgency, agency and possibility are highlighted in political speeches in order to inspire people to mobilize against the state. Urgency is framed as temporality in this context: 'If you act against injustice today, you can ensure the necessary change for tomorrow' is often the tenor of such speeches. In Nepal, the metaphors in the speeches tend to be extremely religious, relying on Hindu metaphors that incite people's sense of agency and responsibility. Such metaphors imply not only that citizens should have rights, but also that it is their responsibility to fight for those rights. These metaphors are also commonly known references that people are familiar with, which can create a feeling of solidarity (Hachhethu 2002a). Metaphors of the nation and land are meant to do this as well: from a shared sense of solidarity, a sense of responsibility to act and support is insinuated. Possibility is set in the past, present, future and in metaphors that transcend temporality.

Media is the other aspect of discourse, but I would argue that there is more negotiation over the framing of meaning with the media. Through social movements, participants seek to use the media as an extension of their voice, but it does not always work out that directly. Gadi Wolfsfeld (1991: 2) argues that there is a 'competitive symbiosis' between the movements and the media because of the asymmetry of their transaction. Social movements need the media to mobilize, validate their cause and enlarge their scope (Gamson and Wolfsfeld 1993: 116). Media publicity can be used as the extension of the social movement: the further it can reach, the more people it can mobilize—perhaps not bringing them to the streets, but moving them to consider the possibilities for which the movement is calling, as this in itself will promote change. The media also has the ability to validate the cause of the movement. Whether it does this depends on the negotiation between how the movement frames the relevance of its cause and how the media understands public sentiment to be (or, more cynically, what the media wants the public sentiment to be). Furthermore, when the media is used as a space for mediators and other partisans to get involved in the production process of movement discourse and debate, this type of dialogue also adds to the performance of the movement and speaks to a larger public in relevant ways.

What do the media get out of this? As I argued earlier, social movements are the contentious part of politics that are open to people and can bring change in ways that institutional politics cannot. These movements are dramatic, sometimes violent, call for justice and create reactions from authority. They are good news to cover, which will sell. Furthermore, the media has a stake in framing the discourse of public sentiment: the media actively uses its power in order to influence how social movements will be perceived, which can determine the level of impact the movements can have on society.

In Nepal, competitive symbiosis between student movements and the media exists, but this is a relationship that has only developed since 1990, when private media began as an enterprise. The portion of the Nepali media that is dedicated to political analysis is large. Political commentary is a media industry. The networks among journalists, editors, political pundits, students and parties fuel political culture in Nepal (Adhikary 2003; Onta 2002). There are some papers that are purely party mouthpieces, while others try to be more broad-based in their analysis of political happenings. The student movements are a popular event for the media and the unfolding of their dramas is always heavily publicized. The students understand this potential publicity that the media provides. They heavily court journalists by providing inside news as well as engaging in dramatic carnival-like protest tactics in the hopes of gaining media attention.

The interesting thing about the media in Nepal is that it really does serve as a democratic form of debate. The political analysis and commentary comes from all corners (factions and partisans), so rather than manufacture consensus, it creates a public space of Habermasian communicative democracy. Does this help the student movements? The media does not necessarily squash or ensure the success of a movement; rather, it propels the movement and all the debate that it entails into a larger public sphere. The media may not ensure the public's reception of student movements, but it aids in the production of politicians by featuring and highlighting particular students' performances, which pushes them along the path of their political careers.

Conclusion

I have sketched various aspects of social movements in order to analyse what informs students' and politicians' conception of Nepali students' movements as social movements. This was meant to demonstrate the process by which students and politicians cast the student movements' positive aspects within the sociological definition while simultaneously downplaying the negatives aspects. It reveals the inherent political limitations.

In Nepal, when you ask someone why he or she has chosen to be a politician, they talk about it as a public service to better the nation. I have asked many people this question and this is the first response that is elicited. What follows varies. Sometimes it is a more refined articulation of what public service should be; at other times it segues into the secondary reasons of why the person has chosen such a path. The current public sentiment holds that those secondary reasons are what truly motivate politicians, just as it is believed that calling politics a 'public service' is mere lip service. But this lip service must matter, because I consistently heard it articulated by politicians and students.

Politicians embody two poles that people have a hard time collapsing in order to make sense of their actions. On the one hand, they charismatically represent all of the possibilities of removing the mundane from public life; on the other hand, they are people who are limited by institutions and human shortcomings—which are more apparent among people in positions of power. Student movements embody this conundrum too, because they are the first step that students take in becoming politicians. Student movements are a training ground for participation in mainstream politics.

Will the public ever be convinced that student movements are social movements? Perhaps not; but even if they were to be, it would no more likely to bring them to the streets. Currently, there is a stagnation of hope in Nepal. This stagnation comes naturally when people have had the life they know uprooted by insurgency and political chaos. The public can be idealistic, but it is first and foremost pragmatic and self-interested. It wants peace and stability. This is more important than the principle of democratic rights (Upadhya 2002). That is the challenge in Nepal: the perceived connection between peace, stability and the democratic rights to self-determination and free speech has been disrupted during the years of democracy. Only when these elements are mutually constitutive will people perceive the students' movements as social movements worth coming to the streets for.

Notes

1. The primary data for this chapter is based on my field observations and interviews, which were accomplished on a Fulbright Research Grant, sponsored by the Fulbright Commission of Nepal, under the Institute for International Education, from September 2003 to July 2004.
2. For reference to this in the Nepali context, please see Panday (2000: 104).
3. Ram Saran Mahat refers to this as the 'politics of underdevelopment' (2005: 371).
4. In his article titled 'Students and Politics', Philip Altbach distinguished between the 'norm-oriented' movement, one concerned with pragmatic goals and generally the product of a specific limited issue, and the 'value-oriented' movement, which is concerned with broad, ideological issues (Altbach 1967: 87).
5. This excludes the judicial branch that has a degree of autonomy, which it has exercised in favour of students at various times during the Panchayat era. The Supreme Court has also been heavily relied upon since 2003, particularly after the 1 February 2005 coup, to review *habeas corpus* filings on the basis that political detainees were being unconstitutionally held. Even though many political detainees were released on these grounds, they were re-arrested within minutes of their release.
6. Interview conducted on 19 December 2004. The translation from Nepali was done by the author.
7. His rule began in 1972. His style was quite different from his father's. Though when he began his rule he planned to enforce his father's constitution of 1962, he was open to reform, working with the liberal Panchayat ministers and at times with political parties.
8. In the context of the political struggle for democracy, black is equated with regression. As a political tactic, protesters will often hold black flags, particularly on 15 December, which marks Mahendra's dissolution of democracy in 1960, and 14 October, when his grandson Gyanendra (the current king) dissolved Parliament in 2001.
9. *Nepal Times*, 19 June 1979 (PD23: 26).
10. Of the 7.1 million registered voters, 2.4 million voted for the Panchayat system and 2 million voted for the multiparty system (Hoftun et al. 1999: 93).
11. I came to recognize this trend by asking shopkeepers, taxi drivers and random citizens who were not affiliated with political parties or movements what they thought of the students' political activities. People often expressed to me the view that the current political leaders were student leaders who had made similar political claims to the ones current students are making, but once they were promoted from student activists to politicians, their agendas changed and they failed the public. Furthermore, the general public views the student organizations

as lackeys of the political parties. These sentiments have not only been expressed to me, but are prominent themes that are addressed in political media commentary and analysis, and also in political speeches.

12. Interview conducted on 28 January 2004. The translation from Nepali was done by the author.
13. The All Nepal National Free Student Union (ANNFSU) is the student affiliate of the Communist Party of Nepal-United Marxist Leninist (CPN-UML), which has historically ranked as one of the two largest parties in Nepal.
14. It makes sense that it took 30 years to get people to the streets for the first restoration of democracy: 30 years was about the span of time in which shared memory no longer included experiences of the democracy in the 1950s. People could be swayed by how the political parties framed democracy in the possibilities of the future with no direct memory or experience of the inefficiency and power politics that it was during the 1950s. This is perhaps why people are not coming to the streets now: many think the parties failed at their project of democracy and that peace and security are more important than the right to vote for ineffective, corrupt politicians (Panday 2000; Upadhya 2002).
15. For details on party organization and hierarchy, see Hachhethu (2002a).

References

Adhikary, Dhruba H. 2003. 'Media: Press, Power, and Pressure', in D.B. Gurung (ed.), *Nepal Tomorrow: Voices and Visions*, pp. 637–49. Kathmandu: Koseelee Prakashan.

Altbach, Philip. 1967. 'Students and Politics', in S.M. Lipset (ed.), *Student Politics*, pp. 74–96. New York: Basic Books.

Assies, W. and T. Salman. 2000. 'Re-visioning Cultures of Politics: An Essay on Social Movements, Citizenship and Culture', *Critique of Anthropology* 20 (3): 289–307.

Buechler, Steven. 1990. *Women's Movements in the U.S.* New Brunswick: Rutgers University Press.

Edelman, M. 2001. 'Social movements: Changing Paradigms and Forms of Politics', *Annual Review of Anthropology* 30: 285–317.

Escobar, Arturo. 1992. 'Culture, Practice, and Politics: Anthropology and the Study of Social Movements', *Critique of Anthropology* 12 (4): 395–432.

Gamson, William A. and Gadi Wolfsfeld. 1993. 'Movements and Media as Interacting Systems', *Annals of the American Academy of Political and Social Science* 528: 114–25.

Giri, Ananta. 1992. 'Understanding Contemporary Social Movements', *Dialectical Anthropology* 17 (1): 35–49.

Hachhethu, Krishna. 2002a. *Party Building in Nepal: Organization, Leadership, and People*. Kathmandu: Mandala Book Point.

———. 2002b. 'Political Parties and the State', in D.N. Gellner (ed.), *Resistance and the State: Nepalese Experience*, pp. 133–75. New Delhi: Social Science Press.

———. 2004. *State of Democracy in Nepal: Survey Report in State of Democracy in South Asia*, International IDEA Report. Institute for Democracy and Electoral Assistance.

Hirschman, Albert O. 1981. *Shifting Involvements*. Princeton: Princeton University Press.

Ho, Ming-Sho. 2003. 'The Politics of Anti-Nuclear Protest in Taiwan: A Case of Party-Dependent Movement (1980–2000)', *Modern Asian Studies* 37 (3): 683–708.

Hoftun, Martin, William Raeper and John Whelpton. 1999. *People, Politics, and Ideology: Democracy and Social Change in Nepal*. Kathmandu: Mandala Book Point.

Hutt, Michael. 2004. 'Introduction: Monarchy, Democracy and Maoism in Nepal', in M. Hutt (ed.), *Himalayan People's War: Nepal's Maoist Rebellion*, pp. 1–21. Bloomington: Indiana University Press.

Jordan, Tim. 2002. *Activism! Direct Action, Hacktivism, and the Future of Society*. London: Reaktion Books.

Joshi, Bhuwan Lal and Leo E. Rose. 2004 [1966]. *Democratic Innovations in Nepal: A Case Study of Political Acculturation*. Kathmandu: Mandala Press.

Kitchelt, Herbert. 1993. 'Social Movements, Political Parties, and Democratic Theory', *Annals of the American Academy of Political and Social Science* 528: 13–29.

Krämer, Karl-Heinz. 2002. 'How Representative is the Nepali State?', in D.N. Gellner (ed.), *Resistance and the State: Nepalese Experience*, pp. 179–98. New Delhi. Social Science Press.

Laclau, Ernest. 1985. 'New Social Movements and the Plurality of the Social', in D. Slater (ed.), *New Social Movements and the State in Latin America*, pp. 27–42. Dordrecht: CEDLA.

Lawoti, Mahendra. 2005. *Towards a Democratic Nepal: Inclusive Political Institutions for Multicultural Society*. New Delhi: Sage Publications.

Linz, Juan J. 2002. 'Parties in Contemporary Democracies: Problems and Paradoxes', in R. Gunther, J.R. Montero and J.J. Linz (eds), *Political Parties: Old Concepts and New Challenges*, pp. 291–317. Oxford: Oxford University Press.

Mahat, Ram Sharan. 2005. *In Defense of Democracy: Dynamics and Fault Lines of Nepal's Political Economy*. New Delhi: Adroit Publishers.

McAdam, Doug, John D. McCarthy and Mayer N. Zald. 1996. 'Introduction: Opportunities, Mobilizing Structures, and Framing Processes—Toward a Synthetic, Comparative Perspective on Social Movements', in D. McAdam, J.D. McCarthy and M.N. Zald (eds), *Comparative Perspectives on Social Movements*, pp. 1–23. Cambridge: Cambridge University Press.

McCarthy, John D. 1996. 'Constraints and Opportunities in Adopting, Adapting, and Inventing', in D. McAdam, J.D. McCarthy and M.N. Zald (eds), *Comparative Perspectives on Social Movements*, pp. 141–51. Cambridge: Cambridge University Press.

Onta, Pratyoush. 2002. 'Critiquing the Media Boom,' in K.M. Dixit and S. Ramachandaran (eds), *State of Nepal*, pp. 253–70. Kathmandu: Himal Books.

Panday, Devendra Raj. 2000. *Nepal's Failed Development: Reflections on the Mission and the Maladies*. Kathmandu: Nepal South Asia Centre.

Pfaff-Czarnecka, Joanna. 2004. 'High Expectations, Deep Disappointments: Politics, State, and Society in Nepal after 1990', in M. Hutt (ed.), *Himalayan People's War: Nepal's Maoist Rebellion*, pp. 166–90. Bloomington: Indiana University Press.

Pradhan, Rajendra. 2002. 'Ethnicity, Caste and a Pluralist Society', in K.M. Dixit and S. Ramachandaran (eds), *State of Nepal*, pp. 1–21. Kathmandu: Himal Books.

Rana, Govardan. 1995. *Prajaataantrik Andolanma Nepaal Bidhyaarthi Sangh* (The Nepal Student Organization in the Democratic Movement). Kathmandu: Prakashak Press.

Rohrschneider, Robert. 1993. 'Impact of Social Movements on European Party Systems', *Annals of American Academy of Political and Social Sciences* 528: 157–70.

Roka, Hari. 2004. 'The Emergency and Nepal's Political Future', in M. Hutt (ed.), *Himalayan People's War: Nepal's Maoist Rebellion*, pp. 261–84. Bloomington: Indiana University Press.

Shah, Saubhaghya. 2004. 'A Himalayan Red Herring? Maoist Revolution in the Shadow of the Legacy Raj', in M. Hutt (ed.), *Himalayan People's War: Nepal's Maoist Rebellion*, pp. 192–225. Bloomington: Indiana University Press.

Snellinger, Amanda. 2005. 'A Crisis in Nepali Student Politics?: Analyzing the Gap between Politically Active and Non-Active Students', *Peace and Democracy in South Asia Journal* 2 (Fall): 14–30.

———. 2006. 'Commitment as an Analytic: Reflections on Nepali Student Activists Protracted Struggle', *PoLAR (Political and Legal Anthropology Review)* 29: (2: November): 351–64.

Tarrow, Sidney. 1990. 'The Phantom at the Opera: Political Parties and Social Movements of the 1960s and 1970s in Italy', in R.J. Dalton and M. Kuechler (eds), *Challenging the Political Order*, pp. 251–76. Oxford: Oxford University Press.

———. 1996. 'States and Opportunities: The Political Structuring of Social Movements', in D. McAdam, J.D. McCarthy and M.N. Zald (eds), *Comparative Perspectives on Social Movements*, pp. 41–61. Cambridge: Cambridge University Press.

———. 1998. *Power in Movement: Social Movements and Contentious Politics*, 2nd ed. Cambridge: Cambridge University Press.

Thapa, Deepak. 2004. 'Radicalism and the Emergence of the Maoists', in M. Hutt (ed.), *Himalayan People's War: Nepal's Maoist Rebellion*, pp. 21–37. Bloomington: Indiana University Press.

Van Cott, Donna Lee. 2003. 'Institutional Change and Ethnic Parties in South America', *Latin American Politics and Society* 45 (2): 1–39.

Zald, Mayer N. 1996. 'Culture, Ideology, and Strategic Framing', in D. McAdam, J.D. McCarthy and M. Zald (eds), *Comparative Perspectives on Social Movements*, pp. 261–90. Cambridge: Cambridge University Press.

Upadhya, Sanjay. 2002. 'A Dozen Years of Democracy: The Games that Parties Play' in K.M. Dixit and S. Ramachandaran (eds), *State of Nepal*, pp. 62–76. Kathmandu: Himal Books.

Wolfsfeld, Gadi. 1991. 'Media, Protest, and Political Violence: A Transactional Analysis', *Journalism Monographs* 127: 1–23.

PART V

Contentious Politics and Democratization

12

A 'Chaos' Ecology: Democratization and Urban Environmental Decline in Kathmandu

ANNE RADEMACHER

In the late twentieth century, a state bureaucratic apparatus for cultivating urban environmental stewardship emerged in Nepal.[1] International development institutions, concerned with issues of bio-diversity protection, environmental conservation, and restoration, provided support to this apparatus in order to promote a variety of conservation-development activities. Among these were projects that addressed specifically urban environmental concerns such as industrial pollution, air quality and sanitation. In the capital city, the challenge of environmental management was formidable, and attempts to improve the urban environment were fraught with expressions of dissent and discontent. If one way of analysing the effectiveness of democracy is through an assessment of how and to what extent the demands of society are formally and substantively met by the government, then the politics of urban environmental improvement projects provide an important lens through which to understand democratization at the bureaucratic centre of the Nepali nation-state.

This chapter understands Nepali democratization as a specific political and cultural experience. Its specificity to the historical period between 1990 and 2001 and its characteristic intersection of both economic liberalization and the opening up of the polity from historically tenacious exclusionary practices make democracy in Nepal a qualitatively different referent than 'democracy' as an abstract form of government. The attachment of democratization in Nepal to its historical moment allows a critical distinction between disaffection with a specific experience of democracy and a rejection of democracy as an ideal governmental form to which a social collective aspires. What follows is a discussion of the critique, and even rejection, of Nepali democracy that followed a conflation of democratization with urban environmental degradation. At issue is the social, cultural and environmental cost of the historical experience of democratization in Nepal's capital city in the 1990s.

The democratic decade produced a complex combination of material, political and cultural changes in Nepal's capital city. Particularly for Kathmandu's expanding middle class, democratization was initially punctuated by high expectations and a sense of unbounded possibilities. Change came with a partner, however: pollution and urban environmental degradation were increasingly identified, discussed and addressed as undeniable aspects of rapid growth and transformation.

As features of an urban landscape with complex cultural, historical and natural importance, the Bagmati and Bishnumati rivers assumed a prominent place among the aspects of the urban environment characterized in official and popular discourses as increasingly degraded.[2] Deteriorating river conditions motivated a variety of state-sponsored and international restoration initiatives that, in turn, drew steady criticism. Although few disputed that the rivers suffered serious degradation or that the degradation had both scientific and cultural facets, precisely *why* river quality continued to decline and exactly *how* to reverse it were matters fiercely contested.

This chapter explores democratization in Nepal's capital city through the lens of urban river politics. In doing so, it treats river decline as both a scientific condition and a culturally mediated social experience. While the degradation of the Bagmati and Bishnumati can be framed and addressed as a development 'crisis' in the classic sense, it can also be understood in terms of its sociocultural implications—how the effects of river degradation are expressed as cultural loss. Both framings enrich our understanding of the experience of democratization in the capital, since the political and cultural costs of accelerated river degradation were often linked to a broader commentary on the proper order of Nepal as a democratic state and a unified nation.

What follows, then, is an exploration of commentaries about democratization that were embedded in debates about river restoration during and immediately following the democratic period. The data presented here are drawn from fieldwork[3] among development professionals, NGO workers and urban environmental activists in Kathmandu[4] between 1997 and 2003—a time of increasing disaffection with democracy, escalating violence in the countryside and the steady decline of urban river vitality. Late in this period, the murder of most of Nepal's royal family and the imposition of emergency brought into sharp relief questions about the stability—and in places, the very existence—of the Nepali state. The political symbolism of the capital city and of its rivers shifted significantly as urban environmental territory assumed new meanings and its management took on a new symbolic urgency.

Since the experience of democratization per se was not the focus of the initial fieldwork, it must be noted here that the data from which this chapter draws cannot provide an exhaustive account of informants' opinions, official ideas or the vast array of news-media representations[5] that spoke directly to the question of democracy in Nepal in the 1990s. Rather, the chapter emphasizes moments when references to democratization made their way into the debates that characterized river politics. There are, therefore, important limits to the claims made herein and an acknowledgement at the outset that, while it raises important questions, this analysis does not pretend to provide a definitive or complete account of the experience of democratization in Kathmandu.

Despite these limitations, however, this essay can enrich our understanding of at least two aspects of democratization. First, river debates in the 1990s highlight how the unstable and ineffective bureaucracy that characterized the democratization period prevented the implementation and practice of effective policies—in this case, comprehensive and sustained river restoration initiatives. The rapid turnover of more than a dozen successive governments during the democratization period not only limited the actions that any single government could take, it also produced a climate of ongoing political—and, by consequence, ecological—flux. For this reason, among many of my environmental activist-informants, democratization in Nepal came to be associated with accelerated environmental degradation itself—so much so that the two were sometimes explicitly or conceptually conflated. In this sense, democracy as experienced in Nepal was seen to exacerbate, and in some instances even catalyze, certain facets of urban environmental degradation. Furthermore, it was often criticized as being ill-equipped to combat challenges as complex and persistent as Kathmandu's ecological decline.

Second, exploring the experience of democracy in Nepal through Kathmandu's river conditions foregrounds a complex calculus of cultural costs and benefits that some informants attached to democratization. While democracy was lauded for bestowing certain freedoms and rights, for instance, it was also derided as generative of a social flux that some regarded as destructive. This destruction was best exemplified, some argued, by the decline of the Bagmati and Bishnumati riverscape, which cultural-heritage activists in particular regarded as much a cultural landmark as an ecological system.[6]

This chapter begins with a review of some ways that river degradation was discussed and described as being associated with, or even driven by, Nepal's experience of democracy. It then reviews how official environmental interventions made in the immediate aftermath of the November 2001 declaration of a state of emergency positioned the post-democracy state in a place of strength and effectiveness relative to the democratic governments that it replaced. While by no means an exhaustive account of the intersections between river politics and the experience of democratization, this discussion suggests that disaffection with democracy in Nepal must be understood not only in terms of unmet material expectations, but also in terms of anxieties over the cultural losses—realized or potential—that were increasingly seen as the cost of democratization.

River Degradation and Democratization: Chaotic Ecology and Unsettled Polity

As urban environmental deterioration intensified through the 1990s, public discontent with the gross imbalance between studies, development investments and official promises on one hand, and the worsening condition of the urban environment on the other, resonated in various fields of public discourse. The capital witnessed a proliferation of citizens' groups and NGOs concerned specifically with the urban environment, with some devoted solely to the cause of Bagmati and Bishnumati River stewardship.[7] Public figures such as cultural-heritage activist Huta Ram Baidya promoted the idea of the 'Bagmati Civilization' (*bagmati sabhyata*) via radio, television and print media,[8] while prominent industrialist Binod Chaudhary issued a high-visibility open appeal to the then Prime Minister Girija Prasad Koirala to either clean up the Bagmati within six months or he would do it himself![9] The year 2001 saw the first of what would become an annual Bagmati rafting event featuring well-known entertainers and media figures braving the 'brown' rapids of the monsoon season to draw attention to the cause. In calling for wider public awareness of, and attention to, the accelerating decline of the city's rivers, these groups also criticized the ineffectiveness of a government and development apparatus that, despite years of studies, policies and projects, had failed to curb the rivers' decline.

In early 2000, a *Kathmandu Post* headline declared, 'Billions Spent But the Rivers Still Polluted'.[10] The article proclaimed the wastage of over Rs 3 billion in investments toward the improvement of the Bagmati and Bishnumati rivers, charging that the countless studies and interventions directed toward river management had produced almost no discernible positive result. A portion of the article read:

> Despite the expenses, Kathmandu Valley's rivers—Bagmati, Bishnumati, Dhobikhola, Hanumante and Tukucha—continue to serve as massive sewerage systems for the Valley's overall population of 1.5 million. Industrial waste is also dumped into them recklessly .... There is a total lack of accountability and co-ordination among more than a dozen authorities that are supposed to be concerned about the plight of the rivers. Experts also stress that the government should come up with laws and regulations clearly defining rivers and their standard widths. They also (criticized) the municipalities, industries, and environment ministry for failing to enforce existing laws.

Although a host of environmental protection laws were established during the 1990s, most lacked effective enforcement mechanisms or clear delineations of bureaucratic responsibility. Several government agencies were assigned the responsibility of protecting and managing the urban environment, but confusion about precisely which ministries should manage what tasks often resulted in cross-agency conflicts rather than actual enforcement or project implementation. Thus the lack of coordination lamented in the selection above.

A few days after the 'Billions Spent' article was published, an editorial response appeared in the same paper under the title 'Protect Valley Rivers'. It argued that ultimately only 'concrete measures' undertaken by a strong and effective state could reverse urban river damage:

> ... There are over a dozen authorities supposed to be concerned with improving the cleanliness of rivers. But lack of coordination and accountability problems mar their performance .... In this backdrop, it can be concluded that serious action must be taken without delay to enforce relevant laws and regulations to improve the plight of the Valley's rivers. Unless the government comes forward with concrete measures, rivers that constitute the foundation of the Valley's old civilization will not stand any chance of survival, forget about improving their condition.[11]

In this framing of river degradation, administrative failure had both immediate environmental implications and the deeper, more far-reaching effect of neglecting history and cultural heritage. Bureaucratic ineffectiveness and weakness, then, risked not only poor public health or poor water quality in the Valley's rivers, but it also held in the balance the heritage narratives through which Kathmandu made cultural and historical sense as the capital city of the Nepali nation-state.

The idea that river degradation was culturally insulting circulated in various media: among the most prevalent were the articles, interviews, speeches and special television coverage that featured the cultural-heritage activist Huta Ram Baidya.[12] Embedded in anxieties over the cultural losses signalled by degraded rivers and templescapes were concerns that democratization encouraged not only excessive individualism, but excessive individual greed. A 1996 *Kathmandu Post* article titled 'How Holy? Much Sewage has Run Down the Bagmati' emphasized stories of personal offence that interviewees associated with river degradation and related them to an emergent 'self-centered attitude' in the Valley. An excerpt reads:

> Recalling from the past, she could not suppress the ecstasy in her eyes when she referred to the purity of the water of the Bagmati just a decade ago. 'We used to bathe in the river and wash our clothes. The water was so clean that people even used to drink it. The self-centered attitudes of the people, together with the deterioration in religious values, have converted the sacred river of the Hindus into an abominable gutter, making a mockery of their own cultural beliefs,' Padma Kumari said.

Later in this piece, the 'self-centered attitude' identified as a catalyst for river degradation is associated with the reinstatement of democracy, which is characterized as a moment when 'like birds released from their cages, (citizens) harboured the misconception that they could do practically anything in a free world'. The article goes on to outline recent assessments of water quality and to identify the familiar lack of coordination among various governmental regulatory bodies and the absence of an overall master plan for riverscape restoration as key obstacles to reversing river degradation.

Later, on 5 April 2000, a *Kathmandu Post* editorial titled 'My House Beneath Bagmati Bridge' offered a direct critique of the Nepali experience of democracy through an expression of dismay over uncontrolled river encroachment and the corruption that seemed to facilitate it. A passage reads:

> This is democracy. Money is the only thing we have left to call our culture. A handful of money can hush them for sure ... you can claim any land in this lustrous city provided you know some officials personally .... So long as the government falls upon the hands of those who never care whether the Bagmati came first or we did, more and more houses will be built along the ever-narrowing banks of the poor Bagmati .... And if you really have power or money in your pocket, join us. It's far more lucrative than crying out for stopping the pollution in the river.

The suggestion that democracy created conditions within which the pursuit of personal financial gain automatically superseded a broader responsibility to steward environmental and cultural resources had direct implications for a diagnosis of urban river degradation and hopes for restoration. Without some evidence that democratic governments not only honoured a wider spectrum of historical and cultural responsibilities, but were also capable of implementing activities that could demonstrate it, envisioning river restoration of any kind seemed an almost hopeless endeavour.

In interviews with river activists about perceived intersections between democratization and river decline, certain features of degradation were particularly prevalent. Among these, encroachment on the riverscape, both by elites and by extremely poor rural-to-urban migrants known as *sukumbasi,*[13] was a condition that seemed to evidence a lack of enforcement—and therefore effectiveness and strength—on the part of the state.

In late December 2001, the author walked along the Bagmati's banks with the activist Huta Ram Baidya and three others: an NGO worker, a writer for a national newspaper and a photojournalist. The three were founders of a small environmental NGO that focused on raising awareness about the plight of the city's rivers. During the walk, members of the group commented on how democracy had worsened Bagmati's degradation, to which the author immediately posed the question: did these young professionals see democracy and urban environmental degradation as in some way directly connected? Following their fervent and unanimous 'yes', they were asked how, with the expectation that we might talk about weak enforcement of regulations or the rapid turnover of successive governments. They explained instead that democracy had brought large numbers of 'outsiders' from beyond the Valley to the city, and not simply the *sukumbasi* migrant poor—the more commonly blamed group. Members of Parliament from districts outside Kathmandu were said to be even more notorious for their lack of 'respect' for the riverscape and the Kathmandu Valley in general. Together, we looked across the river at a large mansion recently constructed, illegally, in the floodplain. The home, presumably belonging to such an 'outsider MP' was offered as evidence of encroachment on river territory by democracy's elites: such homes were an increasingly common sight that testified to an abuse of wealth, power and privilege that to these respondents partly characterized democracy itself.

The group further implied that, contrary to popular conceptions, more blame for river degradation rested with elite riverbank encroachers than with the *sukumbasi* poor. Thus, to add to a more common narrative of democratization as a catalyst for uncontrolled migration of rural Nepalis to the city, the author was encouraged to see the democratic bureaucratic elite as major contributors to both environmental and cultural decline. In this framing, the individual lifestyles of those embedded within democratic rule were seen as a driving force behind river encroachment and therefore river degradation.

The very idea of encroachment, of course, signals some explicit or implicit sense of precisely who is entitled to claim riverscape space. This connects, in turn, to a sense of government and social failure to enforce assumed or prior boundaries around river territory. Again, reference to these issues in certain corners of the Nepali news media is instructive. In 'I Need to Get Back my Bagmati', for instance, author Anu Lohani (1999)[14] describes a visit to Pashupatinath that relates government irresponsibility and ineffectiveness to a general breakdown of the cultural order at this, a highly symbolic historical and contemporary site of both Hindu ritual practice and the reproduction of political order in Nepal (see Sharma 2002). The writer relates being 'shocked to see the rapid growth of (riparian) settlements ... built along the sides of the sanctified shrine'. Lohani asks, 'Is it something that is being allowed by the government ...?'[15]

Such letters not only associated the rivers' condition with a general lack of state order, leadership and strength under democracy, they also lamented a loss of Hindu territorial order on the riverscape. In addition to indicting the government for its practical failures, then, these charges appealed to a specific national imagination of the appropriate cultural and historical order of the capital landscape. It was precisely this order that degradation violated, making proper ecological restoration as much a complex project of cultural salvage as it was a question of water-quality indicators or morphologically transformed riverbeds.

A Government 'Freed to Act': Environmental Order After Democracy

If river encroachment was one metric by which the ineffectiveness of the state under democracy was gauged, then popular representations of an all-out riverscape 'invasion' suggested that degradation (and democracy) had reached a breaking point. By the fall of 2003, some informants linked encroachment and rural-to-urban migration not only to urban environmental decline, but also to the intense political disorder associated with the Maoist insurgency.

A newspaper article titled 'Kathmandu's Malignant Urban Tumor'[16] provides an elaboration of this logic. The piece captured in its title and content perceptions that rural-to-urban migration had become extremely problematic for the Valley's overall environmental 'health', stating that 'urban pressures triggered by insurgency-related out migration from the districts are making the environmental crisis more serious'. It related stories of individual migrants, such as Chandra Raj Bhandari of Nuwakot, whose arrival in the urban riparian *sukumbasi* settlement of Balaju was prompted by an attack in which Maoists assumed that he was an army informer; he was left with no choice but to flee to the Valley for his life. And yet, even as the valley was framed as a refugee from rural violence, new migrant settlements simultaneously stood for an all-out 'invasion' that the city had no choice but to repel. The article quoted the chief of the Urban Development Department, Devendra Dongol, as saying: 'We really need to stop this invasion of people. This is more than the Valley can absorb.' The article then asserted that 'it all falls on the Valley's municipalities to do their best to prevent the city from becoming a malignant urban tumor'.

The state of emergency declared on 26 November 2001 enabled a particular state response to accelerated migration—and, in turn, to river decline—that the democratic era had effectively disabled: the reinstatement of forced evictions in the name of riparian improvement and security objectives. 'Kathmandu's Malignant Tumor' further noted the forced displacement of 142 families from the west bank of the Bishnumati, relating it to the revival of the long-dormant Bishnumati Link Road[17] plan. The refusal by government authorities to compensate evictees was attributed to a suspicion of squatter 'legitimacy':

> Former squatters from the Bishnumati were promised compensation by Mayor Kesab Sthapit in April 2002. 'It never happened,' says Krishna Devi Shahi. The municipality's executive officer Shiva Bhakta Sharma says he will compensate the squatters, but blames them for not furnishing the necessary paperwork. 'Really, I asked them six months ago to give me proof that they are landless. I am still waiting,' he says. Sharma adds that Kathmandu is full of poor people and if the word gets out that the municipality is giving land or money to squatters, thousands more will be tempted to live on government property.[18]

To deal more directly and aggressively with settlements of the landless poor in the riparian zone was one way for the post-democracy emergency government to demonstrate both environmental resolve and intolerance for political threats, real or imagined, in the capital. In a climate in which a strengthening Maoist insurgency cast the resilience of the state into question, a migrant 'invasion' such as that described above was transgressive not only of river territory, but also of a national order of things that held the capital city to be the symbolic and material centre of the Nepali state.

According to members of a prominent housing-advocacy group, official harassment of riparian *sukumbasi* communities increased almost immediately after the emergency was declared.[19] Police actions were formally categorized as a response to security concerns, as *sukumbasi* settlements became the default location of risk to the state within its own capital territory. As bombings and isolated attacks became more frequent in the Valley, so too did raids on *sukumbasi* settlements that were labelled 'security checks'.[20] Evictions from the Thapatali squatter settlements were officially justified on grounds of security concerns in preparation for an upcoming regional trade conference.[21]

A sense of caution soon influenced the activities of housing-rights advocates. When housing advocates were asked about their work with newer settlements in the riparian zone, they reported having withdrawn the outreach component of their operations and that they were, in effect, freezing the number of settlements in which they worked.[22] Entire new settlements, presumably composed of war refugees, were therefore closed off from NGO advocacy. One staff member explained that they 'could not be sure' about the political orientation of the inhabitants of these new settlements.

Unspoken was the assumption that involving an NGO with a settlement in which one might encounter Maoist sympathizers could compromise its very operation.[23] A housing advocacy volunteer described the changed terms under which her organization could engage existing debates in February 2002:

> ... [P]reventative action and delaying tactics like mass demonstrations, press conferences, people blocking the bulldozers—... things (we have) done for past eviction threats—can't be done because the possibility of the squatters and staff getting arrested is too high, and the emergency makes people very afraid that if they go to jail, they won't get out until it's over. Second, (advocates) feel like they can't single out government representatives as targets for action because they're afraid of being called terrorists .... On top of this, if the elections really aren't held this year, then the municipalities are going to grind to a halt.[24]

At some levels, then, as the insurgency intensified and was increasingly felt in the insular urban centre, the disorder of the riverscape seemed to both reflect and contain the magnitude of a revolutionary challenge to the polity itself—a potential for disorder to rival the environmental and cultural breakdown feared or lamented during the democratic decade.

During this period, many state and development officials involved with river restoration turned from a general annoyance with *sukumbasi* settlements as yet another feature of river decline to openly and explicitly identifying them as *the* primary obstacle to restoration of the riverscape. In interviews in late 2001, the director of an extensive riverside park-building initiative, the UN Park project,[25] assured the author that the *sukumbasi* settlements located inside the proposed UN Park boundaries were not only a 'nuisance', but were now the single most important factor limiting international donor interest and involvement in (and therefore the progress of) the UN Park project. 'This land is not clean for donors,' the director said, arguing that it had become extremely urgent for the government to 'manage' or resettle the *sukumbasi*. He said:

> We must either manage these settlements or relocate them, and relocating them is best for the rivers and for the city. Our most important priority has got to be to secure this land that everyone wants. To do this we have to first fence in the area and slowly introduce park construction as the land becomes available.[26]

Existing settlements, he said, simply could not stay where they were. While his immediate goal was to activate the UN Park project by securing donor funding, it was clear that the stakes were much larger: the massive disorder embodied in the Maoist insurgency and signified through river breakdown and migrant 'invasions' threatened not only the capital's territorial order, but also the very financial arrangements through which the bureaucratic apparatus of the Nepali state had been reproduced for decades.[27]

It was only a few weeks later that residents of the Thapatali settlements to which the director had been referring were evicted by state officials, citing a 'security concern'. That same afternoon, the UN Park director met again with the author for a previously scheduled meeting, and he discussed the evictions with elation and relief, saying that the municipality had been 'freed to act' by the state of emergency. If democracy had enabled one sort of freedom, then its converse, the emergency, had enabled another in which the state itself was 'freed' to act with authoritarian impunity. 'Every *sukumbasi* knows he could be next,' he said, pointing out other sites where single-family dwellings had been recently removed. 'As this area opens up, people will start walking along the river again. This is a turning point, because until these local people take care and take interest, this river is not going to change.'[28] He pointed out some riverside walkers in the distance, although it was unclear whether they were the 'legal' inhabitants he hoped would be rediscovering the river or displaced 'illegal' ones assessing losses from the recent eviction. The conversation closed with the director suggesting that in the current political climate, one could not be too careful; 'these settlements must be brought under control,' he said—one facet of a broader ecosystem and polity that had to be reigned in.

Urban Ecology and the Post-Democratic State

The eviction of riparian settlements was by no means the only 'environmental' intervention through which the emergency state showed itself to be an antidote for democratic disorder. Just over a month after the emergency was declared, Kathmandu hosted the eleventh meeting of the South Asian Association for Regional Co-operation (SAARC), a high-profile South Asian summit. In the weeks leading up to the SAARC conference, emergency-bound Kathmandu witnessed a massive beautification campaign, involving extensive demolitions and the rapid construction of new urban parks. While a variety of measures characterized official SAARC preparations in Kathmandu, three most visibly intersected with urban environmental politics. First, there were swift building demolitions and a new park constructed at Tinkune, an area of land in the vicinity of the national airport. This park would be the first to greet visiting SAARC dignitaries on their journey between the airport and the city centre; it featured lush plantings and a large central pond. Second, a cluster of four- and five-storey buildings at a crossroads called Maitighar[29] was demolished and, over the course of a few days, replaced by a small park that featured an enormous mandala, a stupa and two stone waterspouts.[30] Finally, just below the Bagmati Bridge, two informal settlements officially regarded as illegal squatter areas were forcibly evicted, the homes levelled and their residents dispersed. There was a marked lack of protest in all three cases, not only in public discourse, where emergency restrictions limited it, but also in private conversations with activist informants from whom one might reasonably expect expressions of outrage—not over the improvements, but over the authoritarian manner in which urban environmental management was being conducted.[31]

There was a somewhat startling simultaneity between the imposition of the state of emergency and the sudden proliferation of urban beautification. Although officially attributed to preparations for SAARC, these interventions had communicative effects far beyond that of simply cleaning up the city for regional dignitaries and foreign guests. The simultaneity produced a conflation of political and environmental stability such that the boundaries between them seemed to dissolve. Not only was riparian squatting successfully recontextualized as a security threat, but river management itself was subsumed under a broader environmental management that served the performance of a post-democratic state in full control of the capital city.

In discussions with informants, the author expected expressions of reservation, caution or dissatisfaction over the undemocratic context within which SAARC-related environmental improvements took place. Many had spent the previous decade expressing passionate commitments to ecological visions that took concepts such as 'participation' and 'democracy' as central features, and one assumed that they would interpret emergency-era environmental management as a searing violation of these principles. But contrary to such expectations, informants backgrounded their criticisms and offered instead largely positive assessments.

The fact that urban environmental clean-up associated with SAARC preparations had an immediate connection to the image that the city would project to regional and global onlookers seemed to figure into this enthusiasm, reflected, for example, in proud comments made by the UN Park director:

> Kathmandu is the capital. We want to make the city clean for our guests. These parks were a special case because we saw what can happen when we focus our expertise and concentrate our resources. Everyone worked together and something got done. Finally, some action—it is a relief.[32]

As noted previously, the director also expressed relief that the Thapatali squatter settlements were quickly and completely removed. For him, the eviction resolved what he saw as a major obstacle to his own efforts to move forward with UN Park construction. On several occasions, he said that international donors would not get involved with the UN Park until the '*sukumbasi* problem' was resolved. He asserted that only in the context of a state of emergency could such a swift removal of the settlements have taken place.

But expressions of relief and welcome for the changes were expressed even among housing activists. After the Thapatali actions—the first forced *sukumbasi* evictions along the riverbanks since 1996—this author encountered more approval for the state's actions among these informants than criticisms. One prominent activist for urban housing and environmental rights expressed relief that, as she put it, at least 'something' in the way of urban environmental improvement was finally 'getting done', in sharp contrast to the in-effective democratic decade. She emphasized a broader picture in which all SAARC-related improvements were a welcome relief, suggesting that, despite their vulnerability, even the city's *sukumbasi* population had a generally positive reaction to the beautification campaign. After all, she said, the *sukumbasi* were 'just like us:' even they welcomed actions that would evidence a proactive, effective government and promote a cleaner city. She said:

> People [in sukumbasi settlements] are not against [the SAARC-related projects] .... They say they want these development programs. They say they want the city to look clean. The message the people are getting is that the government can do it if they want ... even these big houses [at Maitighar] are demolished in a moment. [The government] can do it if they want to.[33]

While her previous work strongly suggested that she would never approve of forced evictions, her reaction to these particular actions was interesting in that it framed them as almost hopeful, a sign of life for a state empowered to 'do it if they want to'. She went to great lengths to explain that, in a very broad sense, SAARC-related clean-up measures were in themselves desirable, even to communities that could potentially fall victim to evictions.[34]

To interpret such comments as an expression of a desire to do away with democracy altogether would be simplistic and inaccurate, however. In fact, many held on to an *ideal* of democracy quite different from the experience of democratization over the 1990s. For some, salvaging the state by backgrounding dissent during the initial state of emergency also meant preserving the possibility that a more desirable democracy might be forged at some future point. The unspoken trade-off was that if the excesses of the 1990s democratization continued, any hope for a more 'authentic' democracy at some later point would likely be destroyed.

Herein lies an important aspect of emergency-era compromises: while the dissent that might have been openly expressed during the 1990s did not disappear, it was measured, reserved or muted so that the demonstrated effectiveness and functionality of the post-democratic state could be condoned, the Nepali state itself could be reinforced, and the more immediate perceived threats associated with the Maoist insurgency could be curtailed. Ultimate support for an effective, assertive state among environmental activists, particularly in an uncertain time of suspended civil rights, seemed to suggest that democratic environmental management replaced by authoritarian environmental management was still considered environmental, as well as essential political, progress. Even if urban parks were constructed without public consultation or accountability, they were built, demonstrating that, as one informant said, 'the government can do it if they want to'. Perhaps ironically, acts embracing the undemocratic practices of the emergency-era state could also be understood as acts of preservation and salvage consistent with, rather than dismissive of, ultimately democratic political ideals. A certain experience of democratization, then, seemed to give way to support for an authoritarian state of emergency that was seen, at some level, as the only way to ensure that a more authentic democratic Nepal might be possible in the future.

Bringing Order to 'Chaos'

The ordered parks that quickly replaced disorderly and ecologically degraded urban spaces in the immediate aftermath of the November 2001 emergency declaration gave physical testimony to the perceived failures of the previous decade of democracy. By demonstrating what an emergency state order could 'do in a moment', they also demonstrated what interventions undertaken in the context of democratization could not accomplish in 12 years. The active, assertive urban beautification that was embodied in preparations for the SAARC summit made sense locally as the converse of democracy-as-inaction. In this sense, the making of urban parks and the clearing of informal or otherwise undesirable settlements signified a post-democratic state that was aggressive and effective. The SAARC-emergency combination allowed the state to portray itself as a foil to a 'failed' democracy, highlighting what the previous political order had been unable to do and diverting attention from the open question of the sustainability of its own actions and methods.

Thus these environmental transformations did much more than just appropriately welcome and perhaps impress visiting regional dignitaries. They also provided local city residents with spectacles of tangible state action in the wake of a long and frustrating legacy of environmental inaction. Each environmental project seemed tied to show that the emergency state was the converse of its democratic legacy, and, rather than fuel dissent, this initially—though only temporarily—galvanized the support of the urban activists and professionals whose previous political actions and statements conveyed deep commitments to democratic practices.

In the years to follow, many of those who initially welcomed the state of emergency as a consolidation of much-needed order in the capital returned to the streets to demand official accountability, openness and the reinstatement of democratic processes.[35] At the time of this writing, they continued to assume tremendous risks in order to voice their demands not only for the reinstatement of the formal structures of democracy, but also for its substantive realization. Understanding the complexity—and challenges—of the contemporary struggle to reinstate democracy is only possible when one takes into account the experience of democratization in the 1990s, complete with its points of failure and weakness. This chapter has endeavoured to show that in the realm of urban environmental management, democratization was in important ways associated with the seeming intractability of urban environmental degradation. This provided a ready platform for the post-democratic government to demonstrate its contrasting ability to effectively and efficiently meet the demands of a nervous, frustrated and rapidly growing urban populace.

Notes

1. The HMG Ministry of Population and Environment was created in 1995 and an Environmental Protection Act followed in 1996. Since 1997, it has been unlawful to create pollution in a way that causes significant impact on the environment or public health, and there are now national pollution standards and a schedule of fines for development projects that proceed without environmental impact statements (Adhikari 1998).
2. River conditions in Kathmandu have been linked to many interconnected factors. Comprehensive policy and development studies, such as Stanley International's *The Bagmati Basin Water Management Strategy and Investment Plan* (Kathmandu: HMG, 1994), identify the main causes of river pollution inside the urban area as the discharge of untreated sewage and widespread dumping of solid waste into the rivers and on their banks. Excessive sand mining in riverbeds and banks, which supplies mortar and cement materials to the city's construction industry, is blamed for severe morphological and flow pattern changes. In addition to these factors, most policy and development discussions of river degradation identify human encroachment on the banks, floodplains and riverbeds exposed by falling water levels as an element of the degradation

process. Likewise, deteriorating templescapes that line both rivers in their urban reaches are sometimes included in characterizations of river degradation. See also CLEAN-Nepal (2002); Nepal Environmental and Scientific Services (1997); Shrestha and Sharma (1996).

3. The dissertation 'Culturing Urban Ecology: Development, Statemaking, and River Restoration in Kathmandu' (Rademacher 2005) draws from fieldwork conducted in Kathmandu between 1997 and 2003 on competing constructions of the Bagmati and Bishnumati riverscape degradation and restoration. Research conducted in August 1999 and from June to August 2000 was supported by the Edna Bailey Sussman Fund, the Yale Centre for International and Area Studies, the Tropical Resources Institute at Yale, and the Yale Program in Agrarian Studies. Research conducted from November 2001 to April 2002 and October 2002 to January 2003 was supported by the US Environmental Protection Agency (STAR Fellowship Grant 91576401–0) and the Yale Centre for International and Area Studies Henry Heart Rice Research Fellowship. Master's level research was conducted in Kathmandu over six months in 1997–98 with support from the Yale Program in Agrarian Studies and the Tropical Resources Institute at Yale.
4. It is important to note here that the voices of migrants are not presented in this paper. This omission is intended to foreground the voices of those who claimed to represent migrants in official dialogue about the rivers. This focus should not be misinterpreted as a privileging of non-migrant voices, but should be understood instead as a technique for exploring a particular network of actors forging representations of and knowledge about democracy and river degradation.
5. This paper draws from a narrow sample of news media, and as such, references to newspaper articles herein should not be understood as necessarily representative of ideas that were circulating in the vast and diverse Nepali news media.
6. Cf. Dixit (1995). See also the work of Huta Ram Baidya, Note 8.
7. Examples of these include the Friends of the Bagmati (est. 2000), the Save the Bagmati Campaign (est. 1990) and the Nepal River Conservation Trust (est. 1995).
8. See, for example, Baidya 2001, 2002a, 2002b, 2002c and 2002d.
9. On 16 May 2000, Chaudhary's appeal ran in several Nepali newspapers.
10. *Kathmandu Post*, 7 February 2000.
11. Editorial, *Kathmandu Post*, 8 February 2000.
12. See Note 10.
13. There is no easy translation from Nepali to English for *sukumbasi*, although it is most commonly translated to 'squatter'. A related word, *sukumbasa* is the state of having nothing. Used to refer both to people and their settlements, *sukumbasi* refers to those who are assumed to be landless or very poor and who occupy land for which they do not own a legal title. Although technically the term refers to 'the person lacking shelter and food; one having neither' according to *Ratna's Nepali English Dictionary*, the Bagmati–Bishnumati *sukumbasi* population has become permanent enough on the riparian landscape that they cannot be said to be definitely and universally lacking these things.

The population is made up of both rural-to-urban migrants and migrants originating within the Valley. In general, residents of Kathmandu tend to refer to anyone 'illegally' occupying public land as a sukumbasi. It should be recognized that the term can carry negative connotations and, although it is widely used, can be taken as an insult. See Tanaka (1997) for more detailed demographic information on Kathmandu's sukumbasi population during the 1990s. See also Gallagher (1991); Hada (2001); HMG (2006); Hunt (2001); KC (1998); Shrestha (1990); Tiwari (2001).

14. See Anu Lohani. 'I Need to Get Back my Bagmati', *Kathmandu Post*, 7 August 1999.
15. See also, for example, 'Matter of Urgency' by Diwakar Poudyal in a letter to the *Kathmandu Post* on 23 April 2000 and 'Bagmati Needs Help, Not More Pollution' by Mukunda Thapaliya in a letter to the *Kathmandu Post*, 8 July 2000.
16. See Maarten Post, 'Kathmandu's Malignant Urban Tumour', *Nepali Times*, 6–11 September 2003.
17. The construction of this road along the banks of the Bishnumati River was classified as an 'environmental improvement' insofar as it would alleviate several traffic congestion problems in the city and perhaps create a barrier to squatter settlements along the riverbank. According to a report from the housing advocacy group Lumanti dated 10 February 2002, there were five squatter communities (163 families) settled in the planned path of the road and none of these families was guaranteed resettlement or compensation. In 2000, the *sukumbasi* communities located along the Bishnumati received eviction notices from the road construction project, but at that time, the squatters were able to postpone the demolition of their houses. Notice was served again in January of 2001, in which settlers were given seven days to leave. The communities reacted by holding meetings with the Nepal Basobas Basti Samrakshan Samaj (Nepal Settlement Protection Society) and Nepal Mahila Ekata Samaj (Nepal Women's Unity Society), as well as local government representatives, lawyers and Lumanti. They were able to secure a meeting with the Bishnumati Link Road project team on 29 January, thereby delaying the demolition that had been scheduled to start on 27 January. Community members hoped to come away from the meeting with a resettlement plan and guarantee of financial compensation. At the end of the meeting, however, community members were certain that demolition would start in 15 days. See also Strommen (1991).
18. Maarten Post, 'Kathmandu's Malignant Urban Tumour', *Nepali Times*, 6–11 September 2003.
19. Transcript of interview with a Lumanti staff member, 3 January 2003.
20. For example, after an explosion at the Bishnumati bridge at Kalimati on 29 March 2002 injured 24 people, all surrounding *sukumbasi* settlements were raided. In a January 2002 interview, the director of the housing-advocacy NGO Lumanti reported similar raids in Balaju and Kumaristan after an explosion in the Balaju neighbourhood.
21. The SAARC 2002 Summit took place in Kathmandu just after the emergency was declared. See Note 31.
22. Transcript of interview with Lumanti staff member, 3 January 2003.

23. Of course, the individuals who comprised the organization also had personal political affiliations and convictions that may have influenced this decision.
24. Text of an e-mail message from a housing advocacy volunteer, February 2002.
25. In July of 1995, a group of acting and former state ministers, influential scholars and development professionals proposed that a park be built on the Bagmati riverside to commemorate the 50th anniversary of the United Nations (UN). In its earliest formulation, the UN Park plan called for green spaces to replace sandy, flat riverbed on the bank of the Bagmati between Pashupatinath and the Bagmati Bridge. In addition to providing a recreational space, the project was intended to commemorate Nepal's contributions as a member state to the United Nations. Part of the park's stated purpose was '... to mark respect for those Nepalese army, police, and civilians who have died in UN peacekeeping endeavors' (Cosmos Engineering Services 1999: xi). In its early stages, the park boundaries fluctuated; but by 1999, a master plan covered the river corridors from Jorpati Bridge to Chobar Gorge on the Bagmati, the Sangle Khola confluence to Teku Dobhan on the Bishnumati, and the Dhobikhola from Mandikatar to its confluence with the Bagmati (ibid.).
26. Field notes, 8 January 2002.
27. In *Aid in Nepal's Development: How Necessary? Proceedings from a Panel Debate Organized by Udaya-Himalaya Network*, (Kathmandu: Udaya-Himalaya Network, 1992) Meena Acharya demonstrates that foreign aid as a percentage of development expenditure rose steadily from the First Five-Year Plan (1956–61) to the Fourth Five-Year Plan (1970–75). It then rose sharply from the mid-1970s through 1990, which marked the end of the Seventh Plan and the point at which democracy was reinstated. By 1990–91, the outstanding external debt was NRs 46 billion, or 46 per cent of the estimated GDP. By 1997, well over half of the government's budget came from foreign aid, according to Kanak Mani Dixit ('Foreign Aid in Nepal: No Bang for the Buck.' *Studies in Nepali History and Society* 2[1], 1997: 175). This followed the trend set in the 1970s and 1980s, by which Nepal maintained one of the highest per capita levels of foreign aid in the world, as demonstrated by David Seddon, *Nepal: A State of Poverty* (Delhi: Vikas, 1987).
28. Field notes, 8 January 2002.
29. These structures stood in violation of urban development regulations.
30. Michael Hutt (1995: 229) defines the *mandala* as 'a ritual diagram with a principle deity at its centre and the other divinities of this deity's retinue arranged around it. The *mandala* is the model for the design of Nepal's square pagoda temples and also, though less obviously, for the layout of the royal cities of the Valley during the Malla period'. Hutt defines the *stupa* as 'the primary cult object of Buddhism in Nepal and elsewhere. Originally a mound entombing sacred relics, now greatly elaborated' (ibid.: 232).
31. Emergency restrictions did not legally prohibit affected individuals from filing court complaints, yet no complaints in the Thapatali eviction case were filed. Elsewhere, I have problematized my informants' response to SAARC preparations. See Rademacher 2005.
32. Interview transcript, 8 January 2002.
33. Ibid.

34. During this period I was strongly dissuaded from interviewing *sukumbasi* settlers themselves, and I have therefore very limited data about their direct reactions to the Thapatali evictions.
35. Particularly since 2003, Kathmandu's streets have witnessed multiple protests calling for the reinstatement of democracy. Unrest in the capital city culminated in weeks of strikes and protests in April 2006 that brought an end to King Gyanendra's direct rule and the reinstatement of Parliament.

References

Adhikari, Ambika Prasad. 1998. *Urban and Environmental Planning in Nepal: Analysis, Policies, and Proposals*. Kathmandu: IUCN.

Baidya, Huta Ram. 1995. 'Bagmati—The Holy River', *in Images of a Century: The Changing Townscapes of the Kathmandu Valley*. GTZ/UDLE (Deutsche Gesellschaft fur Technische Zusammenarbeit and Urban Development through Local Efforts). Kathmandu: GTZ.

———. 2001. *Bagmati Sabhyatako Khoji (Looking for the Bagmati Civilization). Kantipur*, 7 Mangsir 2058.

———. 2002a. *Bagmati Sabhyatako Jagga Atikraman (Encroaching on Bagmati Civilization Land). Kantipur*, 28 Poush 2058.

———. 2002b. *Bagmati Sabhyatako Garima (The Importance of the Bagmati Civilization). Kantipur*, 2 December.

———. 2002c. *He Bagmati, Timi au! (Dear Bagmati, Please Come Back!). Kantipur*, 22 Jeth 2058.

———. 2002d. *Ranipokhari Bibad (Ranipokhari Debate). Kantipur*, 6 April.

CLEAN-Nepal (Community Led Environmental Action Network). 2002. *Environmental Baseline of Bishnumati Corridor in the Kathmandu Valley*. Kathmandu: World Vision International.

Cosmos Engineering Services. 1999. *Final Report in Preparation of Conservation and Development Master Plan for Bagmati, Bishnumati-Dhobikhola Corridor*. Kathmandu: HMG Ministry of Housing and Physical Planning.

Dixit, Kanak Mani. 1995. 'A Valley Changing'. in *Images of a Century: The Changing Townscapes of the Kathmandu Valley*. GTZ/UDLE (Deutsche Gesellschaft fur Technische Zusammenarbeit and Urban Development through Local Efforts). Kathmandu: GTZ.

Gallagher, Kathleen. 1991. 'An Exploration into the Causes of Squatting in the Kathmandu Valley'. Ph.D. dissertation, Central Department of Sociology/ Anthropology, Tribhuvan University, Kathmandu.

Hada, Jun. 2001. 'Housing and Squatter Settlements', in *City Diagnostic Report for City Development Strategy*. Kathmandu: Kathmandu Metropolitan City (KMC)/ World Bank.

HMG. 1994. *National Shelter Policy 1996*. Kathmandu: HMG.

Hunt, Jacqui. 2001. *Situation Analysis Report: A Study of Poor Urban Communities in the Kathmandu Valley*. Kathmandu: ActionAid/Lumanti.

Hutt, M. 1995. *Nepal: A Guide to the Art and Architecture of the Kathmandu Valley*. Boston: Kiscadale.

Kathmandu Metropolitan City. 2001. *City Diagnostic Report for City Development Strategy.* Kathmandu: KMC/World Bank.

Kathmandu Post. 2000a. 'Billions Spent but the River Still Polluted', Report, 7 February.

———. 2000b. 'Protect Valley Rivers', Edit page, 8 February.

KC, Bal Kumar. 1998. *Trends, Patterns, and Implications of Rural-to-Urban Migration in Nepal.* Kathmandu: Central Department of Population Studies, Tribhuvan University.

Lumanti Support Group for Shelter. 2002. *Report on Evictions at Thapatali.* Kathmandu: Lumanti.

Nepal Environmental and Scientific Services. 1997. *Final Report: Environmental Study of the Bagmati Watershed and Mitigation of River Pollution.* Kathmandu: HMG Ministry of Water Resources.

Rademacher, Anne. 2005. 'Culturing Urban Ecology: Development, Statemaking, and River Restoration in Kathmandu'. Ph.D. dissertation, Yale University.

Seddon, David. 1987. *Nepal: A State of Poverty.* New Delhi: Vikas.

Sharma, Sudhindra. 2002. 'The Hindu State and the State of Hinduism', in Kanak Mani Dixit and Shastri Ramachandaran (eds), *State of Nepal*, pp. 22–38. Lalitpur: Himal Books.

Shrestha, Nanda. 1990. *Landlessness and Migration in Nepal.* Boulder: Westview.

———. 1998. 'Losing Shangri-La?: The Environmental Degradation of Kathmandu', *Education About Asia* 3: 11–18.

Shrestha, R.R. and S. Sharma. 1996. 'Trend of Degrading Water Quality of Bagmati River (1988–1995)'. Paper presented at the Bagmati Environmental Seminar, 11 March 1996. Organized by Water Induced Disaster Prevention Technical Centre/HMG Ministry of Water Resources, Kathmandu.

Stanley International, His Majesty's Government Ministry of Housing, Health, and Population, the World Bank and the Japanese Grant Fund. 1994. *Bagmati Basin Water Management Strategy and Investment Plan: Final Report.* HMG/MHHP, World Bank/Japanese Grant Fund, April 1994, Kathmandu.

Strommen, Katherine, HMG Ministry of Housing and Physical Planning and the University of Trondheim. 1991. *Planning for Urban Development and Environmental Upgrading: An Environmental Impact Assessment of the Bishnumati Link Road.* Kathmandu: HMG.

Tanaka, Masako. 1997. *Conditions of Low Income Squatters in Kathmandu.* Kathmandu: Lumanti.

Tiwari, Sudarshan Raj. 2001. *Nepal's Urbanization and Urban Poverty Alleviation: A Critical Look at the 10th Plan.* Draft paper for the Ministry of Urban Affairs Workshop, Lumanti Support Group for Shelter: Kathmandu: n.d.

Udaya-Himalaya Network. 1992. 'Aid in Nepal's Development: How Necessary?'. Proceedings from a Panel Debate Organized by Udaya-Himalaya Network. Kathmandu.

13

Democratization Promoting and Democratization Hindering Contentious Politics: Lessons from Nepal

MAHENDRA LAWOTI

The contentious activities in Nepal after 1990 have had mixed effects on democratization. Some of the activities furthered democratization. The social-justice movements of the Dalits, Madhesis, women and indigenous nationalities expanded the political space of these traditionally disadvantaged groups. On the other hand, other contentious activities have hindered democratization. For instance, some of the privileged groups have engaged in collective protests to protect their traditional turfs and privileges. This second finding was unexpected, and is in contrast to the general assumption that contentious politics facilitates democratization. I will discuss these ideas in more detail in this chapter.

DEMOCRATIZATION PROMOTING CONTENTIOUS POLITICS

The social-justice movements that emerged and/or became more active after 1990 have contributed to expanding the democratic space to include more groups and individuals. The Dalit, indigenous nationalities', Madhesi and women's movements are some prominent examples. This notion fits well with Robert A. Dahl's (1971) well-known conceptualization of democratization—democratization occurs as more people participate in the polity. The traditionally disadvantaged groups in Nepal became more aware, informed and active citizens, and increased their voice and role in the polity. Some of these groups have received some concessions from the government. In addition, these movements have also generated awareness within the larger society about the complexity of the problems faced by these groups. Chapters 8 and 9 in this book, by Shrestha and Maharjan, on the Newars provide support to the arguments that marginalized groups can organize and mobilize to fight against the inequalities they face as a group and the empowerment of groups empowers individual members of the collectivities and deepens democracy.

However, the reach of social movements has been limited in Nepal. To a large extent, the social movements have been an urban phenomenon. They have occurred around Kathmandu and other urban centres (cities, towns and district headquarters). Many of the people engaged in these movements belong to the middle class or elite section of the society and the groups. Two cases in this book suggest otherwise. Hangen, in Chapter 7, argues that small ethnic parties, which have characteristics of social movements, have provided space to the rural and poor marginalized indigenous nationalities. These people rarely find space in the mainstream political parties and social movements. The ethnic party also raised issues that the mainstream political parties usually do not. Likewise, Lakier in Chapter 10 also discusses the Kamaiya (bonded labour) movement of the Tharus that forced the government to announce an end to the system. It was a movement by a rural indigenous group, although the final protests occurred in the district headquarters and Kathmandu.

In the mobilization of the rural poor and their issues, perhaps the Maoists have played the most significant role. No political party or movement has mobilized the rural people more than the Maoists (see Onesto and Somlai, Chapters 5 and 6). This is significant because the mainstream movements and political parties, despite their claim of representing the rural people, were mostly led by urban and rural elite. If mobilization of hitherto largely neglected people is a contribution toward democratization, the Maoists have played a significant role. However, the violent method they adopted, as will be discussed in the sections that follow, undermined the extant form of electoral democracy (see Khanal, Chapter 3).

Demonstrations, vigils and rallies by human-rights and peace groups also contributed positively to the democratization process. By conducting the activities with voluntary participation, they followed the norms of liberal politics. They also employed innovative strategies to convey their messages and were successful in grabbing media attention. The peace concerts organized by NGOs and music artistes after the turn of the century that toured across the country, for example, expressed the desire for peace for the common people and helped generate attention beyond Kathmandu, the traditional location of such activities. These activities demonstrated that political messages could be conveyed if innovative strategies were employed, even without employing violence or coercion, as many of the regular contentious activities in Nepal did.

A lot has been written about the role of contentious politics in facilitating democratization (see, for example, Chatterjee 2004; McAdam et al. 2001). Some of the chapters in this book and the cases discussed in them support the argument. However, a major finding of this book is that contentious politics can hinder democratization. The following sections dwell on the issue.

Contentious Politics Hindering Democratization

Coercive Protests and Violations of Liberal Rights

The years after 1990 saw plenty of protests and strikes in Nepal. Strikes and protests are, no doubt, an integral part of democracy. They facilitate the expression of unhappiness by societal members and draw the attention of authorities to problems. However, in Nepal, the problem with many of the strikes and protests was that they constrained the liberty of individual citizens. Many of these activities were enforced with violence or the threat of it. The activities restricted the democratic rights of the common people even when they were conducted in the name of protecting democratic rights.

The strikes came in a variety of forms—road blockades, the shutdown of markets, colleges and schools, and *dharnas*. Perhaps the sites that most frequently bore the largest number of strikes were the colleges under the premier Tribhuwan University, where various student organizations led by student activists affiliated with different political parties frequently called strikes and closed down colleges (see Snellinger, Chapter 11). Often these organizations called strikes in the name of the students and people but their activities were in effect an extension of conflicts between their mother parties. The strikes were rarely based on what the people and students wanted. Sometimes, especially in the case of the Maoist student fronts, they also forced closure of institutions such as high schools. These activities not only thwarted students from pursuing a quality education but also constrained the fundamental civil liberties of citizens.

The most well-known public protests were the *bandhs*, which called for the closure of markets, towns, cities or the whole country. Shops, schools and factories were often forcibly closed during the *bandhs*. Vehicles were prohibited from plying. Those who dared to continue with regular activities were often violently stopped. Vehicles that defied the call were broken or burnt, drivers beaten (and once in a while murdered, in the case of the Maoist-organized *bandhs*), shops were vandalized, goods were thrown out, roadside barricades were destroyed and bonfires of tyres and other materials were lit on the roads. Students were prevented from attending schools; small-time retailers were prevented from selling their goods to make a living; common people had to forgo their rights to buy goods and to work and to go on with their normal lives. Often, with the closure of businesses, low-earning labourers lost wage hours as there was less or no work.[1] The common people were thus denied their fundamental political rights and civil liberties. These activities left such a bitter taste in the mouths of the common people that many welcomed the king's interventions in 2002 and 2005 despite their undemocratic nature. The common people did not join the political parties' movement against the king's interventions for a considerable time. They joined the movement only when the royal cabinet began taking away more of the fundamental rights of the people by restricting the media, shutting down telephone lines and showing no signs of response to the peoples' craving for peace either by eliminating the Maoists through force as promised or by initiating a dialogue with the rebels.

Contentious Politics and the Protection of the Privileges of the Traditional Elite

Some of the contentious activities were launched by privileged groups in order to protect their traditional privileges. A good example is provided by Lakier (Chapter 10) when she discusses the power of the transport cartel to close down vehicular movement and prevent new public-transport companies from operating inside the cartel's jurisdiction. The movement succeeded in maintaining the status quo in their favour. It frustrated the government's policy to liberalize the transport sector and deprived consumers from getting alternative and efficient services. This example shows that the privileged groups have used democratic space to mobilize to protect their interests. As the traditionally privileged groups are more resourceful, their ability to resist changes that could foster progress could be formidable.

The activities of the fundamentalist Hindu organizations also fall into this category. After the declaration of the state as secular in May 2006 by the reinstated Parliament, these groups launched various protests to maintain the dominance of the Hindu religion in the state. These groups have also engaged in conflicts with the minority Muslim community, which has often been at the receiving end due to their lower numerical strength and an unsympathetic administration dominated by the Hindus. In Nepalgunj, Hindus and Muslims engaged in violent conflict around five times from 1990 to 1997. In 2001, when Nepali workers were killed by the Muslim fundamentalists in Iraq, the groups are also said to have been behind the rioting that targeted the Muslim institutions, buildings and businesses in Kathmandu. These groups say that they are working to protect the interests of Hindus, but are often working to maintain domination by Hindus.

The Maoists' Challenge to Electoral Democracy

The Maoist insurgency also undermined the emerging electoral democratic practices. For this book, the concern is not whether the insurgency and the issues it is raising are right or wrong. We begin from a normative stand that democracy is a desired objective and activities that constrain it and do not abide by its norms undermine it.

First of all, by the avowed aim to replace the parliamentary democracy for most of the insurgency's lifespan, the insurgency actively opposed the electoral democracy Nepal had been practicing. It killed people it deemed enemies and abducted, tortured and maimed others in the name of the People's War. The security forces killed more people than the Maoists did during the insurgency (see Onesto, Chapter 5) and that should be condemned, but one can argue that it might not have occurred had there been no insurgency.

Beyond such violent and cruel activities, the insurgency also hurt the emerging democracy by restraining free movement, free speech, free association and freedom of faith and ideology. Opposition politicians and others who were deemed as class enemies were expelled from villages, their houses were locked up and their lands and other properties were taken over. Donations (cash and goods) were collected from the government employees, businesses and the common people (often forcibly), many youths were recruited into the Maoist army and militia against their will, and teachers, students and political activists of other parties were made to attend Maoist campaigns for days, weeks and sometimes for months. These activities restricted the freedom of the people and created an atmosphere of fear in the villages. The Maoists engaged in such freedom-restricting activities in the areas under their influence and posed a threat even in areas outside their dominance. Further, due to the creation of unsuitable conditions for elections as a result of the threat from the insurgents, elections were not held after 1999 until 2005, when the royal government attempted to hold local elections, which most of the major parliamentary parties boycotted. The Maoist insurgency directly undermined the emerging electoral democracy by attacking institutions such as elections, local governments and associations that are fundamental for democracy to function.

Democracy is a system of governance where people deliberate, agree or disagree, tolerate, compromise and agree to disagree. Its major element is the procedural process it adopts (Bollen 1991; Przeworski et al. 2000; Young 1995). The Maoists' conception of democracy goes against these fundamental principles, even at the theoretical level. The execution of class enemies, adoption of violent methods and restriction of civil liberties demonstrate their undemocratic practices while the attempts to capture power through violent means show their disregard for procedural process. The residues of such tendencies still remain in the Maoists even after they have professed to join multiparty parliamentary system in 2005. The Maoists still say that the political parties that represent imperialists, expansionists and regressive forces would not be allowed to participate in the multiparty democracy. The issue here is whether it is the

Maoists or the people who will determine which are the undesirable elements. The people, the sovereign power in a democracy, could vote in the Maoists and could throw them out as well.

Even in arenas where the Maoists claim positive contributions, negative consequences have occurred as well. Onesto (Chapter 5) cites the liberation of traditionally disadvantaged groups due to the insurgency. For instance, the Maoists have claimed that they have undermined sexism in society. However, the chapter by Crawford, Kaufman and Gurung (Chapter 4) clearly shows that women have also borne huge costs due to the insurgency. The cost not only came from the killings of dear ones (husbands and other family members), displacement, threats (real or perceived) to life, increased burden (when male members were killed or displaced), but also from the increase of particular kinds of risks for women and children. They argue that daughters of displaced families have higher chances of being trafficked and NGOs working for women's alleviation have been hampered in their work due to the breakdown of law and order and the uncertainty and unpredictability of the situation.

Indirect Consequences: Overwhelming the Fledgling Democracy?

Several indirect negative consequences of contentious activities occurred in Nepal as well. One indirect negative consequence of contentious politics was the perception of social disorder they generated. Rademacher (Chapter 12) shows that by the end of the twentieth century, people in Nepal had increasingly lost hope that the democratic government could enforce law and order. This perception increased—in the case of people concerned with the environment in the Kathmandu Valley in Rademacher's study—with the government's inability to halt the environmental degradation. The coercive street protests and the obstruction and destruction they created, discussed earlier, fuelled these perceptions.

Such perceptions lowered the legitimacy of the democratic regime and developed a yearning for social order and stability. This created a situation whereby autocracy began to appear attractive to some sections of society. They wrongly perceived that it could provide peace, law and order. A state of emergency was declared at the end of 2001. The king topped it off first by dismissing the elected government in 2002 and later on by heading the cabinet himself in 2005. Autocracies come about not only because of autocrats' desires but also because they tend to receive societal support, at least initially. Both the state of emergency declared by the Deuba government in 2001 and those initiated by the king initially received some support from different sections of society[2] that wanted some order and peace.[3] Here it should be noted that even in democratic societies, there are tensions between liberty and order. Even in many democratizing polities and established democracies, when the law-and-order situation deteriorates, many citizens are willing to give up some of their liberties to contain such threats. A good example is the Patriot Act in the USA after 9/11 that has undermined civil liberty.

It could be that some activities may constrain democracy in the short run but may benefit it in the long run. The Maoists could claim that their objective of creating equality, even through violent means, could facilitate democracy in the long run. Other activists engaged in violent and coercive protests could make similar arguments. However, arguments that the ends justify the means do not match well with historical facts. Schumpeter (1950) long ago argued that there is no reason to believe that violent means of heralding a higher 'democracy' are justifiable through the philosophy of ends justifying means, because democracy is a political method of getting to the end and not an end in itself. Likewise, numerous cases of violent changes heralding either counter-violence (France) or the suppression of people's rights (the former USSR and China) abound.

Distinction Between Contentious Politics that Promotes and Hinders Democratization

If some contentious politics hinders democratization while others promotes it, what is it that contributes to the difference? Clearly the use of coercion in the enforcement of calls by the groups engaged in contentious activities does not promote democracy in a democratic regime. On the other hand, non-coercive contentious politics have promoted and expanded democracy. Here I call those contentious activities as coercive where groups that have called for protests forcefully enforce the call: they vandalize shops that open and vehicles that ply the road during the calls for *bandh*s. They violently deny the right of others to disagree with their call. In such instances, peaceful persuasion is not employed to convince people; instead violence, or the threat of it, is used. Here I make a distinction between those activities and others such as rallies that may obstruct traffic for some time but do not employ violent and coercive methods to enforce their call. I do not call the latter activities coercive.

However, as both the first (1990) and the second (2006) people's movements demonstrated, coercive methods were useful in restoring democracy. *Bandhs* and a repertoire of other coercive contentions were also employed during the movements, although they were employed less often in the second people's movement. Hence coercive contentious activities have played a part in restoring democracy during a non-democratic period. Similar contentious activities have contributed in restoring democracy during a non-democratic period while hindering democratization when democracy is operating. A four-fold category presented in Table 13.1 helps to simplify the analysis.

Table 13.1
Contentious Politics and Democratization

	Non-Democratic Regime	*Democratic Regime*
Coercive contentious politics	COULD BE HELPFUL	HARMFUL
Non-coercive contentious politics	HELPFUL	HELPFUL

Table 13.1 shows that non-coercive contentious politics could be helpful for democratization during both democratic and non-democratic regimes. In both types of regimes, they would allow people to express their opinions and make demands for change. Coercive contentious politics is harmful for democratization during a democratic regime, but could be useful for democratization by helping to make a regime change from non-democratic to democratic. The problem, however, is that the activities seem to continue into the democratic period. The actors are familiar with such activities and the activities themselves have gained acceptance due to their success.

Has non-deliverance of non-coercive mobilization led to reliance on coercive methods? This is an important question in Nepal, because if non-coercive methods do not deliver, the proponents could opt for coercive methods in future. The Kamaiya movement shows that reliance on coercive methods could facilitate a quicker response from the government (of course the coercive methods employed, in terms of sitting down on roads, is of a different level from the coercive politics of students burning tyres or vandalizing shops and vehicles). The Kamaiya movement did not depend on violence on their part even though they obstructed traffic for some hours during the day in their sit-in programmes. The indigenous nationalities and Dalits have also obtained concessions, even though minor ones, largely due to peaceful lobbying and protests.[4] Still, the major demands put forward by the peaceful identity movements were largely ignored during the democratic period, suggesting that some groups could perhaps perceive that coercive contentious activities are called for. Thus, if organization and mobilization permit, some of the groups which had not engaged in coercive methods earlier could employ such methods in the future to make their demands, especially if their demands made through non-coercive methods are not met.

Factors Leading to Reliance on Coercive Methods

It is beyond the scope of this chapter to identify the reasons for reliance on coercive methods by various groups. Here, I will hypothesize a few factors.

One factor is the lack of rule of law. In the case of the transport owners' strikes discussed by Lakier (Chapter 10), the transport owners were clearly defying the government policies and were engaged in coercive methods to maintain their privileges. The government was unable to implement its liberalizing policy or break the strike. The government's incompetence could have encouraged such groups. On the other hand, residents alongside the highways often halt the traffic when fatal accidents occur due to their perception that the administration will not punish the drivers and provide compensation unless they compel the administration through such activities.

Another reason for various actors and groups to engage in coercive methods is unresponsiveness of the government. If the government had addressed some of the demands of the non-coercive movements, the incentives to turn coercive would have been less. The underlying reason for the lack of responsiveness from the government could be the centralization of power. Centralization denied power to local authorities. As many of the local issues could not be addressed by local governments, the problems went unresolved. Some of the protests were taken to the centre, but the centre was largely unresponsive due to other preoccupations, lack of sensitivity to the issues, and so on. Alienation among the aggrieved groups increased. The groups also clearly understood that peaceful protests were not yielding results and coercive ones were. Thus, those who could muster organizational and mobilizational power adopted coercive means to draw the attention of the government.

One of the consequences of the centralization has been the absence of autonomy and self-governance rights for various nationalities/ ethnic groups. It has meant that these groups have been compelled to struggle for their rights, as Hangen, Shrestha and Maharjan (Chapters 7–9) show in this volume. Lawoti (Chapter 2) traces the ethnic centralization of the post-1990 democratic years to the 1990 Constitution and its engineering process. The exclusion of non-dominant groups in the constitutional engineering process led to the neglect of their issues and demands in the Constitution.

The centralization also affected the regular political process negatively. The opposition political parties were unable to influence policies as the Nepali state structures concentrated most power in the ruling party and did not give space to the opposition forces. The ruling party often abuses the state power to promote its interests. In such circumstances, the opposition parties are often forced to engage in street politics as it is often the only way to resist the ruling party's political encroachment and influence public policies.

The non-functioning of democracy's various elements due to centralization of power also increased the incentive to contentious activities. For instance, the lack of an independent election commission, which was a result of the ruling party's role in nominating the commissioners and in allocating budget and personnel to the commission, resulted in elections that were perceived to be unfair by the opposition and general public. It contributed to pushing the opposition forces toward coercive methods. As Adam Przeworski has famously said: 'lections are supposed to institutionalize unpredictability. No one should know in advance the outcome of an election. In Nepal, the ruling party has been lessening the unpredictability of the elections by abusing power to influence the elections in its favor. As a result, effective alternation of power among political parties has not taken place.'[5]

This has contributed to the use of coercive contentious activities by opposition parties as they feel that it is the only option they have in a system where the government does not listen to them and it is difficult to change the government through an electoral process.

The lack of truly free and fair elections means that the opposition perceives that the ruling party will rule for perpetuity by abusing elections. It creates a situation of security dilemma. Each party perceives that the others will abuse power when they have it to influence elections in their favour. It has meant that the ruling party perceives that if it does not influence the electoral process to win, the other party will win and abuse power to win again. The lack of fair elections has meant that the ruling party can to some extent extend its tenure non-democratically. It also means that since the democratic process does not function smoothly, the opposition parties have to rely on non-democratic and violent methods to influence government and policy changes. The coercive street protests by the parliamentary parties and the Maoist insurgency are different examples of the coercive activities of opposition parties whose faith in the democratic process has eroded.

Contentious Politics in Fledgling Democracies

Finally, it is imperative that we discuss the lessons from the Nepali experience on the concept of contentious politics itself. Hangen and Snellinger clearly show in this volume (Chapters 7 and 11) that the generally employed definition proposed by McAdam et al. (2001) may have to be revised in the context of new democracies that swing between democratic and non-democratic polities (see Chapter 1 for definitions). McAdam et al. (ibid.: 5) exclude formal politics and agents and activities associated with it—such as 'regularly scheduled events like votes, parliamentary elections'—from contentious politics. However, as Hangen argues, for very small political parties at the margin that act more like social movements than political parties despite their nomenclature and do not have much chance of capturing the state in any foreseeable future, participation in elections could be part of a strategy to push their cause. In such situations, entities such as the MNO may call themselves a 'party' (though it was banned by the government) and may field candidates during elections, but their overall impact is similar to that of a social movement. Thus, participation in the election itself 'was a form of contentious politics'.[6]

Likewise, the student activism in Nepal also brings up other interesting issues. The student organizations are formal sister organizations of the political parties. However, during the non-democratic period, especially between 2002 and 2006, they acted relatively independently. On issues such as the demand for republicanism, they led the political parties toward it. In fact, they also led the movement against the regression, which was a movement in its true sense because civil society, professional organizations, students and other non-political party people played a decisive role in it. This shows that organizations affiliated with formal political parties could be involved in larger socio-political struggles during non-democratic periods. The activities went beyond the formal realm of canvassing for votes for one's party, expanding party organization, and so on. Thus, during non-democratic periods, organizations affiliated with formal political parties could be engaged in activities that are truly contentious politics—those activities may not be part of the regular, formal political practices guided by the larger agenda of contributing to the forming or breaking of governments. The affiliation with political parties should not exclude those activities from being considered as contentious politics.

What these two cases suggest is that perhaps while dealing with fledgling democracies, especially when they are on the swing to the non-democratic side, the criteria for defining contentious politics should take into consideration the different circumstances in such countries. Contentious politics should be defined not solely based on the formal nomenclature of agents and organizations (such as the MNO and student organizations affiliated with political parties—see Hangen and Snellinger, Chapters 7 and 11) and activities (elections, see Hangen, Chapter 7), but more on the consequences of those activities.

Way Forward

We have shown that contentious politics could affect democratization both positively and negatively. The challenge is to promote positive consequences. One way is to recognize the social forces and their causes. In many circumstances, the recognition of issues can defuse the problem. For instance, India witnessed linguistic riots after independence when Nehru tried to divide the country administratively instead of linguistically. After the opposition and riots, Nehru backtracked and re-divided the country linguistically. The problem was defused.

If social forces are not recognized, they could turn into a destructive force. If the demands of the Maoist and ethnic groups had been recognized and addressed earlier, Nepal may not have borne such a huge human and other costs. On the other hand, if social forces are incorporated into governance, they could contribute to reforming the state and society. For instance, to address the Maoist insurgency, the Nepali state is being restructured. It could result in a massive reform that could make the state more inclusive and accountable.

The above discussion shows that the government needs to be responsive. One way to make the government responsive is to increase people's access to the government. In a highly centralized country such as Nepal, extensive devolution of power and power sharing can increase people's access to the government. When power is distributed among different levels and agencies of government, they could become more effective in their own spheres of operation. Good governance would contribute toward promoting law and order, which could lessen the harmful contentious activities as well.

Acknowledgement

I thank Susan Hangen for her insightful comments on an earlier draft of this chapter.

Notes

1. Millions were lost from business transactions that could not take place; tourism industries floundered as tourists were diverted to other destinations—some hotels have gone bankrupt; many industries stagnated due to the political conflicts

and both the owners and the labourers were negatively affected by it. As a result, Nepali businesspersons have diverted capital out of the country, further hurting the economy (based on conversations with businesspersons).

2. The state of emergency declared in November 2001 was supported by all parliamentary parties.
3. The mass participation in the 2006 uprising was to some extent due to the desire for peace and social order among the people. More people increasingly got turned off from the king when he did not reciprocate the ceasefire declared by the Maoists.
4. Some commentators have argued that these concessions were awarded to stop more members of these groups from joining the Maoist insurgency. If that is the case, the peaceful movements could be interpreted as not being successful even in obtaining minor concessions. But we have to recognize the contributions of such movements in not only sensitizing the government, but even the Maoists.
5. Although most political parties participated in the government during the hung Parliament of 1994–99, the Nepali Congress (NC) was in power around 90 per cent of the time during 1990–2002. Hence, effective alternation of power did not occur.
6. E-mail communication with Susan Hangen.

References

Bollen, Kenneth A. 1991. 'Political Democracy: Conceptual and Measurement Traps', in A. Inkeles (ed.), *On Measuring Democracy: Its Consequences and Concomitants*. New Brunswick and London: Transaction Publishers.

Chatterjee, Partha. 2004. *The Politics of the Governed: Reflections of Popular Politics in Most of the World*. New York: Columbia University Press.

Dahl, Robert A. 1971. *Polyarchy*. New Haven: Yale University Press.

McAdam, Doug, Sidney Tarrow and Charles Tilly. 2001. *Dynamics of Contention*. Cambridge: Cambridge University Press.

Przeworski, Adam, Michael E. Alvarez, Jose Antonio Cheibub and Fernando Limongi. 2000. *Democracy and Development: Political Institutions and Well-Being in the World, 1950–1990*. Cambridge: Cambridge University Press.

Schumpeter, Joseph A. 1950. *Capitalism, Socialism, and Democracy*, Third ed. New York: Harper Perennial.

Young, Iris Marion. 1995. 'Survey Article: Rawls' Political Liberalism', *The Journal of Political Philosophy* 3 (2): 181–90.

About the Editor and Contributors

Editor

Mahendra Lawoti, Ph.D., is an Assistant Professor in the Department of Political Science at Western Michigan University, Kalamazoo. He is the author of *Towards a Democratic Nepal: Inclusive Political Institutions for a Multicultural Society* (Sage Publications, 2005, third reprint 2006, Nepali translation 2007), *Samabesi Sambidhan Sabha ra Rajyako Punarsamrachan* (Inclusive Constituent Assembly and Restructuring of the State) (NISP, 2007), *Looking Back, Looking Forward: Centralization, Multiple Conflicts and Democratic State Building in Nepal* (Fortcoming, Washington: East West Center) and many articles and book chapters. He is currently revising his dissertation into a book to be titled *Exclusion in New Democracies: Nepal in a Comparative Perspective.* Professor Lawoti is the President of the Association for Nepal and Himalayan Studies and Non- Resident Associate Fellow of the New York-headquartered Asia Society. His teaching and research interests cover international development, democratization and political institutions, constitutionalism, ethnic politics, social movements and insurgencies, and South Asian politics.

Contributors

Mary Crawford is Professor of Psychology at the University of Connecticut. Books she has authored, co-authored or edited include *Gender and Thought: Psychological Perspectives* (1989); *Talking Difference: On Gender and Language* (1995); *Gender Differences in Human Cognition* (1997); *Coming Into Her Own: Educational Success in Girls and Women* (1999); *Innovative Methods for Feminist Psychological Research* (1999); and the widely used texts *Women and Gender: A Feminist Psychology* (4th ed. 2004) and *Transformations: Women, Gender, and Psychology* (2005). During the academic year 2004–05, she was a Fulbright Senior Scholar based in Kathmandu, Nepal.

Alka Gurung earned her B.A. in sociology and women's studies from Brandeis University, her M.A. and M.Phil. in social anthropology from Cambridge University, UK. She has conducted primary research on female shamans of Darjeeling, India, the 'untouchable' Kami in Kathmandu and the Gorkhas in the UK. Her most recent research was conducted amongst Nepali prostitutes in India and Nepal.

Susan Hangen is Associate Professor of Anthropology and International Studies at Ramapo College, New Jersey. She has conducted research on ethnic politics in Nepal since 1993, in the Ilam and Jhapa districts as well as in Kathmandu. Her articles include 'Race and the Politics of Identity in Nepal' (2005) and 'Boycotting Dasain: History, Memory and Ethnic Politics in Nepal' (2005). She is working on a book to be called *Democracy in the Margins: Ethnic Politics in Rural Nepal in the 1990s.* She is working on a research project on identity politics among Nepalis in New York City, where she currently lives.

Michelle R. Kaufman is a doctoral student in social psychology at the University of Connecticut. Her research interests are in international women's health issues, particularly how gender and power affect women's sexual health. She has conducted research in Nepal on sex trafficking, HIV knowledge and attitudes towards women. In South Africa, she has conducted work on HIV prevention among high-risk men who tend to commit sexual violence. In the US, she has been working on HIV prevention with high-risk populations, including gay men and women.

Shisir Khanal has a master's degree in international public affairs from the Robert M. La Follette School of Public Affairs at the University of Wisconsin, Madison. He has studied Nepal's insurgency for over five years and completed a bachelor's thesis on the Maoist movement in Nepal. He received his B.A. in international political economy from the University of Bridgeport. Currently, he manages Sarvodaya USA, a non-profit organization that supports the work of the Sarvodaya Shramadana Movement of Sri Lanka. He has interests in sustainable development, democratization and conflict resolution.

Genevieve Lakier has a Ph.D. in anthropology from the University of Chicago. Between 2002 and 2004, she conducted dissertation research in Kathmandu on democratic political protest. She currently resides in Cambridge, Massachusetts where she is an Academy Fellow at the Weatherhead Center for International Affairs at Harvard University.

Keshav Lall Maharjan is Professor at the Graduate School for International Development and Cooperation, Hiroshima University. He conducts research and lectures on rural economics and South Asian studies. He is the author of *Peasantry in Nepal: A Study on Subsistence Farmers and Their Activities Pertaining to Food Security* (Research Center for Regional Geography (RCRG), Hiroshima University, 2003) and *Impacts of Irrigation and Drainage Schemes on Rural Economic Activities in Bangladesh* (RCRG, Hiroshima University, 1997). He is also one of the main contributors to H. Ishii (ed.), *Ryudo-suru Nepal* (Social Dynamism in Contemporary Nepal), (University of Tokyo Press, 2005) in Japanese, and has several contributions in books and journals to his credit.

Li Onesto spent several months as a photojournalist in 1999, travelling deep into the guerrilla zones in Nepal. The Communist Party of Nepal (Maoist) gave Onesto, who is a reporter for the *Revolution* newspaper, unprecedented access to party and military leaders, leaders of women's organizations, families of people who had been killed by the police, and common peasants. She also did an extensive interview with Prachanda, the leader of the CPN (Maoist). Her book, *Dispatches from the People's War in Nepal* (Pluto and Insight Press, 2005) is based on this trip.

Anne Rademacher is an environmental anthropologist with an interest in the political and cultural dimensions of urban sustainability. Through studies of rural-to-urban migration, urban conservation and development initiatives, and ideas of nature in cities, Rademacher highlights connections between urban ecology and political transformation. Her work in Kathmandu focuses on the cultural politics of the Bagmati and Bishnumati river restoration project between 1997 and 2003. She currently serves as an Assistant Professor and Faculty Fellow in the Department of Social and Cultural Analysis, New York University.

Bal Gopal Shrestha is currently working on Nepalese democracy as a postdoctoral fellow at the University of Leiden, the Netherlands, and is also lecturer at the Centre for Nepal and Asian Studies (CNAS), Kathmandu, Nepal. He was a postdoctoral fellow at the Centro Incontri Umani, Ascona, Switzerland (2004–06). His Ph.D. dissertation deals with Newar culture and rituals in Nepal and was defended at Leiden University in 2002. He has conducted extensive fieldwork in Nepal and India and has widely published in Newar, Nepali, English and Dutch. His current research focuses on politics, ritual, religion, ethnicity and nationalism in South Asia, particularly in Nepal and India.

Amanda Snellinger is a Ph.D. candidate in anthropology at Cornell University. Her dissertation research focuses on Nepali student politics, particularly the current and historical role of student activism, the impact of the youth on politics, the place of politics in civil society and the political training process that Nepali politicians undergo. Her research has been supported by FLAS Fellowships, a Fulbright Research Fellowship, a Sage Fellowship, an Einaudi Grant, a Fulbright-Hays Dissertation Research Fellowship and a Wenner-Gren Research Fellowship. She has published articles on this research in *The Political and Legal Anthropology Review, Peace and Democracy Journal of South Asia, Loktantra* and *The Nation, Nepal.*

Ivan Gyozo Somlai was educated in Hungary, Canada, Switzerland, Nepal and France. He has an M.A. (in culture) through the King Mahendra Post Graduate Research Scholarship at Tribhuvan University, Nepal, and a Certificate (International Management) from l'Institut Européen d'Administration des Affaires, France. His work has entailed conflict mitigation, multicultural education and project management (health, natural resources, organizational development and indigenous people) with governments, civil society and agencies internationally. Since 1976, he has worked for over 16 years in Nepal and has visited all 75 districts. An accomplished mountaineer and former Olympian, he is currently Associate Director, International Education at Thompson Rivers University, Canada.

Index